PROGRESS IN ASIAN SOCIAL PSYCHOLOGY

PROGRESS IN ASIAN SOCIAL PSYCHOLOGY

Conceptual and Empirical Contributions

Edited by Kuo-Shu Yang, Kwang-Kuo Hwang,
Paul B. Pedersen, and Ikuo Daibo

Contributions in Psychology, Number 42

Westport, Connecticut
London

Library of Congress Cataloging-in-Publication Data

Progress in Asian social psychology : conceptual and empirical contributions / edited by
Kuo-Shu Yang . . . [et al.].
    p.   cm.—(Contributions in psychology, ISSN 0736-2714 ; no. 42)
    Includes bibliographical references and index.
    ISBN 0-313-32463-8 (alk. paper)
    1. Social psychology—Asia. I. Yang, Guoshu, 1932– II. Series.
  HM1027.A78 P76   2003
  302′.095—dc21   2002030337

British Library Cataloguing in Publication Data is available.

Library of Congress Catalog Card Number: 2002030337
ISBN: 0-313-32463-8
ISSN: 0736-2714

First published in 2003

Praeger Publishers, 88 Post Road West, Westport, CT 06881
An imprint of Greenwood Publishing Group, Inc.
www.praeger.com

Printed in the United States of America

The paper used in this book complies with the
Permanent Paper Standard issued by the National
Information Standards Organization (Z39.48–1984).

10 9 8 7 6 5 4 3 2 1

Contents

Preface

Why is Asian social psychology Asian? Asian social psychologists think and do their research in ways different from their colleagues from other parts of the world, especially the West. As psychology becomes more visible in Asia it is becoming more important to reevaluate psychological concepts, research findings, and applications as to their fit with the Asian cultural context.

This book explores indigenous applications of psychology to the Asian cultural context rather than simply transfering psychology from the American–European context without modification. These chapters are comprehensive in reviewing the research findings and rapid growth of psychology in the Asian cultural context. Both the research and the training and teaching applications of psychology are addressed. Conceptual ideas about indigenous psychology in the Asian context are raised for discussion.

The primary audiences for this book are classes in social psychology in Asia and elsewhere that have a global focus that includes the Asian context. In addition, understanding the importance of indigenous psychology will help psychologists identify cultural bias and/or adapt psychology to the international and multicultural community on a global level. The leading social psychologists in Asia have contributed to this book as the most recent in a series of books, conferences, and professional activities to frame psychology in the global context.

The founding of the Asian Association of Social Psychology (AASP) in 1995 marked a new epoch in the development of social psychology in Asia.

The inaugural conference was held in Hong Kong from June 21–23 in the same year, hosted by the Chinese University of Hong Kong. The second biannual AASP International conference took place in Kyoto, Japan during August 4–6, 1997, hosted by Kyoto University. The third conference was held in Taipei, Taiwan on August 4–7, 1999, hosted by Academia Sinica.

As expected, the attendees of successive conferences included increasingly more psychologists from different Asian and non-Asian countries and the diversity of topics that the presentations addressed also increased in scope. These developments all attest to the effort and progress that Asian researchers, and non-Asian scholars as well, have made in their understanding of Asian people's social psychological functioning. This book pursues answers to socially and culturally relevant, practical psychological problems, needs, and issues in various Asian contexts.

In order to provide a forum for Asian and non-Asian scholars to present their theoretical, methodological, and empirical achievements in doing Asian social psychological research for international communication and dialogue, a book series with the general title of Progress in Asian Social Psychology was launched under the able planning of Kwok Leung (originally Professor of Psychology at the Chinese University of Hong Kong and now Professor of Management at the City University of Hong Kong) as the series editor. Each volume published a collection of selected papers from each of the three biannual AASP meetings (Leung, Kim, Yamaguchi, & Kashima, 1997; Sugiman, Karasawa, Liu, & Ward, 1999).

This is the third book in the series on Asian Social Psychology. It contains a collection of papers (each peer-reviewed by three international colleagues) mainly presented at the 1999 Taipei biannual AASP conference, which was organized by the Institute of Ethnology, Academia Sinica, and the Department of Psychology, National Taiwan University. More than 300 scholars in psychology and related disciplines from thirteen Asian countries or districts (Australia, China, Hong Kong, India, Japan, Korea, New Zealand, Pakistan, Philippines, Singapore, Taiwan, Thailand, Vietnam) and eight non-Asian ones (Austria, Canada, Denmark, France, Germany, Israel, Norway, United States) took part in the conference.

During the four-day meeting, 154 oral and 139 poster presentations were made. The 293 presentations covered a large number of academic topics ranging from conceptual, theoretical, and methodological to empirical issues in both basic and applied areas of research on Asian people's social psychological functioning. Quite a number of presented studies were conducted using a cross-cultural indigenous approach, rather than an imposed-etic or pseudo-etic one. These studies were undertaken by investigators from two or more countries, usually one from an Asian and the other from a Western country.

The conference's highlight undoubtedly lay in the systematic, comparative analyses of the similarities, differences, and relationships among the three culturally oriented psychologies: cross-cultural psychology, cultural psychology, and indigenous psychology. Several papers focused on ways to integrate them to create a more viable, productive, culture-based psychology. The plenary keynote speakers at the conference were two cross-cultural psychologists (J. W. Berry, H. C. Triandis), two cultural psychologists (P. M. Greenfield, R. A. Shweder), and two indigenous psychologists (U. Kim, K. S. Yang). Their six papers were published afterward in the *Asian Journal of Social Psychology* in 2000 as a special issue under the guest editorship of K. K. Hwang and C. F. Yang.

The chapters included in this volume were peer reviewed and chosen from a much larger number of submissions made by some of the participants after the conference. This collection of chapters candidly reflects the kinds of research topics or issues in which Asian social psychologists are interested, the ways in which they conceptualize psychological and behavioral phenomena, and the related cultural contexts in which they do their research. The chapters cover the perspectives different authors have adopted in interpreting their research findings both theoretically and practically.

Thanks are due to all the individuals and institutions who made the publication of this volume possible. We are grateful to all conference participants who submitted their papers for consideration for publication in this volume and all the international reviewers for taking their precious time off to evaluate one or more manuscripts for us. We thank Olwen Bedford, Ph.D., for helping edit the volume. Our thanks also go to the Academia Sinica, the ROC Ministry of Education, and the ROC National Science Council for their generous financial support. Last but not the least, we would like to express our gratitude to the editorial staff at Greenwood for their professional effort in publishing the series.

REFERENCES

Leung, K., Kim, U., Yamaguchi, S., & Kashima, Y. (1997). *Progress in Asian psychology*, vol. 1. Singapore: John Wiley and Sons.

Sugiman, T., Karasawa, M., Liu, J. H., & Ward, C. (1999). *Progress in Asian social psychology: Theoretical and empirical contributions*, vol. 2. Seoul, South Korea: Kyoyook-Kwahak-Sa.

Introduction

Modernization and economic development have been the most commonly shared concerns of people in Asian countries. There has been a sustained process of modernization or development in Asia, even though economic growth has been slow in some regions. Asian social psychologists have been more sensitive to the cultures and culture change resulting from this growth than their colleagues in other areas of psychological science. As a result, increasing numbers of Asian social psychologists have been conducting more culturally relevant social psychological research with local people as respondents.

The more rapidly a particular Asian country developed, the more productive social psychologists have been in that country. Two major purposes are behind this trend. First, there was an intention to establish an Asian version of social psychology at both theoretical and empirical levels as the Asian contribution to the development of a balanced human psychology. Second, there was a search for useful social psychological perspectives resulting in better understanding, prevention, and solution of social and individual problems in their respective countries.

These twin purposes have been repeatedly displayed, in one way or another, among the studies presented at the first two biannual international conferences of the Asian Association of Social Psychology (Leung, Kim, Yamaguchi, & Kashima, 1997; Sugiman, Karasawa, Liu, & Ward, 1999). The same is true of the third AASP conference, from which a collection of sixteen papers were selected for publication in this book. These papers are grouped into five broad categories: (1) conceptual perspectives, (2) socialization in family and school, (3) achievement and achievement motivation, (4) group and intergroup dynamics, and (5) deviant behavior and rehabilitation.

Part I includes three chapters, each written by one or two internationally well-known Asian social psychologists, addressing certain important conceptual or theoretical aspects of Asian social psychology. In the first chapter, J.B.P. Sinha, following the late eminent indigenous psychologist D. Sinha's (1998) conceptual lead, systematically reviews six overlapping trends in indigenizing psychology in India. This review includes the purist trend following the ancient Indian wisdom, the trend toward endogenous indigenization, the purist trend in Western psychological tradition, the trend toward exogenous indigenization, the trend toward integrative indigenization, and the trend toward methodological indigenization in India.

India has been one of the most important countries in which indigenous psychologies have developed most rapidly. Basically, these trends represent the relative degrees of identification with both mainstream Western psychology and traditional Indian thinking. Among them, the most promising trend is integrative indigenization, which draws mainly on Indian folkways. This approach shows great eclecticism in the perspective as well as higher elasticity in the choice of research concepts and methods. The Indian experiences in indigenizing psychological theory and research have much to offer to indigenously oriented psychologists in other Asian nations in particular and non-Asian ones in general.

In Chapter 2, S. C. Choi and K. Kim make a highly systematic, penetrating conceptual analysis of the "self" in Korea, by comparison with the Western self, from the perspective of cultural psychology. They point out that Korean people tend to construe their self as a mind-self that is changeable in accordance with social contexts and relationships, whereas American people tend to see their self as an entity-self that is stable across different situations and relationships. This important difference fits with the distinction between the malleable versus fixed self or personality, which has been made by other personality and social psychologists like Dweck and associates (Chiu, Hong, & Dweck, 1997; Dweck & Leggett, 1998). Choi and Kim's analysis is applicable not only in the comparisons of the Korean self with the Western self, but also in comparisons of the Chinese and Japanese self with the Western one.

In Chapter 3, J. H. Liu and S. H. Liu present an interesting, novel attempt to make a cross-cultural comparison between the historical basis for authority in Chinese (more broadly, East Asian) and American (more broadly, Western) societies. Their analyses make it clear that there were historical reasons for the development of a "benevolent authority" system of sociopolitical governance. This system is based on a morally upright leader at the top of a web of hierarchically arranged, harmonious, and interdependent relationships in Chinese and other East Asian societies. This system is in sharp contrast with the

Western case, where a "plurality of power" system has come into existence. The Western case assumes an impartial set of rules (the law) that transcend independent individuals competing with one another.

Based upon this cross-cultural perspective of the historical basis for authority, the authors systematically discuss how and why East Asian social psychologists and other social scientists can exert greater influence on local public policy and debate in their roles as teachers, social scientists, critics, ministers, consultants, and creators of social representations. Their emphasis on the moral aspect of Chinese authority is supported by recent formal empirical research on Chinese leadership behavior. Farh and Cheng (2000) identified, by factor analysis, three major aspects or components of paternalistic leadership in Chinese business organizations, namely, authoritarian leadership, moral leadership, and benevolent leadership, all of which are considered to have their roots in Confucianism.

Part II consists of three chapters related to some aspects of Asian values for arranging interpersonal relationships in the modern age. In order to explain the opposite effects of Chinese filial piety on individual development, K. H. Yeh's chapter proposes a framework to differentiate the reciprocal and the authoritarian types of filial piety in Chinese society. The former can be beneficial to the harmony of family relationship; while the latter can be harmful to the individual's autonomy and creativity. His approach includes core ideas from the indigenous culture that enables us to understand in more detail not only the meaning of the interdependent self in East Asian societies, but also the related socialization process of Asian children in families and schools.

In Chapter 5, parental beliefs about shame and moral socialization in Hong Kong, Taiwan, and the United States are compared by H. Fung, E. Lieber, and P.W.L. Leung with data from two sets of open-ended questions. Their data indicate that Chinese parents tend to believe that an awareness of shame emerges earlier than the ability to tell right from wrong, while most U.S. parents believe the opposite. Their findings reflect cross-cultural differences not only in child-rearing beliefs but also in preferences for disciplinary strategies. Both topics have attracted attention from scholars for years (e.g., LeVine, 1988).

W. Y. Lin investigates the change of parental attitudes toward goals and values to be emphasized in the school education of Taiwan in Chapter 6. Contrary to the popular belief that the Chinese view of education is mainly determined by their cultural tradition, her research proposes an alternative view which emphasizes social adaptation of human needs. Instead of following traditional Chinese child-rearing practices blindly, many parents are trying to find new ways of educating their children under the influence of their traditional culture. The result is a hybrid of new cultural pattern. This and the other two chapters in Part II all provide conceptual and empirical information on the new Asian child-rearing goals, which enable us to have a clearer understanding of parent–child relationships in the changing societies of Asia.

The East Asian economic miracle attracted worldwide attention during the 1980s (e.g., Hofheinz & Calder, 1982). Social scientists have proposed many theories to explain this phenomena (Chen, 1979; Kahn, 1979; McMullen, 1982), and psychologists, in particular, have been quite interested in studying the industriousness and strong work motivation of East Asian people. The three chapters in Part III address this topic. In Chapter 7, E. Leiber and A. B. Yu investigate the cultural difference in achievement motivation as measured by the Individual-Oriented Achievement Motivation (IOAM) scale, the Social-Oriented Achievement Motivation (SOAM) scale, and in prototypical stories collected in Taiwan and the United States. They found that individually and socially oriented achievement motives were meaningful concepts for distinguishing the behavioral domains, primary causes, and primary consequences of achievement experiences in extreme IOAM and SOAM groups in both cultures.

In Chapter 8, W. C. Chang and L. Quan present research findings on the effects of collectivism and situational variations on achievement motivation of school children in Singapore. Their experimental study shows that participants with high collective orientation are higher on overall achievement motivation and its task-related dimensions, but lower on the ego-related dimension. When work and reward distributions are consistent with each other, the work ethic is higher; when reward is distributed on the basis of individual performance, competitiveness is higher.

Finally, in Chapter 9, U. Kim and Y. S. Park adopt an indigenous approach to compare the success attribution made by Korean students and adults. The two groups list the educational success and occupational success as the most important achievement for them respectively. Both groups cite effort and self-regulation as the most important factors contributing to their success and affective support from parents as most helpful to their performance. The study shows the connection between affective support from one's intimate family and motivation for pursuing success in one's operating society. Research as such may expand previous knowledge on this topic to a great extent (e.g., Stevenson & Lee, 1990).

Although much psychological research indicates that Asian people are group-oriented, significant cultural differences have been noted in the group-orientation of Asian people (Tu, Hejtmanek, & Wachman, 1992): The major concerns of Chinese people are focused on the family, whereas the Japanese put their major emphasis on groups in society (Lebra, 1976). Three of the four articles in Part IV are on group dynamics and were all written by Japanese scholars. In Chapter 10, A. Miura describes a laboratory experiment to study the effects of communication medium and goal setting on an idea-generation task of group brainstorming. Results indicate that the computer-mediated groups were more productive than the face-to-face group; those who perceived that they had more opportunity to participate were more motivated in the task than the assigned goal group.

In Chapter 11, F. Murakami utilizes the method of using reward allocation and inviting recipients for dinner as a strategy to uphold the norm of equity and to maintain interpersonal relationships within the group at the same time. In group-oriented Asian societies, the issues of upholding norm of equity and maintaining within-group relationships are both mostly of interest for scholars who are working in the fields of social psychology and management (Amabile, 1983; Leventhal, 1976).

The group orientation of Asian people makes the issue of intergroup dynamics more and more important for maintaining harmony within a larger society. The T. Oe and T. Oka study reported in Chapter 12 deals with effective and ineffective strategies for stereotype suppression in Japan. Their experiments show that the trait-replacement strategy inhibits the "ironic rebound effect" as compared with the group-replacement strategy. On the other hand, both strategies of counterstereotypic trait and neutral trait triggered a stronger rebound effect as compared with the group-replacement strategy.

In Chapter 13, A. Lim and C. Ward present research findings on the effects of some social variables on the perceptions of foreign talent in Singapore. Their data indicated that the country of origin (People's Republic of China and the United States), occupational skills (adequate supply and high demand), and length of residence in the country (short or long term) are significant factors that have strong effects on the evaluation of a hypothetical employee made by Chinese Singaporean adults. This kind of data is invaluable for Asian societies, which are rapidly becoming more global and multicultural (Pedersen, 1999).

There are three chapters in Part V. Deviant behavior exists in every society. There is no exception in Asian societies. One important kind of deviant behavior is school violence, which has been increasing in Asia. In Chapter 14, K. Y. Yang, H. H. Chung, and U. Kim compare the effects of school violence on the psychological adjustment of Korean adolescents. Using the technique of cluster analysis, they identify four groups of adolescents in terms of school violence and label them as bullies, victims, bystanders, and mixed. Their results show distinct psychological and behavioral patterns relating to experience with school violence.

In light of the old controversy about the death penalty (Bailey & Peterson, 1994; Peterson & Bailey, 1991), A. Sakamoto, K. Sekiguchi, A. Shinkyu, and Y. Okada report in Chapter 15 their study on the deterrence effects of media coverage of capital punishment on the occurrence of brutal crimes by analyzing the Japanese time-series data from 1959 to 1990 from a macroperspective.

The last chapter in Part V discusses S. F. Tam, W. K. Man, and Y. Y. Ng's ideas about the conceptualization, application, and implication of Eastern and Western perspectives in social psychological research on rehabilitation. The term *rehabilitation* is used here to denote psychological and physical rehabilitation in a broad sense. Rehabilitation does not imply criminal or deviant behaviors. It is hoped that such a contrast of perspectives may generate new ideas in designing human-services programs (Rothman & Thomas, 1994; Safilios-Rothschild, 1970).

Articles collected in this book represent the diversified research interests of contemporary social psychologists working in Asia. Their performance makes us believe that research on the psychology of Asian people should be done by psychologists with an Asian perspective. It is expected that the publication of this book will stimulate much more research on related topics so as to make more significant contributions to the progress of Asian psychology in particular and world psychology in general.

REFERENCES

Amabile, T. M. (1983). *The social psychology of creativity*. New York: Springer-Verlag.

Bailey, W. C., & Peterson, R. D. (1994). Murder, capital punishment, and deterrence: A review of the evidence and an examination of police killings. *Journal of Social Issues, 50*, 53–74.

Chen, E.K.Y. (1979). *Hyper-growth in Asian economics: A comparative study of Hong Kong, Japan, Korea, Singapore, and Taiwan*. New York: Holmes & Meier.

Chiu, C., Hong, Y., & Dweck, C. S. (1997). Lay dispositionism and implicit theories of personality. *Journal of Personality and Social Psychology, 73*, 19–30.

Dweck, C. S., & Leggett, E. L. (1998). A social–cognitive approach to motivation and personality. *Psychological Review, 95*, 256–273.

Farh, J. L., & Cheng, B. S. (2000). A cultural analysis of paternalistic leadership in Chinese organization. In J. T. Li, A. S. Tsui, & E. Weldon (Eds.), *Management and organizations in the Chinese context* (pp. 84–127). London: Macmillan.

Hofheinz, R., & Calder, K. E. (1982). *Eastasia edge*. New York: Basic Books.

Kahn, H. (1979). *World economic development: 1979 and beyond*. Boulder, CO: Westview Press.

Lebra, T. S. (1976). *Japanese patterns of behavior*. Honolulu: University of Hawaii Press.

Leung, K., Kim, U., Yamaguchi, S., & Kashima, Y. (Eds.). (1997). *Progress in Asian social psychology*, vol. 1. New York: John Wiley and Sons.

Leventhal, G. S. (1976). The distribution of rewards and resources in groups and organizations. In L. Berkowitz and E. Walster (Eds.), *Advances in experimental social psychology*, Vol. 9: *Equity theory: Toward a general theory of social interaction* (pp. 91–131). New York: Academic Press.

LeVine, R. A. (1988). Human parental care: Universal goals, cultural strategies, individual behavior. In R. A. LeVine, P. M. Miller, & M. M. West (Eds.), *Parental behavior in diverse societies* (pp. 5–12). San Francisco: Jossey-Bass.

McMullen, N. (1982). *The newly industrializing countries: Adjusting to success*. Washington: British–North American Committee.

Pedersen, P. (1999). *Multiculturalism as a fourth force*. Washington, DC: Taylor and Frances.

Peterson, R. D., & Bailey, W. C. (1991). Felony murder and capital punishment: An examination of the deterrence question. *Criminology, 29*, 367–395.

Rothman, J., & Thomas, E. L. (1994). *Intervention research: Design and development for the human services*. New York: Haworth Press.

Safilios-Rothschild, C. (1970). *The sociology and social psychology of disability and rehabilitation*. New York: Random House.

Sinha, D. (1998). Changing perspectives in social psychology in India: A journey towards indigenization. *Asian Journal of Social Psychology, 1*, 17–32.

Stevenson, H., & Lee, S. Y. (1990). Context of achievement: A study of American, Chinese, and Japanese children. *Monographs of the Society for Research in Child Development, 55.*

Sugiman, T., Karasawa, M., Liu, J. H., & Ward, C. (Eds.). (1999). *Progress in Asian social psychology*, Vol. 2: *Theoretical and empirical contributions.* Seoul, Korea: Kyoyook-Kwahak-Sa.

Tu, W., Hejtmanek, M., & Wachman, A. (Eds.). (1992). *The Confucian world observed: A contemporary discussion of Confucian humanism in East Asia.* Honolulu, HI: Program for Cultural Studies, East–West Center.

Part I

CONCEPTUAL PERSPECTIVES

CHAPTER 1

Trends toward Indigenization of Psychology in India

Jai B. P. Sinha

Indigenous psychology may be conceptualized as a body of knowledge that derives its principles, laws, and theories from natural taxonomies that the people of a culture employ for organizing their thoughts and actions, constructing their realities, relating with each other, and designing their future.[1] It reflects the collective efforts of a group of social scientists to systematize people's world views into a scientific discipline that is unique to the culture. Naturally, the ethos of a culture plays a seminal role in the growth of indigenous psychology. In case of India, the ethos is expressed most appropriately in *Rig-Veda*[2] in the following words: "Let noble thoughts come to us from all directions" (1.89.9).

When thoughts are welcomed from different directions and diverse groups of people have rich and long traditions of religion and philosophy, centuries of experience of migrations, invasions, and alien rule, and increasing exposure to foreign influences, the culture is rendered highly pluralistic. Naturally, indigenous psychology has to be integrative in accommodating these various forces into a comprehensive framework.

The diverse cultural influences can be arranged into three broad streams. They are the Western influences with a backdrop of colonial experience, the ancient Indian wisdom enshrined in various religious texts and scriptures, and the folkways that reflect the confluence of the two as they filter through people's experiences in coping with their day-to-day realities. The folkways consist of common people's beliefs, preferences, practices, norms, and so on that are acquired in their early socialization and are strengthened, modified, or changed by subsequent social transactions and experiences. The ancient Indian wisdom is believed to permeate folkways through Indians' strong oral tradition, social codes of conduct, and religious practices. Western influences were first experienced during the colonial rule, and are now received through mass media, Western literature, and mobility across boundaries. The three—Western influences, ancient Indian wisdom, and folkways—constitute a triangular space giving rise to five trends toward varying degrees of indigenization of psychology in India. A sixth trend of methodological indigenization manifests in either adapting to the existing methods and procedures or innovating new ones to gain better vantage points for understanding the contents within the trends.

WESTERN INFLUENCE

Western empirical psychology was introduced in India quite early in the first quarter of the nineteenth century. However, its growth remained sluggish until India's independence in 1947. Research facilities were almost nonexistent. Hence, only general and descriptive papers were published on a wide range of topics such as communal conflicts, social organization, social character, religion, poetry, and art. They were superficial, devoid of any serious research, and "followed more or less the beaten tracks" (Bose, 1939, p. 345). There were, however, a few instances of the flashes of a bright idea or the perseverance of individual scholars. Prasad (1935), for example, studied rumors after an earthquake that proved to be "one of the starting points of Festinger's famous theory of cognitive dissonance" (D. Sinha, 1998, p. 21). J. Sinha (1933) wrote two volumes on the nature, types, and theories of perception and emotions in light of Indian philosophical thoughts. Akhilanand (1952) showed the relevance of Indian psycho-spiritual thoughts for enhancing mental health.

Research activities picked up momentum in the 1950s and 1960s. About 90% of pre-1970 publications appeared during this time. The growth rate increased over tenfold from the 1950s to the 1980s (J.B.P. Sinha, 1993), exceeding 900 publications in about 44 journals by over 4,000 psychologists by the first half of the 1980s (Dalal, 1990). Social psychology claimed the lion's share, followed by clinical, industrial–organizational, and personality psychology. Taken together they dominated the field of Indian psychology and set new trends.

Three factors shaped the nature of Indian psychology in the 1950s and 1960s. First was the negative construction of Indian personality and culture by foreign scholars. Second, the separation of psychology from philosophy departments deprived Indian psychologists of the opportunity to draw on the ancient Indian body of knowledge that J. Sinha highlighted so emphatically. Third, in the absence of their own conceptual framework, Indian psychologists had no option but to borrow Western concepts, theories, and methods.

Western scholars were often derogatory in their construction of Indian culture and personality. From their perspective, Indians were authoritarian (Lewis, 1962), narcissistic with a weak superego (Spratt, 1966), obsessive–compulsive, infantile, and neurotic (Berkeley-Hill quoted by Hartnack, 1987). The core of their personality consisted of "an inner sense of instability and insecurity" to the extent that "nothing and nobody can be relied upon, not even one's own self" (Carstairs, 1971, p. 54). This insecure and unstable personality was alleged to express itself in poor emotional involvement, callousness toward others (especially lesser men), mock hospitality, supremely self-centered attitude, and utter collapse of self-control in the face of strong emotions (Carstairs, 1971).

Interestingly, these samples of Western construction of Indian culture and personality were shared by a number of Indian researchers. Educated Indians under the British rule identified with the British, although the latter treated them like slaves (Nandy, 1983) and denigrated them so severely that it was difficult for them to express their Indianness openly (Roland, 1988, p. xxvi). The values and behavior that they frequently attributed to Indians, according to a review by D. Sinha (1986), included fatalism, passivity, dependency, paranoid reaction, narcissism, insecurity, anxiety, authoritarianism, submission, indifference to contradictions (i.e., lack of rationality), and so on. Further, the roots of most of these negative attributes were traced mostly by Western scholars, and also by some Indians, to Indians' other-worldliness, theory of karma, spiritualism, and so forth.

Negation of the cultural heritage and negative construction of Indian culture and personality combined with an utter lack of research facilities created a situation in which Indian psychologists had no choice but to imitate and replicate Western theories and concepts by employing Western methods and tools. Western models and theories such as achievement motivation, two-factors theory of motivation, Maslow's need hierarchy, participative style of leadership, and so on were often shown to be valid in Indian conditions (see Pareek, 1980, 1981 for details). In order to be able to replicate Western studies, psychologists went to the extent of equating castes with race, communalism with anti-Semitism, and untouchables with American blacks (Nandy, 1974). Despite such efforts, some findings were inconsistent with Western models and theories. Such unexplained findings were considered to be "exceptions," and theories and models were left intact. As a result, Indian psychology seemed to be a faint carbon copy of its Western counterpart (Nandy, 1974) or a "replica product" (Adair, 1989).

Another manifestation of dependence on the West was the indiscriminate use of Western scales, measures, and tests. Likert scale of attitude measurement and paper–pencil tests of personality proved to be quite handy for resource-starved psychologists. They employed incidental samples and liberally indulged in establishing relationships of demographic- and personality-related variables with attitudes toward castes, religion, and nationalities (Dalal, 1990). This resulted in what D. Sinha (1981, p. 14) called "questionnaire psychology" yielding little insight beyond common sense.

By the 1970s, Indian psychology was in a crisis (Pareek, 1980, p. vii). The crisis arose out of the realization that (1) psychology had failed to have any impact on the life of the people, (2) its tests and measures were culture blind, and (3) there were too many inconsistent and unexplained findings to be brushed aside (D. Sinha, 1998). This realization, coupled with the advent of a new generation of psychologists who were less constrained by colonial experience, and supported by a number of problem-oriented studies, led to an exploration of more appropriate concepts, theories, and methods which initiated Indian psychology into a phase of indigenization (D. Sinha, 1998). Although a majority of psychologists are still imitating and replicating the concepts and methods of Western psychology, a few of them are establishing a new trend toward indigenization (J.B.P. Sinha, 1993) which, according to Adair (1989), is emerging slowly but surely.

ANCIENT INDIAN WISDOM

The second potential source for developing indigenous psychology is the ancient Indian wisdom enshrined in a variety of texts and scriptures spanning from 2,500 B.C. to A.D. eighth century (Akhilanand, 1952; Misra, in press; Paranjpe, 1984, 1988; Radhakrisnan & Moore, 1954; J.B.P. Sinha, 1982; among others). Broadly speaking, they have given rise to two distinct approaches. The first and the dominant is the devotional approach based on belief in the existence of gods and goddesses whose blessings have to be procured through various rites, rituals, prayers, chanting of mantras, and religious practices. The second is a rational approach emanating from the *Upanishads*, which address philosophical issues regarding life, death, sorrows, and happiness. The two converge in vedantic literature providing a comprehensive psycho-spiritual world view, which is so ingrained in the minds of Indians that unless it is taken into consideration, "it is virtually impossible to comprehend Indian psychological make up, society, and culture" (Roland, 1988, p. 289). It has three main facets: cosmic collectivism, hierarchical order, and spiritual orientation.

Cosmic collectivism posits that the universe consists of diverse forms and elements. They are compatible as well as conflicting, and are interconnected by an underlining sense of unity derived from being part of the same ultimate reality, *Brahman*. The manifest parts of cosmos constitute *maya*, all that is phenomenal, illusory, and deceptive. It is *Brahman* that is real and appears in the *atman* (innermost self) of all beings. Hierarchical order signifies that the whole cosmos and everything within it is arranged in a hierarchical order. Spirituality implies that, although human beings are engulfed in *maya* leading to the experience of *ahamkara* (false ego), *kama* (desire for worldly pleasure), *moha* (attachment), *krodha* (anger), and *lobha* (greed), there also exists in human beings a built-in disposition toward self-transformation of one's spiritual nature (Roland, 1988). Transformation can be realized by cultivating an "observer" (*drashta*) in the mind. The observer enables people to integrate various activities and emotions, expand consciousness, acquire purity in thought and action, and transcend *maya* to realize the *Brahman* that resides in *atman*.

The rational approach was developed by philosopher kings (called Janakas). It was further advanced by the *Samkhya* philosophy of Kapil, the *Yoga Sutra* of Patanjali, *Gita* of Vyas, Bhuddism, Jainism, *Arthshastra* of Kautilya, the *Lokayat* tradition of Charvaka, and so on (P. Sinha, 1987). They had some common and some different elements. They all denied the existence of God, denigrated the importance of rites and rituals, and emphasized the importance of right conduct for liberation from sufferings. They differed in their views on how to cope with desires, which form of *yoga* to practice, and which codes of conduct to follow. *Samkhya*, for example, suggested that one can alleviate pain and attain happiness by regulating sensory and motor functions, which together affect one's intellect and self-awareness. A king, according to *Arthshastra*, has to create, augment, distribute, and protect the resources of society for the well-being of all by establishing a secular administration based on merit, rationality, and judicious use of power (Kangle, 1986). Charvak proclaimed that there is no life after this one. Hence, one must enjoy all pleasures of life. In order to do so, one needs a strong body that can be built by stimulating and activating the energy centres in the body by a proper practice of *hath-yoga*.

The two approaches, despite their manifest contradictions, were integrated or allowed to coexist because of at least three common considerations (Radhakrishnan & Moore, 1954). First, most of them were concerned with the practical problem of how to liberate human beings from the sufferings of life. The shared goal led them to borrow from each other, for no single solution seemed to be sufficient. For example, *Gita*, while propagating the importance of discharging one's duties, also asked devotees to surrender unconditionally to the Almighty.

Second, they all shared the belief that liberation from sufferings lies in cultivating an attitude of detachment. That is, one has to perform one's duties (*dharma*) and get involved in the mundane things of life; but one must not become enslaved by them. Distancing, while remaining involved in earthly pursuits, is the key to liberation. Third, they all subscribed to the doctrine of *karma* (the cause–effect relationship) signifying that good and bad conduct have their inevitable consequences, which, according to some, follow immediately, but, according to others, may occur even in the next life.

It is this integrated as well as not-so-integrated perspective which was expressed in *Gita*, the *Yoga Sutra*, the epics (*Ramayan* and *Mahabjarat*), *Jatakkathas*, Jain literature *Purans*, and other texts on Indian mythology. The epics, for example, externalized people's inner worlds in order to legitimize and validate their thoughts, gain insights into the ways of resolving serious life issues, and create mythic models for emulation. They implied the presence in everyday relationships of the divine and the demonic by generating ego ideals, norms for correct reciprocal behavior in complex hierarchical relationships, as well as negative models that have to be avoided (Ramanujan, 1989; Roland, 1988). Furthermore, even the divine characters were depicted to have vices indicating the complex nature of human beings. The second type of narrative is exemplified in *Panchtantra* in which animals and birds think and behave like human beings. Instead of indulging in divine activities, they demonstrate ways to safeguard against the evils and crooked ones by cultivating practical intelligence in order to identify faithful and skillful friends and relatives who may help in gaining wealth and prosperity.

In sum, ancient Indian wisdom is characterized by a wide variety of concepts and ideas that are at times seen to be integrated, but at other times remain inconsistent and even mutually exclusive of each other. Scholars have to be judicious in selectively focusing on one or another aspect for developing their research paradigms. Further, in the spirit of *Rig-Veda*, the ancient Indian wisdom reflects a "synthesizing tendency of the Indian mind" (Radhakrishnan & Moore, 1954, p. xxv) that tends to see unity amongst diversity, relatedness in seemingly unrelated ideas, and organic unity in the cosmos. In contrast to the Western analytical approach, the ancient Indian approach emphasizes the importance of examining the totality of a phenomenon howsoever complex it may be.

THE FOLKWAYS

The folkways provide an arena where ancient Indian wisdom and Western influences interface with the highly pluralistic societal setting to create a body of beliefs, preferences, and practices that enable common people to regulate their thoughts and actions. As a result, Indians have developed an encompassing cognitive system (Dumont, 1970) and an enfolding mode (Schulberg, 1968). In this world view, seemingly paradoxical and contradictory thoughts, actions, norms, values, and styles of life, instead of being confronted and integrated or rejected, are tolerated, balanced, accommodated, or simply allowed to coexist. For example, Indians acquire the knowledge of modern science, business, and technology, but retain traditional religious lifestyles without experiencing any dissonance (Ramanujan, 1989). They are collectivists (Verma, 1999) as well as individualists (Mishra, 1994; D. Sinha & Tripathi, 1994). They manifest contradictions among as well as across beliefs and practices (Chakraborty, 1993). Their psyche oscillates between erotic and ascetic (Roland, 1988). Organizations, despite modern systems and principles of management, take a cultural detour to get work done (Virmani & Guptan, 1991).

The seemingly paradoxical cognitive algebra may be understood by differentiating (1) the core from the peripheral characteristics of Indians that manifest in their primary and secondary modes of behavior, and (2) delineating the differential impact of situations on them. "A primary mode is triggered by indigenous traditional influences, while a secondary mode may also be manifest because of the more recent Western influences" (Sinha & Kanungo, 1997, p. 99). The primary modes reflect Indians' spiritual and familial selves (Roland, 1988). The familial self is characterized by the enmeshing of persons into their primordial groups to the extent that they are "dividuals" rather than individuals (Marriot, 1990). Consequently, they have permeable ego boundaries, intense emotional connectedness and interdependence, personalized relationships, constant flow of affect in interpersonal transactions, strong mutual caring and dependence, heightened expectations of reciprocity, and so on. The familial self, combined with the spiritual self, ideally expresses itself in refining one's qualities, rising on the scale of spiritual merit and social virtues, and being respectful to one's superiors. There is an obvious parallel in conceptualizing the familial self and Indians' social values. The latter are expressed in the preferences for ingroup members, hierarchical and personalized rather than egalitarian contractual relationships, duty over hedonistic orientation, and harmony rather than confrontation (J.B.P. Sinha, 1990b).

Despite this collectivist orientation, Indians maintain an inner private psychological space that is central to their individuality (Roland, 1988). Paranjpe (1988) observed that "In the intellectual and cultural tradition of India, the individual, rather than the group, has been the focus of moral responsibility" (p. 61) not only for moral responsibility, but also for pleasure seeking. According to the *Lokayat* tradition, individuals should build their bodies through *hath-yoga*.

Thus, an Indian's innermost self is a reservoir of personal and private thoughts, feelings, fantasies, and the need for individual achievements as well as a striving for spiritual transformation. Their behavior, as a result, oscillates in the triangular psychological space where the collective familial and individualized private selves counteract each other or just coexist without causing dissonance. The spiritual self at times combines with a collectivist orientation to express in collectively held socioreligious rituals and activities. At other times, it sides with individualist orientation to manifest in the effort to rise on the scales of merit, personal achievement, virtues, ethics, and integrity. In fact, Indians are likely to use either of the two (collectivist or individualist behavior) as the means to realize either collectivist or individualist goals. The choice of a particular behavior or intention depends on the context (Sinha & Kanungo, 1997), which may be specified in terms of place (*desh*), time (*kaal*), or person (*paatra*). In sum, Indians are particularists and evoke different rules and norms for interacting with others. They draw ideas from different sources, balance and integrate, or let them coexist according to situational requirements.

TRENDS TOWARD INDIGENOUS PSYCHOLOGY

Depending on the degree of proximity to either Western influences or ancient Indian wisdom, D. Sinha (1998) distinguished two major strands of indigenization: exogenous and conceptual or paradigmatic. The latter probably may be renamed more appropriately as endogenous indigenization. Each strand seems to have two variants: The first is a relatively purist one having a deeper anchoring in either the mainstream Western psychology or in ancient Indian thought to the extent that they see Indian reality through only one of the frameworks. The second variant has an allegiance to either of the traditions, but manifests greater flexibility in the choice of concepts and methods. Together they constitute four trends. A fifth may be identified as integrative indigenization drawing mainly on folkways in having greater eclecticism in the approach and elasticity in the choice of concepts and methods of research. D. Sinha (1998) also mentions a sixth trend toward methodological indigenization reflecting attempts to innovate and adapt methods and procedures that are more appropriate for studies of the contents within each of the trends.

These trends are conceptual constructions rather than discrete domains of research. Psychologists are found moving smoothly back and forth between the domains. There are studies that show overlapping trends. All trends address in their own ways the issues that are culturally relevant. They differ mainly in the degree to which they are fixed or just show allegiance to either Western psychology or Indian traditions of thought. A few selective illustrations of each of the trends are given in the rest of the chapter.

The Purist Endogenous Trend of Ancient Indian Wisdom

Those who subscribe to this trend believe that the ancient Indian wisdom is timeless, experientially verifiable (Paranjpe, 1988), and still applicable in its original form. There are three grounds for assuming its continuity. First, through a strong oral tradition, ancient Indian thoughts have been transmitted from generation to generation. Second, instead of creating organized institutions around these thoughts, Hinduism has instilled them in the social codes of conduct that are observed quite strictly even today, constituting an operative culture of the people (Misra, in press). Third, Indians' mythic tradition, through their metonymic thinking, sustains both the orally transmitted ancient knowledge as well as the imperatives to behave according to the social code of conduct (Ramanujan, 1989).

There are two overlapping aspects in the views of those who subscribe to this purist trend: The first one shows the application of the ancient wisdom to the present-day reality. The second one indicates that the ancient Indian wisdom is not only similar to Western psychology in many ways, but has concepts and methods that might enrich psychology in general. Chakraborty (1987), for example, provides evidence that practicing yoga, meditating, controlling breathing, and stilling the turbulent mind can help people purify their *chitta* and make it spiritual, expand their self to include others around them, and orient to self-sacrifice for others instead of expecting reciprocal return. This "giving" (i.e., *dan* involving self-sacrifices) theory of motivation negates the principles of reinforcement and exchange that are so basic to Western psychology. Sharma (1996, 1999) drew ideas from the *Bhagvadgita* and other sources for formulating a number of models that by and large take cognizance of animal impulses in human beings, but recommend transcendence of them in order to cultivate human qualities, realize spiritualism, and ultimately develop harmony with nature. Bhawuk (1999), like many others, recommended the *Gita* model for maintaining mental health. Although the efficacy of these models for an individual's personal growth, mental health, stress management, and so on is beyond doubt, it is still not clear how applicable the ideas are to most of the people in a society that is increasingly subjected to Western consumerism.

Paranjpe (1984, 1988) and Bhawuk (2000) identified many similarities between ancient Indian and Western scientific thoughts. Paranjpe (1988), for example, observed that the triology—capacities of cognition, affect, and conation—that provides the basic framework for the development of modern psychology corresponds to the traditional Indian view of a person being *karta* (doer), *drashta* (observer), and *bhokta* (beneficiary or sufferer). But the latter has made a significant advancement in postulating the superconscious level of mind that "offers a direct experience of an undivided and unchanging self" (p. 356). Bhawuk (2000) suggested a new paradigm drawing on one of the ancient *Upanishads* in which a person's wisdom lies not only in being ignorant (having *avidya*, that is, ignorance or bad knowledge) or having *vidya* (right knowledge) but in knowing both—a synthesized view of the opposites. He argued that the construct of *maya* approximates the Western concept of "social construction," having a subjective view of external reality. He further highlighted the scientific validity of transcendental meditation and its edge over Western techniques of relaxation.

The Trend toward Endogenous Indigenization

This trend is advanced by those who, like the purists, believe in the veracity of ancient Indian wisdom, but examine use with Western empirical methods. A review (Orme-Johnson, Zimmerman, & Hawkins, 1997) of over 500 experimental studies conducted in over 200 universities in 33 countries revealed that Transcendental Meditation helps expand consciousness, decrease oxygen intake and stress levels, increase basal skin resistance and coherence on an EEG, and virtually suspend breathing for up to one minute. All these are related to the health and well-being of all people. Pande and Naidu (1992) reported empirical evidence to show that people with a strong orientation to *nishkam karm* (working sincerely without getting preoccupied about the outcome) experience less work-related stress. Probably, *nishkam karm* implies process rather than goal orientation and thereby emphasizes here-and-now experience rather than uncertain goal anxiety. As a result, it leads to greater intrinsic satisfaction (Misra, 1989). Kaur and A. K. Sinha (1992) confirmed the configurations of three *gunas* (temperamental qualities) in a sample of managers, except that one of them, *rajas*, was bifurcated into two factors: negative (consisting of strife and stress) and positive (composed of love for fame, passion, and power). They further reported that while *sattva* (purity in thought and action) and positive *rajas* had a facilitating effect, *tamas* (inertia or darkness) and negative *rajas* had a debilitating impact on the work ethic, managers' personal effectiveness, and organizational effectiveness. Major issues of organizational behavior have also been conceptualized in terms of

Indian traditional ethos in general and vedantic ideas in particular (N. K. Singh, 1990; N. K. Singh & Paul, 1985).

The Purist Exogenous Trend in the Western Psychological Tradition

This trend reflects a belief in the universal nature of psychological knowledge. Differences in cultural context are supposed to be either irrelevant or instrumental to extending or refining Western theory through empirical, particularly experimental, methods. Many in India, either out of such a belief or because of convenience, still replicate Western studies and use tests and measures developed in the West. They are, however, hardly creative and innovative. One exception is R. Singh (1988, 1995, 1996). He employed rigorous experimental methods, simulations, and the information integration framework to delineate the basic psychological processes involved in reward allocation, intergroup attraction and discrimination, attributions regarding performance, happiness, a leader's perception of situational favor, and so on. Although R. Singh pointed out cross-cultural differences in these basic processes, his efforts have been directed more toward refining information integration models than toward tracing the roots of these processes in Indian culture. As such, his efforts are not quite appreciated in India because of the cultural preference to study complex live issues in their totality rather than simulating them in the information integration framework.

However, there is one area, organizational behavior, that seems to be relatively more conducive to a direct transfer of Western models. Import of Western technology with its values and requirements, management education, and exposure to a Western world view have created a critical mass of managers who share the Western world view. They are highly individualized (Srinivas, 1994). They value achievement, advancement, ability utilization, and personal development (Kumar, 1996; P. Singh & Das, 1977; J.B.P. Sinha, 1990a) and adopt a professional approach in being "strongly influenced by Western norms of personal growth, personal efficacy, [and] pioneering-innovative motive" (Khandwalla, 1994, p. 132). There are, however, reports (Garg & Parikh, 1993) that many of these managers suffer from identity crisis primarily because of the gap between their inner psychological structure formed out of traditional cultural influences and the professional behavior fostered by their organizations.

The Trend toward Exogenous Indigenization

This trend can be distinguished from the purist one on the basis of the relative emphasis placed on the role of Indian culture. The concepts, framework, and methods are still Western in nature, but their applications are culture sensitive. Kanungo and his associates (Kanungo & Jaeger, 1990; Mendonca & Kanungo, 1994), for example, took cognizance of the impact of culture on an organization, but their main prescriptions are essentially culture free. According to them, the core concern in an organization is to ensure high-quality performance that depends on an effective management of rewards backed by an appropriate appraisal system. Performance management involves setting up specific and difficult but attainable goals, arranging training programs, and giving feedback to the employees. While the processes in the three systems are universal, the ways of conducting these processes are postulated to be culture specific. Mendonca and Kanungo (1994, p. 79) advocate blending "firm structured directions" while accommodating cultural expectation.

Another example is Kakar (1978, 1982) who viewed Indian psyche, culture, society, and healing traditions from the psychoanalytic framework and found the latter quite adequate to understand the richness of the former. There are other examples. Pandey (1981) and Tripathi (1981) investigated ingratiation and manipulation to show that ingratiation is more pervasive and risk free in India than in the West. Because of a highly politicized climate in Indian organizations, where hierarchy and personalized relationships play a major role, ingratiation and manipulation are practiced quite often and with a great deal of immunity. Similarly, unlike in the West, the psychological consequences of crowding are not always negative (Jain, 1987). Prolonged prior experience of living in a crowed space (as Indians generally do) may enable people to cope with whatever adverse effects crowding might have, provided they have a sense of control over their life events (Pandey, 1999).

The Western construction of the need for achievement (McClelland, 1975) is another example that has been critically examined. In resource-limited conditions, high need for achievement tends to maximize a person's gains at the cost of the group's achievement, harmony, and quality of relationships (J.B.P. Sinha, 1968). Therefore, need for achievement has to be blended with a culture-specific need, the need for extension (that is, care and consideration for others) (Pareek, 1968), in order to function as the need for social achievement (Mehta, 1987). In fact, achievement goals are found to include social concerns such as being a good person, thinking about the well-being of others, fulfilling one's duties, helping others, and being able to get affection from elders. They can be realized by such means as respecting others, helping others, obtaining elders' blessings, observing social codes of conduct, and so on (Agarwal & Misra, 1989; Misra & Agarwal, 1985).

Distributive justice is another example of a concept that has been picked up from Western psychology and examined from the traditional and contemporary Indian as well as Western perspective (Krishnan, 1997). Similarly, Kohlberg's model of moral development was reformulated in terms of the Hindu conceptualization of morality that stems from the concept of duties and social obligations (Shweder, Mahapatra, & Miller, 1990). The literature is replete with examples of Western concepts and methods being employed to examine Indian issues with or without adaptation. Not that these concepts do not have their equivalents in Indian languages. But the fact that they were coined and researched first in the West and were picked up, often along with their theoretical underpinnings, for application in India places them in the category of exogenous indigenization.

The Trend toward Integrative Indigenization

This trend is anchored in Indian folkways. It differs from exogenous and endogenous indigenization in having an encompassing framework to accommodate both Indian and Western concepts and methods. Pareek (1988), for example, argued that each culture has its strengths in developing modern organizations, but they must also borrow from others. Indians' concern for others, tendency to harmonize and synthesize various points of view, positive regard for different points of view, and general respect of knowledge and expertise can be effectively used for designing effective organizations that should also include Western values such as openness, collaboration, trust, authenticity, autonomy, and confrontation.

Organizational leadership is one area where the integration of Indian and Western thought has been attained to a large extent. Drawing on the work of Gupta (1999), J.B.P. Sinha (1990b), and others, Dayal (1999) showed that effective leaders establish familial relationships with their subordinates as well as create assets, achieve success, mature by learning, enlarge their perspectives, and realize their self. P. Singh and Bhandarkar (1990) reported that transformational leaders create vision, take risk, build teams, and so on. But they also groom, care, and mentor their subordinates. The nurturant-task model of leadership is another example of a blend of Indian familism with Western psychological principles and processes (J.B.P. Sinha, 1980, 1995). An effective leader–subordinate relationship is personalized and bound by *shradha* (deference) for the leader who shows *sneh* (affection) and nurturance for the subordinates. However, this bond is contingent on the leader's role modeling and the subordinates' hard and sincere work. The mutually facilitative relationship and work behavior naturally lead the subordinates to assume greater responsibility for the task and the leader to invite more participation. Thus, culture-specific concepts have been used along with the contingency approach, reinforcement principle, and the quality of dyadic exchange to develop a dynamic and growth-oriented model of leadership.

The Trend toward Methodological Indigenization

"Methodological indigenization" is the attempt to either modify and adapt tests, measures, and procedures of Western psychology or to innovate new ones to make the tool correspond to the trend. For example, D. Sinha used a grains test to measure the villagers level of aspiration. He also adapted a figure-ground test for tribal respondents (D. Sinha, 1986). Mehta (1987) adapted the

TAT test to measure social need for achievement. Sharma (1999) formulated "Rishi" methodology that involves the use of both reason and intuition. J.B.P. Sinha (1990a) found that Indians express themselves more freely and frankly in unstructured interviews and can be observed more accurately in unobtrusive ways than when they are asked structured questions or placed in experimental conditions. Because Indians often live in a crowded or shared space and in collectives, group interviews are not only more feasible but also more useful in getting authentic responses as the members stimulate, counteract, and correct each other. Similarly, information about collectives can be collected more accurately when respondents are asked to put themselves in an observer's role and report on how and what people in the society believe, prefer, practice, appreciate, discourage, reject, and so forth (Sinha, Daftuar, Gupta, Mishra, Jayseetha, Jha, Verma, & Vijayakumar, 1994).

CONCLUSION

The trends suggest that the field of psychology in India is moving toward indigenization through at least five overlapping routes, all contributing in varying degrees to the understanding of Indian realities. Of them, the trend toward integrative indigenization holds greater promise than others because of its reliance on folkways and flexibility in drawing on whatever sources have useful ideas to offer. The process of integrative indigenization needs to be accelerated by highlighting the crucial role of symbiotic interaction between researchers' natural inclinations and values, the state of psychological science, and folkways. The international community of psychologists may facilitate the interaction by being constructive in a critique of the process of integrative indigenization.

NOTES

1. An earlier version of the paper was presented as an invited address during the Third Conference of the Asian Association of Social Psychology, Taipei, Taiwan, August 4–7, 1999. I would like to thank Professor Rajen Gupta for comments and suggestions on the paper.

2. The most ancient text of Hindus, dating back to 2,500–1,500 B.C.

REFERENCES

Adair, J. G. (1989, June). Indigenous developments in Indian psychology: A quantitative assessment. Paper presented at the Canadian Psychological Association, Halifax, Nova Scotia, Canada.

Agarwal, R., & Misra, G. (1989). Variations in achievement cognitions: Role of ecology, age, and gender. *International Journal of Intercultural Relations, 13*, 93–107.

Akhilanand, S. (1952). *Mental health and Hindu psychology*. London: George Allen and Unwin.

Bhawuk, D.P.S. (1999). Who attains peace: An Indian model of personal harmony. *Indian Psychological Review 52* (2–3), 40–48.

Bhawuk, D.P.S. (2000, July 16–21). Science of culture and culture of science: Worldview and choice of conceptual models and methodology. Paper presented at the 25th Congress of International Association for Cross-Cultural Psychology, Poland.

Bose, G. (1939). Progress of psychology in India during the past twenty five years. In B. Prasad (Ed.), *The progress of science in India during the last twenty-five years* (pp. 336–352). Calcutta: Indian Science Congress Association.

Carstairs, G. M. (1971). *The twice born*. Bombay: Asia Publishers.

Chakraborty, S. K. (1987). *Managerial effectiveness and quality of work life: Indian insights*. New Delhi: Tata McGraw-Hill.

Chakraborty, S. K. (1993). *Managerial transformation by values: A corporate pilgrimage*. New Delhi: Sage.

Dalal, A. K. (1990). India: Psychology in Asia and the Pacific. In G. Shouksmith & E. A. Shouksmith (Eds.), *Status report on teaching and research in eleven countries*. Bangkok: UNESCO.

Dayal, I. (1999). *Can organizations develop leaders: A study of effective leaders*. New Delhi: Mittal.

Dumont, L. (1970). *Homo hierarchicus*. Chicago: University of Chicago Press.

Garg, P., & Parikh, I. (1993). *Young managers at the cross-roads: The trishanku complex*. New Delhi: Sage.

Gupta, R. K. (1999). The truly familial work organization: Extending the organizational boundary to include employees families in the Indian context. In H.S.R. Kao, D. Sinha, & B. Wilpert (Eds.), *Management and cultural values: The indigenization of organizations in Asia* (pp. 103–120). New Delhi: Sage.

Hartnack, C. (1987). British psychoanalysts in colonial India. In M. G. Ash & W. R. Woodward (Eds.), *Psychology in twentieth century thought and society* (pp. 233–251). Cambridge: Cambridge University Press.

Jain, U. (1987). *Psychological consequences of crowding*. New Delhi: Sage.

Kakar, S. (1978). *The inner world: A psychoanalytic study of childhood and society in India*. Delhi: Oxford University Press.

Kakar, S. (1982). *Shamans, mystics, and doctors*. Bombay: Oxford University Press.

Kangle, R. P. (1986). *Kautilya's Arthshastra*. Delhi: Motilal Banasidas.

Kanungo, R. N., & Jaeger, A. M. (1990). Introduction: The need for indigenous management in developing countries. In R. N. Kanungo & A. M. Jaeger (Eds.), *Management in developing countries* (pp. 1–22). London: Routledge.

Kaur, P., & Sinha, A. K. (1992). Dimensions of *gunas* in organizational setting. *Vikalpa, 17*, 27–32.

Khandwalla, P. N. (1994). The PI motive: A resource for socio-economic transformation of developing societies. In R. N. Kanungo & M. Mendonca (Eds.), *Work motivation: Models for developing societies* (pp. 114–134). New Delhi: Sage.

Krishnan, L. (1997). Distributive justice in the Indian perspective. In H.S.R. Kao & D. Sinha (Eds.), *Asian perspectives on psychology* (pp. 25–39). New Delhi: Sage.

Kumar, D. S. (1996). Work values and organizational commitment: A study of managers in public and private sector organizations. Unpublished Ph.D. diss., Osmania University, Hyderabad, India.

Marriott, K. (Ed.). (1990). *India through Hindu categories*. New Delhi: Sage.

McClelland, D. C. (1975). *Power: The inner experience*. New York: Free Press.

Mehta, P. (1987). *Scoring imaginations for motivation: A scoring manual for personal achievement, social achievement, and influence motivation*. New Delhi: Participation and Development Centre.

Mendonca, M., & Kanungo, R. N. (1994). Motivation through effective reward management in developing countries. In R. N. Kanungo & M. Mendonca (Eds.), *Work motivation: Models for developing countries* (pp. 49–83). New Delhi: Sage.

Mishra, R. C. (1994). Individualist and collectivist orientations across generations. In U. Kim, H. C. Triandis, C. Kagitcibasi, S. C. Choi, & G. Yoon (Eds.), *Individualism and collectivism: Theory, method, and application* (pp. 225–238). Thousand Oaks, CA: Sage.

Misra, G. (1989). Intrinsic motivation, extrinsic reward, and performance. *Indian Educational Review, 24*, 17–25.

Misra, G. (in press). Implications of culture for psychological knowledge. In J. W. Berry, R. C. Tripathi, & R. Mishra (Eds.), *Psychology in human and social development*. New Delhi: Sage.

Misra, G., & Agarwal, R. (1985). The meaning of achievement: Implication for a cross-cultural theory of achievement motivation. In I. R. Lagunes & Y. H. Poortinga (Eds.), *From a different perspective: Studies of behaviour across cultures* (pp. 250–266). Amsterdam: Swets & Zetlinger.

Nandy, A. (1974). The non-paradigmic crisis in Indian psychology. *Indian Journal of Psychology, 49*, 1–20.

Nandy, A. (1983). *The intimate enemy*. Delhi: Oxford University Press.

Orme-Johnson, D. W., Zimmerman, E., & Hawkins, M. (1997). Maharshi's Vedic psychology: The science of the cosmic psyche. In H.S.R. Kao & D. Sinha (Eds.), *Asian perspectives on psychology* (pp. 282–308). New Delhi: Sage.

Pande, N., & Naidu, R. K. (1992). *Anasakti* and health: A study of non-attachment. *Psychology and Developing Societies, 4*, 89–104.

Pandey, J. (1981). Ingratiation as a social behaviour. In J. Pandey (Ed.), *Perspectives on experimental social psychology* (pp. 157–185). New Delhi: Concept.

Pandey, J. (1999). Socio-psychological dimensions of experience and consequences of crowding. In J. C. Lasry, J. Adair, & K. Dion (Eds.), *Latest contributions to cross-cultural psychology*. Amsterdam: Swets & Zetlinger.

Paranjpe, A. C. (1984). *Theoretical psychology: The meeting of East and West*. New York: Plenum.

Paranjpe, A. C. (1988). A personality theory according to Vedanta. In A. C. Paranjpe, D.X.E. Ho, & R. W. Ribber (Eds.), *Asian contributions to psychology* (pp. 185–213). New York: Praeger.

Pareek, U. (1968). A motivational paradigm for development. *Journal of Social Issues, 24*, 115–122.

Pareek, U. (Ed.). (1980–1981). *A survey of reserach in psychology*, vols. 1 & 2. Bombay: Popular Prakashan.

Prasad, J. (1935). The psychology of rumour. *British Journal of Psychology, 26*, 129–144.

Radhakrishnan, S., & Moore, C. A. (1954). *A sourcebook in Indian philosophy*. Princeton, NJ: Princeton University Press.

Ramanujan, A. K. (1989). Is there an Indian way of thinking? An informal essay. *Contributions to Indian Sociology, 25*, 41–58.

Roland, A. (1988). *In search of self in India and Japan: Towards a cross-cultural psychology*. Princeton, NJ: Princeton University Press.

Schulberg, L. (1968). *Historic India, great ages of man: A history of the world culture series*. Amsterdam: Time-Life International.

Sharma, S. (1996). *Management in new age: Western windows Eastern doors*. New Delhi: New Age International.

Sharma, S. (1999). *Quantum rope: Science, mysticism, and management*. New Delhi: New Age International.

Shweder, R. A., Mahapatra, R. A., & Miller, J. G. (1990). Culture and moral development. In J. Singer, R. A. Shweder, & G. Herdt (Eds.), *Cultural psychology: Essays in comparative human development* (pp. 136–204). New York: Cambridge University Press.

Singh, N. K. (1990). *The dialogue with yati: Insights on man and organization*. New Delhi: Foundation for Organizational Research and Education.

Singh, N. K., & Paul, O. (1985). *The corporate soul: Dynamics of effective management*. New Delhi: Vikas.

Singh, P., & Bhandarker, A. (1990). *The corporate success and transformational leadership*. New Delhi: John Wiley and Sons.

Singh, P., & Das, G .S. (1977). Managerial styles of Indian managers. *ASCI Journal of Management, 7*, 1–11.

Singh, R. (1988). Attitudes and social cognition. In J. Pandey (Ed.), *Psychology in India: The state-of-the-art* (vol. 2, pp. 19–54). Thousand Oaks, CA: Sage.

Singh, R. (1995). "Fair" allocation of pay and workload: Tests of a subtractive model with non-linear judgment function. *Organizational Behaviour and Human Decision Processes, 62* (1), 70–78.

Singh, R. (1996). Subtractive versus ratio model of "fair" allocation: Can the group level analyses be misleading? *Organizational Behaviour and Human Decision Processes, 68* (2), 123–144.

Sinha, D. (1981). Social psychology in India: A historical perspective. In J. Pandey (Ed.), *Perspectives on experimental social psychology in India* (pp. 3–17). New Delhi: Concept.

Sinha, D. (1986). *Psychology in the Third World country: The Indian experience*. New Delhi: Sage.

Sinha, D. (1998). Changing perspectives in social psychology in India: A journey towards indigenization. *Asian Journal of Social Psychology, 1*, 17–32.

Sinha, D., & Tripathi, R. C. (1994). Individualism in a collectivist culture: A case of coexistence of opposites. In U. Kim, H. C. Triandis, C. Kagitcibasi, S. C. Choi, & G. Yoon (Eds.), *Individualism and collectivism: Theory, method, and application* (pp. 123–136). Thousand Oaks, CA: Sage.

Sinha, J. (1933). *Indian psychology*, vols. 1 and 2. London: Kegan Paul.

Sinha, J.B.P. (1968). The nAch/nCooperation under limited/unlimited resource conditions. *Journal of Experimental Social Psychology, 4*, 233–248.

Sinha, J.B.P. (1980). *The nurturant task leader*. New Delhi: Concept.

Sinha, J.B.P. (1982). The Hindu identity. *Dynamic Psychiatry, 15*, 148–160.

Sinha, J.B.P. (1990a). *Work culture in the Indian context*. New Delhi: Sage.

Sinha, J.B.P. (1990b). The salient Indian values and their socio-ecological roots. *Indian Journal of Social Sciences, 3*, 477–488.

Sinha, J.B.P. (1993). The bulk and the front of psychology in India. *Psychology and Developing Societies, 5*, 135–150.

Sinha, J.B.P. (1995). *The cultural context of leadership and power*. New Delhi: Sage.

Sinha, J.B.P., Daftuar, C. N., Gupta, R. K., Mishra, R. C., Jayseetha, R., Jha, S. S., Verma, J., & Vijayakumar, V.S.R. (1994). Regional similarities and differences in people's beliefs, practices, and preferences. *Psychology and Developing Societies, 6*, 131–150.

Sinha, J.B.P., & Kanungo, R. N. (1997). Context sensitivity and balancing in organizational behaviour. *International Journal of Psychology, 32*, 93–105.

Sinha, P. (1987). *The Gita as it was: Rediscovering the original Bhagavadgita*. LaSalle, IL: Open Court.

Spratt, P. (1966). *Hindu culture and personality*. Bombay: Manaktalas.

Srinivas, N. (1994). Management education and work motivation in developing societies: Looking in, looking out. In R. N. Kanungo and M. Mendonca (Eds.), *Work motivation: Models for developing societies* (pp. 230–247). New Delhi: Sage.

Tripathi, R. C. (1981). Machiavellianism and social manipulation. In J. Pandey (Ed.), *Perspectives on experimental social psychology* (pp. 137–156). New Delhi: Concept.

Verma, J. (1999). Collectivism in the cultural perspective: The Indian scene. In J. C. Lasry, J. Adair, & K. Dion (Eds.), *Latest contributions to cross-cultural psychology*. Amsterdam: Swets & Zetlinger.

Virmani, B. R., & Guptan, S. V. (1991). *Indian management*. New Delhi: Vision.

CHAPTER 2

A Conceptual Exploration of the Korean Self in Comparison with the Western Self

Sang-Chin Choi and Kibum Kim

Koreans tend to be at a loss with questions like who they are or what they are. One reason for this is that they are seldom posed with those unspecified questions and so have rare opportunities to think of their reference-free self (Choi, 1992b, 2000, p. 121; Choi & Kim, 1999c, 2000b). Another reason is that those questions are lacking in contextual information. In daily situations, however, Koreans frequently encounter context-specific and intention-oriented questions, such as who they want to be, what sort of job they will pursue, or what they look like in relation to their friends, rather than unspecified questions like who they are (Na & Min, 1998). This may lead Koreans to respond with ease to questions that accompany specific contexts.

Discourse involving ontological definitions of the self is common in Western societies. For instance, casual discussions of concepts and phenomena relating to the self are not uncommon. This discourse is feasible when cognitive systems of the meanings and functions of the self are shared by the people involved in those discussions (Miller, 1999). The shared concept of Western self has several connotations. First, self-representations of the reality of individuals exist in the Western mind with crucial influences on a wide range of psychological variables such as personality, emotion, behavior, and volition (Danziger, 1997). Second, individual uniqueness is inherent in the structure of the self. Third, individuals are aware of and systematize the self on a rational and logical basis (Harré & Gillett, 1994). Fourth, the self plays a critical role as a reference to the behavior of individuals. Finally, individuals lacking in self-identity are judged as anomalous. Thus, Western children are encouraged to seek their self and taught to inquire who they are in discourse with others or in reflection of their deeds (Giddens, 1991).

There are several premises underlying the conceptual meanings of the Western self. First, the self as an entity in nature is subject to rational cognition and analysis. Second, the self is an agent that exercises control over mind and behavior. Third, self differs across individuals, whose life is determined by their unique self. Fourth, self determines reasonably what mind is motivated and what behavior is manifested toward the ultimate goal of self-actualization. These premises suggest that the Western concept of self reflects the core part of materialism, rationalism, individualism, and literalism underlying Western value systems (Bruner, 1990). Things can be seen the other way, such that the very method used by Western people to construct their self rationalizes and justifies their cultural ideologies.

We raise the following questions: Do Koreans possess the same concept of the self as Westerners? If so, is the Korean self the same as the Western self in terms of structure and function? If not, what uniqueness does the Korean self have in comparison with the Western self? We raise these questions in the course of applying the Western self to Korean cultural contexts. We have come to the conclusion that there may be noteworthy differences between the Korean and the Western concept of the self. For instance, Koreans may not regard discovering and organizing the ontological self as important as Westerners do (Choi, 1992b; Choi & Kim, 1999c). Furthermore, the concept of an independent and interdependent self proffered by Markus and Kitayama (1991) enhances our interest in probing the uniqueness of the Korean self. This chapter is designed to compare the Western self with the Korean self.

SELF AND *CHAKEE* AS ITS KOREAN TRANSLATION

The Western concept of the self denotes *I* and the ontological being inherent to *I*. As a conscious being, *I* can objectify, introspect, organize, and restructure the ontological being intrinsic to *I* (Danziger, 1997). However, when this concept of the self is introduced to Koreans, a translation problem occurs since there is no Korean word equivalent to *self*. In this chapter we translate *self* as *chakee*, which literally means "one's own body" and corresponds to *self* in the everyday colloquial activities of Koreans. *Chakee* is used in combination with predicative words that indicate psychological features, such as *chakee-shaping* and *chakee-finding*. The English term *self*, when used in this manner, often has the reflexive connotation of "I am finding myself or shaping myself." *Chakee* is not used in this way, which implies that the conceptual definition of self in terms of personality as in "identifying or making oneself" is inapplicable to *chakee*.

In a culture where one's own native terminology does not correspond to the exotic concept of a psychological construct as with the Korean self and the

Western self, people are likely to have difficulty anchoring phenomena that the exotic construct refers to (Kelly, 1955; Shweder & Miller, 1991). Social representations and phenomena related to that construct are not as salient for the local people as they are for people who are from the culture in which the construct came into being (Harré & Gillett, 1994). Likewise, when *self* is translated as *chakee* in Korean texts, Koreans do not discern all that the original term means. In other words, they are unable to understand the conceptual theory behind the Western concept of *self*. The concept of *self* in the Western sense is alien to Koreans.

Koreans' conceptual lack of a concept of self, however, does not mean that they do not possess self-schema, self-reflection, or self-experience. Traditionally, Koreans place a great deal of emphasis on becoming human beings and acquiring their own humanity. Koreans also seem to assume that they have individual identities similar to the Western self in that they are comprehensible and predictable. For example, words and deeds that suggest "I am a person like this" and "You are a person with a certain personality" are common in social interaction settings.

Observations of Korean usage of *chakee* show that there is a weak tendency to emphasize the self. Instead, Koreans prefer the terms *we* and *our* to the terms *I* and *my* even in situations where the latter is more suitable (Choi, 1993b, 2000, p. 125; Choi & Choi, 1994; Na & Min, 1998). They are likely to use *our school* instead of *my school* and often say *our wife* rather than *my wife*. There are several reasons for the Koreans' reserved attitudes toward *I*. People are seen as individualistic in the Korean culture if they stress *I* in social interactions. Individualism is almost identical to egoism in the eyes of Koreans. In a similar line, emphasis on one's self is interpreted as excluding or rejecting the other person from the social and situational context (Choi & Choi, 1994). The other person in Korean culture has an evaluative connotation of "the person in relation to or opposing me" as well as the neutral meaning of "the third person." Under these circumstances, Korean people have a propensity to use *we* rather than *I*. Also, self-awareness is not highly activated in Koreans in the course of daily conversations, and they try not to draw attention to their self. Instead, both people in a dyadic relationship try to verify their oneness by identifying cues relating to we-ness. In this respect, Koreans are requested, forced, and encouraged to deemphasize their sense of self rather than emphasize the sense of self in social relationships (Choi & Kim, 1999d, 2000b).

WESTERN *I* AND KOREAN *NA* IN RESPECT TO CULTURAL PSYCHOLOGY

There are two general ways of uncovering self: One is to ask people direct questions about their sense of self, whereas the other is to infer it from descriptions or responses to questions about *I*. In the daily discourse of Westerners, descriptions of *I* are often regarded as identical to those of self (Goffman,

1959). As there is no Korean word *self*, examining differences in the concept of *I* between Western and Korean culture will shed light on cultural uniqueness in the concept of self.

The Western View of I and Self

As mentioned earlier, Western concepts and social representations of self and *I* mirror cultural and philosophical ideologies of human beings. Western societies see individuals as unique, able to determine and run their own lives, and endowed with the potential for functional perfection. Similarly, Western social representations of the self conceptualize it as unique and bounded (Danziger, 1997), independent (Markus & Kitayama, 1991), and autonomous (Danziger, 1997; Hofstede, 1980; Miller, 1999; Rose, 1996; Triandis, 1995). This ideology of the self is congruent with the individualism of Western societies (Harré & Gillett, 1994).

Thus, an important task assigned to Western people is to identify, develop, and organize their own self. For example, Westerners are continuously reinforced for discovering their selves. They are also encouraged to develop the characteristics of independence and autonomy and to strengthen the self through reflection on their selfhood. Further, the self that is constructed and integrated into a structural system is seen as complete. Note that the term *system* or *set* is frequently adopted to explain the construct of self, as in a set of theories, a value or belief system, a set of concepts, and so on. These terms imply that the self is seen as an object having the quality of structure and entity, which enables individuals to objectify, observe, and introspect their internal self. Nonetheless, the self is not observable with so much ease and reliability as is an external object. Individuals must make a special effort and pay much attention to identifying their own self.

Self-actualization for Western people is accomplished when their sense of self underlies their behavior and life (Wertsch, 1991). Westerners try to connect their behavior to their self by referring to the self in forming behavior (Giddens, 1991). For Westerners, the self is clear-cut evidence of their existence. Westerners frequently objectify and observe themselves to discover their self. It is also necessary for individuals to focus their attention on analyzing and articulating the personalities and dynamics of their self in order to understand their reality. In fact, Westerners are accustomed and habituated to introspection and analyzing their inner self.

One of the items on the Self-Concept Clarity scale developed by Campbell and Lavallee (1993) is as follows: "It is often hard for me to make up my mind about things because I don't really know what I want." This item reflects the following postulates:

1. Knowing what I want is an important factor in decision making.

2. Ignorance of self makes it difficult to select appropriate behaviors.

3. Knowing what I want can be accomplished by observing the inner self with self-focused attention. Behind the idea that observing the inner self is important is the presupposition that the real self is stable and its components are compatible with each other (Holland, 1997).

4. The self exerts a critical influence on selecting a variety of forms of behavior.

These postulates suggest that social representations of the Western self comprise beliefs in its material stability, mechanical order, and prototypical existence.

The Korean View of *Na* and Mind

The Korean word *na* is identical to *I* in English. *Na* in a daily conversation indicates anything and everything about oneself within the semiotic context. For example, *na* denotes personality in "I am impatient," intellectual ability in "I am smart," employment in "I work at City Bank," and family line in "My last name is Choi." Thus the context in which *na* is used determines what the word indicates in relation to the self. According to the results from our data sets, a coherent structure or system of responses does not emerge when Korean students are asked to describe *na*. Instead, they list personality adjectives and statements pertaining to relationships piece by piece, so that the lists are not intertwined with each other in logical coherence and relevance of content. This result suggests that the Korean concept of *na* is anchored around personality and relationships (Choi & Kim, 1999c).

The same result occurred when Korean students were asked to describe what their friends would think of them: There was no organized structure of the responses and the content centered around personality and relationships. However, in all responses, particularly those related to relationships, responses were more related to a friend's perception than self-perception. This result suggests that providing a context may facilitate Koreans in describing *na*.

Further examination revealed that self-descriptions of Koreans are made in terms of socially desirable personality traits (i.e., sincerity, truthfulness, emotional stability, and consideration). Also, the content of ideal *na* comprises interpersonal relationship dimensions that are considered desirable in the Korean society. These findings suggest that the Korean *na* has its root in a socially desirable personality that is of service to harmonious social relationships.

The Korean concept that is similar in function to *self* is *mind*. The term *mind* is used in Korean cultural contexts to cover the whole range of content and function of the mental world of individuals, including intentionality, spirit, thinking, and so forth. *Mind* exists in consciousness and emotion. However, it is most frequently referred to in the contexts in which it indicates consciousness or a state of consciousness involving intentionality. Mind containing intentionality emerges with or without volition. *Mind* is seen as correspondent to the Western self in that mind is established over a long period of time and plays a crucial role in determining what behavior is selected and what that selected behavior is oriented toward.

Many Asian countries, including Korea, place a high social value on improving one's own mind up to the socially or religiously idealized level. For example, Buddhism cherishes identification with the universal real self as its ideal, which can be achieved by getting rid of the selfish mind that motivates individuals toward material satisfactions and self-interest. From the Buddhist perspective, the personal self bearing Western meanings is mundane and should be discarded. Instead, the universal real self, an essence of self above and beyond the mundane self, can be found by liberating oneself from constraints derived from mundane experiences (Lee, 1996; Park, 1998).

Confucianism conceives human nature as *given*, and the expression of this given nature is defined as *cheong* (Kum, 1998). In addition, Confucianism regards human beings as good natured and regards the four virtues embedded in this nature as goals individuals should pursue throughout their lives: generosity, righteousness, courtesy, and wisdom. The mind exercises control over one's given nature and *cheong*, and so an individual can be a saint, great person, and scholar if his or her mind follows its given nature. Self-discipline in developing the four virtues is designed to sustain and nurture one's given nature.

Given these religious thoughts and ideals, Eastern culture takes a social-oriented view of the self where the individual mind should be congruent with social norms and goals. This perspective sees individuals as a part of the whole, not as separate from each other, which is not the case in Western societies. A belief that persons of maturity should possess a mind and personality consistent with those of public persons rather than private persons is pervasive in Korea. Likewise, the Korean educational system places its focus on the harmony between individuals and society, public goals, and interpersonal cooperation rather than on self-centered individuals, individual uniqueness, and independence (Choi, 1991). The question can be raised as to whether those values are still cherished and realized in the Eastern capitalistic competitive societies. It seems safe to say that those values are still weighted at least in the school or family contexts (Choi & Kim, 1999c, 2000b).

As mentioned, the Korean concept corresponding to the Western self is *mind*. However, as stated earlier, Western *self* is given the quality of entity and structure, whereas Korean *mind* is given the quality of agency or potency and interpreted in the form of existence and state. Although self can be objectified, analyzed, and articulated, this is not the case for the concept of *mind*. The failure of Korean philosophers in uncovering *mind* suggests that it is hard to observe and articulate this concept. For Koreans, it is very common to infer their own mind from observations of their behavior, consistent with Bem's (1972) self-perception theory. Koreans convey their mind to others relying on a storytelling method in which they describe the occurrences and variations of their mind as a function of events. This phenomena serves as indirect support for Bem's self-perception theory. Further, Koreans frequently say, "My mind is such and such" or "I feel or think that my mind is such and such" in social interaction settings. The expressions imply that Koreans speculate on their mind by observing how they feel (Choi & Kim, 1999d).

The objective self is possibly less developed for Koreans than for Westerners. The Korean self works as a reference to behavior in limited situations and so ontological self-involving uniqueness, autonomy, and independence of individuals are not much required in the Korean cultural context. Furthermore, there is no need to reflect frequently on one's own self. Low social need for the Western type of self results from the features of Korean culture. For Koreans, it is more important to internalize sociocultural values and ideals afforded by society than to develop their individuality. In these respects, the Korean self is likely formed by internalizing and practicing personalities and values socially defined as ideal and desirable rather than by discovering and establishing something new within their own self. It is a more important task for Koreans to internalize and grow a socially idealized self than to identify their own unique self. Self-reflection means regretting one's behavior that falls short of the socially idealized self rather than identifying one's self. For Koreans, it is not important to achieve self-actualization, but instead, control over the mind is critical in order to refrain from mundane desires or thoughts. That is, self-actualization for Koreans is social self-actualization or success in life. Success in life means becoming a socially respectable person and, in its mundane usage, gaining a position of high power and status. There has been an idea in Korean history that learned and virtuous people are politicians. In this tradition, Koreans have developed the view of status–personality correspondence (Choi & Kim, 1998, 1999b, 2000a).

The sociocultural contextualism in Korea also impedes the development of an individual self. Koreans tend to adjust their behavior according to the persons they interact with and the situations in which those interactions occur. Several studies (Jang & Kim, 1996; Kim, 1998) indicate that Koreans' behavior varies tremendously by the type of relationship and psychological distance with others. This is why Westerners may form the impression that Koreans have a dual personality. Koreans' behavior is determined by their mind in close relationships, but they manifest other-oriented behavior when others are not close to them. This contrasting behavior suggests that in shaping their behavior, Korean people regard its situational appropriateness as more important than its consistency.

In a given culture where words and behaviors are forced to adjust by situation, to define self clearly may not be judged as important in shaping behavior and as necessary to develop. In this vein, Koreans do not have a strong need to construct the Western type of self in their mind, instead it is more important for them to perform behavior appropriate to situations and to keep their mind in line with social values.

COMPONENTS OF WESTERN ENTITY-SELF
AND KOREAN MIND-SELF

Recall that the Western *I* is defined as an entitative self, whereas the Korean *na* is mind as a psychological existence or state. When the self is defined as an entity, there is a clear boundary between one's self and others' selves. Also, the self is recognized in the same way as attributes of materials. Self is conceived of as something that exists self-evidently like an object that is subject to objective analyses and reconstructions and that possesses specific and structural qualities. The Western self is structured like a material framework and is available as a stable and reliable reference to reflective evaluations of behaviors or thoughts. Further, self is an object of reasoning (i.e., one can ask of oneself, "Who are you?" "What do you want?" or "What do you consider valuable?"). However, when self is composed of mind as with Korean people, the attributes and functions of the self described earlier may be weakened (Choi & Kim, 1999c).

Mind, unlike material objects, is mainly not of objective and realistic characteristics. *Mind* lacks characteristics embedded in objects—a clear boundary between two objects, self-evident existence, and adequacy for objective analyses. This makes it difficult to perceive one's own mind in confidence. Mind is changeable and unstable, which makes it hard to grasp. Also, components of mind are not understood with ease when the same analytic ways are applied as those used for material objects. Instead, mind is understood and described in the abstract form of disposition. *I* is conceptualized not as *what*, but as a person with a great deal of (or a paucity of) a specific disposition.

Koreans' discovery and construction of *I* heavily rely on extracting their own major dispositions, whereas Westerners construct a variety of components of self in the form of an integrated whole. Koreans turn to the modes of inferring and reasoning in order to discover *I*. It is believed that one's own mind is distributed over the wide range of behavior and thought. Mind is a set of representative and principal dispositions extracted from behaviors and thoughts. Although dispositions are generally regarded as at least somewhat stable and unchangeable, mind is very susceptible to situational influences, so that Koreans do not turn to their mind as a reference for thoughts and behaviors as frequently as Western people do. The Korean's *na* does not contain so much of a material quality as does the Western self, such that a boundary between individual *na*'s is rather fuzzy. Taken together, the Korean's *na* has a strong characteristic of *subjective I*.

Given the differences between the Western self and Korean *chakee* or *na*, the Korean *chakee* is termed *inferential mind-self* and the Western self *referential entity-self* (Landrine, 1995; Choi & Kim, 1999c, 2000b). So, the Koreans' inferential mind-self concerns the processes of drawing self-portraits whereas the Westerner's referential entity-self can be defined as the process of articulation and identification of self.

Referential Entity-Self	**Inferential Mind-Self**
entative	mental (unstable)
ontological	dispositional
structured	nonstructured
real	psychological
referential	configurational
transcendental	contextual

I and *self* in Western culture are a reference to verify my existence against others. Independence from others is proclaimed on the basis of self. Self is also given a transcendental characteristic where self is considered constant across objects and situations (Holland, 1997). In relation-oriented societies like Korea, however, an individual's mind is qualified contextually by situations and objects (Kim, 1998). This renders *mind* as not consistent and constant relative to Western self. The transcendental property of *mind* is less in relation-oriented Korean culture (see Figure 2.1).

Relational-Contextual Mind of Koreans

In most cases, words and behaviors of Koreans vary as a function of the situation (Choi, Yamaguchi, & Kim, 1998). In interpersonal relations and interactions, taking into account others' expectations or their relationships is given priority over presenting straightforward ideas or opinions of a given

Figure 2.1
Westerner's Self and Korean's Mind-Self

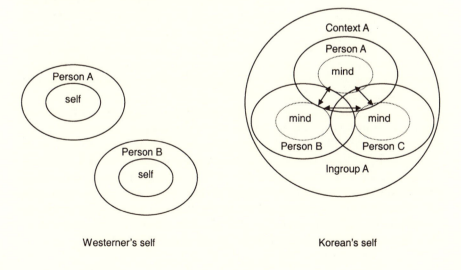

Westerner's self   Korean's self

issue. Koreans tend to behave in a manner that is quite often discrepant from who they are. However, others do not interpret this behavior as hypocritical. *Chemyon* or social face (Choi, 1997, 2000; Choi & Kim, 1998, 1999b, 2000a; Choi & Yu, 1992), *uireysung* or ritualized behavior (Choi, 1997, 2000; Choi & Yu, 1994a), and *noonchi* or tact (Choi, 1997, 2000; Choi & Choi, 1989, 1990) are closely linked to considering others' expectations, authority, competence, social status, and private mind (Choi, 1998).

These phenomena take place dramatically at formal meetings in organizations. For example, although a consensual decision has been made at a meeting, Koreans involved in the decision will often say in the informal discourse setting that in reality they did not agree with the decision. Foreigners will be puzzled at why they did not voice their disagreement in the meeting. They likely regard this behavior as inconsistent and self-deceptive. However, Koreans do not necessarily perceive this as negative, but as adequate for the particular situation. For example, suppose that the person presiding over the meeting is a senior or closely related to me. If I put forth an opinion opposing the chair's preference, that person will consider my behavior inadequate for the situation regardless of the validity of my opinion. Further, I will cause loss of the chair's face, and disregard the chair's authority, and show disrespect by not considering the chair's private mind.

Korean people are sensitive to reading another's mind. If the other reveals clearly a preference or expectation orally, people do not have to read that person's inner mind. However, Koreans expect others to be aware of their inner mind, even without directly conveying their mind to the other. Koreans prefer to form close relationships with someone through the sense of reading the other's mind. Indeed, when Koreans display straightforward expressions of their mind, this suggests that they do not have full trust of or are not close to the other (Choi & Kim, 1999a, 1999d).

Noonchi, reading others' minds, is highly developed in Korean relationships (Choi & Choi, 1989, 1990). *Noonchi* is the ability to read what others have in their minds on the basis of experiential knowledge of them as well as situational cues. A Korean proverb suggests "with *noonchi*, you could beg pickled shrimps even at temples." That is, although seafood is rare at temples, to act in accordance with others' preference using *noonchi* makes it available (Choi, 1997, 2000).

Uireysung denotes the phenomenon that an individual expresses words and behaviors inconsistent with their mind in order to conform to another's private mind (Choi & Yu, 1994a). Although the other senses the inconsistency, he or she does not consider this unpleasant because it is perceived as due at least partially to the individual's consideration. Westerners are often told not to believe Koreans when they say "yes." This is because "yes" can be a ritualized word, but *uireysung* does not necessarily cause discomfort or unpleasantness on the part of another Korean. These types of words are seen as adequate for the situation and whether they are true or not does not matter.

Korean people frequently use the term *shimcheong* indicating the inner mind, which is felt or read through feeling (Choi, 1993a, 1994; Choi & Kim, C-W, 1998; Choi & Kim, 1999a, 1999d; Choi & Yu, 1996). This is different from *mind* as articulated by reasoning or objective analysis. *Shimcheong* is a most important psychological medium for formation and maintenance of interpersonal intimacy. Koreans do not regard as friends those who do not show consideration for their *shimcheong*. In addition, exchanges of *shimcheong* underlie a formation of friendship with others. *Shimcheong* is also subject to emotional rather than objective rules. *Cheong* is the raw material of *we-ness*. *Cheong* is the mind of consideration and care for others (Choi, 1997, 2000; Choi & Choi, 1990; Choi & Kim, 2000; Choi, Kim, & Kim, 1999, 2000). In Korea, individuals with no *cheong* are judged as inhumane and undesirable. So, Koreans' interpersonal relations are characterized more by emotional bonds than rational judgments.

People get their *shimcheong* hurt in close relations when the behavior of the partner falls short of or is in opposition to their expectations (Choi, 1997, 2000). In these cases, people spell out such words in tones of disappointment or rejection as "How come you treat me like that?" or "How can you say that in front of me?" (Choi & Kim, 1998). *Shimcheong* is supposed to be taken into account by others and so self-adjusting behavior with reference to others' *shimcheong* occurs constantly. When *shimcheong* plays an important role in a variety of interpersonal situations, self-expressive behavior as observed in Western culture may be interpreted as selfish and so self-consistency may not be judged as so important (Choi & Kim, 1999a).

CONCLUSION

This paper highlights crucial differences between Western and Korean people in conceptualizing self. For Western people self reflects their unique and unchangeable reality and so functions as a reference to determining and evaluating behavior. In the same line, Western people place high value on behavior congruent with the self concept across situations and time and so view life consistent with the self as self-actualization.

However, the Korean self is not concerned so much with ontological aspects of individuals, like uniqueness and independence, as the Western self. Instead, the Korean self is oriented toward shared ethics and values of importance to the society. For Koreans, *self* concerns mainly assessment and evaluation of their place in those ethics and value dimensions. This awareness induces, in turn, intentions and motivations in Koreans to be socially more desirable. When Korean students are asked to describe self-actualization, the content of their responses is mainly concerned with social self-actualization rather than self-actualization in the Western sense (Choi & Kim, 1999c). In this respect, the Korean self is more future-oriented and goal-directed than the Western self and also more specific and realistic in that the Korean self fully reflects social realities.

There may be a generation gap in conception of the Korean self. Young Koreans, unlike the older generations, seem ready to accept the Western value system and establish the Western self-view in their mind. Nonetheless, it is hard to say that psychological characteristics of young Koreans are void of traditional views of the world, including the self developed in Korean culture. For example, *cheong, shimcheong, chemyon, uireysung, noonchi,* relationalism, and collectivism are still prevalent across highly educated college students. These psychological characteristics are manifested quite frequently in informal relationship settings. Nonetheless, affairs in the public, political, and social areas of Korean societies are increasingly handled by Westernized methods.

REFERENCES

Bem, D. J. (1972). Self-perception theory. In L. Berkowits (Ed.), *Advances in experimental social psychology,* 6: 2–62. New York: Academic Press.

Bruner, J. (1990). *Acts of meaning.* Cambridge, MA: Harvard University Press.

Campbell, J. D., & Lavallee, L. F. (1993). Who am I?: The role of self concept confusion in understanding the behaviour of people with low self-esteem. In R. F. Baumeister (Ed.), *Self-esteem: The puzzle of low self-regard* (pp. 3–20). New York: Plenum.

Choi, S. C. (1992b, October). Koreans' cultural self. Paper presented at the Annual Conference of the Korean Psychological Association, Seoul, Korea.

Choi, S. C. (1993a, October). Shimcheong psychology of Koreans: Phenomenological understanding of Han and Cheong. Paper presented at the Annual Conference of the Korean Psychological Association, Seoul, Korea.

Choi, S. C. (1993b). A Comparative analysis of the We-ness of Koreans and Japanese. Paper presented at the Annual Conference of the Korean Psychological Association, Seoul, Korea.

Choi, S. C. (1994). Shimcheong psychology. *Studies on Social Sciences, 7* (by Institute of Social Sciences, Chung-Ang University), 213–237.

Choi, S. C. (1997). Psychological characteristics of Koreans. In KPA (Ed.), *Understanding contemporary psychology* (pp. 695–766). Seoul: Hakmunsa.

Choi, S. C. (1998). The third-person psychology and the first-person psychology: Two perspectives on human relations. *Korean Social Science Journal, 25,* 239–264.

Choi, S. C. (2000). *The Korean psychology.* Seoul: Chung-Ang University Press.

Choi, S. C., & Choi, S. H. (1990, October). Psychological Structure of Cheong. Paper presented at the Annual Conference of the Korean Psychological Association, Seoul, Korea.

Choi, S. C., & Choi, S-H. (1994). We-ness: A Korean discourse of collectivism. In J. Yoon & S. C. Choi (Eds.), *Psychology of the Korean people* (pp. 57–84). Seoul: Dong-A.

Choi, S. C., & Choi, Y. H. (1989, October). The social psychological structure of NoonChi: A heuristic approach to its conceptualization. Paper presented at the Annual Conference of the Korean Psychological Association, Seoul, Korea.

Choi, S. C., & Kim, C-W. (1998). "Shim-Cheong" psychology as a cultural psychological approach to collective meaning construction. *Korean Journal of Social and Personality Psychology, 12* (2), 79–96.

Choi, S. C., & Kim, J-Y. (2000, July 16–21). Cultural emotion of Korea: Cheong. Paper presented at the Fifteenth Congress of the International Association for Cross-Cultural Psychology, Warsaw, Poland.

Choi, S. C., Kim, J-Y., & Kim, K. (1999, August 4–7). Sweet Cheong and hateful Cheong. Paper presented at the International Conference of the Asian Association of Social Psychology, Taipei, Taiwan.

Choi, S. C., Kim, J-Y., & Kim, K. (2000). The structural relationship among Cheong, its expressive behavior and functions. *Korean Journal of Social and Personality Psychology, 14* (1), 203–222.

Choi, S. C., & Kim, K. (1998, October). The internal structure of Chemyon. Paper presented at the Annual Conference of the Korean Psychological Association, Seoul, Korea.

Choi, S. C., & Kim, K. (1999a, August 4–7). *Shimcheong*: The key concept for understanding Koreans' mind. Paper presented at the International Conference of the Asian Association of Social Psychology, Taipei, Taiwan.

Choi, S. C., & Kim, K. (1999b, August 4–7). The psychological structure of the Chemyon. Paper presented at the International Conference of the Asian Association of Social Psychology, Taipei, Taiwan.

Choi, S. C., & Kim, K. (1999c). A conceptual exploration of the Korean self. *Korean Journal of Social and Personality Psychology, 13* (2), 275–292.

Choi, S. C., & Kim, K. (1999d). Psychological characteristics of Shimcheong and its transactional forms and discourses. *Korean Journal of Psychology, 18* (1), 1–16.

Choi, S. C., & Kim, K. (2000a). The psychological structure of Chemyon (social face) in Korea. *Korean Journal of Social and Personality Psychology, 14* (1), 185–202.

Choi, S. C., & Kim, K. (2000b, July 16–21). A conceptual exploration of the Korean self. Paper presented at the Fifteenth Congress of the International Association for Cross-Cultural Psychology, Warsaw, Poland.

Choi, S. C., Yamguchi, S., & Kim, K. (1998, October). The cultural difference of social justice and group-orientedness in conflict situations. Paper presented at the Annual Conference of the Korean Psychological Association, Seoul, Korea.

Choi, S. C., & Yu, S-Y. (1992). A social psychological analysis of Chemyon (social face). *Korean Journal of Social Psychology, 6* (2), 1–10.

Choi, S. C., & Yu, S-Y. (1994a, October). Formal behavior and its function in Koreans. Paper presented at the Annual Conference of the Korean Psychological Association, Seoul, Korea.

Choi, S. C., & Yu, S-Y. (1996, June 27–29). An exploration of a conceptual framework of Shimcheong psychology. Paper presented at the Annual Conference of the Korean Psychological Association, Seoul, Korea.

Danziger, K. (1997). *Naming the mind: How psychology found its language.* London: Sage.

Giddens, A. (1991). *Modernity and self-identity: Self and society in the late modern age.* Stanford, CA: Stanford University Press.

Harré, R., & Gillett, G. (1994). *The discursive mind.* London: Sage.

Hofstede, S. (1980). *Culture's consequences: International difference in work-related values.* Beverly Hills, CA: Sage.

Holland, D. (1997). Selves as culture: As told by an anthropologist who lacks a soul. In R. D. Ashmore & L. Jussim (Eds.), *Self and identity: Fundamental issues* (pp. 161–190). New York: Oxford University Press.

Kelly, G. A. (1955). *The psychology of personal constructs*. New York: Norton.

Kim, D-I. (1998). *Self-concept clarity in Korea: Personality, self-consciousness and behavioral correlate*. Unpublished master's thesis, Chung-Ang University, Seoul, Korea.

Kum, J-T. (1998). *The philosophy of Toegey*. Seoul: Seoul National University Press.

Landrine, H. (1995). Clinical implications of cultural differences: The referential versus the indexical self. In N. R. Goldberger & J. B. Veroff (Eds.), *The culture and psychology* (pp. 744–766). New York: New York University Press.

Lee, K-J. (1996). *The psychotherapy in Korea*. Seoul: Hang Lim.

Markus, H. R., & Kitayama, S. (1991). Culture and the self: Implications for cognition, emotion, and motivation. *Psychological Review, 98*, 224–253.

McAdams, D. P. (1997). The case for unity in the (post) modern self. In R. D. Ashmore & L. Jussim (Eds.), *Self and identity: Fundamental issues* (pp. 46–78). New York: Oxford University Press.

Miller, J. G. (1999). Cultural psychology: Implications for basic psychological theory. *Psychological Science, 10* (2), 85–91.

Na, E-Y., & Min, K-H. (1998). Discrepancies between formal/explicit and informal/implicit norms in Korea and generational gaps: Theoretical points and evidence from existing survey data. *Korean Journal of Psychology: Social Issues, 4* (1), 75–93.

Park, A-C. (1998). *Exploration of self*. Seoul: Kyo-uk-kwa-hak-sa.

Rose, N. (1996). *Inventing our selves: Psychology, power, and personhood*. Cambridge: Cambridge University Press.

Shweder, R. A., & Miller, J. G. (1991). The social construction of the person: How is it possible? In R. A. Shweder (Ed.), *Thinking through cultures: Expeditions in cultural psychology* (pp. 156–185). Cambridge, MA: Harvard University Press.

Triandis, H. C. (1995). *Individualism and collectivism*. Boulder, CO: Westview Press.

Wertsch, J. V. (1991). *Voices of the mind: A sociocultural approach to mediated action*. Cambridge, MA: Harvard University Press.

CHAPTER 3

The Role of the Social Psychologist and Social Science in the "Benevolent Authority" and "Plurality of Powers" Systems of Historical Affordance for Authority

James H. Liu and Shu-hsien Liu

Social psychology should be intimately concerned with its effect on society. Research in core areas, such as prejudice, stereotyping, intergroup and inter-personal relations, attribution, social influence, and persuasion all have practical implications, and have from time to time been brought to bear on the practical elements of social issues (see the *Journal of Social Issues* or the Society for the Psychological Study of Social Issues (SPSSI) Web site, http://www.spssi.org/).

However, critics have charged that as a whole social psychology has failed to affect social policy or input much into the public debate of important issues facing society (Harris, 1997). It has also been to a significant degree noncumulative (Liu & Liu, 1997). In the United States, where the vast majority of social psychologists reside, the field appears to have lost confidence in its ability to comment effectively on social policy since the great debate over busing (Cook, 1988; Gerard, 1988) and its "crisis of confidence" (Elms, 1975; Gergen, 1973). In recent times, it appears as committed to protecting its funding for research as it is to any particular social policy or policy direction. The lack of enthusiasm within the Society for the Psychological Study of Social Issues for service within the organization (Unger, 1999) is probably a reflection of the feeling of powerlessness that afflicts American (and hence mainstream) social psychology today.

Perhaps in this era of increasing pluralism, it should not be expected that the field should be unified behind any particular social policy or policy objectives. Perhaps it would be more fruitful to look at how individual social psychologists have achieved positive outcomes in governments, schools, or other institutions. However, even during the heyday of its social movement, seminal social psychologists such as Goodwin Watson (Nicholson, 1998) and George Hartmann (Harris, 1998) who tried to change the system found themselves either absorbed or destroyed. Today such figures hardly appear on the social or political landscape, even as great failures. The era of the great humanistic psychologists such as Maslow or Fromm appears to be long gone. The most influential of social psychologists in the United States today pale in their ability to influence public policy and debate compared to talk show hosts and famous athletes.

Taking a broader look at social science in the world, it seems apparent that the area with the most significant impact on public policy and debate is economics. There is good reason for this. The variables that economics bring to bear on social policy, like manipulating money supply, taxation policy, or trade tariffs, appear infinitely more powerful than any variables that social psychology has to offer because they represent collective outcomes directly aligned with institutional structures. The variables of social psychology are almost without exception at the individual level: how to reduce prejudice in the individual, how to persuade the individual, what kinds of situations affect individual attributions (Ho, 1998). Even if aggregated or conceived of as a collective (Moscovici, 1988), these variables are unrelated to actions institutions might take. Further, the empirical data base for social psychology has almost invariably been gathered from individuals of lower or equal status (e.g., students; see Sears, 1986) to practitioners. Social psychology has little to say about how people with power act within their sphere of influence (but see Gold & Raven, 1992; Simonton, 1988, for interesting exceptions). Hence, as an empirical science, social psychology has studied the wrong individuals if it wants to exert influence. It has interesting wares, but they can hardly appeal to policymakers the way a theory about taxation can.

It is important to acknowledge this basic limitation at the outset, so as not to entertain false expectations that cannot be achieved. The basis of social psychology as individual centered and unaligned with institutional structures will not change overnight. However, its basic philosophy can be changed to open the way for social psychologists to reanalyze the kinds of social roles they can play for the benefit of society. In doing so, in time social psychologists may be able to realign portions of the field to become more socially significant. And social psychologists do have time, perhaps twenty or thirty years at minimum to fifty or sixty years at most, before the twin forces of environmental degradation and population demographics are likely to demand more functional rather than theoretical social sciences (Brown, 1997; Moghaddam, 1990; Liu, Bonzon-Liu, & Pierce-Guarino, 1997; Liu & Liu, 1999).

In writing this chapter, issues familiar to Asian social psychologists, for whom collectivism and service to society are millenia-old traditions, are addressed and homage is paid to the founders of social psychology, who have sometimes expressed disappointment at contemporary activism and relevance (McGarty & Haslam, 1997; Rodrigues & Levine, 1999). While we cannot claim to be entirely interdisciplinary in our outlook, we do invite scholars from related fields to compare notes and consider whether the philosophy we espouse may be useful to them. The ideas in this essay can be applied broadly to any social scientist, though we aim some specific comments at social psychologists as our main target audience.

As Chinese, we draw on Confucian and Neo-Confucian philosophy to provide us with an indigenous theory of statecraft and personhood that Western social psychology lacks. The benevolent authority system of governance we describe is by no means restricted to Confucian societies, however. Chinese attempted to perfect such a system of centralized bureaucracy, but this type of system is used to a greater or lesser extent by many preindustrial societies of large scale. In modern times, Korea is far more representative of traditional Confucian theory and practice than any extant Chinese society (Kim, 1996). So while we use the terms *East Asian, Confucian*, and *benevolent authority* systems of governance somewhat interchangeably, they should be understood to refer to similar concepts varying in precision and scope, and not boundary conditions. Though we cannot speak with confidence for others, we hope that our comments about East Asia will find resonance with people in other parts of the world.

HISTORICAL AFFORDANCES FOR AUTHORITY IN GOVERNANCE

Confucianism was formed with the explicit goal of providing a moral and ethical framework for living and a theory of statecraft (see Tu, 1984, 1996 for contemporary applications). It evolved over centuries to provide not only a philosophy proper, but also a popular set of beliefs, and the underpinnings of a system of governance (S. H. Liu, 1989). Politicized Confucianism was indicted as part of the feudal society that retarded China's evolution toward modernity (Weber, 1964; King, 1996). Hence, contemporary scholars have treated this part of the Confucian legacy with caution.

The Confucian model of person and state contains insights that can be rehabilitated within the modern practice of social psychology and social science to provide an answer to the question: "How can social science be effective in providing advice for society and government?" Of course any treatment of Confucianism provided in this chapter will be a simplification and used as a vehicle for discussion rather than as a statement of historical fact about the 2,000-year-old legacy of Confucian models of governance. The discussion must begin with the fact that Confucius tried his whole life without success to become a minister for the ruler of a state. Confucianism was not adopted as a ruling ideology until the Han dynasty hundreds of years after his death. So there always has been and always will be a gap between the ideals of Confucianism and its practice. S. H. Liu (1993) suggested that a "height psychology," a psychology of possibilities and aspirations, may be one way to not only take advantage of the psychological ramifications of this gap, but also act to bridge it.

The role of Confucianism in feudal bureaucracy can be captured by the saying that classical Chinese civilization was characterized by a "Confucian Yang and Legalist Yin." That is, the bright face of Confucius's moral teachings on human benevolence were underpinned by the dark reality of legalized oppression and harsh punishment as advocated by Han Fei-tsu. While the Confucian model was capable of producing superb civil servants (a characteristic used to great advantage by Singapore and Japan; see, for example, Kuo, 1996), it also has had grave difficulties constraining corruption at the top, especially on the part of the ruler, and managing transitions of power on the death of the ruler.

The Confucian model of statecraft begins with an assumption about the basic benevolence of human nature (*ren*) (S. H. Liu, 1998). In the midst of warring states, Confucius had the idea that it might be possible to have a "sage–emperor" characterized by a moral rectitude and a high level of self-cultivation. Rather than implement specific policy, the sage–emperor was to provide a moral and ethical foundation to make the ground fertile for a multitude of undertakings. Confucius's examples of sage–emperors were stories about Yao and Shun in the dawn of Chinese civilization. Confucian statecraft was a theory, not a practice of rule. In effect, Confucian political theory centered around the person of the political leader, whose virtue attracted a talented group of ministers who dealt with actual policy. The cultivation of the person of the emperor was critical, because the emperor's influence was thought to filter through all society via social relations (see Hwang, 1987, 1997, 1998).

As long as the ruler was moral and virtuous, he maintained the "Mandate of Heaven," was regarded as the "Son of Heaven," and merited the dedication of his ministers. Hence, the basis for legitimate rule was perceived to stem from the person of the ruler. The protocol for relations between the ruler and ministers filtered down through society in a rigid order. Norms governing relations between the leader and the ministers were outlined as part of the *wu lun*, the five basic relations ordering Chinese society. Most of these relationships are hierarchical rather than equal. The reification of *wu lun* into rigid forms was actually a Legalist rather than a Confucian innovation (S. H. Liu, 1998). The system outlined by Confucius himself was rather too idealistic to actually hold and maintain power, so it was augmented by Legalism. Therefore, the political system in China from the Han dynasty on is more accurately described as Confucian–Legalist rather than simply Confucian.

Ths person–relationship centered model of authority (Pye, 1985; Redding, 1996) contrasts with the contemporary Western model, in which the mandate of authority rests in the law, an impartial set of rules that transcend the individuals who occupy positions mandated by law. "No one is above the law" and "justice is blind," according to Western ideals, whereas in the Confucian model, the person of the ruler, the benevolent authority, is at the top of the authority structure (see Figure 3.1).

At the top of Figure 3.1 are two ideals, and at the bottom is contained some of the struggle that goes into maintaining an actual system of governance: For

Figure 3.1
Historical Affordances for Authority

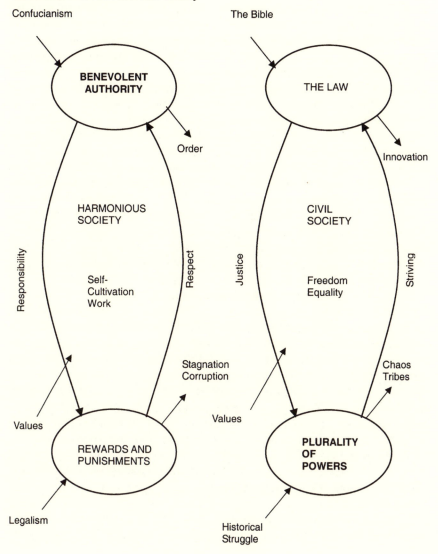

East Asians, a strict, centralized, and hierarchical system of rewards and punishments; in the West, a host of competing powers and groups striving against one another to further their own interests under the rule of law. The model society in traditional East Asia is harmonious: The ruler looks after the people, the people respect the ruler, and at each level an unequal but reciprocal system of exchange serves to maintain order. The model society in the West is a civil society, where competing interests strive against one another under the rule of law, which administers justice to keep the struggle within boundaries. The virtues of self-cultivation and work are central to the former system, just as the values of freedom and equality are central to the latter. In the East Asian model, principle dangers are stagnation and corruption. If the person of the ruler becomes corrupt, there is almost nothing to stop the spread of corruption down through society. Hence, transitions in rulership are dangerous moments. In the Western model, principle dangers are that the struggle will devolve into chaos, where the competing interests no longer form a civil society but warring tribes. Rule by law is very difficult under extreme factionalism.

The models depicted should be thought of as historical affordances for authority rather than any actual systems active today. Almost all extant models of governance have been influenced by the Western model, and the Western model itself retains historical resonance with traditional ideas about benevolent authority (e.g., the divine right of kings, the Papacy). The Western system was earned through centuries of conflict, between kings and nobles, nobility and merchants, mercantile interests and workers, so rule by law is today not an empty phrase but a sophisticated system of checks and balances. The East Asian system as well emerged through centuries of refinement in developing a centralized bureaucracy capable of managing the competing interests in society. All actual systems of governance today are hybrids, a mix between person–role centered and legal–individual centered systems.

Japan would be the most obvious hybrid, impossible to describe in the simple terms of a dichotomy. It has a constitutional and democratically elected government that now changes hands with regularity. Yet the same cast of political leaders appear under different party names, and the system of patronage between universities and companies and political parties is entrenched through complex relationships. There is no cult of personality surrounding leaders, yet there is an oligarchy and entrenched bureaucratic elite that maintains continuity. The emperor still retains a degree of moral authority above day-to-day political machination, perhaps as a consequence of the historical division of authority between emperor and shogun. Our intention by hypothesizing person–relationship and legal–individual centered affordances for authority is not to set up a false dichotomy but to point out different possibilities for social psychologists and other social scientists to take action, especially if they live outside of the West.

Asian rulers like Lee Teng-hui, Chiang Kai-Shek, Lee Kwan-Yew, Deng Xiao-Ping, Mahathir, Mao Ze-Dong, and Suharto have had longer tenures of rule than their counterparts in the West and considerably greater personal power at their peak. Some were constitutionally elected, some were not. But each of these individuals manipulated the law to provide a system of rewards and punishments to further his objectives. None of them treated the law as something above and beyond the domain of their personal powers. Some have been more benevolent than others. Each has shaped the course of his nation to a greater extent than any postwar Western political leader with the possible exception of Germany's Kohl. Each has been perceived as a benevolent authority in his country and in his time. To serve as an advisor to men like these has significant implications in many ways that we shall explore.

In the United States, President Clinton was able to remain in office despite his obvious loss of moral rectitude following the Monica Lewinsky affair because he was perceived to have not sufficiently broken the law to warrant removal. American public opinion polls were squarely behind him. A system of checks and balances is in place in the United States so that there is little to fear from a morally corrupt ruler. Instead, there is a plurality of powers, where each sector or faction contests with the others for power under the rule of law. Americans could comfort themselves with the notion that Clinton was a victim of political attack by a rival political party, or alternatively that Clinton was a lame duck who would soon be out of office. The law and office of state continue while the person passes through.

The legal basis for the mandate of authority ensures that challenges to this authority are also framed in legal terms. Moreover, challenges are expected. Politicians are perceived as the least trustworthy persons in Western society even though they wield great power. The law provides an arena for civilized combat between various individuals and factions. The perceived moral rectitude of political leaders has been a frequent casualty of this combat. But the system itself has proven robust beyond the rise and fall of any particular individuals.

The plurality-of-powers system evolved over centuries of struggle and conflict to attain its current equilibrium. Westerners would be foolish to be overly complacent about their system, however. The forces of globalization may have unleashed social, political, and economic forces well beyond what the current system of checks and balances can contain (Chomsky, 1994; Rosenau, 1997). Global capital has given birth to distance transcending superorganisms such as multinational corporations and billion-dollar mutual funds that may be beyond the capability of any elected government to control. The voice of the voter has become increasingly a cry in the wilderness of moneyed interests that hover over the lobbies of Washington and Brussels. The power of political money has given rise to voter apathy, which in turn gives moneyed interests even more power (Hout & Knoke, 1975; Miller, 1992; Southwell, 1995).

In this emerging epoch (Liu & Rosenau, 1999), the ideal of benevolent authority may once again become useful in providing for an alternative source of direction to that of mercantile interests. For example, within business, a long-term, relationship-oriented East Asian model has resisted the dictates of global capital to shed workers for maximum stockholder profit. China has had many dictators and autocrats, but they have generally not been puppets of commercial interests, which are principal among the forces driving environmental degradation (Brown, 1997). While Asian leaders have yet to act in a concerted way on behalf of the natural environment, we suspect that if and when they choose to, they may do so more decisively than their Western counterparts.

The American reaction to Clinton contrasts with the idea of benevolent authority. Though there is hybridity across cultures, Clinton would probably have had to resign in an East Asian country once his scandal became public. In East Asia, where the ideal of a benevolent authority has had a longer historical lineage than the law, and the notion of a plurality of powers runs counter to the cherished notion of centralized bureacracy, shame has a greater role in constraining the power of the ruler than in the West. Clinton may have lost face in East Asia. He could not likely continue to govern after having demeaned himself. The second author has a favorite saying that captures the function of shame in East Asian systems of authority: "A false gentleman is superior to a truly small man."

The false gentleman has a real sense of shame restraining his abuse of money and power. Loss of face is a severe consequence to someone who wants and needs the appearance of propriety to function in a powerful way (Choi & Kim, 1997; Hwang, 1987). Conversely, without a sense of propriety, the behavior of the truly small man cannot be constrained by shame. As many scholars have argued, shame is a central emotion for social control in collectivist societies (Markus & Kitayama, 1991; Hwang, 1997, 1998). Outside observers may wonder what has happened to shame in the United States. Everyone is a victim, even the ruler of the most powerful country in the history of the world. As long as Americans are rich, Americans are happy, never mind about the moral authority of their leaders. Under such an operant ideology, it is difficult to imagine any political leader being able to stand up to mercantile interests. In the talk show paradigm that has gripped the United States, everyone is a victim and no one is responsible.

East Asian rulers are different politically. Rulers such as Lee Teng-hui and Mahathir have in recent years spurned mercantile interests to an extent that would be unthinkable in the West. Every time Lee Teng-hui talked about Taiwanese statehood, Mainland China rattled its sabers and the Taiwanese stock market plummeted. Yet he is still perceived as a benevolent authority by many Taiwanese, perhaps because he tookk on such a dangerous (and popular) view. Mahathir told the World Bank and the IMF to get out of Malaysia with their economic reforms. He took the ringgit out of the international monetary exchange, froze foreign assets, put the champion of Western economic reform in jail on sodomy charges, and blamed the collapse of the currency on foreign capital. This strategy has been surprisingly effective. A political leader who is perceived as a benevolent authority in Asia by a significant percentage of voters can operate with a kind of autonomy unavailable to Western leaders.

Whether their motivations are for the good of the people or for raw power is another issue entirely.

If Mahathir or Lee Teng-hui fail in the high-stakes games they are playing, they will pay the price, and so will their people. Herein lies the great irony of individualism and collectivism and the independent and interdependent self (Hofstede, 1980; Triandis, 1995; Markus & Kitayama, 1991). In Asia, where people are supposed to be more collectivist, individuals at the top of a social hierarchy have greater autonomy of political power than in the West. The primary constraints on their behavior are internal (e.g., a feeling of responsibility), relational (e.g., advice from ministers) and socioemotional (e.g., shame), rather than rule by law or a system of checks and balances underpinned by money and factional power. The latter are much more limiting. The exception to this rule appears to be Japan, where there was a historical balance of power between the emperor and the shogun, and memories of the consequences of blindly following authority in World War II are still salient.

THE ROLE OF THE TEACHER

The historical affordances we have described are not limited to the authority of the ruler, but can be applied to the position of any person in authority. Teachers, according to Choi and Kim (1997) are one group that has *chemyon* (the Korean term for face). Social psychologists and others who work in universities as teachers are subject to similar constraints and affordances for their power.

A teacher in East Asia can have considerably greater influence than a teacher in the West. In the West, students tend to consider the teacher a conveyor of knowledge, whose job is to transmit information about the field. In East Asia, students still consider the teacher to be a figure of respect, and the purpose of teaching may be moral and ethical as well as functional (Cheung, 1999; *Hong Kong Book Review*, 1999). Moral rectitude on the part of the teacher is very important. The role relationship between the student and teacher tends to be more enduring, whereas in the West the relationship can move from student–teacher to collegial or even friends with greater ease.

All these factors suggest that it may be more important for social psychologists and other teachers in East Asia to have a moral and ethical rather than purely empirical approach to their work. Liu and Liu (1999) proposed that interconnectedness and truth are fundamental values of scholarly inquiry resonant with the cultural traditions of both the East and West. They suggested that both are necessary for a social psychology of practical value. Truth underlies the empirical approach of social psychology to its teaching and research. Social psychologists should be willing to subject their beliefs to empirical scrutiny and allow them to be disconfirmed.

At the same time, social psychologists need more than the attitude of healthy skepticism and empiricism to have a positive impact on society. They must believe in something, some higher goal or aspiration. Liu and Liu (1999) proposed that this higher goal should be interconnectedness. Interconnectedness is the perception of unity in differentiation and differentiation in unity. It brings about greater harmony. It is about contemplating the *Is–Can*. It means seeing clearly the possibilities identified by empirical research (the *Is*) and acting in a way to realize the best of these possibilities (the *Can*) (Liu & Rosenau, 1999).

To fill the role of a teacher fully in the historical affordances provided by the benevolent authority model, one should have more than a Faustian thirst for knowledge. In the Confucian model, figures of authority teach through moral example as well as through their specific functions as conveyors of knowledge.

This moral aspect has deep implications for what the goal of Asian social psychology should be. The goal of an Asian social psychology should be to cultivate individuals who are exceptional in the integrity and humanity of their dealings with others. The responsibility of the teacher to the student is much greater under a system of benevolent authority because the loyalty and respect of the student for the teacher is also greater.

Anyone can teach a t-test or experimental design. But true teachers in a Confucian tradition need to be able to do more. Teachers must pass on their humanity, their *ren* (a whole benevolence of being) to their students, which must truly challenge the individuality and interindividuality of the teacher and the student. Even if this sort of interconnectedness only happens once or twice during an entire career, it is to be cherished, as much or more than the publication of one's best papers or books. They are tasks of comparable magnitude and difficulty in the value system we are proposing.

THE ROLE OF THE SOCIAL SCIENTIST

Closely related to the functional differences in the role of teacher across cultures is the role of the social scientist. For social psychologists in the West to speak with authority, they must speak with respect to data. Outside of their area of expertise, scholars have no particular authority. Impartiality and scientific objectivity appear to be the main ways in which the discourse of the social psychologist is warranted in public communications (Gilbert & Mulkay, 1984). Any hint of underlying values on the part of the scholar is treated with suspicion, as it represents a deviation from the script of the impartial scientist speaking with objectivity. For example, the American Psychological Association (APA) maintains a congressional science fellow in Washington, but it is perceived on Capital Hill as a left-wing organization, especially by those on the right. The agenda of the press to sell controversy (Liu, Bonzon-Liu, & Pierce-Guarino, 1997) rarely allows psychological discourse to hold sway, even if it is founded on very strong science.

Given these constraints, there is little wonder that social psychologists in the West are rarely if ever given voice to discuss in a public forum the great issues of the day. The press sets the agenda, and academics are called upon for sound bites. There is no presumption of moral authority for their pronouncements except for a certain degree of respect for what is labelled as science. This respect is balanced by a certain degree of contempt by the media for the ivory tower that academics supposedly inhabit.

The first solution to this problem is to align research so that its outcomes are more closely related to the outcomes and measures sought by institutions. Do not just do research on memory, do research on memory for learning foreign languages. Do not just study achievement motivation, study achievement motivation with student performance on a standardized test used by qualifications authorities as a dependent measure. Social psychology should make greater effort to align its dependent measures to variables that have meaning to society and its institutions. A natural focus in this regard should be on educational outcomes (and this is already in place in many parts of Asia). But aligning dependent measures is playing the game as defined by the West, and few win at it. Andrews's (1989) work on criminal recidivism, for example, has fallen on deaf ears in Washington even though it employs meticulous metaanalytic techniques to show that longer prison sentences do not function as deterrents.

Social scientists appear to have a greater latitude of authority in East Asia, so much so that in some places it is deemed necessary to restrict their ability to speak out. It is much more typical in Hong Kong or Taiwan for academics to be able to speak out in a highly accessible forum on public issues related to public interest, regardless of how closely it intersects with their area of academic expertise. The scholar is presumed to have a certain degree of competence and authority to speak on issues of relevance to society. This again flows from the benevolent authority model which affords the Eastern scholar a greater latitude of commentary on society than Western scholars. In classical Confucian tradition, it is the responsibility of the scholar to have political vision (Tu, 1984). It is their reputation for integrity that gives them a right to speak.

Given this state of affairs, truth and interconnectedness are again paramount. To speak wisely about public affairs, it is necessary to have a firm grasp on the truth—to have knowledge about society. To speak wisely about public affairs it is necessary to have a firm grasp on how one's commentary will relate to society at large. Scholarship needs breadth as well as depth to serve in this capacity (Shils, 1996). It must have interconnectedness.

There are only a few social psychologists who have been able to act as spokespersons for the field (see, for example, Tavris, 1989; Taylor, 1989). The vast majority of writing is directed internally to other social psychologists. It takes somewhat different qualities and skills to reach the wider audience of society, in both writing and speech. Hence, practitioners of the different arts of writing, working with others, conducting an experiment or theorizing, and communicating verbally all may serve society in different ways. Individuals with people skills, courage, analytical ability, or quick wit may find some of these roles more conducive than others.

There are three ways that a scholar can be of service to society in political matters. The first is the role of critic and conscience, the second is the role of minister, and the third is the role of consultant. In certain respects, the first two roles are mutually exclusive, but it may be possible for both to make different contributions to society. Depending on the qualities of the government in power and the individual, one may be more suitable than the other.

THE ROLE OF CRITIC AND CONSCIENCE

Both Western ideals of democracy and individual autonomy and Confucian ideals of interdependence and moral rectitude offer social psychologists a role as critic and conscience. The critic and conscience of society is not required to be loyal to anyone in particular, but rather is responsible to their own conscience and scholarship and to the welfare of society as a whole. This role is enshrined in the charter of some universities, including Victoria University of Wellington. There is no equivalent legal precedence in traditional East Asian society, where so much is contingent on role relationships and the prestige of the scholar is high.

Critic and conscience function more safely under the protection of the law and freedom of the press, but these two factors exert significant constraints on the role in the West just as the use of power by authority does in the East. In order to have a practical freedom, the press must be willing to give voice for dissent. This is a problem, because media are often owned by either multinational corporations or controlled by the state (Bagdikian, 1997; Herman & Chomsky, 1988).

Within the plurality of powers system, the main danger is simply of being ignored. The so-called free press has little interest in publishing anything that criticizes capitalism, for example, and relatively little interest in anything that is not controversial (Herman & Chomsky, 1988). However, modern information technologies such as the World Wide Web allow any academic to publish commentary (e.g., http://www.socialpsychology.org or more radically, http://www.zmag.org). This forum provides an unprecedented opportunity for social scientists, but there appears to be no rush of scholars to fill this role. Serving as critic and conscience requires courage, quick wits, breadth, and the ability to communicate clearly and succinctly—not typical qualities that graduate students are selected and trained for. It is also not a very secure occupation.

Within the system of benevolent authority, the role of critic and conscience can be more powerful and more dangerous (to both the critic and the government). Given the greater access of scholars to popular media, and their stronger position of moral authority, the critic and conscience in East Asian societies can potentially have greater impact than in the West. This potential impact makes some governments extremely sensitive to criticism. In Singapore, for example, scholars can publish freely in academic journals, but must be careful what they say in the popular press.

However, as long as the government's mandate to rule is not directly challenged, East Asian scholars may experience considerable latitude of effectiveness in their ability to comment on societal affairs (Gold, 1996). In Taiwan, K. S. Yang was instrumental in developing two popular magazines that gave intellectuals and political thinkers considerable voice in Taiwan during critical periods of the nation's development. The collective contribution of *Da Xue Za Zhi* (*The Intellectual*) and *Zhong Guo Lun Tan* (*China Tribune*) to Taiwanese national development should not be underestimated. Yang's contribution to the political discourse of a nation of 21 million is largely unparalleled in the history of Western social psychology and he was able to do it because of his standing as an intellectual among a group of intellectuals rather than any specific attributes as a social psychologist. His success in these endeavors was a function of not only scholarly abilities, but people skills. A social psychology that values interconnectedness would want to understand the conditions that allowed *Da Xue Za Zhi* and *Zhong Guo Lun Tan* to flourish and wane. It would be far more reflexive in attempting to understand the flows of knowledge, influence, and resources into and out of the field (Moscovici, 1993).

THE ROLE OF MINISTER

While the roles of social scientist, teacher, and even critic and conscience are familiar to most Western-trained social psychologists, the role of minister is less familiar, but deeply rooted in Eastern traditions. The role of minister was sought by Confucius. His ideal was to advise a ruler. Generations of Chinese, Korean, and Japanese scholars have aspired to this, and a system of civil examinations and centralized bureacracy was set in place to implement it.

To function capably in this role, ministers must know their place. Loyalty, trustworthiness, judiciousness, and competence become paramount virtues (Shils, 1996). To offer reliable and effective service is the duty of the minister. This is a different approach to that assumed by the critic and conscience, whose first duty is to the truth, value, and integrity of their assertions. The Confucian system is hierarchical. It specifies role relationships, sometimes involving unequal duties and obligations. Interconnectedness here means a system of social relations that is not predominantly spiritual or intellectual. It concerns responsibilities and obligations, a system of material and moral exchange.

When one's superior is virtuous there is no conflict of interests. The problem of what to do when there is an impropriety on the part of the superior runs to the very core of Confucian ideals of authority and civil service. Ministers must be loyal. They should not act to make their superior lose face. The job of the minister is to guide the ruler to make the best decisions. However, the minister also has an obligation to try and correct superiors if they are in the wrong. But good Confucian ministers were often powerless when faced with a bad ruler. Under someone like Chu Yuan-chang, the first Ming emperor, they died by the hundreds.

In essence, the Confucian role of minister is to serve. It is self-sacrificing. If ministers disagree with a policy adopted by the ruler, they may discuss the issue with the ruler in private but should not oppose the ruler in public. If called upon to implement a policy disagreed with, the scholar may resign as the last resort. In an earlier age, such an option would have been associated with exile or death. Confucian ministers had little ability to actively resist, even if their superiors were terribly in the wrong.

In East Asia, both past and present, the political careers of persons in power tend to be longer than their counterparts in the West. This makes the old Confucian strategy of loyalty, guidance, and remonstrance a fairly effective strategy. The cultivation of relationships with superiors is still among the most effective ways for a scholar to have impact on social policy. This is true in any country but particularly important in Asia where there are clear social rules for different kinds of relationships (Hwang, 1998). But it has never been terribly effective in constraining the corruption of a ruler, especially in old age. The Confucian model seems to privilege the morality of the individual to a greater extent than modern social science would deem realistic (e.g., Asch, 1955; Milgram, 1965). Even though this is a weakness, the ideal of honorable civil service is something that still draws talent into government, and has surely been part of the success of Japan and the four minidragons.

Such a strategy has not been followed by Western social psychologists to any great extent. The experience of several prominent Western social psychologists was that they were swallowed up by the bureaucracy of government or else they were chewed up and spit out (Harris, 1998; Nicholson, 1998). Like their Western counterparts, most Asian scholars who have entered into government are faced by virtually insurmountable situational pressures. Yet the alternative is to criticize from the sidelines.

So there is no easy solution to the problem of the engagement of the scholar with government. Social psychologists who enter into government will become different from those in academia. The same purity of ideals cannot be expected. Nor can the same autonomy of action be expected. It is quite likely that a social psychologist filling the role of politician or bureaucrat would be no different from any other person in the position, except for that such a person would have certain knowledge structures and be connected to a particular network of colleagues, who may attempt to activate their relationship in a variety ways. Perhaps one side might try to capture more resources from the government for their field, or the other might try to use research from their field as support for their policies.

The benevolent authority system cuts both ways: It demands duties and obligations on the part of the lower-power person such that their service will operate within the power of the superior. The scholar who works in government will serve the aims of the government, not vice versa (Wong, 1996). It is possible that the right form of interconnectedness might yield positive results, but once again, this is a situation that is little understood by social scientists. How can positive links between colleagues in academia and government be maintained? Are there any general rules or is it primarily a property of the situation and the particular individuals involved?

THE ROLE OF CONSULTANT

The role of consultant offers a hybrid position between the minister and the critic and conscience. The possibilities for such a position depend on the particulars of the situation. For example, in New Zealand, there is probably less corruption in politics than in most countries. Of course, New Zealand has a population of less than 4 million. The amount of money available to the two major political parties combined to contest the 1996 election was about $NZ6 million (less than $US3 million). This is less than the cost of a campaign for a single seat in the American House of Representatives. The presidency of the United States costs in excess of $US50 million in campaign money, which means that the power of moral benevolence to exert influence on the eventual ruler would be insignificant next to the debts incurred by the $50 million. The main problem in New Zealand is not corruption, but a lack of long-term political and economic vision.

Consultants do not need to be as quick-witted or courageous as the critic and conscience, nor as loyal and reliable as the minister. They do require superior analytical abilities and good connections. In the course of his teaching at Victoria University (located in New Zealand's capital), the first author made acquaintance with the man who ran the advertising campaigns for the Labour Party in 1996 and 1999. We spent many afternoons discussing strategy and direction for the nation. It was a typically Chinese notion on the part of the first author to ask his friend to pass on a memo to the then candidate for Prime Minister from the Labour Party, Helen Clark.

The memo was quite different from academic writing. First, it contained a value statement. The author made no attempt to disguise his distaste for certain economic policies of the New Right, such as cutting taxes for the rich and privatizing schools. The memo contained words about vision, a topic outside of the author's empirical work, but central to his view of why New Zealand has not prospered as much as other developed countries in the last thirty years. The message was pragmatic. It did incorporate lessons from the author's work on identity, politics, and history (Liu, Wilson, McClure, & Higgins, 1999; Liu & Temara, 1998), but these were used to suggest ways of avoiding certain political errors in dealing with bicultural issues. The message was concise, containing a total of 2,560 words. It focused not on the "why" question that authors in academia pursue but the "how" of a consultant. The "how" question anticipates the future, whereas the "why" question tries to explain the past. In social science, these two questions have become too far separated.

The memo could not have been written under a purely Western notion of social psychology as objective and nonpartisan. It was a compromise between the demands of being a good scholar and the demands of attempting to influence or be of service to a political party that eventually became the next ruling party in New Zealand. The meaning of service is something that has become completely underrated in today's world of scholarship. The moment advice contains a value judgment it cannot be objective. It is far more important to have a standpoint rather than to pretend to be objective when the goal is to take action (Liu & Liu, 1997; Liu & Liu, 1999).

THE ROLE OF GENERATING
SOCIAL REPRESENTATIONS

All the roles mentioned so far have been for individuals, and, except possibly for the role of minister, they are relatively circumscribed in effect. A final, more collective role pertains to the ability of social psychology as a field to generate and maintain new social representations—new ways to conceive of our social environment (Moscovici, 1993). Psychology is by far the most popular among the "Big Three" of the social sciences (sociology, psychology, and anthropology) because it fits with the zeitgeist of the times—it is a science, it is empirical, and it focuses on the individual. The only two social scientists to make it into *Time's* list of the 100 great thinkers of the twentieth century were Freud and Piaget. Freud's contribution in particular was in creating social representations. His work is known today for its impact on culture more than its scientific value.

Among all the things psychologists study, the one that could have the maximal impact on society is social representations. For instance, work of Asch (1955) and Milgram (1965) has created a uniquely social psychological representation of the individual as someone vulnerable to the pressures of the situation. As a social psychologist, the first author is operating under no illusion that he will be able to influence the trajectory of politicians and government. It is far more likely that he will lose some of his current idealism. The lesson of the "power of the situation" is one of the most enduring social representations of social psychology.

But social psychology is only one source of social representations. Hollywood films and television would be another, far more powerful source. While the cumulative impact of any academic field should not be underestimated, the field currently sends out a plurality of messages, based only on its empiricism.

It is unknown whether any of these views will gain popular currency. The communication medium of choice for social psychology, its journals, are formalistic and not meant to be read by outsiders. Thus, it must rely on translators or popularizers to communicate more broadly. Many of these popularizers combine the grossest cultural stereotypes with their reading of the field.

Psychology Today was supposed to be the American Psychological Association's flagship publication to communicate social representations to the general public, but the magazine has had difficulty maintaining a balance between popularizing and conveying facts about psychological research. A magazine of this nature could be a powerful instrument, but recently the writing of *Psychology Today* has been delegated to journalists, who have created a magazine like any other highbrow pop magazine. The new editorial regime has promised changes, and their effects remain to be seen.

However, it is doubtful whether the American Psychological Association has any particular message that it wants to communicate other than to publicize psychological research and practitioner concerns. Psychology as a whole is probably too disparate a field to expect any other outcome. Psychology does contain a clear message that empiricism is its approach to finding the answers. But outside of this general methodology, psychological research has produced a massive pluralism of theory and results not united by any recipe other than methodological individualism (Ho, 1998). On the practical side, its main message seems to be the following: See your clinician if you have a problem. The psychologizing of issues that were once the province of religion must be one of psychology's most powerful social impacts (Murray, 1962).

Social psychology, as a smaller field within the whole, could be capable of generating a more focused social representation that can have a more direct impact on how its students conceive of themselves and their society. Specific subfields within social psychology can be even more focused: For instance, the most coherent body of indigenous Asian social psychology today is probably from Taiwan. The overwhelming message from this body of work is that historical concepts from traditional Chinese society are crucial to understanding modern Chinese social behavior. As yet, this body of work has yet to be collected into the single most powerful source of social representations under the direct control of social psychologists: the undergraduate textbook. Given the rapid development of an indigenous psychology happening concurrently in several parts of Asia, why not develop a textbook for Asian social psychology that combines the empirical message of the field with its moral and ethical implications?

If, as the authors have speculated, the benevolent authority model still exerts a significant influence on East Asian populations, would it not be a powerful and effective device to create a textbook that functions precisely within that role? Instead of just reporting research on loneliness, for example, the text could also comment on case studies on how to avoid loneliness. Instead of just describing research on prejudice, it can outline how to avoid behaving in a prejudiced way, or how prejudice in a community was changed.

Such a text could be absolutely rigorous in the way that it reports research and research findings (the *Is*), but it could mark off special sections where it offers advice on what to do about it (the *Can*). It would have to be culturally grounded in order to be able to achieve this goal, and so either examples must be given from many countries, or different versions of the text would have to be developed for different parts of Asia. It would have to adopt a standpoint in offering advice instead of couching it in more abstract or objective terms. It would also require updating, due to feedback from current research and teacher–student use. It would create a social structure that could anchor the field to topics of practical value.

The effect of such a text on student opinions could be very powerful. The first author's own experience is that what makes pop psychology popular is that it answers the questions of "How?"; "How do I avoid loneliness?"; "How do I get a date?"; whereas scientific psychology answers the question, "Why?"; "What are the predictors of loneliness?"; and "What are the predictors of date selection?" These are not separate questions, but are portrayed as such in pop and scientific psychology. Such a textbook would be not only an object of social knowledge but a conscious and reflexive attempt to affect the process of creating such knowledge. It would be a good site for integrating reflections from social psychologists in all the roles described, and would provide a greater vision of possible futures for students. It could be the ultimate positive feedback loop. Psychology as a science has not yet in its hundred-year history produced mathematical equations or foundational taxonomies that have captured human behavior successfully. What it has produced are sophisticated verbal descriptions. What we propose elevates the verbal description into an acting and active body of knowledge.

The production of an action-oriented text in the United States has not been met with success, in part because of the demands of the publishers, in part because they preach diverse values (e.g., women-oriented, black-oriented, cultural diversity-oriented, etc.) that many lecturers might not agree with (Tavris, personal communication). In the plurality-of-powers environment of America, it is much safer to cling to objective science. In the benevolent authority environment of East Asia, a text that clearly demarcates empirical results (the *Is*) and potential for positive outcomes (the *Can*, case studies of applications, successful or partially successful) might be more favorably received, especially if edited by a benevolent authority (e.g., a senior figure in East Asian social psychology who is widely admired).

At this stage, such a text is nothing more than an idea. As such, it should be made open for discussion. It may be a radical suggestion, as is our previous suggestion of civil service. It may be that the authors are dreaming in the wrong direction, and that social psychology would prefer to be rigorous in its own field of inquiry, without worrying about how it is received by society at large. However, if we are currently approaching the end of a golden age, the Pax Americana that emerged as a consequence of World War II (Liu & Rosenau, 1999; Huntington, 1996), then the multipolar, disaggregated, and culturally diverse world that is emerging may well offer a different set of problems and challenges than what we currently face. The demographics of increasing globalization, population increase and aging, and environmental degradation suggest that the next century may well have a greater need for a more actively influential social psychology than the present era will support. But steps toward such an entity need to be taken today.

REFERENCES

Andrews, D. A. (1989). Recidivism is predictable and can be influenced: Using risk assessments to reduce recidivism. *Forum on Corrections Research, 1* (2).

Asch, S. E. (1955). Opinions and social pressure. *Scientific American, 193* (5), 31–35.

Bagdikian, B. H. (1997). *The media monopoly*, 5th ed. Boston, MA: Beacon Press.

Brown, L. R. (1997). *The world watch reader on global environmental issues*. New York: W. W. Norton.

Cartwright, D. (1979). Contemporary psychology in historical perspective. *Social Psychology Quarterly, 42* (1), 82–93.

Cheung, C. Y. (1999). The scholarship of Liu Shu-hsien from my perspective. *Hong Kong Book Review* (pp. 37–45). Hong Kong: Committe for the Development of the Arts.

Choi, S. C., & Kim, U. (1997). Multifaceted analyses of *chemyon* ("social face"): An indigenous Korean perspective. In K. Leug, U. Kim, S. Yamaguchi, & Y. Kashima (Eds.), *Progress in asian social psychology* (vol. 1, pp. 3–22). New York: John Wiley and Sons.

Chomsky, N. (1994). *World orders, old and new*. London: Pluto Press.

Cook, S. W. (1988). The 1954 social science statement and school desegregation. In P. A. Katz & D. Taylor (Eds.), *Eliminating racism: Profiles in controversy* (pp. 237–256). New York: Plenum Press.

Elms, A. C. (1975). The crisis of confidence in social psychology. *American Psychologist, 30*, 967–976.

Gerard, H. B. (1988). School desegregation the social science role. In P. A. Katz & D. Taylor (Eds.), *Eliminating racism: Profiles in controversy* (pp. 225–236). New York: Plenum Press.

Gergen, K. J. (1973). Social psychology as history. *Journal of Personality and Social Psychology, 26*, 309–320.

Gilbert, G. N., & Mulkay, M. (1984). *Opening Pandora's box: A sociological analysis of scientists' discourse*. Cambridge: Cambridge University Press.

Gold, T. B. (1996). Civil society in Taiwan. In W. M. Tu (Ed.), *Confucian traditions in East Asian modernity* (pp. 244–258). Cambridge, MA: Harvard University Press.

Gold, G. J., & Raven, B. H. (1992). Interpersonal influence strategies in the Churchill–Roosevelt bases-for-destroyers exchange. *Journal of Social Behavior and Personality, 7* (2), 245–272.

Harris, B. (1997). Repoliticizing the history of psychology. In D. Fox & I. Prilleltensky (Eds.), *Critical psychology: An introductory handbook* (pp. 21–33). London: Sage.

Harris, B. (1998). The perils of a public intellectual. *Journal of Social Issues, 54* (1), 79–118.

Herman, E. S., & Chomsky, N. (1988). *Manufacturing consent: The political economy of the mass media*. New York: Pantheon.

Ho, D. (1998). Interpersonal relationships and relationship dominance: An analysis based on methodological relationism. *Asian Journal of Social Psychology, 1* (1), 1–16.

Hofstede, G. (1980). *Culture's consequences: International differences in work-related values*. Beverly Hills, CA: Sage.

Hong Kong Book Review. (1999). An interview with leading Neo-Confucian scholar Liu Shu-hsien (in Chinese; pp. 4–36). Hong Kong: Committee for the Development of the Arts.

Hout, M., & Knoke, D. (1975). Change in voting turnout: 1952–1972. *Public Opinion Quarterly, 39* (1), 52–68.

Huntington, S. (1996). *The clash of civilization and the remaking of world order*. New York: Simon and Schuster.

Hwang, K. K. (1987). Face and favor: Chinese power game. *American Journal of Sociology, 92*, 944–974.

Hwang, K. K. (1997–1998). Guanxi and mientze: Conflict resolution in Chinese society. *Intercultural Communication Studies, 7* (1), 17–42.

Hwang, K. K. (1998). Two moralities: Reinterpreting the findings of empirical research on moral reasoning in Taiwan. *Asian Journal of Social Psychology, 1* (3), 211–238.

Kim, K. O. (1996). The reproduction of Confucian culture in contemporary Korea. In W. M. Tu (Ed.), *Confucian traditions in East Asian modernity* (pp. 204–227). Cambridge, MA: Harvard University Press.

King, A.Y.C. (1996). State Confucianism and its transformation: The restructuring of the state–society relation in Taiwan. In W. M. Tu (Ed.), *Confucian traditions in East Asian modernity* (pp. 228–243). Cambridge, MA: Harvard University Press.

Kuo, E.C.Y. (1996). Confucianism as political discourse in Singapore. In W. M. Tu (Ed.), *Confucian traditions in East Asian modernity* (pp. 294–309). Cambridge, MA: Harvard University Press.

Leuers, T.R.S., & Sonoda, N. (1999). Independent self bias. In T. Sugiman, M. Karasawa, J. H. Liu, & C. Ward (Eds.), *Progress in Asian social psychology* (pp. 87–104). Seoul: Kyoyook-kwahak-sa.

Liu, J. H., Bonzon-Liu, B., & Pierce-Guarino, M. (1997). Common fate between humans and animals? The dynamical systems theory of groups and environmental attitudes in the Florida Keys. *Environmental and Behavior, 29* (1), 87–122.

Liu, J. H., & Liu, S. H. (1997). Modernism, postmodernism, and neo-Confucian thinking: A critical history of paradigm shifts and values in academic psychology. *New Ideas in Psychology, 15* (2), 159–178.

Liu, J. H., & Liu, S. H. (1999). Interconnectedness and Asian social psychology. In T. Sugiman, M. Karasawa, J. H. Liu, & C. Ward (Eds.), *Progress in Asian social psychology* (pp. 9–32). Seoul: Kyoyook-kwahak-sa.

Liu, J. H., & Rosenau, J. N. (1999, August 4–7). *The psychology of fragmegration: On the uses of a simultaneity of consciousness in the "New World Order."* Presented at the Third Conference of the Asian Association of Social Psychology, Taipei, Taiwan.

Liu, J. H., & Temara, P. (1998). Leadership, colonization, and tradition: Identity and economic change in Ruatoki and Ruatahuna. *Canadian Journal of Native Education, 22* (1), 138–150.

Liu, J. H., Wilson, M. S., McClure, J., & Higgins, T. R. (1999). Social identity and the perception of history: Cultural representations of Aotearoa/New Zealand. *European Journal of Social Psychology, 29*, 1021–1047.

Liu, S. H. (1998). *Understanding Confucian philosophy: Classical and Sung-Ming*. Westport, CT: Greenwood Press.

Liu, S. H. (1993). The psychotherapeutic function of the Confucian discipline of Hsin (mind–heart). In L. Y. Cheng, F. Cheung, & C. N. Chen (Eds.), *Psychotherapy for the Chinese* (pp. 1–17). Hong Kong: Department of Psychiatry, Chinese University of Hong Kong.

Liu, S. H. (1989). Postwar Neo-Confucian philosophy: Its development and issues. In C.W.H. Fu & G. E. Spiegler (Eds.), *Religious issues and interreligious dialogues*. New York: Greenwood Press.

Markus, H., & Kitayama, S. (1991). Culture and the self: Implications for cognition, emotion, and motivation. *Psychological Review, 98* (2), 224–253.

McGarty, C., & Haslam, S. A. (Eds.). (1997). *The message of social psychology: Perspectives on mind in society*. Oxford: Blackwell.

Milgram, S. (1965). Some conditions of obedience and disobedience to authority. *Human Relations, 18* (1), 57–76.

Miller, W. E. (1992). The puzzle transformed: Explaining declining turnout. *Political Behavior, 14* (1), 1–43.

Moghaddam, F. M. (1990). Specialization and despecialization in psychology: Divergent processes in the three worlds. *International Journal of Psychology, 24* (1), 103–116.

Moscovici, Serge. (1993). *The invention of society: Psychological explanations for social phenomena* (Halls, W. D. Trans.). Oxford: Polity Press.

Moscovici, S. (1988). Notes towards a description of social representations. *European Journal of Social Psychology, 18* (3), 211–250.

Murray, H. A. (1962). The personality and career of Satan. *Journal of Social Issues, 18* (4), 36–54.

Nicholson, I.A.M. (1998). The approved bureaucratic torpor: Goodwin Watson, critical psychology, and the dilemmas of expertise. *Journal of Social Issues, 54* (1), 29–52.

Pye, L. (1985). *Asian power and politics*. Cambridge, MA: Harvard University Press.

Redding, S. G. (1996). Societal transformation and the contribution of authority relations and cooperation norms in overseas Chinese business. In W. M. Tu (Ed.), *Confucian traditions in East Asian modernity* (pp. 310–327). Cambridge, MA: Harvard University Press.

Rodrigues, A., & Levine, R. A. (Eds.). (1999). *Reflections on 100 years of experimental social psychology*. New York: Basic Books.

Rosenau, J. (1997). *Along the domestic–foreign policy frontier: Exploring governance in a turbulent world*. Cambridge: Cambridge University Press.

Sears, D. O. (1986). College sophomores in the laboratory: Influences of a narrow database on psychology's view of human behavior. *Journal of Personality and Social Psychology, 51*, 515–530.

Shils, E. (1996). Reflections on civil society and civility in the Chinese intellectual tradition. In W. M. Tu (Ed.), *Confucian traditions in East Asian modernity* (pp. 228–243). Cambridge, MA: Harvard University Press.

Simonton, D. K. (1988). Presidential style: Personality, biography, and performance. *Journal of Personality and Social Psychology, 55* (6), 928–936.

Southwell, P. L. (1995). "Throwing the rascals out" versus "throwing in the towel": Alienation, support for term limits, and congressional voting behavior. *Social Science Quarterly, 76* (4), 741–774.

Tavris, C. (1989). *Anger: The misunderstood emotion* (rev. ed.). New York: Touchstone Books.

Taylor, S. E. (1989). *Positive illusions: Creative self-deception and the healthy mind.* New York: Basic Books.

Triandis, H. C. (1995). *Individualism & collectivism.* Boulder, CO: Westview Press.

Tu, W. M. (1984). *Confucian ethics today: The Singapore challenge.* Singapore: Curriculum Development Institute of Singapore, Federal Publications.

Tu, W. M. (Ed.). (1996). *Confucian traditions in East Asian modernity.* Cambridge, MA: Harvard University Press.

Unger, R. (1999, April). President's message. *SPSSI Newsletter, 208,* 1–2.

Weber, M. (1964). *The religion of China* (H. H. Gerth, Trans.). New York: Free Press.

Wong, J. (1996). Promoting Confucianism for socio-economic development: The Singapore experience. In W. M. Tu (Ed.), *Confucian traditions in East Asian modernity* (pp. 278–293). Cambridge, MA: Harvard University Press.

PART II

SOCIALIZATION IN FAMILY
AND SCHOOL

CHAPTER 4

The Beneficial and Harmful Effects of Filial Piety: An Integrative Analysis

Kuang-Hui Yeh

The concept of filial piety contains important rules that children should follow regarding how they treat their parents and take care of them. It has played a crucial role in Chinese society through the influence of Confucianism. As the interpretation of traditional Confucian thought has changed over time, so have the implications of filial piety changed in the context of modern Chinese life. Conflicting findings and debates have arisen over the impact of filial piety on individual development in Chinese and other Asian societies.

Some scholars claim that filial piety has a beneficial effect on personal growth and interpersonal relationships. Findings in empirical studies support the idea that the values embodied in filial piety support warmth, love, harmony, and close family ties, all of which facilitate intergenerational relationships (Sung, 1990, 1995). In addition, filial piety correlates with some positive aspects of personality (E.K.F. Ho, 1994; Zhang & Bond, 1998), makes children feel more obligated to support their elderly parents and more responsible for caring for them (Ishii-Kuntz, 1997), and reduces parent–child conflicts (Yeh, 1999).

In contrast, other scholars have found that filial piety entails some harmful effects on personal growth and interpersonal relationships. Boey (1976) found that Chinese parents' attitudes toward filial piety were positively correlated with their children's rigidity, and negatively correlated with their children's cognitive complexity. Other research also indicated that filial piety resulted in an uncreative character, a poor cognitive development, and a negative personality orientation (D.Y.F. Ho, 1994, 1996).

No matter whether filial piety is considered to be beneficial or harmful, it definitely has an essential influence on many aspects of human development, including personality, interaction, socialization, and the parent–child relationship. This study first reviews past studies regarding the concept of filial piety and its effects. A discussion of the historical development of the concept of filial piety in Chinese society is then provided to enhance the readers' understanding of its complex aspects. Next, the aspects of filial piety are integrated into a dual framework derived from factor analysis of empirical data and supported by the analysis of historical development. Finally, the framework is applied to a review of relevant findings.

BENEFICIAL PERSPECTIVES

As an essential traditional guiding principle of parent–child relations, there are a number of good reasons for the concept of filial piety to have persisted for such a long time. Results of empirical studies have suggested that filial attitudes have a facilitating effect on social interactions and intergenerational relationships. This beneficial effect could in fact be the very reason that the concept of filial piety has persisted for centuries.

Filial attitudes have been found to have a positive relationship with personality in the domain of agreeableness and, to a lesser extent, conscientiousness, two factors of the Five-Factor Model (FFM) of personality (Costa & McCrae, 1992). These two factors are related to social interactions (E.K.F. Ho, 1994). Filial attitudes can also be predicted by two Chinese indigenous personality traits, harmony and *renqing* (Zhang & Bond, 1998). These two traits are interpersonally focused. Harmony refers to inner peace of mind and contentment, particularly with respect to interpersonal concerns. *Renqing* measures interpersonal sensitivity to social favors that are exchanged according to an implicit set of rules that are dependent on the category of social ties between the individuals involved in the interaction. Results of the studies mentioned earlier indicated that people holding filial attitudes tend to possess personality characteristics that are helpful to their social interactions.

With respect to intergenerational relations, filial obligation has been found to affect adult children's attachment to and support of their parents (Cicirelli, 1983a), and to motivate adult children to take care of their parents (Selig, Thomlinson, & Hickey, 1991), especially during illness (A.E.Y. Lee, 1997). Recently, Ishii-Kuntz (1997) researched adult children's support of their parents in three different Asian American populations: Chinese, Japanese, and Korean. For all three types of Asian Americans he found that adult children's filial piety positively affected the provision of three kinds of support for elderly parents, which include financial assistance, service, and emotional support.

In another study, Yeh (1999) surveyed the association between filial piety and intergenerational conflict, with emphasis on parent–child conflict with adolescents. Yeh confirmed that a high level of filial piety corresponds to a low frequency of parent–child conflict. Since filial piety implies respect, warmth, and harmony in interpersonal relationships, mutual affection, propriety, and good order between children and parents are likely to occur when relations are based on the attitude of filial piety (Sung, 1990, 1995). Lawrence, Bennett, and Markides's (1992) findings support the idea that an attitude of filial piety results in good intergenerational relationships. They found that the psychological distress of caregivers was less when caregivers had positive affect toward the care recipients.

Filial piety is a mediator that sustains familial solidarity, including consensus, association, and affection (Roberts & Bengtson, 1990). There is a relatively strong relationship between family cohesion and the attitude of filial piety (Cheung, Lee, & Chan, 1994). The relation of family cohesion to filial piety suggests that filial piety is most likely an affect-based concept in parent–child relations rather than a norm or a rational choice. In sum, results of numerous empirical studies suggest that filial attitudes have a beneficial effect on many aspects of interpersonal interaction, including social interactions and intergenerational relationships.

HARMFUL PERSPECTIVES

Although filial piety appears to be quite a helpful and constructive concept in many aspects of social life in the studies reviewed, other scholars have pointed out the harmful influences of filial piety. Boey (1976) observed that Chinese parents' attitudes toward filial piety are positively correlated with children's rigidity and negatively associated with children's cognitive complexity. He suggested that strong parental emphasis on filial piety might have an adverse effect on children's cognitive development. This argument is supported by D.Y.F. Ho's summary paper (1996) in which he detailed the relationship between filial attitudes and what he called cognitive conservatism.

In previous research Ho explored the relationship of Confucian filial piety to parental attitudes, function of personality, and social cognition (1994). He found that filial attitudes are related to a number of parental attitudes toward child training, including obedience, indebtedness to one's parents, impulse control, and proper conduct. Related parental attitudes toward child training were tight control, overprotection, harshness, emphasis on proper behavior, and neglect or inhibition of the expression of opinions, self-mastery, creativity, and all-round personal development. All these negative parental attitudes are closely associated with an authoritarian parenting style.

Ho terms the influence of filial piety on parental attitudes toward child training *authoritarian moralism*. The influences of filial piety on children include a sense of obedience and indebtedness to one's parents instead of a need for self-fulfillment, a tendency toward impulse control instead of self-expression, and feelings of moral correctness in place of psychological sensitivity. The result of applying filial piety in child training is cognitive conservatism in personality and social cognition. Children are poorer in verbal fluency, adopt a passive, uncritical, and uncreative orientation toward learning, hold fatalistic, superstitious, and stereotypic beliefs, and are authoritarian, dogmatic, and conformist. The results of Ho's study showed that the concept of filial piety, which underlies the authoritarian moralism and cognitive conservatism in Ho's arguments, seems to have a negative impact on development.

So far I have reviewed the two opposing positions on the impact of filial piety on personal growth and interpersonal relationships. Why do these contradictory descriptions exist? In the next section I review the historical development of the concept of filial piety in Chinese society to enhance understanding of the many facets of this concept. In the final section of this chapter, I offer a theoretical model of filial piety that encompasses its disparate influences.

THE HISTORICAL DEVELOPMENT OF FILIAL PIETY

The historical development of filial piety can be divided into three main stages of Chinese society: the pre-Chin era (551 to 221 B.C.), the Han to Ch'ing dynasties (206 B.C. to A.D. 1911), and the early period of the Republic of China (1911) to the present. Aspects of the concept of filial piety revealed in this examination of historical development will then be used in the final section to support a dual framework. Influences of filial piety will then be explored under the new framework.

The Pre-Chin Era (551 to 221 B.C.)

In Chinese society the earliest significance of filial piety was religious and associated with ancestor worship. It was not until the pre-Chin era and Confucius's time that filial piety was construed as a virtue of parent–child interaction (Wei, 1969; Hsu, 1975).

Ren (love for humanity) is a focal virtue in Confucianism and is the basis for measuring and understanding the feelings of others in every relationship. During Confucius's time, filial piety became defined as children's love toward their parents. In fact, the love of children for their parents was seen as the very root of *ren*. The practice of filial piety became the practice and the cultivation of the virtue of *ren*. Confucius considered filial piety to be every person's obligation in daily life and the key point of social order. However, he did not recognize that children's obligations of filial piety were superior to or greater than the obligations of the parents. Obligations derived from each person's virtues. Since virtues were equal, obligations were reciprocal, not partial or based on external authority (Hsu, 1975).

At this stage of Chinese history, affection for one's parents and the reciprocal nature of virtue were both fundamental to the concept of filial piety, and closely corresponded to traditional Confucian principles. The traditional Confucian principle of favoring the intimate teaches that one should always give preferential treatment to the people with whom one has close relationships. Affection for one's parents corresponds to this principle. The Confucian principle of reciprocity is based on the idea that helpful or generous behavior should be returned in kind. The nature of virtue corresponds to this principle.

The Han to the Ch'ing Dynasty (206 B.C. to A.D. 1911)

Before the Han dynasty, the line distinguishing service to parents and treatment of superiors was very clear. However, with the appearance of the Apocryphal Filial Book and other historical events, filial piety began to acquire more authoritarian characteristics (Hsu, 1975). Especially important in the Han dynasty was the reification of the precepts of *san-kang* (the three bonds) in governing: father–son, emperor–official, and husband–wife relationships. The idea that in each of these three types of relationships the inferior must submit to the superior helped to maintain orderliness in the world by treating hierarchy as an immutable part of nature's way (Hamilton, 1990).

According to the laws of this time, unfilial children could be punished severely (Lin, 1975). Children who physically attacked their parents were beheaded, and even swearing at parents could result in death by hanging. Children were regarded as the property of their parents, and parents could do whatever they liked to their children. During this period a proverb developed to support the idea that the child must always defer to the parents: If the father demands that his son die, the son dare not stay alive. These concepts all show the authoritarian characteristics that became embedded in filial piety.

The Confucian principle of respecting the superior dictates that those in inferior positions always defer to those in superior positions. This pattern of deference is characteristic of authoritarianism. In the period from the Han to the Ch'ing dynasty, filial piety was mostly defined by this principle, in contrast to the principles of favoring the intimate and reciprocity, which were emphasized in the pre-Chin era.

The Early Period of the Republic of China (1911) to the Present

After the monarchism of the Ch'ing dynasty, the concept of filial piety retained an important position in the everyday lives of most Chinese until Chen Du-Hsiu presented an antifilial essay in a journal called *La Jeunesse* in 1915. Chen claimed that the authoritarian characteristics of filial piety were the core source of damage to independence of personality, obstruction of freedom of thought, deprivation of equality in law, and damaged productivity by fostering dependence. Wu Yue supported and elaborated these ideas in the same journal in 1917. He concluded that if filial piety could not be totally destroyed, people's autocratic thinking could never be overcome, and democracy could never be truly established. From that time, the value of filial piety in the minds of many Chinese has been gradually diminishing, reaching its lowest point during the

Cultural Revolution. It should be noted that the aspect of filial piety that was so strongly opposed at this stage was authoritarianism, and not the attributes of reciprocity and affection as advocated in the pre-Chin era.

Contemporary researchers point out that with the process of industrialization and modernization of Chinese societies, beliefs in filial piety are decreasing (Yeh, 1997). The same effect has been noted among overseas Chinese (Liu, Ng, Weatherall, & Loong, 2000). People have adjusted their lifestyles and value systems in order to adapt to the changes in social, cultural, and economic structures. Consequently, some attributes of filial piety are gradually eroding at a conceptual level, although other attributes are still crucial to people's everyday lives (Yang, 1988; Yeh, 1997). People now embrace a new type of filial piety that is adapted to societal changes (Hwang, 1977, 1982; H. Lee, 1983; Yang, Yeh, & Huang, 1989). Changing beliefs about filial piety coincide with Sung's (1990, 1995) opinions about the changing forms of respect for the aged in modern society. He predicted that these changes would occur due to the trend toward smaller families, the expansion of the female labor market, the geographic mobility of villagers, and the tendency of the young toward a more individualistic lifestyle.

A DUAL FRAMEWORK OF FILIAL PIETY

Two Aspects of Filial Piety

So far I have shown that filial piety can have both beneficial and harmful consequences on personal growth and interpersonal relationships, and that the negative effects of filial piety can be traced to particular historical attributes of the concept. I will now offer a more integrative framework of conceptualization that encompasses the broader meanings of filial piety in order to resolve its contrasting aspects.

Based on extensive content analysis of relevant quotations from various Confucian classics and other reference materials on filial piety, Yang (1988) suggested there were fifteen subcategories of meaning included in the concept of filial piety. Examples of these subcategories include tender-heartedness toward parents, obedience to parents, and protection of parents. Through factor analysis of a fifty-two item scale developed from the fifteen subcategories of meaning, Yang, Yeh, and Huang (1989) extracted four common factors: Respecting and Loving Parents, Supporting and Memorializing Parents, Oppressing Oneself, and Glorifying Parents. The nine highest loading items representing the four common factors were then selected as a short-form filial scale (items l_1 through l_9 in the key to Figure 4.1). Two distinctive superfactors were extracted from this scale with confirmatory factor analysis (Yeh, 1997; see Figure 4.1). These two higher order factors correspond to two of the focal filial piety attributes in the first two stages of historical development of the concept, namely reciprocity and authoritarianism. These two superfactors are the fun-

Figure 4.1
Two Aspects of Filial Piety: An Empirical Test

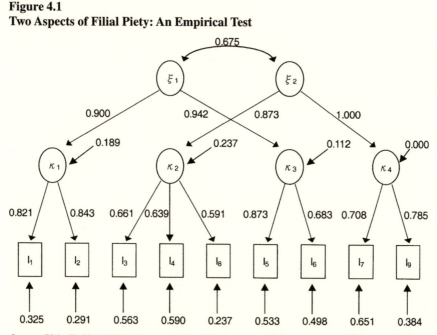

Source: Yeh, K. H. (1997). Changes in the Taiwanese people's concept of filial piety. In L. Y. Cheng, Y. H. Lu, & F. C. Wang, (Eds.), Taiwanese society in the 1990's (pp. 171–214.). Taipei, Taiwan: Institute of Sociology, Academia Sinica (in Chinese).

Key: ξ_1 = Reciprocal filial piety; ξ_2 =Authoritarian filial piety; κ_1 = Respecting and loving parents; κ_2 = Oppressing self; κ_3 = Supporting and memorializing parents; κ_4 = Glorifying parents; l_1 = Be grateful to parents for their upbringing; l_2 = Be kind and nice to parents regardless of how badly one has been treated by them; l_3 = Give up his or her own plans for the future in order to comply with parents' wishes and expectations; l_4 = Live with parents even after marriage; l_5 = Be responsible for making parents' life more comfortable; l_6 = Hurry home upon the death of the parent, regardless of how far away he or she lives; l_7 = Compliment his or her parents when it is needed to save their face; l_8 = Give birth to at least one son for the succession of the family name; l_9 = Do something to glorify the family.

damental values underlying the filial piety concept. Each includes different subfactors and follows distinctive principles.

Reciprocal Filial Piety

The first superfactor underlying the dual framework of filial piety is reciprocity. According to empirical analyses (Yang, Yeh, & Huang, 1989; Yeh, 1997), reciprocal filial piety consists of two subfactors: Respecting and Loving Parents, and Supporting and Memorializing Parents. The first subfactor implies respecting and attending to one's parents out of gratitude for their effort in raising and caring for you. Respecting and Loving Parents is shown emotionally and spiritually. The second subfactor indicates supporting and caring for one's parents when they are aged in order to repay their effort in raising and caring for you, and memorializing them when they are dead for the same reason. In this factor, Support and Memorializing of parents is shown physically and financially.

Because this aspect of filial piety indicates that people should comply with filial piety partly for reasons of reciprocity and partly out of natural intimate affection, I propose that the dimension of reciprocal filial piety mirrors filial piety during the pre-Chin era. It is based on two important Confucian values: the principle of reciprocity and the principle of favoring the intimate.

Numerous studies have indicated the importance of the principle of reciprocity in the construction of filial piety (Sung, 1990, pp. 610–611; 1995, pp. 240–241). In Confucianism, the principle of reciprocity as applied to filial piety implies that the first and most important gift that children receive from their parents is life itself. The origin of a person's life is that person's ancestors. According to Chinese thought, children should repay their parents and ancestors with reverence and by honoring their memory. Children owe their parents all the nurturance, comfort, and aid that they are capable of providing. Throughout the lives of the parents and until their deaths, children should offer their parents complete deference and support.

The second Confucian principle that reciprocal filial piety is based on is the principle of favoring the intimate. This principle means that people usually feel more intimate toward those who are closest in their interaction networks. It can be viewed as the motivation behind supporting, accompanying, comforting, and caring for parents, which is most likely based on affective involvement and recognizing parental needs. Research has shown that family cohesion is an important antecedent to filial attitude (Cheung, Lee, & Chan, 1994), and that individuals from a disrupted family are less likely to feel filial obligation and to help their parents (Cicirelli, 1983b). Family cohesion promotes filial attitudes because it fosters the development of children's empathy toward their parents. It is based on the notion that children's filial piety is in response to their parents' needs. This empathic response is only fostered in a cohesive family environment (Hoffman, 1984). In other words, perceived intimacy promotes helping (Dunkel-Schetter & Bennett, 1990).

In the tradition of Confucianism, the cardinal rule between parents and children is that parents must love their children out of benevolence, and that children must respect and support their parents out of filiality. The basic feelings of filial piety are love for humanity rooted in the goodness of human nature. These feelings should be encouraged in family life. Family orientation or familism is understood to be an ideology closely connected to filial piety (Choi, 1970; Kim, Cho, Choi, & Yu, 1986). From an early age every person learns to think of family first, and the maintenance of family solidarity, harmony, and prosperity reinforces the familial orientation of filial piety.

Authoritarian Filial Piety

The second superfactor of the dual framework of filial piety is authoritarianism. According to empirical analyses (Yang, Yeh, & Huang, 1989; Yeh, 1997), authoritarian filial piety may also be broken down into two subfactors: Oppress Oneself and Glorify One's Parents.

Oppressing Oneself implies sacrificing one's own wishes and complying with and deferring to one's parents' wishes because of their seniority. Glorifying One's Parents implies continuing the succession of the family lineage and maintaining the parents' reputation because of the force of role requirements. Since authoritarian filial piety is characterized by submission to hierarchical authority and the oppression of self-autonomy, this superfactor is likely to mirror filial piety from the Han to the Ch'ing periods and is based on the Confucian principle of respecting the superior.

The principle of respecting the superior means that people should always defer to their superiors in their relational network, no matter how these superiors treat them. According to the Oppressing Oneself subfactor, there are at least three types of sacrifices in filial behavior: physical, financial, and social (Sung, 1990). In the Confucian configuration of ethical arrangements within a family, juniors should submit themselves to seniors to ensure family solidarity and harmony. Thus, the concept that children should repress their own needs in order to fulfill parental desires is a distinguishable characteristic of authoritarian filial piety.

According to normative socialization theory, people are socialized to act according to social norms (Simmons, 1991). Performing filial duties toward parents is obligatory for Chinese individuals to maintain psychological homeostasis (K. K. Hwang, 1999). Ho (1987, 1994, 1996) argues that authoritarian moralism, which is molded by the moral imperative of filial piety, is a central characteristic of the Chinese pattern of socialization. Authoritarian moralism embodies a significant feature of Chinese society: the hierarchical structure of authority ranking in the family. It is also believed that filial piety justifies absolute parental authority over children, and, by extension, the authority of anyone senior in generational rank to those who are junior in generational rank (Ho, 1994). The superiority of the father's role is especially emphasized (Hamilton, 1990), and may be the reason obedience to parents is more strongly supported by Chinese than by Europeans (Ng, Loong, Liu, & Weatherall, 2000).

The ultimate goal of filial piety has much to do with continuing the life and culture of the family. The authoritarian approach of filial piety was established by social and family organizations in the form of laws, public opinions, family rules, and education to make sure interaction between family members is smooth and harmonious. With a structure of unbalanced power and resources between parents and children as a foundation for family relations, the norm that people should respect and treat their parents kindly is accepted and internalized by the Chinese. This norm can be viewed as a strategy of social control, yet it is also what D. H. Chen (1915) and Wu (1917) opposed most because submissive relationships damage individuality and independence.

Two Aspects of Filial Piety in Modern Chinese Society

After examining the historical development of the concept of filial piety and elucidating the dual framework, we are now more capable of understanding the following phenomenon: Both beneficial and harmful aspects of filial piety simultaneously exist in contemporary Chinese society. The experiential result of each aspect can be quite different. For this reason some researchers think the concept of filial piety shows both continuities with and departures from tradition (Ho, 1996).

Examining the concept of filial piety from the perspective of changes in modern Chinese society reveals a trend. A group of scholars known as the New Confucianists have proposed a definition of filial piety that coincides with reciprocal filial piety (T'ang, 1978; Hsieh, 1982; Fung, 1986; Cheng, 1986; Liang, 1988). In contrast, the filial piety that was denounced by liberals during the May Fourth period (D. H. Chen, 1915; Wu, 1917; Hu, 1919; Lu 1990), as well as by the Red Guards in the Cultural Revolution, was authoritarian filial piety. Certain aspects of filial piety (the reciprocal attributes) persist due to their relevance to human nature while other aspects (the authoritarian characteristics) gradually fade away and decline with the time (Yeh, 1997).

The facts of the historical development of filial piety and the concepts embodied by the dual framework of filial piety are compatible. The proposed framework was developed through analysis of empirical research. It reflects the actual implications of the concept. If the dual factors of the filial piety concept are ignored, the concept cannot be fully comprehended, and research results will be partial and problematic. For example, Ho (1994, 1996) stated that the essential aspects of filial piety were obedience, respect, ancestral worship, support for one's aged parents, and ensuring the continuity of the family line, all of which encompass reciprocal and authoritarian meanings of filial piety. However, in his actual research measures, some of the wording in his scale seemed to be highly culture-specific (Gallois et al., 1999, p. 196), and placed greater emphasis on the authoritarian meaning, and so resulted in slanted research findings. Ho's Filial Piety Scale contained twenty-two items (Ho, 1994, appendix). The number of items belonging to either the reciprocal or authoritarian categories from the dual framework was calculated: Eighteen items were related to authoritarian filial piety. Examples of these items include the following two statements: Sons and daughters should not go to faraway places while their parents are still living. As a son or daughter, one must obey one's parents no matter what. Only five items (one item was counted twice because it could not be categorized) contained reciprocal filial piety traits. Examples of these items include the following: The great debt that you have to repay your parents is as boundless as the sky. And, the main reason for sons and daughters not to do dangerous things is to avoid worrying their parents.

In contrast, in his study of filial piety Sung (1990) emphasized reciprocal aspects. Sung claimed that the most outstanding dimensions underlying filial piety were respect, responsibility, family harmony, and sacrifice. Ishii-Kuntz also used a problematic measure of filial piety. His questionnaire was too simple to allow for speculation about filial piety factors.

SOME EVIDENCE FOR THE DUAL FRAMEWORK

To date, there has been no complete study testing the dual framework. However, there are two related analyses that partially support it. First, Yeh (1999) explored the conflict-related factors between parents and children. In addition to the usual explanation of poor parenting styles and skills that have been proposed by many Western researchers (Crockenberg, 1987; Crockenberg & Litman, 1990; Kuczynski & Kochanska, 1990; Martin, 1981; Osborne & Fincham, 1994; Parpal & Maccoby, 1985; Patterson, 1982), Yeh found that filial piety factors should also be considered when discussing parent–child conflict in Chinese societies.

Applying the dual framework to the relationship between filial piety and parent–child conflicts suggests that filial piety not only has an effect on the frequency of parent–child conflicts and the solution strategies selected, but also that different filial attributes have different effects. For example, the lower reciprocal filial attitudes of adolescents are associated with higher parent–child conflict frequencies and escaping (doing nothing or removing oneself from the conflict situation) and egocentric (putting personal benefit ahead of parental benefit) conflict solution strategies. Children with higher authoritarian filial attitudes are inclined to use deferential solution strategies (sacrifice personal benefits to achieve parental demands) in parent–child conflict situations. Even under the condition of controlling for variation in parenting style, reciprocal filial piety was influential in determining both the frequency and the solution strategy in parent–child conflict situations.

Second, according to social domain theory, there are at least two kinds of regulations: moral guidelines and social conventions (Nucci & Turiel, 1978; Smetana, 1989, 1997; Turiel, 1983). These two types of regulations roughly correlate to the principles underlying reciprocal and authoritarian filial piety.

Moral guidelines are shaped by principles of justice, fairness, rights, and trust. Behavior that transgresses morality includes hurting others' physical and psychological beings, violating others' rights, depriving others of something they own, and so forth. Social conventions are the common consensus of specific social groups on the regulations for the proper interaction of individuals. However, social conventions can be determined by authoritarian sources, and are affected by certain situations, for example, wearing uniforms at school (Nucci & Turiel, 1978; Smetana, 1997). Behaviors that are contrary to social convention include not acting in accordance with the expectations of the authorities, and knocking the social order out of balance (Nucci, 1981; Smetana, 1989).

Reciprocal filial piety is dominated by the principles of reciprocity and favoring the intimate. These principles are based on the goodness of humanity, including love, empathy and benevolence, and so on, and can be expected to correlate more with morality than with social convention. Authoritarian filial piety is dominated by the principle of respecting the superior, which is more of a culture-specific principle, and so related to social convention more than to morality. Authoritarian filial piety does have a relation to morality, but the association is weaker than or even mediated by reciprocal filial piety.

Using the datasets of the 1995 Taiwan Social Change Survey, the relationship of filial piety to morality and social convention was supported by a model designed as suggested earlier (see Figure 4.2). Individual attitudes toward morality were measured by six Likert-type items such as the following: to tell lies, to do shoddy work and use inferior materials, to discard garbage outside the home, and so forth. Individual attitudes toward social convention were measured by three items: having premarital sex, having extramarital relations, and being a homosexual. The model's normal theory weighted least squares chi-square was 0.18 (P = 0.67, df = 1, N = 934), MSEA = 0.0 (P = 0.89), ECVI = 0.019, Critical N = 34230.06). Results show that reciprocal and authoritarian filial piety are two separate aspects based upon different principles, and confirm that reciprocal filial piety is based on the goodness of humanity and correlates more closely with moral guidelines than with social conventions (0.31 versus 0.17). Authoritarian filial piety is a kind of normative principle that is more closely related to social convention than to morality (0.14 versus 0.0). Its association with morality is mediated by reciprocal filial piety. This mediating effect is likely due to the fact that reciprocal and authoritarian filial piety are moderately related to one other (0.52).

These empirical studies may not fully test the dual framework of filial piety, but they do show there are at least two distinguishable aspects of filial piety that have different effects on interpersonal behaviors and personality orientation. They also underscore the necessity of continued research into the nature of filial piety.

CONCLUSION

In this chapter I have presented two sets of empirical findings on the effects of filial piety. Several scholars, including Sung, Zhang, Ishii-Kuntz, and Yeh, found evidence supporting the beneficial effects of filial piety, which encompass agreeable personality traits, filial support, and intergenerational and family cohesion. Other studies, including those of Boey and Ho, emphasized the harmful effects of filial piety, which include children's rigidity, poor cognitive complexity, an uncreative character, and a negative personality orientation.

Figure 4.2
A Test of the Dual Framework of Filial Peity

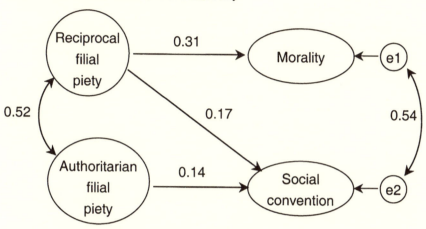

Under the dual framework, the reciprocal filial factor represents beneficial effects, while the authoritarian factor represents harmful ones. Any study of filial piety that examines only the effects from one side will be incomplete and unbalanced. The dual framework allows for a better and more integrative way to view the concept of filial piety by integrating both beneficial and harmful effects.

Hsu (1975) proposed that the appearance or existence of every idea is for adapting to certain kinds of situations and requirements in history. Each idea is constrained by the conditions of that time. When the situation and the requirements change, the content and validity of certain cultures also changes. If a concept is viewed as static and unchangeable and is applied to different individuals and times, convincing results cannot be obtained. Since filial piety has persisted for such a long time and has so many practical implications in Chinese social life, any attempt to restrict this concept to the choice of giving it up or keeping it would not be an appropriate and responsible way of dealing with such a complex concept. Future research will contribute to the understanding of this complex concept and the contributions it makes to contemporary Chinese societies.

REFERENCES

Boey, K. W. (1976). *Rigidity and cognitive complexity: An empirical investigation in the interpersonal, physical, and numeric domains under task-oriented and ego-oriented conditions.* Unpublished Ph.D. diss., University of Hong Kong.
Chen, D. H. (1915). Thinking differences between the East and the West. *La Jeunesse, 1* (4) (in Chinese).

Cheng, C. Y. (1986). On the modernization of the Confucian ethics of filial piety: Rights, duties and virtues. *Chinese Studies, 4* (1), 83–106 (in Chinese).

Cheung, C. K., Lee, J. J., & Chan, C. M. (1994). Explicating filial piety in relation to family cohesion. *Journal of Social Behavior and Personality, 9* (3), 565–580.

Choi, J. S. (1970). Comparative study on the traditional families in Korea, Japan and China. In R. Hill & R. Koenig (Eds.), *Families in East and West* (pp. 202–210). Paris: Mouton.

Cicirelli, V. G. (1983a). Adult children's attachment and helping behavior to elderly parents. *Journal of Marriage and the Family, 45* (4), 815–825.

Cicirelli, V. G. (1983b). A comparison of helping behavior to elderly parents of adult children with intact and disrupted marriages. *Gerontologist, 23* (6), 619–625.

Costa, P. T., Jr., & McCrae, R. R. (1992). *Revised NEO personality inventory (NEO PI-R) and NEO five-factor inventory (NEO-FFI) professional manual.* Odessa, FL: Psychological Assessment Resources.

Crockenberg, S. (1987). Predictors and correlates of anger toward and punitive control of toddlers by adolescent mothers. *Child Development, 58*, 964–975.

Crockenberg, S., & Litman, C. (1990). Autonomy as competence in two-year-olds: Maternal correlates of child defiance, compliance, and self-assertion. *Developmental Psychology, 26*, 961–971.

Dunkel-Schetter, C., & Bennett, T. L. (1990). Differentiating the cognitive and behavioral aspects of social support. In B. R. Sarason, I. G. Sarason, & G. R. Pierce (Eds.), *Social support: An interactional view* (pp. 267–296). New York: Wiley.

Fung, Y. L., (1986). *San sung t'ang ch'uan chi*, vol. 4. Ho-nan, China: Ho-nan People's Publisher (in Chinese).

Gallois, C., Giles, H., Ota, H., Pierson, H. D., Ng, S. H., Lim, T.-S., et al. (1999). Intergenerational communication across the Pacific Rim: The impact of filial piety. In J. C. Lasry, J. Adair, & K. Dion (Eds.), *Latest contributions to cross-cultural psychology* (pp. 192–211). Lisse, Netherlands: Swets & Zeitlinger.

Hamilton, G. G. (1990). Patriarchy, patrimonialism, and filial piety: A comparison of China and Western Europe. *British Journal of Sociology, 41* (1), 77–104.

Ho, D.Y.F. (1987). Fatherhood in Chinese culture. In M. E. Lamb (Ed.), *The father's role: Cross-cultural perspectives* (pp. 227–245). Hillsdale, NJ: Erlbaum.

Ho, D.Y.F. (1994). Filial piety, authoritarian moralism, and cognitive conservatism in Chinese societies. *Genetic, Social and General Psychology Monographs, 120*, 349–365.

Ho, D.Y.F. (1996). Filial piety and its psychological consequences. In M. H. Bond (Ed.), *The handbook of Chinese psychology* (pp. 155–165). Hong Kong: Oxford University Press.

Ho, E.K.F. (1994). *Validating the five-factor model of personality: The Hong Kong case.* Unpublished bachelor's thesis, Chinese University of Hong Kong.

Hoffman, M. L. (1984). Empathy, its limitations, and its role in a comprehensive moral theory. In W. M. Kurtines & J. L. Gewirtz (Eds.), *Morality, moral behavior, and moral development* (pp. 283–302). New York: John Wiley and Sons.

Hsieh, Y. (1982). The properties of filial piety and its necessity. In the Council of the Chinese Cultural Renaissance (Ed.), *The theory and practice of ethic* (pp. 229–250). Taipei, Taiwan: Council of the Chinese Cultural Renaissance (in Chinese).

Hsu, F. K. (1975). Formation, change and problems in history of Chinese filial thoughts. In F. K. Hsu (Ed.), *The collected papers of Chinese ideological history* (pp.

155–200). Taipei, Taiwan: Taiwan Student Bookstore (in Chinese).

Hu, S. (1919). My son. *Weekly Review, 33*, 3 (in Chinese).

Hwang, C. H. (1977). Filial piety from a psychological point of view. *Bulletin of Educational Psychology, 10,* 11–20 (in Chinese).

Hwang, C. H. (1982). The practice of filial piety in modern times. *Proceedings of the conference on traditional culture and modern lives* (pp. 283–297). Taipei, Taiwan: Committee of Recovering and Promoting Chinese Culture (in Chinese).

Hwang, K. K. (1999). Filial piety and loyalty: Two types of social identification in Confucianism. *Asian Journal of Psychology, 2,* 129–149.

Ishii-Kuntz, M. (1997). Intergenerational relationships among Chinese, Japanese, and Korean Americans. *Family Relations, 46,* 23–32.

Kim, H. C., Cho, N. J., Choi, S. J., & Yu, I. H. (1986). *Development of a standard model of the Korean family.* Seoul, Korea: Academy of Korean Studies.

Kuczynski, L., & Kochanska, G. (1990). Development of children's noncompliance strategies from toddlerhood to age five. *Developmental Psychology, 26,* 398–408.

Lawrence, R. H., Bennett, J. M., & Markides, K. S. (1992). Perceived intergenerational solidarity and psychological distress among older Mexican-Americans. *Journal of Gerontology, 47* (2), S55–S65.

Lee, A.E.Y. (1997). *Family social support patterns of the Chinese elderly in Beijing, Shanghai, Guangzhou, and Los Angeles: The role of filial piety.* Unpublished Ph.D. diss., University of California, Los Angeles.

Lee, H. (1983). The meaning of filial piety in modern times. In *Proceedings of the conference on filial piety and related behaviors* (pp. 19–22). Taipei, Taiwan: Committee of Recovering and Promoting of Chinese Culture (in Chinese).

Liang, S. (1988). *The essences of Chinese culture* (rev. ed.). Taipei, Taiwan: Wu-Nan (in Chinese).

Lin, Y. J. (1975). *Chinese traditional law and morality.* Taipei, Taiwan: Chung Shan Cultural Foundation.

Liu, J. H., Ng, S. H., Weatherall, A., & Loong, C. (2000). Filial piety, acculturation, and intergenerational communication among New Zealand Chinese. *Basic and Applied Social Psychology, 22* (3), 213–223.

Lu, H. (1990). *Fathers do their duties as fathers and sons do their duties as sons.* China: People's Literature (in Chinese).

Martin, J. A. (1981). A longitudinal study of the consequences of early mother–infant interaction: A microanalytic approach. *Monographs of the Society for Research in Child Development, 46,* 1–58.

Ng, S. H., Loong, C.S.F., Liu, J. H., & Weatherall, A. (2000). Will the young support the old? An individual- and family-level study of filial obligations in two New Zealand cultures. *Asian Journal of Social Psychology, 3,* 163–182.

Nucci, L. (1981). Conceptions of personal issues: A domain distinct from moral or societal concepts. *Child Development, 52,* 114–121.

Nucci, L., & Turiel, E. (1978). Social interactions and the development of social concepts in preschool children. *Child Development, 67* (4), 1870–1886.

Osborne, L. N., & Fincham, F. D. (1994). Conflict between parents and their children. In D. D. Cahn (Ed.), *Conflict in personal relationships* (pp. 117–142). Hillsdale, NJ: Lawrence Erlbaum.

Parpal, M., & Maccoby, E. (1985). Maternal responsiveness and subsequent child compliance. *Child Development, 56,* 1326–1334.

Patterson, G. R. (1982). *A social learning approach to family intervention: A coercive family process.* Eugene, OR: Castalia.

Roberts, R.E.L., & Bengtson, V. L. (1990). Is intergenerational solidarity a unidimensional construct? A second test of a formal model. *Journal of Gerontology, 45* (1), S12–S20.

Selig, S., Tomlinson, T., & Hickey, T. (1991). Ethical dimensions of intergenerational reciprocity: Implications for practice. *The Gerontologist, 31* (5), 624–630.

Simmons, R. G. (1991). Altruism and sociology. *Sociology Quarterly, 32,* 1–22.

Smetana, J. G. (1989). Toddler's social interactions in the context of moral and conventional transgressions in the home. *Developmental Psychology, 25* (4), 499–508.

Smetana, J. G. (1997). Parenting and the development of social knowledge reconceptualized: A social domain analysis. In J. E. Grusec & L. Kuczynski (Eds.), *Parenting and children's internalization of values: A handbook of contemporary theory* (pp. 162–192). New York: John Wiley and Sons.

Sung, K. T. (1990). A new look at filial piety: Ideas and practice of family-centered parent care in Korea. *The Gerontologist, 30,* 610–617.

Sung, K. T. (1995). Measures and dimensions of filial piety in Korea. *The Gerontologist, 35,* 240–247.

T'ang, C. (1978). *The consciousness of culture and the rationality of morality,* vol. 1. Taipei, Taiwan: Taiwan Students Book Company (in Chinese).

Turiel, E. (1983). *The development of social knowledge: Morality and convention.* Cambridge: Cambridge University Press.

Wei, C. T. (1969). The change and problems of Chinese filial thoughts. *Universitas: Monthly Review of Arts and Sciences, 3* (5), 1–10 (in Chinese).

Wu, Y. (1917). Chinese family and autocracy. *La Jeunesse, 2* (6), 1–4 (in Chinese).

Yang, K. S. (1988). Chinese filial piety: A conceptual analysis. In K. S. Yang (Ed.), *The Chinese mind* (pp. 39–73). Taipei, Taiwan: Laureate Book Company (in Chinese).

Yang, K. S., Yeh, K. H., & Huang, L. L. (1989). A social attitudinal analysis of Chinese filial piety: Conceptualization and assessment. *Bulletin of the Institute of Ethnology, 56,* 171–227 (in Chinese).

Yeh, K. H. (1997). Changes in the Taiwanese people's concept of filial piety. In L. Y. Cheng, Y. H. Lu, & F. C. Wang (Eds.), *Taiwanese society in the 1990's* (pp. 171–214). Taipei, Taiwan: Institute of Sociology, Academia Sinica (in Chinese).

Yeh, K. H. (1999, August 4–7). *Parent–Child conflicts and filial piety: A preliminary study in Taiwan.* Paper presented at the Third Conference of the Asian Association for Social Psychology, Academia Sinica, Taipei, Taiwan.

Zhang, J., & Bond, M. H. (1998). Personality and filial piety among college students in two Chinese societies: The added value of indigenous constructs. *Journal of Cross-Cultural Psychology, 29* (3), 402–417.

CHAPTER 5

Parental Beliefs about Shame and Moral Socialization in Taiwan, Hong Kong, and the United States

Heidi Fung, Eli Lieber, and Patrick W. L. Leung

Every culture attempts to socialize its youngsters into culturally desirable, mature members. What is seen as desirable and how such a goal is achieved may vary across different cultural groups. This study examines whether and how the sociomoral emotion may play a role in this process. After a long period of relative neglect, there has been a renewed interest among psychologists and psychiatrists in the concept of shame. Coupled with the recent rise of the functionalist approach to emotions, shame is now increasingly being treated as a differentiated, complex, and important emotion. Nevertheless, its sociomoral functions are often seen as mere responses to external forces caused by a real or imaginary audience, having little to do with the long-term socializing effect. Moreover, since Freud, a frequent association with narcissism and loss of self-esteem has aroused anxiety about the consequences of excessive shame, if not about shame itself, and a tendency to dismiss the legitimate functions of shame (Schneider, 1977; Broucek, 1991; Sabini & Silver, 1997). With few exceptions, shame is often viewed negatively as a problem to be solved or a disease to avoid, and its adaptive form is often overlooked (Schneider, 1977, 1987; Creighton, 1990). In order to restore shame to its rightful place in the moral spectrum, in this study parents of preschoolers from three different sociocultural groups were directly asked about when and in what situations they believed that their children had begun to know shame and distinguish right from wrong.

SHAME IN AMERICAN AND CHINESE CULTURES

Shame, along with guilt, pride, and embarrassment, is considered a secondary or self-conscious emotion emerging later in life as opposed to the inborn primary emotions (e.g., anger, fear, joy) (Lewis, 1992; Stipek & DeCotis, 1988; Ferguson & Stegge, 1995; Ferguson, Stegge, & Damhuis, 1991; Lewis, Alessandri, & Sullivan, 1992; Lewis, Sullivan, Stanger, & Weiss, 1989). Due to the clinical presumption of shame as a much less desirable, mature, prosocial, and adaptive emotion than guilt, when studying shame, the most common approach is to make comparisons with and differentiate it from guilt (Tangney, 1998; Tangney, Burggraf, & Wagner, 1995; Stipek, 1983; Freud, 1923; Lynd, 1958; Zahn-Waxler & Kochanska, 1990). Guilt is reportedly located in the moral domain, and involves actions perceived as controllable, such as inadequate effort. In contrast, shame is more likely to be associated with competence and deals with situations involving inadequate ability or competence, which are perceived as uncontrollable (Ferguson & Stegge, 1995; Weiner, 1986). Guilt arises internally from one's own conscience, focusing on one's own opinion of the self. The intense focus of shame, however, comes from others' opinions of the self (Ferguson, Stegge, & Damhuis, 1991). In guilt, the individual tends to make negative attributions to specific actions—things done or not done, while in shame the individual makes attributions globally to the total self (Lewis, 1992). Therefore, an individual experiencing guilt would be aware of personal power—self as agent—and actively seek control over the consequences of specific actions through confession and reparation. Behavioral responses to guilt characterize one as an amender (Barrett, Zahn-Waxler, & Cole, 1993). In contrast, when one experiences shame, the entire person becomes a recognized object being evaluated by others—self as object (Barrett, 1995, 1998). The shamed individual is hence compelled to hide the malignant and weak self and behave as an avoider (Barrett, Zahn-Waxler, & Cole, 1993). The individual passively withdraws from interaction with others or defensively externalizes humiliation and anger at the risk of serious damage to interpersonal relationships (Ferguson & Stegge, 1995; Tangney, Wagner, Fletcher, & Gramzow, 1992; Scheff, 1987, 1990), which may lead to a range of psychopathological symptoms (Tangney, Wagner, & Gramzow, 1992, 1995; Cook, 1996). As maintained by Lewis (1992), "the emotion of guilt lacks the negative intensity of shame. It is not self destroying and, as such, can be viewed as a more useful emotion in motivating specific and corrective action" (p. 77).

This negative view of shame, considered only at the cognitive and affective level, may not be historically validated or universally shared. In his recent review, Kilborne (1995) noted that, "from Ancient Greece to the present . . . there has been an evolution culturally from shame as socially intelligible related to honor, to shame as emblematic of a basic flaw in the self, a deep, narcissistic vulnerability, and bewildering identity confusion" (p. 296). What seems to explain this shift is the absence of the moral element in shame. As denoted in most Indo-European languages, there are dual aspects of shame—disgrace-shame versus discretion-shame (Schneider, 1977; Twitchell, 1997). Disgrace-shame involves negative affect, an intrapsychic state that is painful, disorienting, and often unexpected. In contrast, discretion-shame can be seen as an ethical virtue, a positive quality, which falls into the moral domain and reflects and sustains social values and order. Although they seem to be two strikingly different conceptions, both are necessary for an accurate and complete representation of shame. Accordingly, though an individual experiencing shame may feel self-contempt and a motivation to withdraw, there is also a deeper meaning to the experience that incites the "better" self and encourages the strengthening of character. These aspects can be understood as critical to a full understanding of the concept because, "where despair rules, there is no shame" (Schneider, 1977, p. 28).

Under the influence of Confucianism, shame has been not only a hypercognized emotion, but also an underscored moral value in Chinese culture. A significant part of the Confucian Analects dealt with the value of shame (Chu, 1972). According to Confucian ideology, "a false gentleman can be superior to a truly small man." The distinction between them is that since the former still wants and needs the appearance of propriety to rule his behavior he can be constrained by shame, whereas the latter does not even have a sense of shame (Liu & Liu, 1999). Even to this day, compared to the West, shame plays a greater role in constraining the power of the ruler in Chinese societies (Hwang, 1987; Liu & Liu, 1999). The importance of the Chinese experience of shame is well reflected in the emphasis on saving face, criticism, and evaluation in interpersonal relationships (Ho, 1976; Hu, 1944; King & Myers, 1977; Chu, 1972; Zhai, 1995; Hwang, 1987, 1997; Schoenhals, 1993). Further emphasizing this centrality is the rich variety and complexity of lexical terms and labels for shame, humiliation, embarrassment, face, and related notions (Mascolo, Fischer, & Li, in press; Her, 1990; Russell & Yik, 1996; Wilson, 1981; Shaver, Wu, & Schwartz, 1992).

In primary schools in Taiwan, shame anxiety or shaming with a component of ostracism and abandonment by the group was found to be a major moral training technique, serving to not only correct the wrongdoer, but also to corroborate and reinforce the rectitude of the others (Wilson, 1970, 1981). In a recent ethnographic study on the paradoxical relationship between teachers and students in a high school in China, Schoenhals (1993) concluded that Chinese culture is a "shame-socialized culture," in which members are strongly socialized to be sensitive to other people's criticisms, judgments, and evaluations and are encouraged to act so as to maximize positive esteem while avoiding disapproval and contempt from others.[1] The consequences of not doing so are much greater than in nonshame-socialized cultures. As remarked by Mascolo, Fischer, and Li (in press), "Whereas shame in the U.S.A. carries stigmatizing connotations, shame among the Chinese offers the promise of reintegration into the family or community following reestablishment of appropriate behavior. As such, shame is not primarily a threat to self-esteem; instead, it is a vehicle for social cohesion and the development of self" (p. 29).

SHAME AND MORAL SOCIALIZATION

The overarching goal of moral socialization is internalization of rules and norms. How might this process work, particularly for children of a young age? Does emotion play a part in such a process? As shame is deployed as a moral training strategy in Chinese societies, does it contribute to the process of internalizing rules? Kochanska and her colleagues (Kochanska & Aksan, 1995; Kochanska, Tjebkes, & Forman, 1998) distinguished two kinds of compliance for young children: situational and committed. While the former is context-specific in nature—merely a momentary response to explicit external force—the latter reflects an emerging conscience, a complete and autonomous commitment to rules. Committed but not situational compliance represents an early form of internalization. Further, the less parental power-assertive control, stress, and negative affect are involved, the faster the child's internally based discomfort (i.e., guilt), positive esteem, and readiness to embrace parental standards will develop (Kochanska, 1991; Kochanska & Thompson, 1997). To be effective, optimal levels of discomfort and stress need to be aroused in the child (Hoffman, 1982, 1983, 1984, 2000). Too little arousal may prompt the child to ignore the standard, while too much may provoke unnecessary conflict or negative reactions (e.g., anger, resentment, anxiety, or fear). Either problem could interfere with the process of facilitating the child's internalization of rules and values—a child's compliance under these pressures would be only situational surrender to external force (Kochanska & Thompson, 1997). Guilt, based on empathetic concerns for the bad consequence caused by the child's misconduct, is believed to be an important affect in this process (Hoffman, 1982, 2000). Overall, moral affect has to be socialized, because "even when children have the cognitive and affective requisites of guilt, they may not actually experience it unless an external agent such as the parent is present to compel them to attend to the harm done to the victim and to their own role in the victim's plight" (Hoffman, 1982, p. 98).

For Chinese parents, it might be shame that serves to achieve optimal levels of arousal in moral socialization, with the goal of committed compliance in the child. In an ethnographic work (Fung, 1994, 1999; Fung & Chen, 2001), the daily interactions of nine Taiwanese children with their family members were intensively observed and videotaped over a period of two years. It was found that shaming occurred at a regular rate (2.5 events per hour) across all families at all sampling ages (2.5, 3, 3.5, and 4). The majority (78%) of these spontaneous events, seen as prototypical, were in response to the child's precipitating transgression, while the remainder involved invocations of the child's past transgression. In an attempt to forestall the transgression or to remind the child of the rules, shame feelings were elicited through the deployment of a variety of communicative resources, verbal, nonverbal, and paralinguistic, to put the focal child in an unfavorable light. Although during parental interviews shaming was never mentioned as a disciplinary measure, parents believed that their youngsters understood shame at an early age and that this rudimentary sense of shame could be used as a tool to teach the ability to tell right from wrong.

These parents' actions exemplified an endorsed training method referred to by the parents as "opportunity education" (*jihui jiaoyu*). This method implies two connecting notions. First, instead of teaching in the abstract, the child's immediate experience, including his or her own or others' negative and positive behaviors, provides an opportunity to situate the lesson in concrete terms (immediacy, situatedness, and concreteness). And second, parents should take every opportunity to educate. Charging these occasions with shame allows them to put extra weight to the situated lesson. By provoking shame feelings (disgrace-shame), parents intentionally or unintentionally socialize the child toward the culturally desirable values of shame (discretion-shame).

The effectiveness and meaning of these practices and beliefs are best understood in terms of their situated cultural context and historical heritage. Chinese parenting is often reported as authoritarian, controlling, restrictive, or even harsh (Ho, 1986; Lin & Fu, 1990). However, Chao (1994, 1995, 1996) pointed out that existing measures of parenting styles originate from an American sociocultural context, which is rooted in evangelical and Puritan religious influences and in firm beliefs in individualism and independence. As such, they cannot but fail to fully capture the prevailing parenting styles held by Chinese (or even most Asians) who do not necessarily share the same sociocultural traditions and values. The indigenous concepts of Chinese parenting, *training* (*jiaoxun* and *guan*), refer to the earliest possible introduction to government and guidance by exposing the child to explicit examples, or by comparison to other children while in close proximity to and with high involvement of the caregivers. Unlike its English translation, *guan* has a very positive connotation, because, based on an immense demand for parental responsibility, devotion, and sacrifice, it can mean "to care for" or "to love" as well as "to govern" (Chao, 1994). Taken together, parental shaming practices can take place in a supportive and loving context and may involve a variety of meanings.

THE CURRENT STUDY

A previous ethnographic study was conducted with a small sample of families in Taiwan, but whether the findings hold with larger samples remains in question. Do most Chinese parents believe that their children have some knowledge of shame by preschool age? How do they perceive shame? Will shame also be located in the moral rather than competence domain, serving adaptive functions in moral socialization? Do cultural comparisons shed some light on the possible relationship between having a sense of shame and telling right from wrong in the early years of life? While acknowledging the child as an active agent and the bidirectional nature of family dynamics, parents are still believed to be the most important and influential feature of the socialization equation (Kuczynski & Grusec, 1997). Combining both qualitative and quantitative approaches, this study directly asks parents in different cultural and subcultural groups about the ages and the occasions in which their preschool-aged children began to understand shame and were able to tell right from wrong. This study does not intend to differentiate shame from guilt or develop measures of shame. Nor does it attempt to identify any causal relation between a sense of shame and knowing right from wrong. Rather, by inviting parents to write freely to open-ended questions, we sought to explore and understand parents' observations and interpretations of shame in relation to the child's moral development. Building on our earlier investigations (Fung, 1994, 1999; Fung & Chen, 2001; Fung, Leung, & Yeh, 1998; Lieber, Fung, Leung, & Leung, 1997), our expectations regarding parental ethnotheories are as follows:

1. Most parents from the three research sites—Taiwan, Hong Kong, and the United States—will report that their children have acquired a sense of shame and some knowledge of right and wrong by preschool age.

2. Chinese (Taiwan and Hong Kong) parents will believe that their children's knowledge of shame emerges earlier than the ability to tell right from wrong, whereas U.S. parents will believe that the reverse is true.

3. A much greater proportion of U.S. parents will be reluctant to talk about shame as compared to their Chinese (Taiwan and Hong Kong) counterparts, reflecting American psychological theories that emphasize its negative self-focus and perceived threat to self-esteem.

4. Regarding the occasions when the child was thought to begin to have a sense of shame, U.S. parents will be more likely to report instances related to the child's competence, whereas responses from their Chinese counterparts (Taiwan and Hong Kong) will tend to fall into the moral domain.

5. The parents' reports regarding occasions of telling right and wrong will demonstrate their demands or expectations of the ability of committed compliance in their children.

6. The reported occasions about children's acquisition of telling right from wrong will also, to some extent, illustrate their endorsed disciplinary strategies, for instance, opportunity education for Chinese (Taiwan and Hong Kong) parents.

Design and Method

Procedure

This study was part of a larger survey on parental child-rearing beliefs across cultures, involving ten open-ended questions, eighty-five six-point Likert items, and demographic information. The questionnaire was first established in Chinese and then translated into English for the U.S. data collection. School administrators in seven daycare centers and preschools in Taipei, Taiwan; six in Hong Kong; and nine in Los Angeles, California, helped to first distribute informed consent letters, and then distribute questionnaires to children's parents and collect them once completed. The return rate in each school varied from 60% to 94%.[2] In this particular study, we examined parental beliefs on the child's acquisition of sense of shame and ability to tell right from wrong by analyzing two straightforward open-ended questions from the survey. The two questions examined here are the following: (1) At about what age do preschool-age children begin to have a sense of shame (*xiukuigan*)? If your child has begun to understand shame, please give an example of an occasion when he or she showed this understanding; and (2) At about what age do preschool-age children begin to be able to tell right from wrong (*bianbie shifeishane*)?[3] If your child has begun to be capable of telling right from wrong, please give an example of an occasion when he or she showed this understanding.

Since these questions belonged to a much larger survey, only those who provided answers (including "not yet" and "cannot remember") to both the knowing shame and knowing right from wrong questions were processed in this study. For easier management, the age questions and the occasion questions were analyzed separately. Answers to the age questions were analyzed with quantitative approaches, while the effective answers for each occasion question in each research site were analyzed with qualitative approaches. Codes (or subcategories) were derived in an iterative grouping and regrouping of the emerging similar wording, characteristics, or themes in the caregivers' answers in their original languages. Subcategories that were similar in nature were then grouped into larger categories. In order to enhance reliability of the coding system, two coders each independently coded the same randomly selected Taiwan, Hong Kong, and U.S. data. In each case, one of the two coders was a native of the research site. For the question regarding the child's knowledge of shame, the intercoder reliability check was performed on 36.4% of the Taiwan data, 47.9% of the Hong Kong data, and 46.0% of the U.S. data, with kappa coefficients of 0.95, 0.92, and 0.82, respectively. For the question on knowing right from wrong, the intercoder reliability check was performed on 37.5% of the Taiwan data, 47.9% of the Hong Kong data, and 49.7% of the U.S. data, with kappa coefficients of 0.91, 0.78, and 0.81, respectively.[4]

Subjects

There were 1,249 Taiwanese parents, 710 Hong Kongese parents, and 162 American parents who participated in this study. The mean ages in months of their children (and standard deviation) at the time were 57.4 ($SD = 11.6$), 50.7 ($SD = 12.0$), and 50.7 ($SD = 10.2$), respectively. Taiwanese children were significantly older than their Hong Kong and U.S. counterparts ($F(2, 2061) = 82.66$, $p < 0.001$; also supported by a post-hoc Tukey HSD test). These children were equally distributed in terms of gender: 53.7% boys and 45.3% girls in the Taipei sample (1.0% unknown), 49.7% boys and 49.2% girls in the Hong Kong sample (1.1% unknown), and 56.2% boys and 43.8% girls in the Los Angeles sample. Questionnaires were completed mostly by mothers (i.e., 67.1% in Taiwan, 63.4% in Hong Kong, and 86% in the United States), followed in frequency by both parents (i.e., 16.5% in Taiwan, 17.7% in Hong Kong, and 9.1% in the United States), and then fathers (i.e., 15.6% in Taiwan, 16.6% in Hong Kong, and 4.9% in the United States).[5] The mean age of parents at each research site was similar: Most mothers were in their mid-thirties: 35.1 in Taiwan, 33.3 in Hong Kong, and 34.6 in the United States; while the fathers were in their late thirties: 38.0 in Taiwan, 36.9 in Hong Kong, and 37.5 in the United States). The majority of the parents had received an education of at least twelve years—96.9% of fathers and 97.5% of mothers in Taiwan, 66.1% of fathers and 68.5% of mothers in Hong Kong, and 96.7% of fathers and 100% of mothers in the United States. The racial makeup of the subsamples was predominantly Chinese for the Hong Kong and Taiwan samples and Euro-American for the U.S. sample.[6] Finally, after conversion to U.S. dollars, average household annual income was reported at $31,530, $35,290, and $61,400 for Taiwan, Hong Kong, and the United States, respectively. Given the difference in cost of living from site to site, these annual family incomes are roughly comparable and correspond to middle and upper-middle class levels.

Results

Acquisition Age and Developmental Sequence

One of the central questions here focuses on the age at which parents report their children to demonstrate knowledge of shame and being able to tell right from wrong and how the ages for these two types of knowledge are related to each other. In the analyses related to age acquisition, answers of "not yet" and "cannot remember" were treated as missing values. For the age of acquiring knowledge of shame, the effective answering rates were 94.8%, 93.1%, and 89.5% for Taiwan, Hong Kong, and the United States, respectively. Further, the average reported ages of acquisition (in months) were 35.83 ($SD = 10.22$), 31.27 ($SD = 9.89$), and 36.43 ($SD = 11.67$) in Taiwan, Hong Kong, and the United States, respectively. For the knowing right from wrong question, the effective answering rates were 94.6% for Taiwan, 91.6% for Hong Kong, and 96.9% for the United States. And, the average reported ages of acquisition (in months) were 39.02 ($SD = 10.48$), 34.44 ($SD = 10.56$), and 32.29 ($SD = 10.26$) in Taiwan, Hong Kong, and the United States, respectively.[7]

An issue arose regarding how the child's present age might influence parents' reports of the age at which the child acquired a sense of shame or ability to tell right from wrong. To address this concern, correlation analyses were performed among these variables. Significant positive relationships were found for each subsample between the child's age and the reported age at which the child began to know shame: r's = 0.30, 0.40, and 0.35 for the Taiwan, Hong Kong, and U.S. groups, respectively (all at $p < 0.01$). A similar pattern was found for the relation between the child's age and the parents' report of the age at which the child knew right from wrong: r's = 0.35, 0.44, and 0.25 for the Taiwan, Hong Kong, and U.S. groups, respectively (all at $p < 0.01$). These findings indicate that attention should be paid to the child's age in any such analysis. However, as will be described, such a bias is eliminated in our analysis here related to developmental sequence by the creation of difference scores that remove these age effects.

The developmental sequence of the age of knowing shame in comparison to knowing right from wrong was examined by subtracting the reported age at which the children know shame from the age at which they can tell right from wrong within each research site.[8] Three groups were then created based on the parents' beliefs. Parents reporting the belief that knowing right from wrong occurs earlier than knowing shame were coded < 0. If the reverse were true, they were coded as > 0. And parents reporting the same age for knowing shame and right from wrong were coded as = 0.

As shown in Figure 5.1, the U.S. developmental pattern is distinctive from both of the Chinese groups. Nearly half (45.9%) of the U.S. parents believed that telling right from wrong came earlier than knowing shame, while almost all of the Chinese parents believed that knowing shame came either earlier than (Taiwan = 41.9% and Hong Kong = 42.3%) or concurrently with the ability to tell right from wrong (Taiwan = 42.2% and Hong Kong = 42.8%). Significant group effects were confirmed by a two-tailed chi-square analysis $[\chi^2 (4, N = 1988) = 86.96, p < 0.001]$. Additional pairwise comparisons re-

Figure 5.1
Developmental Sequence (Age of Knowing Right and Wrong–Age of Knowing Shame)

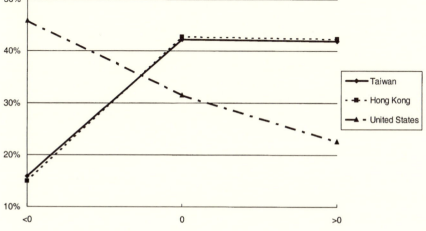

vealed significant group effects between the United States and Hong Kong for the code < 0 ($z = 4.41$, $p < 0.001$) and the code > 0 ($z = 2.18$, $p < 0.05$), and between the United States and Taiwan for both the code < 0 ($z = 4.94$, $p < 0.001$) and the code > 0 ($z = 2.19$, $p < 0.05$). Finally, as described, these developmental sequence findings were consistent regardless of the child's current age in each subsample.[9]

Occasions When Children Begin to Understand Shame and Right from Wrong

Response Rates and Effective or Ineffective Answers

Turning to the qualitative data, compared to the questions about specific age, fewer parents provided answers to both open-ended occasion questions: 997 (79.8%) Taiwan, 511 (72%) Hong Kong, and 111 (68.5%) U.S. parents. However, the characteristics of these children and their families were similar to those of the larger sample.[10] The responses "not yet" and "cannot remember" to these questions were treated as missing values and excluded from further analysis. For the knowing shame question, the effective response rates for each site were 93.3% in Taiwan, 91.6% in Hong Kong, and 81.1% in the United States. For the knowing right from wrong question, the effective response rates were 91.6% in Taiwan, 88.7% in Hong Kong, and 94.6% in the United States.

The U.S. parents seemed to have relatively more difficulty answering the question regarding knowing shame than their Chinese counterparts and indicated stronger opinions about the question. For example, as one U.S. parent said,

"Shame" we see as a deeply negative emotion related to *loss of self-esteem* [emphasis added]. Thus, it's stronger (and less useful and more damaging) than "guilt" as in a guilty conscience from knowing one has done something wrong once a conscience (or internalized values of right and wrong) has begun to develop. A discipline system that frequently conveys a sense of low worth can cause a child to sense shame very early, without accompanying comprehension—this can constitute abusive child-rearing, and is not necessary to successful teaching of norms of conduct and appropriate discipline. (3180US)

Among the Taiwan parents who objected to the question, there tended to be a feeling that "shame" was too heavy and serious a word for young children at this age. For example, "In principle, I hope my child understands right and wrong of things, rather than worries about losing face or not" (1853TW).

Examples of Occasion When the Child Began to Understand Shame

Of all effective answers, the first noticeable phenomenon was that explicit shame labels were often applied.[11] Such labels occurred in 43.8% of all the occasions reported by Taiwan parents, 27.2% of those from Hong Kong, and 34.8% of those from the United States. A breakdown of the occurrence rates of these explicit labels for shame (including embarrassment, shyness, face, and related mixed emotions) is presented in Table 5.1. Although simple word counts at the lexical level do not reflect much of the complexity of cultural meanings, it remains intriguing to note that that there were a far greater variety of shame labels expressed in Chinese than in English.

In addition, *zizunxin* (literally self-respect heart, which is the closest translation for self-esteem in Chinese) was spontaneously brought up by eight Taiwanese parents and one Hong Kongese parent in their reported occasions. Other than in the earlier noted American quote expressing the loss of self-esteem as her reason for opposing shame, no other American parent made mention of self-esteem. However, the connotation of self-esteem in the Chinese parents' words is likely somewhat different from the American parents'. Although the Chinese parents mentioned a possible threat to self-esteem and the child's defensive reaction of turning to shame-anger, they did not seem to worry much about a crisis of losing self-esteem due to shame. Further, they did not consequently reject the idea of knowing shame. Instead, the acquisition of shame (*xiuchixin* or *xiuchigan*) and positive self-esteem seemed to coexist without much contradiction, perhaps because they both point to respect for rules and sensitivity to evaluations and criticisms, as shown in the following examples:

Since my child started preschool, whenever he does something wrong or doesn't behave at home, I would pretend as if I am going to report to his teachers and fellow students. Due to his *zizunxin* and *xiuchigan* [emphasis added], he would cry and say no. (2100TW)

When he was 1½ years old, one day when we had dinner with several family friends, he ate a lot and very fast. I inadvertently said to him, "You are eating too much, swallowing like a wolf and tiger." He immediately turned red and cried aloud. I suddenly realized that he had already acquired *zizunxin* and *xiuchixin* [emphasis added]. (0220HK)

As stated earlier, codes or subcategories were derived through iterative grouping and regrouping of similar themes arising from caregivers' answers to the open-ended occasion questions within each group. For the open-ended question regarding occasions of knowing shame, the subcategories fell into four major categories, the general pattern of which is shown in Figure 5.2. Significant group effects were found by a two-tailed chi-square analysis [$\chi^2(8, N = 1,582) = 63.69, p < 0.001$]. Pairwise post-hoc tests further confirmed that, for the category of "transgression," there was a significant group effect between the United States and Taiwan ($z = 4.33, p < 0.001$), between the United States and Hong Kong ($z = 6.63, p < 0.001$), and between Taiwan and Hong Kong ($z = 3.72, p < 0.001$). For the category of "shyness," significant group differences were found between Hong Kong and the United States ($z = 18.78, p < 0.001$), between Hong Kong and Taiwan ($z = 9.88, p < 0.001$), and between Taiwan and the

Table 5.1
Explicit Shame Labels Applied to the Focal Child

	Taiwan	Hong Kong	United States
Shame/Shameful	*Xiuxiulian*	*Xiuxiu*	Shame
	Xiuxiu	*Haoxiu*	Shameful
	Xiuchigan	Shame	Humiliated
	Haoxiu	*Mengxiu*	
	Xiuchi		
	Xiuhonglelian		
	7.9%	3.1%	21.9%
Ashamed	*Xiukuei*	*Xiukuei*	Ashamed
	Xiukueigan	*Xiukueigan Xiukueixin*	
	Xiukueixin	*Yixiaozhekuei*	
	Cankuei		
	Kueijiu		
	Youkueiyuxin		
	34.1%	76.7%	46.9%
Embarrassed/Shy	*Buhaoyisi*	*Buhaoyisi*	Embarrassed
	Haixiu	*Haixiu*	Embarrassment
	Haixiugan	*Paxiu*	Shy
	Xiuse	Shy	
	Xiusegan	*Xiuse*	
	Nanweiqing	*Hanxiudada*	
	52.1%	13.9%	31.2%
Shame-face	*Diulian*	*Wudizirong*	
	Meimianzi		
	Diudiulian		
	Wudizirong		
	3.8%	0.8%	--
Shame-anger	*Naoxiuchengnu*	*Naoxiuchengnu*	
	Naoxiuchengkuei		
	Xiufen		
	2.0%	0.8%	--
Shame-ugly		*Chou*	
		Chouchou	
		Chouguai	
		Chouxiu	
		Yixiaozhechou	
	--	4.7%	--
Total	100%	100%	100%

Note: Labels for shame in each category are listed in the order of their occurring rates. Although Taiwan and Hong Kong parents spoke different dialects, they shared the same writing system and the romanization presented here is in Mandarin.

Figure 5.2
Occasion When C Began to Understand Shame

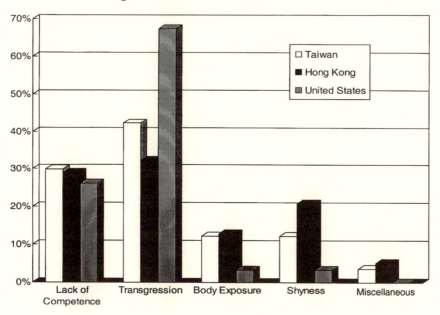

United States ($z = 2.57$, $p < 0.05$). Finally, for the category of "body exposure," group effects were found between Hong Kong and the United States ($z = 2.64$, $p < 0.01$), and between Taiwan and the United States ($z = 2.57$, $p < 0.05$).

The list and distributions of these categories and their subcategories are presented in Table 5.2. These data-driven categories and subcategories are defined as follows:

1. *Lack of competence.* Instances in this category belong to the competence domain, in which the child's behavior failed to match up with his or her age, gender, or standards set by himself, herself, or others. The specific subcategories include the following: (a) Age-inappropriate behaviors, which include accidents in toilet training (i.e., wetting or soiling pants), sucking the fingers, pacifier, or blanket, and drinking from a bottle. As reported by one U.S. parent, "While sucking her binky in a public place—someone remarked that she no longer needed such a thing. She quickly hung her head" (3163US); (b) gender-inappropriate behaviors, in which gender was an issue explicitly raised, for example, a girl behaved like a rough boy or failed to sit properly, or a boy was teased for going into the wrong restroom with his mom; (c) weakness or special needs in body or character, such as having oversensitive skin or specially thin hair; (d) failure to recognize own parents or relatives, for instance, mistakenly identifying or calling one person for another; and (e) failure to achieve a goal or losing when competing or being compared with other children, such as losing in a game, and failing to tie shoelaces indepen-

Table 5.2
Examples of Occasions When a Child Began to Understand Shame

	Occasion	Taiwan	Hong Kong	U.S.A.
Lack of competence	•age-inappropriate behavior	23.9%	20.1%	26.1%
	•gender-inappropriate behavior	0.2%	0.4%	--
	•weakness in body or character	0.6%	0.2%	--
	•failure to recognize own parents or relatives	0.3%	1.3%	--
	•failure to achieve a goal or loss in competition or social comparison	4.9%	6.9%	--
		29.9%	28.9%	26.1%
Rule violation or transgression	•as soon as transgressing rules	16.3%	12.1%	43.5%
	•being punished/publicly reprimanded	18.5%	15.5%	15.2%
	•when invoking C's past misdeed	4.7%	1.9%	2.2%
	•when making parents upset or hurt	0.6%	1.7%	5.4%
	•being punished by teacher in school	1.4%	0.8%	--
	•shame brought by other's transgression	0.3%	0.2%	--
	•when being disliked by others	0.4%	--	1.1%
		42.2%	32.2%	67.4%
Body exposure	•exposing own body	11.1%	12.3%	3.3%
	•being exposed to other people's intimate behavior	1.1%	0.4%	--
		12.2%	12.8%	3.3%
Shyness	•when performing in public	1.5%	0.6%	1.1%
	•meeting strangers	4.6%	12.3%	--
	•being praised	1.8%	2.9%	--
	•being the center of attention	3.4%	5.0%	2.2%
	•wearing inappropriate clothes	0.9%	--	--
		12.2%	20.9%	3.3%
Miscellaneous		3.6%	5.2%	--
Total		100.0%	100.0%	100.0%

dently or answer a teacher's question in class. One Hong Kong parent wrote, "When she was four, all her fellow students left school except her, because she hadn't finished her schoolwork yet. After finally finishing it, she felt very ashamed and started to cry" (0375HK).

2. *Rule violations or transgressions.* Subcategories in this category differ from one another as to when and how the child's shameful expressions occurred in relation to his or her transgression. They include the following: (a) As soon as the child transgressed, in which the child's expression of shame occurred before being corrected or reprimanded by an adult (or at least, with no description of any adult's intervention after the child's transgression). Over 40% of U.S. answers belonged to this subcategory, for instance, "My child felt ashamed when he broke a statue of mine. He had been told not to throw his ball in the house and he did it anyway, hitting the statue and breaking it. He said he wouldn't do it again" (4210US); (b) When the child was punished or publicly reprimanded. Punishment or reprimand was overtly and explicitly depicted here, as described vividly by a Taiwan parent: "One day, after my daughter wet her clothes in school, the teacher mistakenly changed her with another kid's clothes. I found that out when I later picked her up and asked her to change back. She was very reluctant, because she loved that dress. While that child and her mom were waiting aside, I forced her to take it off, which made her cry badly. I acted as if I were mad, walking home quickly and leaving her behind. She chased after me. I turned back and asked if she had done anything wrong. She finally apologized" (1444TW); (c) When the parents invoked or related the child's past misdeed or bad habit to others; (d) When the child physically hurt or emotionally upset or disappointed the parent; (e) After the child was punished or corrected by teachers in school; (f) When the child felt ashamed by his or her parent's or sibling's transgression: In other words, the child's shame was brought on by other family members, as in the following report: "My boy shed tears and didn't talk to his dad when his dad accidentally drove through a red light. He thought his dad did it intentionally" (2230TW); and (g) When the child was disliked or rejected by peers due to his or her wrongdoing.

3. *Body exposure.* Body exposure references can be divided into two subcategories: (a) exposing one's own body—when the child did not allow others to get close to him or her when he or she was undressed or in the bathroom; and (b) when being exposed to other people's intimate behavior or bare body in person or in the media (such as TV, movies, books, or magazines).

4. *Shyness.* Occasions here concern the child's experiences of being shy due to the following situations: (a) when the child was asked to perform or act in public, and when his or her private dancing or singing was being observed by others; (b) when meeting strangers, including a relative whom the child had not seen for a while, or a child's opposite-sex friend; (c) when being praised or receiving an award or gift from others; (d) when becoming the center of attention, in situations when people watched, laughed at, or paid particular attention to the child for his or her cute, funny, or mischievous behavior (though not perceived as a transgression), or simply for being the youngest in the group; and (e) when wearing inappropriate clothes, for instance, missing the required accessories (such as a name tag or a handkerchief) to go with the preschool's uniform, or wearing pajama-like pants, with or without other's comments and laughter.

Taken together, across all research sites, parents overwhelmingly located shame in the moral domain, with significant group differences not only between Americans and Chinese, but also between Taiwanese and Hong Kongese. The subcategory of "shame occurring as soon as the child transgressed without the parents' reprimand" was most frequently cited among American parents, whereas Chinese parents' reports in this category mostly fell into two subcategories: "as soon as transgressing" and "after being punished or reprimanded." "Occasions with regard to the competence domain" were the next most frequently reported category across all research sites with no significant group difference emerging; almost all instances belonged to the subcategory of "age-inappropriate behaviors," which ranks the highest across all subcategories for Chinese parents, and the second highest for American parents. Compared to their American counterparts, Chinese parents came up with a more varied range of answers in this category. Instances involving body exposure and being shy ranked the lowest, particularly among American parents. Significantly more Hong Kongese parents reported instances regarding shyness, most of which fell into the subcategory of "meeting strangers."

Examples of Occasions When the Child Began to Understand Right from Wrong

The overall pattern of responses to occasions when the child began to understand right from wrong are shown in Figure 5.3. Significant chi-square analysis results were found for the distribution of these responses across groups $[X^2(10, N = 1,560) = 170.01, p < 0.001]$. Post-hoc pairwise comparisons confirmed significant group differences for the category of "recognizing rules" between American and Taiwanese parents ($z = 22.24, p < 0.001$) and between American and Hong Kong parents ($z = 30.26, p < 0.001$). For the category of "correcting other," significant group effects were also revealed between Taiwan and the United States ($z = 9.09, p < 0.001$) and between Hong Kong and the United States ($z = 8.96, p < 0.001$). Finally, for the category of "confession," significant differences were found between American and Taiwanese parents ($z = 14.90, p < 0.001$), between American and Hong Kongese parents ($z = 3.07, p < 0.01$), and between Hong Kongese and Taiwanese parents ($z = 2.89, p < 0.01$).

All the categories and subcategories of responses to the right versus wrong occasion question are presented in Table 5.3. The following is a description of the five major categories and their subcategories derived from the parents' freely written answers:

1. *Autonomous self-discipline.* This category involves instances in which the child was able to take the initiative to observe rules, which can be decomposed into the following specific subcategories: (a) Self-initiating or invoking rules, which refer to instances when the child specifically and correctly spelled out rules by himself

Figure 5.3
Occasion When C Began to Understand Right from Wrong

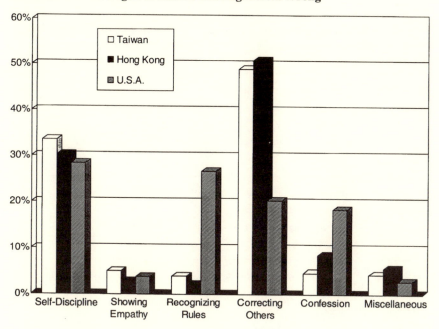

or herself, as shown in the following example: "When crossing the street at the traffic light, my child said to me, 'Daddy, don't cross the street when the little man (the figure on the traffic light) is red; cross it when the little man turns green'" (0187HK); (b) Refusing to transgress even when being tempted or under pressure; (c) Internalizing rules or showing self-discipline. What distinguishes this subcategory from "self-initiating" is that "self-initiating" emphasizes what the child has said, and "internalizing" focuses on the child's spontaneous behavior. For example, "After buying her favorite food in the supermarket, she could bear waiting to open it until after paying the bill and arriving home" (1330TW).

2. *Showing empathy.* This category involves occasions when the child demonstrated a sense of justice or the ability to be altruistic: (a) Showing sympathy to people or animals or protecting and taking care of family members;[12] (b) Being considerate. This subcategory refers to occasions when the child showed consideration and understanding, and was willing to please others.[13]

3. *Recognizing rules, although not necessarily following them.* According to the parents' descriptions, this category involves three subtly different subcategories: (a) Transgressing while knowing the rule. This refers to instances in which, according to the parent, the child knowingly violated the rule, mainly due to a lack of self-control; (b) Recognizing transgression without reparation. Parents believed that the child understood rules, because after transgressing, although the child did not confess, she ran away to hide or pretended that nothing had happened. For

Table 5.3
Examples of Occasions When a Child Began to Understand Right from Wrong

	Occasion	Taiwan	Hong Kong	U.S.
Autonomous self-discipline	•self initiating or invoking rules	10.5%	7.9%	5.5%
	•refusing to transgress even when being tempted	0.9%	0.9%	--
	•internalizing rules or showing self-discipline	22.1%	21.5%	22.9%
		33.5%	30.3%	28.4%
Showing empathy	•showing empathy to people or pet or protecting family members	3.6%	2.8%	3.7%
	•being considerate	1.3%	--	--
		4.9%	2.8%	3.7%
Recognizing rules (although not necessarily having self-control)	•transgressing while knowing the rule	0.7%	0.4%	8.3%
	•recognizing transgression with no reparation	1.5%	1.5%	14.7%
	•checking adult's reaction before or during transgression	1.6%	0.2%	3.7%
		3.8%	2.1%	26.6%
Correcting others	•pointing out other child's misdeed	14.3%	17.2%	13.8%
	•pointing out adult's wrongdoing	11.1%	10.7%	4.6%
	•identifying moral or distinguishing good and bad characters in story	22.1%	21.5%	1.8%
	•learning from observing others being reprimanded	1.5%	1.5%	--
		49.0%	50.9%	20.2%
Confession	•accepting punishment after violating rules	1.0%	2.8%	0.9%
	•confessing and apologizing after transgression	3.6%	5.6%	17.4%
		4.6%	8.4%	18.3%
Miscellaneous		4.2%	5.6%	2.8%
Total		100.0%	100.0%	100.0%

example, "He took some candy from his grandma and hid in his closet and ate it. When I found him and asked him what was happening. He told me he took the candy and was hiding because he was being bad and didn't want anybody to know" (4032US); (c) Checking the adult's reaction before or while transgressing the rule. In this case, the child would check, test, or watch the parents' reaction or seek their approval.[14]

4. *Correcting or identifying others' wrongdoings.* (a) Pointing out other children's misdeeds. Instances include when the child pointed out, corrected, or reported to an adult about other children's wrongdoings, which the child witnessed or experienced as a victim. For instance, "When my daughter saw a child throwing a tantrum on the street, she said, 'Mommy, he's not a good child'" (0403HK); (b) Pointing out the adult's wrongdoing. Similar to the former subcategory, but the target here is someone in an older generation rather than the child's peer; (c) Identifying the moral or distinguishing between the good and the bad characters in stories, films, cartoons, soap operas, or news reports. Here is one Taiwan parent's report: "Once we watched a cartoon on TV, which was about a boy who played with a ball while walking on the street, and it almost caused a car accident. I therefore conveniently gave her an 'opportunity education' (*jihuijiaoyu*) and asked her, 'Is it alright to cross the street as that boy did on TV? Can we do that?' She immediately answered, 'Mama, it's not alright, because it's very dangerous and would make his daddy upset'" (1158TW); (d) Learning from observing others (e.g., a sibling or peer), being punished or reprimanded. Instances here refer to the child's ability to draw lessons from witnessing how siblings or fellow students are being taught, punished, or reprimanded by an adult.

5. *Confession.* (a) Accepting punishment after violating rules. Instances reported here refer to situations in which the child was able to accept punishment as the consequence of his or her transgression; (b) Confessing and apologizing after a transgression. Examples include the child admitting his or her own mistake, saying sorry, or asking for forgiveness, with or without punishment, as shown in the following: "During a mommy-n-me class, she bit another child. I immediately removed her from the area and gave her a time-out. We made a fuss over the other child and later I told her she was not allowed to hurt other children. She commented that the bite was 'bad' and that she was sorry" (3114US).

In sum, about one-third of parents reported instances regarding the child's ability to autonomously display self-discipline. This category ranked the highest for American parents and the second highest for Taiwanese and Hong Kongese parents, with no group effect. Moreover, the subcategory, "internalizing rules," ranked the highest across all subcategories in all groups. Half of the occasions reported by both Taiwanese and Hong Kongese parents fell into the category of "correcting others"—it not only was the most highly ranked, but also contained the top three subcategories. It is particularly common for Chinese parents to report instances regarding "identifying the moral in stories." Significant group difference was also found in the category of "recognizing rules," which ranked the second highest for American parents but was the least frequent among Chinese parents. Moreover, compared to Chinese parents (Taiwanese in particular), a significantly greater proportion of American parents' answers fell into the category of "confession," particularly the subcategory, "confessing and apologizing after transgression." Group difference also exited between Hong Kongese and Taiwanese for this category. Finally, "showing empathy" was the least frequently reported category for Americans and the second least for Chinese parents, with no group difference.

CONCLUSIONS

Based on two sets of open-ended questions concerning when a child had acquired a sense of shame and some knowledge of right and wrong, remarkable similarities as well as significant differences, particularly between Chinese (Hong Kong and Taiwan) and American parents, were found. As expected, all parents believed that their youngsters had begun to demonstrate a sense of shame and some knowledge of right and wrong by preschool age. Despite the fact that American parents seem to have relatively more difficulty answering questions regarding shame, they are more likely to associate shame with transgressions of sociomoral rules than their Chinese counterparts. In other words, all parents unanimously locate shame in the moral domain, followed by the lack of competence domain. In terms of developmental sequence, Chinese parents believe that knowing shame precedes knowing right and wrong, while American parents believe the reverse. Recognized autonomous self-discipline appears equally salient to parents in all surveyed groups indicating unanimous demands and expectations for committed compliance in the child. This expectation for committed compliance is strongest for Chinese parents. While half of the Taiwanese and Hong Kongese parents reported instances regarding the child's ability to point out and correct others' wrongdoings and learning from others' experiences, only about 20% of the American parents did so. In contrast, nearly half of the American parents related occasions when their child was able to confess and apologize, and display some recognition of the rules even if a transgression had occurred, while only about 10% of the Chinese parents reported similar events. Taken together, these parental reports not only reveal their beliefs about development of their children, but also, to some extent, reflect their child-rearing attitudes and strategies.

In the other open-ended question in the survey we asked parents to offer the most effective way of teaching right and wrong to their children, "opportunity education" and its related notions came up as a popular category among Chinese, particularly in Taiwan (Fung, Leung, & Yeh, 1998). While 53.5% (ranked the highest) of Taiwanese and 37.0% (ranked the second highest, after "verbally explaining and reasoning") of Hong Kongese parents endorsed opportunity education, only 11.6% of U.S. parents did so. Specific methods included exposing the child to real-life examples, teaching through morals in stories shown on TV programs, cartoons, or in books and magazines, and promptly pointing out and correcting the child's misdeeds. In contrast, for American parents, the most frequently endorsed teaching method was "modeling and setting example by parent" (39.4%), while only a small proportion of Taiwanese and Hong Kongese parents offered such an answer (7.9% and 9.5%, respectively).

Another noticeable point was raised by some Taiwanese parents. While *shifeishane* is how we phrased the question regarding right and wrong, 2.1% of Taiwanese parents, but no Hong Kongese parents, spontaneously made a clear distinction between *shifei* and *shane* in their reports. According to these Taiwanese parents, the acquisition of the knowledge of *shifei* came earlier than that of *shane*. This is because the former involves relatively absolute standards and values (such as traffic laws), whereas the latter may go beyond the absolute (for instance, although carrying guns is bad, police carrying guns is good), and may involve the weak and dark side of human nature (for instance, although most policemen are good, some can be bad). Since *shane* is highly context-dependent and has to be individually judged, it takes much longer to learn (even an entire lifetime, as indicated by one parent, 1882TW). The distinction between *shifei* and *shane* might also help explain why Chinese parents endorsed opportunity education, because each opportunity offers a unique context for a set of rules in concrete terms.

In contrast, instead of pointing out and correcting the child's misdeeds, and taking every opportunity to educate the child, U.S. parents seem to be much more relaxed and willing to grant the child the ability to tell right from wrong as soon as the child recognizes his or her transgression or says sorry, even if the child may not yet be able to control his or her impulses. To some extent, this tendency may be consistent with an emphasis on protecting and enhancing the child's self-esteem, what Harwood, Miller, and Irizarry (1995) term *self-maximization*, common among Euro-American child-rearing beliefs and practices. Interestingly, several Chinese parents also spontaneously brought it up, though with somewhat different connotations than in English. To them, provoking shame does not seem to be a serious threat to positive self-esteem, and having too high self-esteem can be equally damaging as having too much shame. Hence, having a reasonable amount of both shame (*xiuchixin*) and self-esteem (*zizunxin*) seems to be a healthy balance between sensitivities to others and concerns for the self (see also Fung & Chen, 2001). The issue regarding the relationship between shame and self-esteem well reflects parental ethnotheories about the child's psychological well-being, which is inevitably culturally embedded, and shaped by moral visions of the good or ideal person (Christopher, 1999).

If American parents do not share such a cultural belief about the possible role of shame in moral socialization, why do nearly 70% of them associate shame with transgression of sociomoral rules? One possibility is that it has to do with the child's age. At such a young age, instances regarding the competence domain as reported by American parents are all related to age-inappropriate conduct. Future research might explore whether there is a developmental increase in occasions of incompetence and a decrease in morality when academic achievements become more important in the children's later lives. Moreover, the question may be raised as to whether the American parents in our study collectively confused shame with guilt. In a cross-cultural survey in thirty-seven countries, Wallbott and Scherer (1995) concluded that "real-shame" is predominant in collectivistic, high-power-distance, and high-uncertainty-avoidance cultures, which usually are more closed, primitive, and norm guided. In contrast, "guilt-shame" (i.e., shame experiences with features very similar to those of guilt experiences) is predominant in individualistic, low-power-distance, and low-uncertainty-avoidance cultures, which usually are more open and modern, and less norm guided. Along these lines, we could have treated cultures as a polar dichotomy assuming that American parents report guilt-shame instead of real-shame, and collectively mistake shame for guilt.

For cross-cultural research such as this, it is important to bear in mind that no single component of any theory or concept can be simply transported from one culture to another without risk of misrepresentation and misunderstanding. Further, as is the nature of open-ended questions, it is also difficult to know how similarly or differently parents might have interpreted these questions within the group as well as across groups. We have indeed raised more questions than what could possibly be answered, which calls for more empirical work with different cultural and subcultural groups in the future. Nevertheless, without imposing any presupposing theories, questions of this sort did lead the parents in our study to offer an abundant variety of answers from their own perspective. They not only are ready to report shame as an indicator for their young child's moral knowledge, but may well use it as one effective means of teaching right from wrong, particularly Chinese parents. Indeed, due to the dual aspects of shame as both an affect and a moral value, a full definition of shame may well consist of elements of both real-shame and guilt-shame. The discretional, healthy, and adaptive form of shame should be acknowledged, as should its possible role in the process of moral socialization.

NOTES

1. This is different from a "shame culture." For criticisms of the dichotomy of guilt versus shame cultures, please see Chapter 8 in Schoenhals (1993) as well as other sources (e.g., Piers & Singer, 1953; Lebra, 1971, 1983; Creighton, 1990; Fung, 1994, 1999).

2. The disproportionate numbers of schools and children from the United States, relative to Hong Kong and Taiwan, stems from big differences in the typical number of children in U.S. preschool programs (roughly 50–100) as compared to hundreds or more than a thousand in Hong Kong and Taiwan.

3. Literally, *shifeishane* means "right-wrong-virtue-vice." However, *bianbie shifeishane* is usually the way Chinese say "telling right from wrong." Since the translation of this questionnaire into English and administration of the survey in the United States did not begin until the Taiwan and Hong Kong surveys were completed, "telling right from wrong" was the phrase adopted in English.

4. Due to the incompatible sample size, the U.S. data were used as a contrast, rather than a comparable, group.

5. The remaining 0.7% in Taiwan and 2.3% in Hong Kong were completed by others, usually an extended family member who shared childcare responsibility on a daily basis.

6. Approximately 85.5% of the U.S. parents originated from North America, 9.2% from an Asian society, and the remaining from Europe, South America, or India.

7. ANOVA's were conducted for both age variables by research site and parent sex. No significant main effect results emerged for parent sex indicating that the age variables reported were not influenced by the sex of the parent completing the questionnaire.

8. Please note that if the parent provided a specific age for one question but answered "not yet" for another, the response was included in this analysis.

9. While positive relations appeared to exist between the children's age and the age at which parents believed their children acquired the types of awareness under investigation here, no such relationship was found to influence the analyses of developmental sequence. Computation of difference score used in the analysis of developmental sequence for shame and right from wrong awareness proved to eliminate any influence of the response bias observed in parents' reports of the specific ages at which children know shame or can tell right from wrong.

10. The mean ages (in months) of their children at the time were 57.6 (ranging from 25.7 to 81.4, $SD = 11.3$), 53.0 (ranging from 24.2 to 76.8, $SD = 11.3$), and 49.3 (ranging from 26.4 to 77.0, $SD = 10.0$), respectively. Again, Taiwanese children were significantly older than their Hong Kongese and American counterparts, $F(2, 1564) = 45.02$, $p < 0.001$ (also supported by a post-hoc Tukey HSD test). These children were equally distributed in terms of gender—53.4% boys and 45.4% girls in the Taipei sample (1.8% missing), 48.3% boys and 49.9% girls in the Hong Kong sample (1.4% missing), and 54.1% boys and 45.9% girls in the Los Angeles sample. These occasion questions were mostly written by the mother (65.3% in Taiwan, 59.7% in Hong Kong, and 82.9% in the United States), followed by both parents, and then the father. The mean age of the parents in each research site was similar—most mothers were in their mid-thirties (35.2 in Taiwan, 33.5 in Hong Kong, and 33.9 in the United States) while most fathers in their late thirties (38.3 in Taiwan, 37.3 in both Hong Kong and the United States).

11. Please note that these labels all belong to the "shame" family (for example, "anger" alone was not included, but "shame-anger" was). Also, they were counted only when applied to the focal child's behaviors and reactions.

12. In this subcategory, a similar proportion of parents at each research site (40% for Taiwan and the United States and 44% for Hong Kong) reported instances related to family members (including younger siblings or a cousin or mother). Compared to their Chinese counterparts, there were more American parents who reported occasions that involved animals (none for Hong Kong, 26% for Taiwan, mainly referring to stray dogs, and 60% for American parents, all referring to family pets).

13. In Chinese, this is often described as "good at reading the other's mind" (*shantirenyi*) or "close to [the other's] heart" (*tiexin*).

14. In Chinese, this is often described as "looking at [the other's] face color" (*kanlianse, kanyanse*, or *chayanguanse*).

REFERENCES

Barrett, K. C. (1995). A functionalist approach to shame and guilt. In J. P. Tangney & K. W. Fischer (Eds.), *Self-conscious emotions: The psychology of shame, guilt, embarrassment, and pride* (pp. 25–63). New York: Guilford Press.

Barrett, K. C. (1998). A functionalist perspective to the development of emotions. In M. F. Mascolo & S. Griffin (Eds.), *What develops in emotional development?* (pp. 109–133). New York: Plenum Press.

Barrett, K. C., Zahn-Waxler, C., & Cole, P. M. (1993). Avoiders vs. amenders: Implications for the investigation of guilt and shame during toddlerhood. *Cognition and Emotion, 7*, 481–505.

Broucek, F. J. (1991). *Shame and the self.* New York: Guilford Press.

Chao, R. K. (1994). Beyond parental control and authoritarian parenting style: Understanding Chinese parenting through the cultural notion of training. *Child Development, 65*, 1111–1119.

Chao, R. K. (1995). Chinese and European American cultural models of self reflected in mothers' child-rearing beliefs. *Ethos, 23*, 328–354.

Chao, R. K. (1996). Chinese and European American mothers' beliefs about the role of parenting in children's school success. *Journal of Cross-Cultural Psychology, 27*, 403–423.

Christopher, J. C. (1999). Situating psychological well-being: Exploring the cultural roots of its theory and research. *Journal of Counseling and Development, 77*, 141–152.

Chu, C. L. (1972). On the same orientation of the Chinese from the interrelationship among society, individual, and culture. In Y. Y. Lee & K. S. Yang (Eds.), *Symposium on the character of the Chinese: An interdisciplinary approach* (pp. 85–125). Taipei, Taiwan: Insitute of Ethnology, Academia Sinica (in Chinese).

Cook, D. R. (1996). Empirical studies of shame and guilt: The internalized shame scale. In D. L. Nathanson (Ed.), *Knowing feeling: Affect, script, and psychotherapy* (pp. 132–165). New York: W. W. Norton.

Creighton, M. R. (1990). Revisiting shame and guilt cultures: A forty-year pilgrimage. *Ethos, 18*, 279–307.

Ferguson, T. J., & Stegge, H. (1995). Emotional states and traits in children: The case of guilt and shame. In J. P. Tangney & K. W. Fischer (Eds.), *Self-conscious emotions: The psychology of shame, guilt, embarrassment, and pride* (pp. 174–197). New York: Guilford Press.

Ferguson, T. J., Stegge, H., & Damhuis, I. (1991). Children's understanding of guilt and shame. *Child Development, 62*, 827–839.

Freud, S. (1923). The ego and the id. In J. Strachey (Ed. and Trans.), *The complete psychological works of Sigmund Freud* (vol. 19, pp. 3–66). London: Hogarth Press.

Fung, H. (1994). *The socialization of shame in young Chinese children.* Unpublished Ph.D. diss., University of Chicago, Illinois.

Fung, H. (1999). Becoming a moral child: The socialization of shame among young Chinese children. *Ethos, 27* (2), 180–209.

Fung, H., & Chen, E.C.H. (2001). Across time and beyond skin: Self and transgression in the everyday socialization of shame among Taiwanese preschool children. *Social Development, 10*, 419–436.

Fung, H., Leung, K. W., & Yeh, Y. H. (1998, July). *Growing up the Confucian way: Child-rearing beliefs and practices in Taiwan and Hong Kong.* Poster session presented at the fifteenth biennial meetings of the International Society for the Study of Behavioral Development, Bern, Switzerland.

Harwood, R. L., Miller, J. G., & Irizarry, N. L. (1995). *Culture and attachment: Perceptions of the child in context.* New York: Guilford Press.

Her, E.H.L. (1990). *A phenomenological explication of shame in a shame culture: A cross-cultural perspective.* Unpublished Ph.D. diss., Southern Illinois University, Carbondale.

Ho, D.Y.F. (1976). On the concept of face. *American Journal of Society, 81,* 867–884.

Ho, D.Y.F. (1986). Chinese patterns of socialization: A critical review. In M. H. Bond (Ed.), *The psychology of the Chinese people* (pp. 1–37). Hong Kong: Oxford University Press.

Hoffman, M. L. (1982). Affect and moral development. In D. Cicchetti & P. Hesse (Eds.), *Emotional development* (New Directions for Child Development No. 16, pp. 83–103). San Francisco: Jossey-Bass.

Hoffman, M. L. (1983). Affective and cognitive processes in moral internalization. In E. T. Higgins, D. Ruble, & W. Hartup (Eds.), *Social cognition and social development: A sociocultural perspective* (pp. 236–274). New York: Cambridge University Press.

Hoffman, M. L. (1984). Interaction of affect and cognition in empathy. In C. E. Izard, J. Kagan, & R. B. Zajonc (Eds.), *Emotions, cognition, and behavior* (pp. 103–131). Cambridge, UK: Cambridge University Press.

Hoffman, M. L. (2000). *Empathy and moral development: Implications for caring and justice.* New York: Cambridge University Press.

Hu, H. C. (1944). The Chinese concept of "face." *American Anthropologist, 46,* 45–64.

Hwang, K. K. (1987). Face and favor: The Chinese power game. *American Journal of Sociology, 92,* 944–974.

Hwang, K. K. (1997). *Guanxi* and *mientze*: Conflict resolution in Chinese society. *Intercultural Communication Studies, 7* (1), 17–42.

Kilborne, B. (1995). Truths that cannot go naked: Shame in many forms. *Psychiatry, 58,* 278–297.

King, A.Y.C., & Myers, J. T. (1977). *Shame as an incomplete conception of Chinese culture: A study of face* (Social Research Center Occasional Paper No. 63). Hong Kong: Chinese University of Hong Kong.

Kochanska, G. (1991). Socialization and temperament in the development of guilt and conscience. *Child Development, 62,* 1379–1392.

Kochanska, G., & Aksan, N. (1995). Mother–child mutually positive affect, the quality of child compliance to requests and prohibitions, and maternal control as correlates of early internalization. *Child Development, 66,* 236–254.

Kochanska, G., & Thompson, R. A. (1997). The emergence and development of conscience in toddlerhood and early childhood. In J. E. Grusec & L. Kuczynski (Eds.), *Parenting and children's internalization of values: A handbook of contemporary theory* (pp. 53–77). New York: John Wiley and Sons.

Kochanska, G., Tjebkes, T. L., & Forman, D. R. (1998). Children's emerging regulation of conduct: Restraint, compliance, and internalization from infancy to the second year. *Child Development, 69,* 1378–1389.

Kuczynski, L., & Grusec, J. E. (1997). Future directions for a theory of parental socialization. In J. E. Grusec & L. Kuczynski (Eds.), *Parenting and children's
internalization of values: A handbook of contemporary theory* (pp. 399–414).
New York: John Wiley and Sons.

Lebra, T. S. (1971). The social mechanism of guilt and shame. *Anthropological Quarterly, 44*, 241–255.

Lewis, M. (1992). *Shame: The exposed self*. New York: Free Press.

Lewis, M., Alessandri, S. M., & Sullivan, M. W. (1992). Differences in shame and
pride as a function of children's gender and task difficulty. *Child Development,
63*, 630–638.

Lewis, M., Sullivan, M. W., Stanger, C., & Weiss, M. (1989). Self-development and
self-conscious emotions. *Child Development, 60*, 146–156.

Lieber, E., Fung, H., Leung, P.W.L., & Leung, K. W. (1997, August). *Chinese child
rearing beliefs: The use of an indigenous perspective in scale development*.
Paper presented at the second conference of the Asian Association of Social
Psychology, Kyoto, Japan.

Lin, C. C., & Fu, V. R. (1990). A comparison of child-rearing practices among Chinese, immigrant Chinese, and Caucasian-American parents. *Child Development, 61*, 429–433.

Liu, J. H, & Liu, S. H. (1999, August). *The role of the social psychologist in the
benevolent authority and plurality of powers: Systems of historical affordance
for authority*. Paper presented at the third conference of the Asian Association
of Social Psychology, Taipei, Taiwan.

Lynd, H. (1958). *On shame and the search for identity*. New York: Harcourt, Brace.

Mascolo, M. F., Fischer, K. W., & Li, Jin. (in press). Dynamic development of component systems of emotions: Pride, shame, and guilt in China and the United
States. In R. Davidson, K. Schery, & H. Goldsmith (Eds.), *Handbook of affective science*. Oxford, UK: Oxford University Press.

Piers, G., & Singer, M. B. (1953). *Shame and guilt: A psychoanalytic and a cultural
study*. New York: W. W. Norton.

Russell, J., & Yik, M. (1996). Emotion among the Chinese. In M. H. Bond (Ed.), *The
handbook of Chinese psychology* (pp. 166–188). Hong Kong: Oxford University Press.

Sabini, J., & Silver, M. (1997). In defense of shame: Shame in the context of guilt and
embarrassment. *Journal for the Theory of Social Behaviour, 27*, 1–15.

Scheff, T. J. (1987). The shame-rage spiral: A case study of an interminable quarrel. In
H. B. Lewis (Ed.), *The role of shame in symptom formation* (pp. 109–149).
Hillsdale, NJ: Erlbaum.

Scheff, T. J. (1990). *Microsociology: Discourse, emotion, and social structure*. Chicago: University of Chicago Press.

Schneider, C. D. (1977). *Shame, exposure, and privacy*. New York: W. W. Norton.

Schneider, C. D. (1987). A mature sense of shame. In D. L. Nathanson (Ed.), *The
many faces of shame* (pp. 194–213). New York: Guilford Press.

Schoenhals, M. (1993). *The paradox of power in a People's Republic of China middle
school*. Armonk, NY: M. E. Sharpe.

Shaver, P. R., Wu, S., & Schwartz, J. C. (1992). Cross-cultural similarities and differ-
ences in emotion and its representation: A prototype approach. In M. S. Clark
(Ed.), *Review of personality and social psychology* (pp. 175–212). Newbury
Park, CA: Sage.

Stipek, D. J. (1983). A developmental analysis of pride and shame. *Human Development, 26,* 42–54.

Stipek, D. J., & DeCotis, K. M. (1988). Children's understanding of the implications of causal attributions for emotional experiences. *Child Development, 59,* 395–406.

Tangney, J. P. (1998). How does guilt differ from shame? In J. Bybee (Ed.), *Guilt and children* (pp. 1–17). San Diego, CA: Academic Press.

Tangney, J. P., Burggraf, S. A., & Wagner, P. E. (1995). Shame-proneness, guilt-proneness, and psychological symptoms. In J. P. Tangney & K. W. Fischer (Eds.), *Self-conscious emotions: The psychology of shame, guilt, embarrassment, and pride* (pp. 343–367). New York: Guilford Press.

Tangney, J. P., Wagner, P., Fletcher, C., & Gramzow, R. (1992). Shame into anger? The relation of shame and guilt to anger and self-reported aggression. *Journal of Personality and Social Psychology, 62,* 669–675.

Tangney, J. P., Wagner, P., & Gramzow, R. (1992). Proneness to shame, proneness to guilt, and psychopathology. *Journal of Abnormal Psychology, 101,* 469–478.

Twitchell, J. B. (1997). *For shame: The loss of common decency in American culture.* New York: St. Martin's Press.

Wallbott, H. G., & Scherer, K. R. (1995). Cultural determinants in experiencing shame and guilt. In J. P. Tangney & K. W. Fischer (Eds.), *Self-conscious emotions: The psychology of shame, guilt, embarrassment, and pride* (pp. 465–487). New York: Guilford Press.

Weiner, B. (1986). *An attributional theory of motivation and emotion.* New York: Springer-Verlag.

Wilson, R. W. (1970). *Learning to be Chinese.* Cambridge, MA: MIT Press.

Wilson, R. W. (1981). Moral behavior in Chinese society: A theoretical perspective. In R. W. Wilson et al. (Eds.), *Moral behavior in Chinese society* (pp. 117–136). New York: Praeger.

Zahn-Waxler, C., & Kochanska, G. (1990). The origins of guilt. In R. Thompson (Ed.), *Nebraska Symposium on Motivation,* vol. 36: *Socioemotional development* (pp. 183–258). Lincoln: University of Nebraska Press.

Zhai, X. W. (1995). *The Chinese concepts of face.* Taipei, Taiwan: Gui Guan (in Chinese).

Chapter 6

The Role of Social and Personal Factors in the Chinese View of Education

Wen-ying Lin

Education is commonly viewed as an aspect of culture and is a very difficult concept to define adequately. In a general sense, education designates "the broader process whereby we come to accept the goals and values of our society" (Hobson, 1987, p. 1). Views of education may encompass a range of beliefs from the process of education to its aims. As Goodnow and Collins (1990) observed, "The goals parents emphasize provide clues to the relative importance of various sources. Some goals, for instance, may reflect ongoing environmental factors, while others reflect traditions that no longer have a clear anchor in today's pressures" (p. 17). Educational aims are of particular interest in this study on views of education.

The roots of modern Chinese views of education have been attributed almost universally to traditional Chinese cultural influences. Chinese researchers, like their Western counterparts, expect culture to play a role in many contexts, despite the absence of either a theoretical basis or empirical support for this assumption (e.g., Lau & Yeung, 1997; Wu, 1997). Statements like "Chinese culture and tradition have always enshrined the entrance examination system" (Lau & Yeung, 1997, p. 36) demonstrate this tendency.

Researchers have paid too little attention to the literature examining cultures in real-world contexts. They answer empirical questions by simply adopting a Chinese ideology (such as Confucianism or Taoism) or cultural factors (such as collectivism or an emphasis on diligence) as their sole framework without enough relevant empirical evidence (e.g., Chen, Lee, & Stevenson,

1997; Chao & Sue, 1997; Hau & Salili, 1997). This practice is simplistic, if not wrong. Although a few studies (e.g., Wu, 1997) have made impressive efforts to document the causal role of culture, culture has remained a very general concept, and consequently not fully explanatory in understanding Chinese education. The obvious result of this bias is that conclusions about the influence of culture may not be generalizable. For instance, if Chinese parents' expectations of academic success are found to be critical, the prescriptive assumption of cultural influence may preclude consideration of other important alternative explanations such as psychological needs. Indeed, the assumption that modern Chinese society can be understood using Chinese culture or philosophy clearly demands clarification and empirical support (Lin & Wang, 1995).

Using corporal punishment as the core issue, Lin and Wang (1995) attempted to explore whether the traditional Chinese family precept of education has an important impact on contemporary views of education. They maintained that traditional views of education might still deeply influence the educational styles of parents and teachers in Taiwan today (such as in widespread acceptance of corporal punishment). However, they also remarked that the traditional idea of strict education has lost its social foundation grounded in the traditional concept of superiority and inferiority in terms of social status and seniority. Lin and Wang believed that this dislocation of traditional ideas might be the crux of Taiwan's current educational problems. Specifically, traditional ideas (e.g., absolute respect for the teacher and the teaching) have been confronted with social change (e.g., the trend toward democratic equality) and have consequently generated the characteristics of contemporary education as well as some of its problems. Lin and Wang's conclusion challenged a fundamental assumption concerning the role of culture in understanding contemporary educational phenomena.

At this point it is legitimate to hope for some clarification of the still-unspecified relationship between Chinese culture and modern Chinese educational phenomena. Unless some satisfactory answers are given, it will remain unclear why ancient tradition should be accepted as sufficient explanation for modern people's behavior. Before speculating on possible answers, I first examine the origin of Chinese educational thought.

THE HISTORY OF CHINESE
EDUCATIONAL THOUGHT

Almost all documents exploring ancient Chinese education indicate that education came into being in response to social needs, including the need to train productive talent, the need to maintain social life, and the need to inherit and pass on culture (Mao, Shao, & Chu, 1989; Hu, 1986). Understanding the implications of these needs for Chinese culture requires understanding of the unique Chinese social context. For instance, low-cost labor provided by a huge population and slaves taken in wars resulted in the absence of a motive to save labor (Huang, 1993). Because of the minimal progress made in production technology and long-time reliance on cheap labor and simple production skills, productive talent was naturally insignificant in educational thinking as a whole. This lack of emphasis on productive talent is a crucial point in Huang's argument against a cultural interpretation of Chinese educational thought, which roughly originated during the Spring and Autumn Period and the Warring States Epoch (Wang, 1990; Hu, 1986), a time of political and social chaos and collapse. To educational thinkers of that time such as Mencius, the chief way to save society was to rebuild traditional rites and advocate education. Changing society through education was the focus of their concern. Teachings and writings of educational thinkers stressed the art of governing to change human behavior in order to put down rebellions and restore order. Because their original goal in talking about education was to use it to reform politics and society, their chief interest remained politics and society, not the people being educated. A clear proof of education as the art of governing is provided in the fact that the Chinese legal concepts contained in famous writings (e.g., Yang, 1964; Chang, 1994) are virtually isomorphic to the ideas of famous educational thinkers (Wang & Lin, 1999). To be exact, however, both education and law are actually tools of politics.

In response to a chaotic social environment, Chinese educational thought was used to emphasize political and social control, as well as the inheritance and passing on of culture (Wang & Lin, 1998). Starting with Confucius, Chinese educational thinkers emphasized the education of human relationships and ethics based upon social roles to fulfill the mission of social and political control. They also developed a unique concept of the orthodoxy of precepts, making the inheritance and passing on of this orthodoxy the major task of education.

In such anarchic times, many powerful and ambitious figures contended for ascendancy. Members of the nobility, feudal princes, and even ministers and officials with ulterior motives were either seeking to protect themselves or to vanquish others in order to gain superiority. The greatest need they experienced was perhaps not to rebuild orthodox rites and music, but, conversely, to break through the norms of existing rites and music to win through unconventional means. More ideally, they sought to use the rites and music for their own ends, and not to be bound by them. Feudal princes and nobles were in more need than ever of large quantities of talent in rites, music, politics, and military to produce their own rites and music and carry on their own punitive expeditions. As a result, an increasing number of rites came into being, replacing older ones, and more and more scholars were needed who were well versed in these rites. The impact of this situation on education was most obvious: prosperity of the Confucian school. The traditional role of education in training productive talent was thus converted into training political and military talent and experts in financial matters. In modern parlance, the aim of education was to create the utilizable value of the individual, especially the value utilizable by officialdom and the rich. The Confucian educational tradition started by Confucius thenceforth became a tradition for scholars to attain riches and rank. This result is probably due to human nature; even Confucius could do nothing about it.

CHARACTERISTICS OF TRADITIONAL CHINESE EDUCATIONAL THOUGHT

This analysis pinpoints an important feature of the history of Chinese educational thought. Throughout the following two thousand or more years, Chinese educational thought changed in step with special social and political needs. In a time of pandemonium, two political and social needs were particularly urgent: first, the need to rebuild social and political order, and second, the need to train a large amount of political talent in view of the extraordinary times. Thus, in China education finally evolved to a state where ethical education based on the Three Bonds of Human Relationships and Five Cardinal Virtues became the core, and the training of bureaucratic talent appropriate to the feudal autocratic society its main goal.

These characteristics of the origin of Chinese educational thought are very different from those of most other cultures. The comparison of educational thought between East and West is particularly striking when one explores its period of inception in the West, in particular the philosophy behind the liberal education of ancient Greece. The educational tradition of ancient Greece with its democratic political system focused from the beginning on the recipient of education as the primary subject. To a large extent, the aim of education was to promote the humanism of students and to expand their learning and thinking abilities so that they attained a more complete subjective character—a clearer head, more mature personality, more stable moods—in society as a whole. That is to say, the recipients were expected to become more like citizens of a democratic society who controlled the direction of the society. "The daily lives of the Greeks were imbued with a sense of choice and an absence of social constraint that were unparalleled in the ancient world" (Nisbett, Peng, Choi, & Norenzayan, 2001, p. 292).

In contrast, pre-Ch'in education in China, at least in its initial aim, was strongly oriented toward society and politics. Since the greatest concern of educational thinkers at the time was to reform people to conform to customs, the type of education given to the people naturally depended on what kind of customs society needed, not on the subjective needs of individual development. According to the same reasoning, if education was meant to train talent, then the type of talent it should train also depended on social and political needs, not the potential of the recipient of the education. Today this is what is called *manpower planning*. Educational activity is planned for the specific purpose of building manpower, hence selective talent development is presupposed.

If the social-context based analysis in my historical review of Chinese education is acceptable, it leads to the question: Can the contemporary Taiwanese view on education be understood from the perspective of its unique social and political context? Educational views here refer to ultimate and abstract goals of education, such as self-realization or social order, in contrast to the specific and particular aims at hand, such as mastering English or mathematics (Park, 1997). If the goal of the ancients was to maintain the social order by keeping the upper classes superior and the lower ones inferior, in modern democratic societies where equality is taken for granted, the goal of education must necessarily be different. This chapter proposes that the core of Chinese thought (that education serves society, and humans are tools for satisfying social needs) remains true, but that the society it serves has changed—hence so has Chinese education. Cultural and philosophical aspects of Chinese ideology take a secondary position relative to the social forces of modern society.

EDUCATIONAL THOUGHT IN MODERN TAIWAN

Precisely speaking, the concept of social-tool orientation can be divided into two categories: (1) that which considers education a tool of social control (Social Norms Orientation), and (2) that which considers education a means to skills that create talent (Talent Orientation) and thus a tool for social development that allows the individuals themselves to earn fame and fortune (Wang & Lin, 1999). In modern Taiwan, society has begun to transform itself into a democratic mode, and economics stand at the forefront of people's motives to obtain fame and fortune. Also, it appears that people would rather be taught skills through which they can prosper than be taught to be submissive (cf. Stevenson & Haberman, 1998).

The first specific hypothesis derived from the historical analysis is that the main thrust of educational thought in modern Taiwan will be the Talent Orientation, with the Social Norm Orientation being of lesser importance. In other words, Taiwanese are not only imbued with a social-tool oriented educational view, but are also particularly inclined toward its Talent Orientation component. Moreover, if individual differences are evident in educational views, they will be explained by social background variables such as age or education, or personal variables such as psychological needs or life experience.

In general, the main purpose of this research is to provide the impetus for reconsidering social scientists' overall conceptualization of the relationship between Chinese education and Chinese culture.[1] It has a twofold focus: (1) to reexamine and question some commonly held beliefs about the effect of culture on Chinese education phenomena in general and educational views in particular, and (2) to stimulate new thinking on educational research by closely investigating whether there are factors or mechanisms that buffer the impact of culture. This chapter reports two studies conducted to meet these aims. The first study was designed to provide evidence for the link between ancient and contemporary Chinese educational views by addressing the inferential links that characterize social environments. On the basis of the historical review, Study 1 was designed to assess the relationship between characteristics of educational thought and its social environment. I used empirical methods to examine the two hypotheses derived from the historical review in order to clarify whether the Chinese view of education today is really a reflection of ancient Chinese thought. The second study was aimed at providing evidence for specific personal factors that may link an individual's educational thought to his or her social context. In Study 2, I predicted that the effect of personal developmental variables on educational views would be greater than that of culture.

STUDY 1

The primary purpose of Study 1 is to examine the impact of traditional concepts on modern educational views. It demonstrates the two inferential hypotheses previously described: (1) educational views of modern Taiwan are mainly characterized by the Talent Orientation, and (2) there is a relationship between educational views and individual backgrounds.

As Park (1997) noted, "All sorts of particular aims of specific educational activities are to be analyzed in terms of different ways instrumental to the ultimate aim of education; most people are not conscious of their own ultimate intention of educational activity" (p. 8). Assessing seemingly vague concepts such as people's general view of education is difficult. In order to elicit a true view on education, this study extended previous works on educational views, focusing on the relationship between ancient Chinese educational thought and contemporary educational views in Taiwanese society. The initial pool of data was derived from Lin's 1992 work. Lin identified twenty educational maxims as the most often purported reasons for a teacher's choice of educational methods. In a follow-up study, Lin and Wang (1995) used these twenty maxims to represent the working definitions of six educational (methods) views, and asked respondents to indicate their agreement with these constructs on a four-point scale. The maxims Lin and Wang used not only pertained to educational methods, but also to educational aims. For instance, the maxim "dutiful sons come from the end of a rod" not only proposes the educational method of "using the rod," but also the educational aim of "turning out dutiful sons." There is an obvious correlation between educational methods and educational aims. This correlation is why, although Lin and Wang (1995) used the maxims as definitions of educational methods, it is also appropriate to reorganize these same maxims as indicators of educational goals. For this study I reanalyzed Lin and Wang's (1995) data from the perspective of educational goals.

Method

Respondents

The sample consisted of 1,321 teachers and 2,188 parents, totaling 3,509 respondents recruited from nine junior high schools located in north, south, and central Taiwan. Their ages are listed in Table 6.1. Generally, teachers were slightly younger than parents. The former averaged thirty-five, the latter forty. Standard deviations were fourteen and thirteen, respectively.

Procedure

Three academic researchers selected the ten maxims that most obviously pertained to educational goals from the original twenty. For consistency with the previous historical analysis in this study, these maxims were further divided into two categories: six represented the (traditional) Social Norms Orientation, and four represented the Talent Orientation.

Traditional Social Norms Orientation:
1. Dutiful sons come from the end of a rod.
2. Being teacher for a day makes a man a father for life.
3. Parents can never be wrong.
4. Kill a chicken to warn the monkey.
5. Reward and punishment must be clear.
6. Children should be seen and not heard.

Table 6.1
Age Distribution of Participants (number and percentage)

Age	Parents	Teachers	Total
under 30	208 (9.5%)	421 (31.9%)	629 (17.9%)
31 – 45	1,403 (64.1%)	623 (47.2%)	2,026 (57.7%)
46 – 60	528 (24.1%)	244 (18.5%)	772 (22.0%)
over 61	49 (2.2%)	33 (2.5%)	82 (2.3%)
Total	2,188 (62.4%)	1,321 (37.6%)	3,509 (100%)

Talent Orientation:

1. Crude jade must be painstakingly worked to produce precious gems.
2. Only when a person goes through the most rigorous hardships can he become outstanding among men.
3. Strict teachers turn out outstanding students.
4. Steel comes from tempering.

Each respondent's view of education was indexed by his or her total score on these maxims. The extent of agreement respondents indicated with each maxim ranged from 1 (disagree very strongly), 2 (disagree), 3 (agree), to 4 (agree very strongly). The total score of each respondent on the six maxims in the Social Norms Orientation category was designated the respondent's Social Norms Orientation Index. Similarly, the total score of each respondent on the four maxims in the Talent Orientation category was designated that person's Talent Orientation Index. For example, a respondent who very strongly disagreed with all maxims received six points (one point for each maxim). Conversely, a respondent who very strongly agreed with each maxim would receive a score of twenty-four points (four for each maxim). A person scoring fifteen points neither agreed nor disagreed with the traditional concepts.

Since the number of maxims in the two categories differed, the ranges of the two indices were different and had to be standardized to facilitate direct comparison. Accordingly, the two indices were transformed to 100-point scales.

Results

Since the maxims in the Social Norms Orientation category reflect the ideology of traditional society (the unconditionally obedient dutiful son, or the teacher revered as a father), this category is regarded as an index of traditional concepts. The average score of all respondents on this index was only slightly higher than the noncommittal level (fifteen points), indicating that there is little support for cultural persistence in tradition of educational concepts (teachers averaged 15.7, whereas parents averaged 16.5). Results obtained from comparing the Social Norms Orientation to the Talent Orientation were clearer and more meaningful. Figure 6.1 shows the results after conversion to standardized scores. From Figure 6.1, it is evident that, among both parents and teachers, the Talent Orientation (79.5 and 76.7, respectively) is higher than the Social Norms Orientation (58.4 and 53.7). A 2 × 2 (parent/teacher status × views of education) ANOVA yielded a significant main effect of status ($F = 54.825$, $df = 1, 3178$, $p < 0.0001$). These results conform to the hypothesis previously specified that traditional concepts may still be influencing the modern generation through cultural infiltration. However, if there is a predominant and subordinate relationship between the two various orientations, the possibility that the Talent Orientation is predominant is far greater. In other words,

Figure 6.1
Distribution of Views of Education of Parents and Teachers

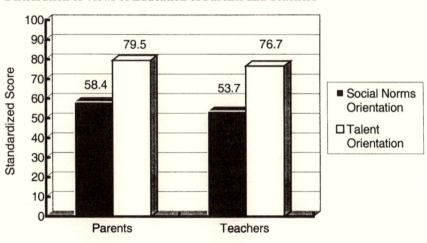

the educational views of modern Taiwanese are primarily characterized by the Talent Orientation rather than traditional concepts.

Although both parents and teachers have an inclination toward the Talent Orientation, parents' preference for the Talent Orientation was stronger than that of teachers. A significant status × views interaction ($F = 8.750$, $df = 1$, 3178, $p < 0.0001$) demonstrated the trend. This finding bears out the second hypothesis that educational views are associated with personal backgrounds. Teachers, due to their exposure to a variety of modern educational concepts in their work environments, do manifest different educational views from nonteachers. Related evidence includes the significant difference between teachers and parents in the Social Norms Orientation Index ($t = 8.64$, $df = 2815$, $p < 0.001$), as well as in the Talent Orientation Index ($t = 4.812$, $df = 3348$, $p < 0.001$). Although the difference may be trivial due to large sample size, this finding strengthens the indication that educational views may be predicted from respondents' experience with educational concerns.

Similarly, correlation analysis suggested that there was a positive relationship between age and views of education (for Social Norms Orientation, Pearson's $r = 0.098$, $p < 0.01$; for Talent Orientation, Pearson's $r = 0.124$, $p < 0.01$). This result also speaks to the prediction about individual life experience rather than cultural influence with respect to educational views.

STUDY 2

Study 1 illustrated the ascendancy of the Talent Orientation over the Social Norms Orientation in a basically liberal capitalistic society. It indicated that contemporary utilitarian educational views, which are obviously very different from Confucius's educational philosophy, might not be a legacy of traditional educational thought. That is to say, educational views of contemporary people may be more a function of social adaptation than of traditional culture. Study 1 also demonstrated that people's views of education might reflect the consequence of individual social adaptation such as their social roles or occupational experiences.

In Study 2, I further examined the relative impact of culture and social factors on Chinese educational views. In specific terms, if there is strong cultural influence on educational views, a common pattern in educational views should be observed in all walks of life. In contrast, if educational views are found to differ systematically across demographic variables such as age or education and individual developmental variables such as personal psychological needs, then social and personal factors can be said to have more influence than cultural factors.

Among these variables, personal psychological needs are viewed as primary regulators of educational views in contemporary society (Kneller, 1982) due to the nature of social adaptation. Hoffman (1988) reported an interesting cross-national study concerning parents' needs and child-rearing goals. Various needs such as economic help, primary ties and affection, expression of self, and adult status or social identity were assessed. His study suggested that the utilitarian value of children seems likely to meet parents' own needs. In a similar vein, LeVine (1974, 1988) gave detailed attention to parents' needs. Comparing aims across diverse cultures, LeVine suggested that parents set their aims in a hierarchical way. The hierarchy starts from physical health and survival, progressing through the acquisition of economic capacities (e.g. good job, self-supporting), and then moves up to the attainment of cultural values. LeVine's results are reminiscent of Maslow's (1970) hierarchical theory of psychological needs, and imply possible links between parents' psychological needs and the underlying goals of child-rearing. In other words, what parents want their children to become may reflect their own psychological needs.

Method

Prestudy

Tape-recorded interviews of twenty-three fathers and thirty-three mothers were conducted prior to designing the questionnaire. The interviews were conducted for several purposes: (1) to reestablish the focus of interest of the study, (2) to discover if there were any significant views of education that had not emerged in the first study, and (3) to provide a general framework for more specific structured questions in preparation for developing the questionnaire. The interviewers were intensively trained and instructed to ask open-ended questions about events, experiences, and feelings of personal life history that included educational, social, and occupational experiences. A description of the respondents in terms of age and education is presented in Table 6.2. Content analyses by three judges of the parents' transcript statements of their educational goals in the prestudy (98% interjudge consensus) resulted in the generation of three categories of aims: social norms orientation, individual instrumental orientation (utilitarian orientation), and self-cultivating orientation. The last category reflects a modern humanistic view of education (Bell & Schniedewind, 1989).

Respondents

The sample included 644 fathers and 613 mothers recruited from selected schools. The schools were sampled on the basis of school type and location area. One primary school, one junior high, one senior high, and one vocational school was selected from each of three regions, including Taipei (north-

Table 6.2
Cross-Tabulation of Respondents' Age and Education*

Education level	Age				Total
	Under 30	31-40	41-50	Over 51	
Formal Study (Questionnaire)					
Junior high and under	8	120	285	51	464
High school	10	95	230	30	365
College and beyond	36	55	206	26	323
Total	54	270	721	107	1152
Prestudy (Interview)					
High school and under		11	14		
College and beyond		19	12		
Total		30	26		56

*Missing data were excluded.

ern Taiwan), Kaohsiung (southern Taiwan), and Chia-yi (central Taiwan). One class was randomly selected from each grade level, except in the primary school, which was divided into three levels: low (grades 1–2), middle (grades 3–4), and high (grades 5–6). Altogether twelve schools and thirty-six classes participated. The respondents' ages and education levels are listed in Table 6.2. None had participated in Study 1. Generally, most respondents' ages were between 41–50, and the mean was 41.2 (valid N = 1240). About 70% of the respondents had not completed college. Younger parents (under 30) were mostly college graduates, in contrast, 30% of older parents (over 51) were only primary school graduates. Male and female participants were roughly equivalent in number. Because no gender effects were found in this study, gender is not included in the analyses reported.

Materials and Procedure

Respondents completed a questionnaire consisting of measures of educational aims and psychological needs. These measures were imbedded in a battery of other questions designed to inquire about life experience, life satisfaction, the realization of minimum required educational level as well as their expectations for their children's educational level.

Measure of Views on Education

Parents' views of education aims may seem infinite in their variety. They can, however, be conceptualized to a manageable number (Goodnow & Collins, 1990). Based on previous survey interviews and the research items from Lin, Wang, and Chen (1992) and Lin and Wang (1995), a set of three questions was designed to determine participants' views on education: (1) What is the purpose of schooling? (2) What do you want your children to be like? (3) What do you not want your children to be like? These three questions respectively addressed the parents' view of the purpose of the school, their goals for their children's development, and the unbearable outcome parents do not desire for their children. Based on the analysis of the prestudy interview, several statements were developed to represent each orientation category. Each statement tapped one simple, unitary belief in the aim of education. The following are the statements representing each orientation:

Social Norms Orientation

Purpose of Schooling

To develop the individual's talent in order to meet the needs of society

To improve the economic condition of the lower economic classes

To elevate the moral standards of the country

To accumulate and pass on the inheritance of society

To create and develop culture

Goal of Children's Development

To glorify the family

To be able to support his or her own parents

Unbearable Outcome of Children's Development

To disgrace the family's name

Not to have the ability to support his or her own parents

Individual–Instrumental Orientation (Utilitarian Orientation)

Purpose of Schooling

To gain a diploma in order to enhance one's life and status

To obtain the skills of a breadwinner

Goal of Children's Development

To have a stable and respectable occupation

To be popular and attractive among peers

To lead a safe and sound life

To be successful and prosperous

To have a happy family life

Unbearable Outcome of Children's Development

Not to have a respectable job

Not to have friends

To live a poor and insecure life

To lead a trivial bread-and-butter life

Not to have a happy family

Humanistic Orientation

Purpose of Schooling

To achieve self-actualization

To enrich one's spiritual life

Goal of Children's Development

To freely develop oneself

To be oneself

Unbearable Outcome of Children's Development

To live a catch-as-catch-can life

Not to have courage to pursue one's dream

Measure of Personal Psychological Needs

The theoretical grounding of the measure of personal psychological needs is Maslow's (1968, 1970) hierarchical psychological need theory. Previous works concerning sense of security, interpersonal relations, (Gorlow & Barocas, 1965), self-esteem (Crandall, 1973; Lorr & Wunderlich, 1986), sense of well-being, (Diener, 1984; Diener, Emmons, Larsen, & Griffin, 1985; Robinson, 1969), and life attitude (Constantinople, 1967; Levitin, 1968) were also examined. I chose life attitude as an index to assess psychological needs. Statements representing each stage were generated from related theory and measurements of value and life attitude (Braithwaite & Law, 1985; Brogden, 1952; Handy, 1970; Lynn, 1974; Rokeach, 1973; Schwartz & Bilsky, 1987). The index was thus developed from theoretical postulates rather than from empirical evidence concerning mutual exclusiveness of the alternatives. The Life Attitude Index was designed to assess preferences among various psychological needs: safety, love and belonging, esteem, and self-actualization. Items of the value valence assigned to the fulfillment of those psychological needs were also included. Changes in wording were made based on a pretest sample of thirty respondents varying in age and education. The stimulus materials were then sent to sixteen academic professionals to evaluate the correspondence of the statement to each of various psychological needs. The professionals independently judged that the scale was face valid. The concurrence rate among the sixteen professionals was high, ranging up to 95%. The statements on which the professionals disagreed were either eliminated or modified. A second pretest was administered to another thirty subjects for the final version. One week later, the same subjects were retested. The concordance rate for the final version was 94.8%.

Results

Relation of Views on Educational Aims to Personal Background

Table 6.3 demonstrates that parents' educational aims differed when they were considering the purpose of schooling versus children's individual development goals. They were, for instance, more likely to endorse socially oriented aims in response to the purpose of schooling ($\chi^2 = 35.665$, $df = 4$, $p < 0.0001$). In contrast, parents were more likely to endorse utilitarian and humanistic self-cultivating aims when considering their own children's development in optimal expectation ($\chi^2 = 20.168$, $df = 4$, $p < 0.0001$), as well as in unbearable outcome ($\chi^2 = 17.186$, $df = 4$, $p < 0.002$). How may such differences be accounted for? Socialization into a view of education is certainly one possible explanation. Parents' views of the purpose of schooling may reflect the position selected from a number of views available in the culture as socially acceptable. An apparently reverse expectation emerges when an educational aim is self-concerned, that is, concerns their own children. What gives

Table 6.3
Views on Educational Aims among Different Education-Level Groups

Educational Aims	Education Level	Social	Utilitarian	Humanistic	Total
Purpose of Schooling**	Junior and under	73.4% (351)	18.0% (89)	8.6% (41)	100% (481)
	High school	75.0% (276)	17.7% (65)	7.3% (27)	100% (368)
	College and up	73.5% (236)	8.4% (27)	18.1% (58)	100% (321)
Positive Goal **	Junior and under	11.6% (55)	66.3% (315)	22.1% (105)	100% (475)
	High school	7.2% (25)	69.9% (241)	22.9% (79)	100% (345)
	College and up	4.8% (15)	63.2% (196)	31.9% (99)	100% (310)
Unbearable Outcome*	Junior and under	41.6% (195)	21.5% (101)	36.9% (173)	100% (469)
	High school	30.5% (106)	27.7% (96)	41.8% (145)	100% (347)
	College and up	29.1% (90)	26.5% (82)	44.3% (147)	100% (319)

$*p < 0.01; **p < 0.001.$

rise to variations in such aims? Overall, the utilitarian aim was mentioned more often in the optimal context, while "being an independent person" was felt to be the minimum requirement of an educated person.

To test the assumption that a person's view on education is a matter of social adaptation rather than cultural effect, the effects of basic personal factors, such as age and education, were examined. As demonstrated in Table

6.3, more highly educated parents emphasized the humanistic self-cultivating purpose of education more than the less-educated parents, and the opposite pattern emerged for the utilitarian purpose. Age also influenced the perception of the aim of education in a similar manner. A higher percentage of younger parents demonstrates preference for the Humanistic Orientation while more older parents endorsed the utilitarian orientation ($\chi^2 = 27.308$, $df = 6$, $p < 0.000$). However, due to the negative correlation found between education and age ($r = -0.271$, $p < 0.01$), the age difference may be caused by education differences (or vice versa). The contrast test between groups also showed that the education effect occurred across all three conditions. Life experience was also marginally associated with views regarding educational aims.

Relation of Views on Education to Personal Needs and Values

The validity of the psychological needs measure, based as it was on theoretical rather than empirical analysis, was evaluated using three indicators: (1) distribution of various psychological needs, (2) the relationship between the respondents' background and the psychological needs, and (3) the predicative validity of the measure. The results seem to imply that the Life Attitude Index was an appropriate index in accordance with Maslow's psychological-need hypotheses. Firstly, the percentage of participants assigned to "self-actualization" based on the Life Attitude Index was 28%, approximating to the percentage suggested by Maslow. Second, different psychological need patterns were found among various educational level groups ($\chi^2 = 30.081$, $df = 6$, $p < 0.0001$), which was also emphasized by Maslow. Third, the responses of self-actualization needs obtained from the Life Attitude Index have more emphasis on the fulfillment of one's potential, more meaning-oriented, and nonsafety oriented needs than do the other needs. This finding coincides with the definition of self-actualization.

Table 6.4 displays the contingency table analysis of psychological needs and views on educational aims. Results indicated that people with various psychological needs may have different views regarding the purpose of schooling ($\chi^2 = 21.315$, $df = 6$, $p < 0.005$) and optimal expectation of children development ($\chi^2 = 26.458$, $df = 6$, $p < 0.0001$), but do not differ on unbearable outcomes. In a broad sense, Study 2 generated data similar to Study 1. In the case of the purpose of schooling, over two-thirds of the parents emphasized social value as the aim of education. However, there was an apparent trend among groups endorsing the other two orientations. Only the self-actualization group evidenced a preference for humanistic-oriented responses over a utilitarian orientation. The esteem group placed relatively greater emphasis on the utilitarian purpose of education. When rating the desirable outcomes of children's development, again, the self-centered value preference rather than social value was supported among all groups. The discrepancy in such cases lies mainly between the social recognition of educational aim and parents'

Table 6.4
Cross-Tabulation of Psychological Needs and Views of Educational Aims

Psychological Needs	Purpose of Schooling**			Total
	Social	Utilitarian	Humanistic	
Safety	74.7% (293)	15.1% (59)	10.2% (40)	100% (392)
Love and Belonging	67.6% (201)	18.2% (54)	14.1% (42)	100% (297)
Esteem	71.7% (205)	21.0% (46)	7.3% (16)	100% (219)
Self-Actualization	77.0% (264)	6.6% (34)	13.1% (45)	100% (343)
Total Sample	73.1% (915)	15.4% (193)	11.4% (143)	100% (1251)

Psychological Needs	Positive Goal***			Total
Safety	8.5% (32)	70.3% (266)	20.5% (77)	100% (375)
Love and Belonging	13.7% (40)	66.4% (194)	19.9% (58)	100% (292)
Esteem	8.8% (19)	66.5% (143)	24.7% (53)	100% (215)
Self-Actualization	6.4% (21)	60.8% (200)	32.8% (108)	100% (329)
Total Sample	9.2% (112)	66.3% (803)	24.4% (296)	100% (1211)

Psychological Needs	Unbearable Outcome			Total
Safety	35.0% (131)	25.9% (97)	39.0% (146)	100% (374)
Love and Belonging	39.9% (166)	25.1% (73)	35.1% (102)	100% (291)
Esteem	34.0% (72)	24.1% (51)	42.0% (89)	100% (212)
Self-Actualization	31.3% (104)	23.2% (77)	45.5% (151)	100% (332)
Total Sample	35.0% (423)	24.6% (298)	40.4% (488)	100% (1209)

$*p < .1; **p < 0.01; ***p < 0.001.$

own expectations of themselves. Thus, these findings may be best explained by assuming that people always pursue their own aims in public goals.

Regardless of personal psychological needs, over half of the respondents clearly recognize that a college education is necessary in modern Taiwanese society ($\chi^2 = 20.48$, $df = 18$, $p > 0.10$). Since this social belief reflects social reality, the fact that there was no difference between groups provides evidence for the validity of the responses. However, a difference was found among various psychological need groups in the educational expectation for one's own children ($\chi^2 = 37.28$, $df = 18$, $p < 0.01$). Most self-actualizers and safety pursuers expected their children to achieve higher education, while few showed indifference to the acquisition of the diploma. Since education is a means-in-itself, it can serve as a means to gain power, fortune, social status, as well as self-actualization. Therefore, the result suggests further scrutiny of the education aims that are manifested in education requisition.

In conclusion, parents' aims for their children's education may well be influenced by what the parents need or want for themselves. Social aims may only reflect traditions that no longer have a clear anchor in today's Taiwan.

CONCLUSION

The findings suggest that societal context and personal variables may be quite important in determining the educational aims of modern Chinese in Taiwan. This chapter began with a discussion of the origins of education and showed that education was developed to answer specific, socially determined needs. Education became a social tool, and the recipients of education became tools to attain social aims as well as to satisfy social needs. From this perspective, the social conditions at the time at which educational thinking had its inception, and the concerns of thinkers at the time would naturally affect the basic characteristics of the educational thinking of society. The demands of rebuilding political and social order and the need for training large numbers of people with political talent imbued Chinese educational thinking at the start with the manifest characteristic of being a tool for social control (Social Norms Orientation) and skills training (Talent Orientation). Most pre-Ch'in educational thinkers neglected the fact that education lacked nurturing and respect for the subjective character of the education recipient (Humanistic Orientation). One of the reasons may have been that to these educational thinkers, the object of greatest concern was politics, not education. Nevertheless, Confucius was eventually able to develop progressive educational thinking. In the modern context, when the cultural inheritance of education is mentioned, it specifically refers to Confucius, not others.

I reframed the problem with which many researchers have been concerned by asking the following question: Is culture or are social and personal factors of primary importance in understanding Chinese views of education? Reanalyzing Lin and Wang's (1995) questionnaire data, I found strong Talent Orientation responses in the educational aims of respondents. Theirs was not Confucian thought. However, the methodological limitations made it difficult to determine whether statistical differences reflected respondents' views on educational aims or on educational methods. I conducted another study to examine exclusively the effect of social and personal variables on views of educational aims. The results showed personal variables such as age, education, life experience, as well as psychological needs influenced views of education. On this basis, views on education may be interpreted as indicating achievement of goal-oriented action rather than as mere statements of opinion or knowledge. The results not only reflect individual adaptiveness to societal requirements, but also the manner in which people's educational aims are sensitive to their personal expectations. It is possible that in Taiwanese society, people are no longer so involved in real sharing with certain Chinese traditions due to social change. However, some further divisions among aims are clearly needed, along with further evidence as to why some are more highly valued than others.

The results also bear on the interesting issue that operational ideas are less likely to be put into words than are representational ideas (Caws, 1974, in Goodnow & Collins, 1990). When asked to make explicit statements about their educational values and beliefs in formal interviews or daily discourse, people must account for themselves. In so doing, they may present views that reflect social representations rather than opinions carefully constructed on the basis of individual operational meanings. The distinction may well be demonstrated in notions such as global belief and practical belief. In the current research, beliefs about the purpose of school were challenged by beliefs about individual aims that are met through schooling. The former involves the kind of social information communicated through socialization, whereas the latter is knowledge gained through personal experience. The individual can actually choose according to his or her personal needs or world views from multiple perspectives available in the social context. In this research, parents demonstrated an awareness of the formal social norms orientation aims concerning the public purpose of schooling, whereas they instead chose a self-serving, utilitarian view concerning the practical educational aims of their own children.

The time has not yet come for any single grand theory of Chinese educational views, but it is possible to propose some promising general perspectives that serve as an alternative to simple cultural interpretations. One such perspective has to do with the need to ask how far culture is shared. To what extent do people from various occupational or experiential groups share the same views on parenting, or the same goals of child development? The finding that parents endorse more than one educational aim suggests that social scientists may need to be concerned with the extent to which parents may disagree with propositions that are considered common in Chinese tradition. I have called attention to the processes through which parents' needs come to influence their educational views, but I have left it to others to delineate the psychological needs and other individual variables that constitute the connotative foundations of what might be called the educational view. I also leave to others the question of how to justify an answer to culture attribution. I would like to conclude with the thought that these findings may encourage researchers in the future to take account of the very powerful personal goal systems that affect people's views on education and behavior.

NOTE

1. This research was funded by National Science Council Grant NSC 84-2413-H-030-002. I am grateful to Dr. Bill Gabrenya for his insightful comments and valuable suggestions on an earlier version of this chapter.

REFERENCES

Bell, L., & Schniedewind, N. (1989). Realizing the promise of humanistic education: A reconstructed pedagogy for personal and social change. *Journal of Humanistic Psychology, 29* (2), 200–223.

Braithwaite, V., & Law, J. (1985). Sturcture of human values: Testing the adequacy of the Rokeach Value Survey. *Journal of Personality and Social Psychology, 49*, 250–263.

Brogden, J. (1952). The primary personal values measured by the Allport-Vernon test: A study of values. *Psychological Monographs, 66* (348).

Caws, J. (1974). Operational, representational, and explanatory models. *American Anthropologist, 76*, 1–11.

Chang, K. H. (1994). *Revised history of Chinese legal thought.* Taipei, Taiwan: Yangchi Publisher (in Chinese).

Chao, R. K., & Sue, S. (1997). Chinese parental influence and their children's school success: A paradox in the literature on parenting styles. In S. Lau (Ed.), *Growing up the Chinese way: Chinese child and adolescent development* (2d ed., pp. 93–120). Hong Kong: Chinese University Press.

Chen, C., Lee, S., & Stevenson, H. W. (1997). Academic achievement and motivation of Chinese students: A cross-national perspective. In S. Lau (Ed.), *Growing up the Chinese way: Chinese child and adolescent development* (2d ed., pp. 69–91). Hong Kong: Chinese University Press.

Constantinople, A. (1967). Perceived instrumentality of the college as a measure of attitudes toward college. *Journal of Personality and Social Psychology, 5*, 196–201.

Crandall, R. (1973). The measurement of self-esteem and related constructs. In J. Robinson & P. Shaver (Eds.), *Measures of social psychological attitudes* (pp. 45–167). Ann Arbor: University of Michigan, Survey Research Center, Institute for Social Research.

Diener, E. (1984). Subjective well-being. *Psychological Bulletin, 95*, 542–575.

Diener, E., Emmons, A., Larsen, R., & Griffin, S. (1985). The satisfaction with life scale: A measure of life satisfaction. *Journal of Personality Assessment, 49*, 71–75.

Goodnow, J., & Collins, W. (1990). *Development according to parents: The nature, sources and consequences of parents' ideas.* London: Lawrence Erlbaum Associates.

Gorlow, L., & Barocas, R. (1965). Value preferences and interpersonal behavior. *Journal of Social Psychology, 66*, 271–280.

Handy, R. (1970). *The measurement of values.* St. Louis, MO: Warren H. Green.

Hau, K., & Salili, F. (1997). Achievement goals and causal attributions of Chinese students. In S. Lau (Ed.), *Growing up the Chinese way: Chinese child and adolescent development* (2d ed., pp. 121–145). Hong Kong: Chinese University Press.

Hobson, B. (1987). *Theories of education: Studies of significant innovation in Western educational thought,* 2d ed. Brisbane, Australia: John Wiley and Sons.

Hoffman, L. W. (1988). Cross-cultural differences in childrearing goals. In R. A. LeVine, P. M. Miller, & M. M. West (Eds.), *Parental behavior in diverse societies* (pp. 99–122). San Francisco: Jossey-Bass.

Hu, M. C. (1986). *History of education of the Chinese.* Taipei, Taiwan: Sanming (in Chinese).

Huang, Y. J. (1993). *The great history of China.* Taipei, Taiwan: Lienching (in Chinese).

Kneller, G. F. (1982). *Educational anthropology: An introduction.* Malabar, FL: Robert E. Krieger (original in 1965).

Lau, S., & Yeung, P.P.W. (1997). Understanding Chinese child development: The role of culture in socialization. In S. Lau (Ed.), *Growing up the Chinese way: Chinese child and adolescent development* (2d ed., pp. 29–44). Hong Kong: Chinese University Press.

LeVine, R. A. (1974). Parental goals: A cross-cultural view. *Teachers College Record, 76* (2), 226–239.

LeVine, R. A. (1988). Human parental care: Universal goals, cultural strategies, individual behavior. In R. A. LeVine, P. M. Miller, & M. M. West (Eds.), *Parental behavior in diverse societies* (pp. 5–12). San Francisco: Jossey-Bass.

Levitin, T. (1968). Values. In J. Robinson & P. Shaver (Eds.), *Measures of social psychological attitudes* (pp. 405–501). Ann Arbor: University of Michigan, Survey Research Center, Institute for Social Research.

Lin, W. Y. (1992). Study into corporal punishment: From theory to practice. *Journal of Chinese Applied Psychology, 1*, 53–77 (in Chinese).

Lin, W. Y., & Wang, J. W. (1995). Chinese parents' view of education: Strict education view or scolding and beating concept? *Indigenous Psychological Research in Chinese Societies, 3*, 2–92 (in Chinese).

Lin, W. Y., Wang, J. W., & Chen, H. C. (1992). Chinese parents' choice of education allocation. Research report of Institute of National Policy Study. Taipei: Chang Jung-Fa Foundation (in Chinese).

Lorr, M., & Wunderlich, R. A. (1986). Two objective measures of self-esteem. *Journal of Personality Assessment, 50*, 18–23.

Lynn, R. (1974). Review of "The nature of human values" by M. Rokeach. *British Journal of Psychology, 65*, 453.

Mao, L. J., Shao, H. T., & Chu, C. N. (1989). *History of education of the Chinese.* Taipei, Taiwan: Wunan (in Chinese).

Maslow, A. H. (1968). *Toward a psychology of being* (2d ed.). New York: Van Nostrand Reinhold.

Maslow, A. H. (1970). *Motivation and personality* (2d ed.). New York: Harper and Row.

Nisbett, R. E., Peng, K., Choi, I., & Norenzayan, A. (2001). Culture and systems of thought: Holistic versus analytic cognition. *Psychological Review, 108* (2), 291–310.

Park, Y. (1997). Rationality and human dignity: Confucius, Kant and Scheffler on the ultimate aim of education. In H. Siegel (Ed.), *Reason and education: Essays in honor of Israel Scheffler* (pp. 7–18). Dordrecht, The Netherlands: Kluwer Academic.

Robinson, J. (1969). Life satisfaction and happiness. In J. Robinson & P. Shaver (Eds.), *Measures of social psychological attitudes* (pp. 11–41). Ann Arbor: University of Michigan, Survey Research Center, Institute for Social Research.

Rokeach, M. (1973). *The nature of human value.* New York: Free Press.

Schwartz, S., & Bilsky, W. (1987). Toward a universal psychological structure of human values. *Journal of Personality and Social Psychology, 53*, 550–562.

Stevenson, L., & Haberman, D. (1998). Evolutionary psychology: Lorenz on aggression. In L. Stevenson & D. Haberman (Eds.), *Ten theories of human nature* (3d ed., pp. 207–222). New York: Oxford University Press (original in 1974).

Wang, F. C. (1990). *History of education of the Chinese*. Taipei, Taiwan: National Bureau of Edition and Translation (in Chinese).

Wang, J. W., & Lin, W. Y. (1998). Punishment and acculturation: An exploration of Chinese naïve psychology. *Fu-Jen Studies, 26*, 181–214 (in Chinese).

Wang, J. W., & Lin, W. Y. (1999). Mechanism of the construction of educational view: Performance of human nature under environmental restrictions. *Formosan Journal of Applied Psychology, 7*, 1–16 (in Chinese).

Wu, D.Y.H. (1997). Parental control: Psychocultural interpretations of Chinese patterns of socialization. In S. Lau (Ed.), *Growing up the Chinese way: Chinese child and adolescent development* (2d ed., pp. 1–28). Hong Kong: Chinese University Press.

Yang, H. L. (1964). *History of Chinese legal thought*. Taipei, Taiwan: Taiwan Shanwu (in Chinese).

Part III

ACHIEVEMENT AND ACHIEVEMENT MOTIVATION

CHAPTER 7

Individual Differences and Prototypical Stories: Achievement Motivation in Taiwan and the United States

Eli Lieber and An-Bang Yu

Research distinguishing between individualistic and collectivist cultures has suggested that achievement experiences may differ across cultures (Hofstede, 1980; Salili, 1995; Triandis, 1972). An obstacle to distinguishing achievement motivation (AM) characteristics across cultures has been that the majority of research methods have been developed for application within individualistic cultures (McClelland, Atkinson, Clark, & Lowell, 1953; McClelland, 1961; Murray, 1943; Weiner, 1985). For instance, Yang and Yu (1988) argued that AM theory would better describe Chinese culture if it incorporated a social perspective along with the traditional individual one. Since Chinese culture has been described as involving a relatively social perspective (Bond & Hwang, 1986; Yang, 1986), aspects of AM that reflect issues of face (Gabrenya & Hwang, 1996; Hwang, 1987), filial piety, or relational determinism (Ho, 1994; Yang, 1995) are not likely to be assessed from an individual AM perspective.

In this study, we build on conclusions drawn by Yang and Yu (1988) by applying individual difference and social cognitive approaches to AM in Taiwan and the United States. We found individual and social perspectives to be meaningful and distinct concepts in both cultures. Further, a content analysis was conducted to search for indigenous characteristics of behavioral domain, causes, and consequences in stories of prototypical achievement experiences. Sets of characteristics were identified that distinguish between the two cultures and between extreme individual oriented (IO) and social oriented (SO) groups within a culture. Distinguishing characteristics were consistent with sociohistorical differences between the cultures. Furthermore, though individual and social conceptions of achievement are meaningful to the study of AM in both cultures, they must be understood in terms of the relevant sociocultural context.

INDIVIDUAL DIFFERENCE PERSPECTIVE

Amidst a history of efforts to describe and develop instruments for assessing AM characteristics from individual difference perspectives, Yang and Yu (1988) distinguished between individual and social perspectives. They argued that given the rich sociohistorical context of Confucian values in Chinese culture, AM research methods with Chinese populations were incomplete without full representation of a social perspective. The argument that both individual and social perspectives may coexist in a complementary manner within Chinese culture is consistent with findings related to Chinese AM values and beliefs (Feather, 1986; Lau, 1988; Salili, 1995). This notion should, in general, not be underestimated as a focus on what may be false dichotomies, which risks obscuring an appreciation for the often more natural experience of complement among varying perspectives (e.g., Lieber, Yang, & Lin, 2000). As for individual and social perspectives on AM, key distinctions include variations in goal definition, achievement behavior, behavioral consequences, and outcome evaluation.

Individually oriented achievement orientation (IOAM) tends to invoke the self as the primary source for achievement definition, behavior, and evaluation, while socially oriented achievement orientation (SOAM) tends to invoke membership in groups and social roles as the primary source for these aspects of the achievement experience. IOAM and SOAM have been found to represent relatively independent characteristics—through their unique associations to other variables—and arise through separate aspects of socialization (see Yu, 1996, for a review). Research delineating a social perspective on achievement experiences has exposed limitations in how individual differences in achievement motivation are understood when the construct is applied in collectivist societies (Ho, 1994; Salili, 1996; Triandis, 1990; Yu & Yang, 1994; Yu, 1996). Yang and Yu (1988) suggested that Chinese conceptions and implications of AM differ in important ways from research findings in Western cultures. While Western cultures may be subject to the influences of a social perspective, they tend to emphasize a more individual perspective on AM. As such, prior research methods and findings have been adequate to represent and understand the construct in these Western contexts, but inadequate in Chinese cultures, which emphasize a socially oriented AM and cannot be adequately studied through existing conceptions and methods. Thus, we argue that individual and social represent distinct aspects of AM and the incorporation of both perspectives in AM research is critical for a full description of AM in Chinese populations and may prove equally valuable in research with Western populations.

SOCIAL COGNITIVE APPROACH

Attention to individuals' thoughts, feelings, and perceptions in achievement situations has provided researchers with a second approach to exploring and understanding achievement behavior. These methods are useful in evaluating cultural differences in the meaning of achievement and linkages between sociocultural contexts and cognitive processes. Salili (1994) argued that the influence of social context and culture on conceptions of achievement has been neglected. Moreover, situational influences have been demonstrated to impact the way individuals perceive and subsequently respond in achievement situations (Ames & Ames, 1984; Nicholls, 1984; Lieber, 1990). For example, Lieber (1990) elicited either a learning or performance perspective in a learned helplessness research paradigm by controlling verbal feedback on an achievement task. Subsequently, significant differences were observed between the two perspective groups in the subjects' beliefs about the cause of their success and failure and objective task performance following a series of failures. Further, Dweck (1986) and Dweck and Leggett (1988) argued that differential patterns of social influence foster cognition associated with variation in learning versus performance goals—mastery versus helpless perspectives. Dweck's theory speaks well to the broad influence of culture on the development and maintenance of particular AM orientations. Moreover, Dweck emphasized the importance of understanding cognitive processes as related to achievement behavior variation and the mechanisms by which social experience determines the nature and meaning of this cognition.

THE PRESENT STUDY

We believe that with varying emphasis, the conception of AM in all cultures includes aspects of both individual and social perspectives. Given the expansion of AM research across multiple cultures, method can no longer be limited to any one perspective. As multiple AM conceptions may operate in both individualistic and collectivist cultures, all relevant conceptions should be identified and explored simultaneously. That is, those characteristics that distinguish cultures may be found in the relative emphasis of one perspective versus another—as opposed to an exclusive reliance on one orientation or another. The challenge is to identify and validate social aspects of the AM construct that will complement the predominant individual one. Once such aspects are elucidated, research can apply both perspectives to examine the prevalence of and relations between these aspects both within and across cultures.

As such, we argue that currently available methods fail in their capability to allow for the discovery of distinctive perspectives on achievement motivation and their associated psychological and social implications. While existing strategies are applicable in new cultural contexts, they must be understood as limited in their utility to assess only those aspects of AM for which they were developed and have proven useful. On the other hand, where new cultural contexts are to be considered, so should the possibility that new perspectives and methods may be necessary to fully recognize the unique influences social context and culture may have on the achievement construct. In an effort to justify the utility of a social AM perspective, this study sought to identify the levels of and relations between individual and social AM in Taiwanese and American culture, link the individual difference results to characteristics of prototypical achievement experiences from each culture, and reconcile both sets of evidence with reference to the relevant sociocultural context.

Method

Participants

Undergraduate university students in Taiwan ($n = 148$) and the United States ($n = 77$) participated as subjects for this study. The Taiwan sample included 105 females and 43 males, averaged 19.5 years of age and two years of university study, and was all of Chinese racial background. The American participants included 56 females and 21 males, averaged 21.2 years of age and two years of university study, and was 57.5% Caucasian, 17.5% African American, 5% Asian, 4% Latino, and 16% of unknown racial background due to missing data. Both samples were representative of populations in public universities in metropolitan areas in their respective countries.

Measures

Materials were prepared in Chinese (Mandarin) and English simultaneously. An iterative process involving native speakers of both languages was taken toward the development of functionally equivalent instruments (Brislin, 1986). Individual differences in AM were assessed with the Individual Oriented Achievement Motivation and Social Oriented Achievement Motivation instrument (Yang & Yu, 1988). The IOAM-SOAM consists of sixty Likert-scale items that provide two scores for respondents, indexing their beliefs about individual- and social-oriented achievement motivation. Respondents indicate on a six-point scale how true they believe each statement is for them (e.g., 1 = Completely Untrue of Me to 6 = Completely True of Me). Items range from expectations and performance related to specific tasks, for example, "I try my best on school work in order to impress my teachers," to general reference to tasks or expectations, for example, "Before I do anything, I first consider whether my goals fit my parent's expectations." This instrument was developed in Chinese for use with Taiwanese populations and required translation to English for this study, a process which involved minor modifications to the original Chinese version to insure operational equivalence.

Social cognitive aspects of AM were assessed through an open-ended story-writing task. In this task, respondents were asked to write freely in describing what they believe to be a prototypical achievement experience in their life. There were no restrictions on the domain or nature of achievement experience to be described or that the experience was one of their own or someone they knew well. While largely unstructured, in order to assure the stories included details relevant to the research questions, instructions provided a checklist of details respondents were encouraged to include in their description (i.e., context, persons' roles, time of life, location, major causes, and the nature of event consequences).

Procedures

Procedures for data collection were similar in both Taiwan and the United States. Students were recruited for participation through university-required participation in subject pools and as extra course credit. Informed consent was obtained and all data collection materials were distributed and explained during course time. Where possible, all data were collected during a class period with an option to complete the story-writing task away from class if required—in this case the story materials were returned within one week of their distribution.

Results and Discussion

The analysis and subsequent interpretation of these data were framed by principles inherent in socioecological and indigenous psychology. These guides are appropriate because, given the limits of existing work in this area, this study represents a starting point for an understanding of how achievement motivation within and across culture may be examined from a more comprehensive perspective. Drawing on previous work, we argue that the conception of AM, and hence its precursors, causes, consequences, and broader implications, necessarily differs from one social context to another. While the IOAM-SOAM provided data in a standardized format, the story-writing task allowed for broad freedom in describing the form and nature of prototypical achievement. Using results from both of these tasks, we sought to address the main questions of how conceptions of AM differ within and across cultures, how we can best pursue an understanding of these differences, and what the implications of these differences may be.

Individual Difference (IOAM-SOAM) Findings

The individual difference approach, represented by the IOAM-SOAM, provides a comparison of broad AM characteristics across the cultural groups. No sex differences in these variables were found within either group and, accordingly, there were no further attempts to explore differences between males and females. Table 7.1 includes IOAM and SOAM descriptive results for both groups. Both scales proved to be internally consistent in Taiwan and the United States, indicating the cohesive structure of the constructs in each culture as assessed and conceptualized by this measure. As expected, the American sample reported significantly higher ratings of IOAM than the Taiwanese sample ($t(244) = 2.42, p < 0.05$). In contrast, and somewhat surprising, no significant SOAM differences were observed. As will be reported, the story-writing task findings indicate the anticipated divergence in social oriented achievement between the populations. Discussion of these findings and some explanation for the methodological inconsistencies will be provided.

Turning to a within-culture analysis, bivariate correlations between IO and SOAM scores were conducted to examine the relations between the social and individual AM perspectives. In support of our argument that a social AM perspective is distinct from an individual one, no significant relationships between IO and SOAM were found for the total, Taiwan, or U.S. samples, $r = 0.01, -0.09$, and 0.13, respectively. Moreover, as a second check on the influence of sex on these variables, partial correlations (controlling for sex) were calculated for IO and SOAM relations and, again, no significant results emerged. These results indicate that, separately for both cultural groups, individual and social perspectives seem to represent complementary aspects of AM. Furthermore, this evidence suggests that when individuals hold beliefs that emphasize one aspect of AM they do not necessarily deemphasize the other (Feather, 1986; Lau, 1988; Yang & Yu, 1988).

Overall, while meaningful for descriptive purposes, the emergence of IO and absence of SOAM differences tell us relatively little about the sociocultural implications of these results from one cultural context to the next. Theoretical differences in the socialization of AM beliefs raises the question as to whether the conceptions of AM and their consequent implications can be found to differ across sociocultural groups (Stein & Bailey, 1973; Gilligan, 1982;

Table 7.1
IOAM-SOAM Descriptive Results by Culture

	Taiwan					United States			
	M	Range	SD	*		M	Range	SD	*
IOAM	4.67	3.0-5.9	.55	.89		4.87	2.1-5.8	.64	.91
SOAM	3.42	1.5-5.2	.80	.93		3.54	1.8-5.9	.87	.90

Note: Taiwan $n = 148$; United States $n = 77$. Scores on the IOAM and SOAM can range from 1 to 6, with higher scores indicating greater endorsement of IO or SO aspects of motivation.

•Indicates Cronbach's alpha coefficient.

Salili, 1994). The content analysis of prototypical stories, presented next, was intended to address these questions from a more foundational and culturally sensitive perspective.

Social Cognitive (Prototypical Achievement Stories) Findings

The prototypical achievement stories collected for analysis provide a window on the subjective sociocultural meaning of achievement as reported in these cultures.[1] Content analysis of the stories was carried out to identify characteristics related to the behavioral domain, causes, and consequences of achievement experiences. It is important to recall that there were few restrictions placed on the participants in their decision about what constituted a prototypical achievement event. Thus, in contrast to AM work focused on a particular reference task or behavioral domain (e.g., Chang, Wong, & Teo, 2000), this method provided respondents great latitude in determining what was, for them, an appropriate example of achievement.

Results reported here are based on a coding system developed along apriori notions—albeit flexible—and as emerging from work processing preliminary story data. The system was then applied to the entire set of stories and refined as necessary in response to encounters with data that could not be properly represented by the existing code structure. Whenever any modification was necessary, previously coded stories were reviewed to assure their coding continued to correspond with the most current code structure. This development was further challenged by the desire to balance complete representation of the experiences on common grounds; that is, with concern for both allowing cultural comparison and properly representing the stories with sensitivity to culture-specific meaning—with appreciation and respect for indigenous perspectives (Geertz, 1984). As such, the goals of the system's evolution were influenced by both etic and emic factors—apriori theory-based views and representation of the story writer's voices and the content through which they expressed their beliefs (Berry, 1989).

The strategy taken to accomplish these goals involved having native individuals of each culture initially read sample stories from their cultural group and work to develop codes that would fully represent the content with respect to their own culture. Consequently, two sets of codes were initially developed and defined. These two sets were examined and, following discussion among research team members from both cultures, comparable code categories were defined based on story evidence provided by participants from both cultural groups. Where codes emerged that were specific to only one culture, they were similarly defined based on story evidence and included in the code system.

Following the development of the coding system, all stories were coded independently by two research assistants. For the twenty-seven variables included here, Cohen's kappa coefficient for interrater reliability ranged from 0.50 to 1.0 and averaged 0.75. The average kappa rose to 0.85 when excluding the four codes rated with the poorest reliability. These results indicate that an acceptable level of confidence can be placed in the coding system and its application to the data. Finally, wherever discrepancies between raters occurred, the item was discussed among the study's raters and researchers until consensus on a coding decision was achieved.

Findings from analysis of these stories are organized to address three main questions:

1. Are there overall differences between Taiwan and the United States in the meaning of achievement as represented through prototypical achievement experience stories?

2. As significant differences between Taiwan and the United States were observed for IOAM scores, how does prototypical achievement story content differ between extreme IO groups across cultures?

3. While no significant differences between Taiwan and the United States were observed for SOAM scores, does prototypical achievement story content differ between extreme SO groups across cultures?

Achievement Story Domain

True to traditional distinctions between the cultures represented here, some of the most dramatic differences between groups emerged in the behavioral domain or function referenced in the achievement stories. The vast majority of stories were organized into seven nonexclusive categories: academic, affiliation, interpersonal positive impression, future employment, nonacademic learning, security, and the avoidance of fears or disapproval. Significant differences were found between the samples in four of these seven categories (see Figure 7.1). For the relatively individualistic American culture, the prospect of future employment, and security (personal) goals may all be interpreted as reflecting the pursuit of more individual success and accomplishment (Hofstede, 1980). These beliefs are apparent in many of the American stories referring to academic accomplishment and progress and the purchase of large items (such as a house or car). For example, one participant wrote, "Getting accepted into college was an achievement for me. . . . This is an achievement because so many students do not go on to college after high school but I wanted to go on because I wanted more for myself." Another stated, "I believe my job was the greatest achievement in my life. The company I work for requires the best employees with outstanding work ethics. It takes a lot of hard work to become a permanent employee with high wages, excellent benefits, and weeks of paid vacation." On the other hand, in the relatively collectivist Taiwanese culture, emphasis on affiliation and nonacademic learning (frequently referring to how to get along with others or understand groups) are consistent with a more social perspective (Ho, 1994). These views are exemplified in one Taiwanese student's writing:

Figure 7.1
Achievement Story Behavioral Domains Referenced

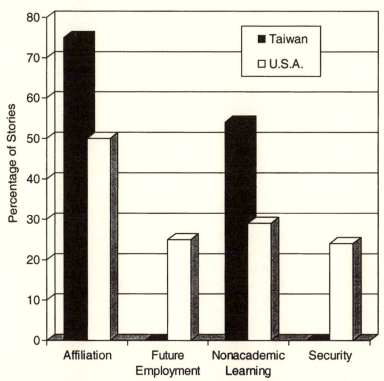

Note: Significant differences were found between Taiwanese (n = 24) and Americans (n = 72) in the percentage of stories referencing the domain.

During the winter holidays of this year, my classmates and I enrolled to participate in a "play camp for children." At first, from hearing the name, we felt it should be fun! However, it was completely different from our expectation . . . the first three days, we had to prepare activities. At that time, we really resented it. . . . Although it was very tiresome to take care of the children, we were very happy to see that they learned all the things we had just learned. . . . Our complaints and resentments of the past three days were all gone . . . there was satisfaction and achievement. Even now, those children still keep in touch with me.

Seeing these data as reflecting meaningful aspects of AM conception, these findings support earlier notions (Triandis, 1990; Yu, 1996) about how achievement motivation is differentially conceived in individualistic and collectivist cultures.

Self-Based Causes of Achievement Experiences

In coding causes for achievement it became clear that while the actor's efforts were frequently indicated as a primary force in both cultures, there were important distinctions in how the self was represented. Moreover, we found that variation in this representation suggested differences between stories across cultures. Two variables distinguishing between the self and individual (i.e., references to "I" or "my") and within a social role (i.e., references to "as a son," "student," "sibling," or "friend") were created. Marginally significant differences were found in the percentage of stories referring to the individual self versus the social-role self as a cause: 58% and 33% in Taiwanese stories compared to 82% and 17% in the American stories ($\chi^2(6, 96) = 12.13$, $p < 0.06$).

Achievement Experience Consequences

Achievement experience consequences were first classified into six categories: approval, emotional, instrumental, problem or obstacle, self-satisfaction, and tangible reward. The stories were clearly rich with variation across these categories, yet the analyses carried out here did not serve to distinguish between the cultures for most categories. Though beyond the scope of this study, a future more specific investigation would likely discover meaningful variation in consequences as a function of achievement story domain and specific causes. However, though no differences across cultures were found in the number of emotion terms used, significant differences were observed in the expression of particular emotions. Figure 7.2 presents the percentage of stories in each culture reporting experiences of emotions that differed significantly between the groups: excitement, frustration, love, and pride. American stories included significantly more mention of excitement and pride than the Taiwanese stories. Focused more on end products, these emotions can be seen as associated with the desire for, and anticipation and achievement of successful achievement outcomes. Further, the story descriptions showed a tendency to center on the individual (i.e., the frequent use of "I" and "me"). For example, one student wrote, "My mom and dad have never let me settle for second best. They helped me set goals and meet them . . . [after the achievement] I felt absolutely elated. I was as proud as I have ever been . . . my parents were glowing with pride and excitement for me." On the other hand, the Taiwanese stories included significantly more mention of frustration and love than the American stories. These emotions are understood in terms of progress toward goals—persistent efforts and appreciation for supportive others—as opposed to the achievement outcome itself. For example, "Because I will not give up in anything until I get it done perfectly, I don't have much sense of frustration. But to me, a sense of achievement is only an emotion. I would not feel that sense of achievement, that is, the sense of achievement is the same as the sense of frustration." This student seems to be suggesting that frustration is an

Figure 7.2
Achievement Story Experiences for Emotions Referenced

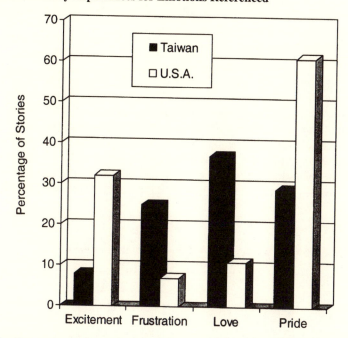

Note: Significant differences found between Taiwanese (n = 24) and Americans (n = 72) in the percentage of stories referencing the emotion. χ^2 (1, 96) = 5.21, $p < 0.05$; 5.78, $p < 0.05$; 8.60, $p < 0.01$; and 8.15, $p < 0.05$ for excitement, frustration, love, and pride, respectively.

inseparable aspect of achievement striving. Moreover, reports of love and attention to social relationships are frequent in the Taiwanese stories. For example, "Then I can achieve the goal as a good teacher. At the same time, I won't fall short of my family's expectations." Another wrote, "My performance tells my parents not to worry about me. They follow the norms and standards of society. That's why this is my greatest achievement." While both the American and Taiwanese stories reference other persons with regard to positive emotions, the Taiwanese stories included more frequent reference and concern for these others' perspective as integral to their own experience.

Extreme Group Comparisons

Beyond the general descriptive IOAM-SOAM results, a great deal of variability was observed along the IO and SO variables. In order to elucidate the characteristics of the more extreme groups within each culture, the groups were divided into quartiles based on each of these variables. Four comparisons were made between cultures for the upper and lower quartiles of each

AM variable: high IO, low IO, high SO, and low SO. The results of these analyses help illustrate the meaning of being classified into one of these groups for Taiwanese and American individuals.

High IO Comparisons

Significant results across cultures for high IO groups were observed for three achievement story domain variables: Taiwanese stories more frequently referenced affiliation and interpersonal positive impressions and American stories more frequently referenced future employment (see Figure 7.3). The affiliation and future employment findings directly reflect the overall group results as discussed previously. However, 36% of the Taiwanese and none of the American stories in the high IO group included mention of positive impressions on others. In the overall analysis, the parallel results were equal (17%

Figure 7.3
Achievement Story Characteristics, Individual Orientation I

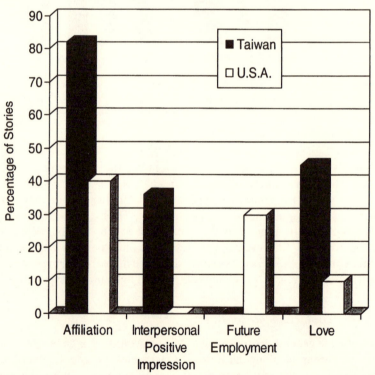

Note: Significant differences found between high IO Taiwanese (n = 11) and American (n = 10) participants in the percentage of stories referencing the characteristic. χ^2 (1, 21) = 3.88, $p < 0.05$; 4.49, $p < 0.05$; and 3.85, $p < 0.05$ for references to affiliation, interpersonal positive impression, and future employment, respectively.

and 19% for the Taiwanese and American stories, respectively). As such, it is striking that the stories of high IO Taiwanese students are distinguished by reference to a clearly socially oriented characteristic and at rates higher than observed in the overall Taiwanese sample. Thus, even extreme high IO members in Taiwan appear to recognize social relations in their AM conceptions.

Low IO Comparisons

Within the low IO groups Taiwanese stories again more frequently referenced the affiliation domain. Further, Taiwanese stories more frequently referenced the social-role self as a cause for achievement, while American stories more frequently included reference to the individual self as a cause for achievement and to the experience of pride (see Figure 7.4). As within the high IO group, the low IO group results were quite consistent with the overall analy-

Figure 7.4
Achievement Story Characteristics, Individual Orientation II

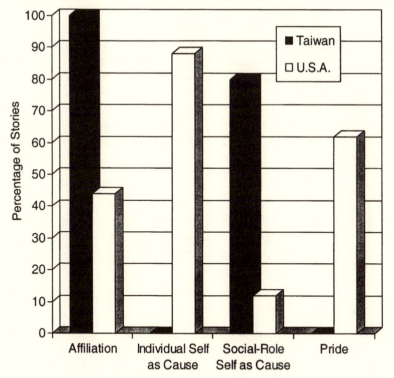

Note: Significant differences found between low IO Taiwanese (n = 5) and American (n = 16) participants in the percentage of stories referencing the characteristic. χ^2 (1, 21) = 4.92, $p <$ 0.05; 15.49, $p < 0.01$; and 5.97, $p < 0.01$ for references to affiliation, the individual self and/ or social-role self as cause, and the experience of pride, respectively.

ses. Yet in these results the emergence of significant differences in the representation of self can be seen as a cause for achievement events. In this group, these differences are dramatic (differing by over 60%) and are consistent with the classical understanding of self in individualistic and collectivist cultures (Markus & Kitayama, 1991).

High SO Comparisons

While the SOAM mean scores did not differ across cultures, there were a variety of differences found in the stories for the high SO group. This group represents the stereotypical social-oriented individual, often argued to be more characteristic of collectivist cultures. Yet the two differences observed here, related to academics and fear avoidance, are consistent with traditional characteristic differences between the cultures. As expected, the Taiwanese stories showed significantly less reference to academic domains and more reference to fear avoidance than the American stories (see Figure 7.5). Furthermore, significant differences were observed for the representation of self as a cause for achievement events. Taiwanese stories involved less reference to the individual self and more reference to the social-role self than American stories, less reference to the experience of pride than those of the United States, and more reference to happiness than those of the United States (see Figure 7.5). These results demonstrate that substantive cultural differences appear to exist among high social-oriented individuals. Further, while these findings help explain particular assumptions, they place the overall results in the context of the variation present in each cultural context. In a pattern opposite to that of the high IO group, high SO American participants who hold beliefs atypical of their culture remain focused on behavioral domains typical of their culture in reporting AM.

Low SO Comparisons

Only two significant achievement story differences were found in the low SO group. Consistent with the overall results, Taiwanese stories included significantly less reference to future employment and security than the U.S. stories (see Figure 7.6).

Extreme Group Analysis Summary

Though the results reflect somewhat artificial groups distinguished by IO and SO variables, the magnification of differences serves to expose particularly salient areas of discrepancy between how prototypical AM is reported by parallel subsets of individuals in these cultures. Particularly for those groups that report beliefs atypical of their primary culture (i.e., high IO in Taiwan and high SO in the United States), the findings draw our attention to aspects of

Figure 7.5
Achievement Story Characteristics, Social Orientation I

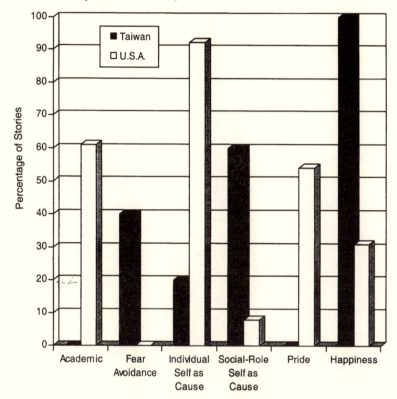

Note: Significant differences found between high SO Taiwanese (n = 5) and American (n = 13) participants in the percentage of stories referencing the characteristic. χ^2 (1, 18) = 5.54, $p <$ 0.05 and 5.85, $p < 0.05$ for references to academics and fear avoidance, respectively.

AM that may be of particular use in future investigations. Moreover, these results help researchers to more fully understand how overall group findings may be accounted for by particular subsets of the population as well as how representative these subsets are amidst the variability observed in a particular group.

GENERAL DISCUSSION AND CONCLUSIONS

This study demonstrates that assessing AM from both individual and social perspectives exposes information relevant for the study of AM within and across cultures. In the interest of similar future efforts, the IOAM-SOAM proved psychometrically sound for use in Taiwan and the United States and, as expected, distinguished individual and social aspects of AM in meaningful ways

Figure 7.6
Achievement Story Characteristics, Social Orientation II

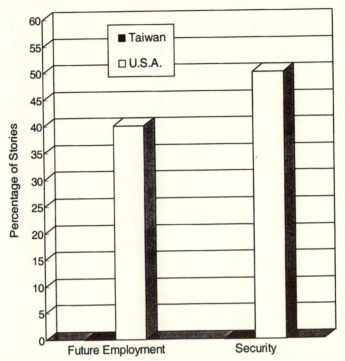

Note: Significant differences found between low SO Taiwanese (n = 9) and American (n = 10) participants in the percentage of stories referencing the characteristic. χ^2 (1, 18) = 9.66, $p <$ 0.01; 4.41, $p < 0.05$; and 6.92, $p < 0.01$ for references to the individual and/or social self as cause, experience of pride, and happiness, respectively. χ^2 (1, 19) = 4.56, $p < 0.05$ and 6.11, $p < 0.01$ for references to future employment and security, respectively.

as reflected in associated differences in the prototypical achievement stories. The story findings indicate the richness of information available through the open-ended method. Moreover, these findings demonstrate the complexity of cognition related to AM and that the cross-sectional examination of the story characteristics taken here can be enriched by a more idiographic study of the linkages between behavioral domains, causes, and consequences for achievement experience. Finally, while many commonalties in AM conception across cultures were observed, the uniqueness of each culture was clearly reflected in a number of aspects of achievement story description.

The combination of methods as applied here in examining AM revealed some inconsistency in findings between the strategies. There are at least three plausible explanations for these inconsistencies. First, a direct comparison between cultural groups of mean scores failed to account for the possible effects of response bias error. In these data, and true for both the IOAM and SOAM, one group's idiosyncratic tendency to respond higher or lower on the scales could have the effect of masking or exaggerating group differences. Second, while these populations represent distinct sociocultural backgrounds, both samples represent university student populations. Similarities in developmental stage and the experiences of higher education may also contribute to reducing differences that may exist and may be more easily detected in the more general population. Finally, a preliminary content analysis was conducted on items making up the IOAM and SOAM scales. The IOAM scale items are relatively homogeneous with respect to individual self-promotion and self-determination. In contrast, the SOAM scale items are less consistent in focus, including emphases on performance, reward, or effort and reference to peers, parents or ancestors, or teachers. The range of items represented in the SOAM scale corresponds to the relative complexity of the social domain. This range of items, and domain complexity, may explain the absence of findings between groups. That is, one group may score higher on some aspects and lower on others, essentially masking differences that may be found in an examination of the specific aspects. Thus, it will be important for future work to attend to the underlying meaning of SOAM. Factor analysis of the measure across groups may serve to disentangle distinct aspects of the social domain and how they relate to AM. Together, these possibilities suggest that valuable work may be done in the future to better understand AM in differences between cultural groups' response patterns to specific measures, more diverse samples within particular cultures, and with respect to the complexity of social orientations.

With regard to the prototypical achievement stories, overall differences between Taiwan and the United States were consistent with traditional descriptions of Asian and Western sociocultural contexts (Hofstede, 1980; Salili, 1995; Triandis, 1990; Yang & Yu, 1988). The content of the stories provided a new look at AM conception within and across cultures. Taiwanese stories told of goal seeking involving affiliations with important others in nonacademic learning situations and focused more on process than on outcome—being fulfilled. American stories told of individual striving in more academic or competitive situations toward future job and life security and focused more on the achievement outcome itself—being outstanding. These interpretations are further supported by reference to particular causal beliefs and emotions. Taiwanese stories focused more on social roles and emotions related to goal striving, and American stories focused more on the individual self and emotions related to ego enhancement and goal attainment.

Finally, the findings here generally support the notion that meaningful variation in the IO and SOAM variables exists between Taiwan and the United States. Extreme group analyses provided a backdrop on which to evaluate the variation within each group. These results demonstrated the following: (1) story characteristics that distinguish culture appear consistent across the subgroups, (2) particular subgroups account for large portions of the differences observed between cultures in the overall comparisons, and (3) nontraditional groups (e.g., high IO Taiwanese students or high SO American students) are still distinguished by traditional sociocultural characteristics as reflected in their stories. The approach taken here demonstrates the potential of multiple perspectives to the study of AM and indicates three areas for further AM investigation: characteristics that distinguish the overall groups, differences between more traditional and nontraditional groups within a culture, and dynamics between achievement experience domain, cause, and consequence.

NOTES

Eli Lieber, Department of Psychiatry and Biobehavioral Sciences, UCLA, United States, and An-Bang Yu, Institute of Ethnology, Academia Sinica, Taipei, Taiwan. This research was supported in part by a Pacific Cultural Foundation research grant (PCF-96-0317) awarded to Eli Lieber. The authors also wish to express appreciation to Ms. Shih Chen-Chen, Ms. Chen Weiyin, and Ms. Chau Lai Ling for their tireless efforts in translating, understanding, and coding the qualitative data for this study.

1. Achievement stories were collected from subsamples of participants (Taiwan = 24 and the United States = 72).

REFERENCES

Ames, R., & Ames, C. (Eds.). (1984). *Research on motivation in education: Student motivation in education*. New York: Academic Press.

Berry, J. W. (1989). Imposed etics–emics-derived etics: The operationalization of a compelling idea. *International Journal of Psychology, 24*, 721–735.

Bond, M. H., & Hwang, K. K. (1986). The social psychology of Chinese people. In M. H. Bond (Ed.), *The psychology of the Chinese people* (pp. 213–266). Hong Kong: Chinese University Press.

Brislin, R. W. (1986). The wording and translation of research instruments. In W. J. Lonner & J. W. Berry (Eds.), *Field methods in cross-cultural research* (pp. 137–164). Beverly Hills, CA: Sage.

Chang, W. C., Wong, W. K., & Teo, G. (2000). The socially oriented and individually oriented achievement motivation of Singaporean Chinese students. *Journal of Psychology in Chinese Societies, 2* (1), 39–64.

Dweck, C. S. (1986). Motivational processes affecting learning. *American Psychologist, 41* (10), 1040–1048.

Dweck, C., & Leggett, E. L. (1988). A social-cognitive approach to motivation and personality. *Psychological Review, 95*, 256–273.

Feather, N. T. (1986). Value systems across cultures: Australia and China. *International Journal of Psychology, 21*, 697–715.

Gabrenya, W. K., & Hwang, K. K. (1996). Chinese social interaction: Harmony and hierarchy on the good Earth. In M. H. Bond (Ed.), *The handbook of Chinese psychology* (pp. 309–321). Hong Kong: Oxford University Press.

Geertz, C. (1984). "From the native's point of view": On the nature of anthropological understanding. In R. A. Shweder & R. A. LeVine (Eds.), *Culture theory: Essays on mind, self, and emotion* (pp. 123–136). Cambridge: Cambridge University Press.

Gilligan, C. (1982). *In a different voice: Psychological theory and women's develop-ment*. Cambridge, MA: Harvard University Press.

Ho, D.Y.F. (1994). Cognitive socialization in Confucian heritage cultures. In P. M. Greenfield & R. R. Cocking (Eds.), *Cross-cultural roots of minority child de-velopment* (pp. 285–313). Hillsdale, NJ: Lawrence Erlbaum Associates.

Hofstede, G. H. (1980). *Culture's consequences: International differences in work-related values*. Beverly Hills, CA: Sage.

Hwang, K. K. (1987). Face and favor: The Chinese power game. *American Journal of Sociology, 92* (4), 944–974.

Lau, S. (1988). The value orientations of Chinese university students in Hong Kong. *International Journal of Psychology, 23*, 583–596.

Lieber, E. (1990). *The role of verbal feedback in the elicitation of learned helplessness.* Unpublished master's thesis, University of Illinois, Urbana–Champaign.

Lieber, E., Yang, K. S., & Lin, Y. C. (2000). An external orientation to the study of causal beliefs: Applications to Chinese populations and comparative research. *Journal of Cross-Cultural Psychology, 31* (2), 160–186.

Markus, H., & Kitayama, S. (1991). Culture and the self: Implications for cognition, emotion, and behavior. *Psychological Review, 98*, 224–251.

McClelland, D. C. (1961). *The achieving society*. Princeton, NJ: Van Nostrand.

McClelland, D. C., Atkinson, J. W., Clark, R. A., & Lowell, E. L. (1953). *The achieve-ment motive*. New York: Appleton-Century-Crofts.

Murray, H. A. (1943). *Thematic apperception test manual*. Cambridge, MA: Harvard University Press.

Nicholls, J. G. (1984). Achievement motivation: Conceptions of ability, subjective experience, task choice, and performance. *Psychological Review, 91*, 328–346.

Salili, F. (1994). Age, sex, and cultural differences in the meaning and dimensions of achievement. *Personality and Social Psychology Bulletin, 20* (6), 635–648.

Salili, F. (1995). Explaining Chinese students' motivation and achievement: A socio-cultural analysis. *Advances in Motivation and Achievement, 9*, 73–118.

Salili, F. (1996). Learning and motivation: An Asian perspective. *Psychology and De-veloping Societies, 8* (1), 55–81.

Stein, A. H., & Bailey, M. M. (1973). The socialization of achievement orientation in females. *Psychological Bulletin, 80* (5), 345–366.

Triandis, H. C. (1972). *The analysis of subjective culture*. New York: Wiley-Interscience.

Triandis, H. C. (1990). Cross-cultural studies of individualism and collectivism. In J. J. Berman (Ed.), *Nebraska symposium on motivation, 1989: Cross-cultural per-spectives* (pp. 41–133). Lincoln: University of Nebraska Press.

Weiner, B. (1985). An attributional theory of achievement motivation and emotion. *Psychological Review, 92* (4), 548–573.

Yang, K. S. (1986). Chinese personality and its change. In M. H. Bond (Ed.), *The psychol-ogy of the Chinese people* (pp. 106–170). Hong Kong: Chinese University Press.

Yang, K. S. (1995). Chinese social orientation: An integrative analysis. In T. Y. Lin, W. S. Tseng, & E. K. Yeh (Eds.), *Chinese societies and mental health* (pp. 19–39). Hong Kong: Oxford University Press.

Yang, K. S., & Yu, A. B. (1988, August 28–September 2). Social-oriented and indi-vidual-oriented achievement motivation: Conceptualization and measurement. Paper presented at the symposium on Chinese personality and social psychol-ogy, Twenty-Fourth International Congress of Psychology, Sydney, Australia.

Yu, A. B. (1996). Ultimate life concerns, self, and Chinese achievement motivation. In M. H. Bond (Ed.), *The handbook of Chinese psychology* (pp. 227–246). Hong Kong: Oxford University Press.

Yu, A. B., & Yang, K. S. (1994). The nature of achievement motivation in collectivist societies. In U. Kim, H. C. Triandis, C. Kagitcibasi, S. C. Choi, & G. Yoon (Eds.), *Individualism and collectivism: Theory, method, and applications* (pp. 239–250). Thousand Oaks, CA: Sage.

CHAPTER 8

The Impact of Collectivism and Situational Variations on the Motivation to Achieve in Singapore

Weining C. Chang and Lilian Quan

Since McClelland's seminal publication *The Achieving Society* (1961), achievement and achievement motivation in collectivist cultures have been an area of research fraught with conceptual confusion and contradictory findings (e.g., Sagie, Elizur, & Yamaguchi, 1996). Forty years after McClelland's original studies, researchers have now gained a better understanding of both the concept of culture as well as the concept of the motivation to achieve. Specifically, two lines of development are pertinent here: (1) a broader definition of collectivism as both a culture dimension and an individual difference construct—at both levels, the construct could be multidimensional (Triandis, 2000), and (2) a multidimensional conceptualization of the motivation to achieve construct that takes into consideration both task-oriented motives as well as social-ego-oriented motives that might be associated with the former (Spence, 1983). With these theoretical advances, researchers are now addressing both culture and achievement motivation in ways that take into consideration the multidimensional and multilevel nature of culture and psychological processes. Furthermore, it has been increasingly recognized that within different cultures, collectivism and individualism may operate differently (Sinha & Tripathi, 1994). In East Asian countries, these two dimensions are sometimes positively correlated with each other (see, e.g., Chan & Koh, 2000), suggesting that individualism and collectivism might be two separate but parallel constructs. It follows that collectivism and individualism might have different impacts on individual psychological variables, and these impacts have to be analyzed separately.[1]

These theoretical advances also lead to questions about some of the research practices used in culture and motivation studies: First of all, researchers often confuse the cultural level of analysis with the individual level of analysis. Second, drawing the conclusion that motive is higher in certain cultures and lower in certain other cultures requires the assumption that the construct is the same in structure and in meaning across cultures. Neither of these assumptions can be made across a large number of cultures (D'Andrade, 1992; Maehr & Nicholls, 1980; Spence, 1985). Third, the motivation to achieve has been treated as a trait, or a dispositional construct. Situational variations of the motive have been less attended to. These confounding practices must be addressed before the question as to whether collectivism has any effect on the motivation to achieve can be answered.

In this study focus is on identifying the relationship between individual differences in collectivism, termed allocentrism (Triandis, 2000), and the individual's motivation to achieve.[2] In other words, a within-culture design with the individual level of analysis was used. In line with the within-culture design, a measure of achievement motivation that has been extensively validated to incorporate the local meaning of achievement and the motivation behind it (Chang, Wong, Teo, & Fam, 1997) was chosen as the dependent variable. Addressing discussions on the trait-state variation of basic human psychological process (Mischel & Shoda, 1995), the fluctuations of motive in situations that involved different incentive structures were investigated.

The motivation to achieve may assume different meanings in different cultural communities, depending on the culture-specific meaning of achievement (Maehr & Nicholls, 1980). Within the collectivist context, achievement and achievement motivation tend be more socially oriented in their meanings and goals. Motives in the West tend to be associated with individually oriented meanings and goals (Yu & Yang, 1994). With the socially oriented meanings of achievement, the motivation to achieve may involve both task-oriented motives as well as socially or ego-oriented motives. This mixture of task-oriented and ego-oriented dimensions in the motivation to achieve construct was found to be the case in Singapore (Chang, Wong, & Teo, 2000). Owing to this difference in the meanings and goals for achievement, the relationship between collectivism and individuals' motivations to achieve may differ with the cultural context: In a low collectivist context, high individual allocentrism may be associated with low motivation to achieve; however in a high collectivist context, high allocentrism may be associated with high motivation to achieve.

MULTILEVEL ANALYSIS OF COLLECTIVISM

In Singapore, collectivism and individualism have been found to be positively correlated with each other (Chan & Koh, 2000). In other words, individuals who are high on collectivism may not necessarily have low individualism. If independence, which implies individualism, supports the motivation to achieve, as proposed by McClelland (1961), it does not necessarily follow that interdependence, a consequence of collectivism (Triandis, 2000) suppresses the development of this motive. Furthermore, individualism and collectivism do not exist in a vacuum, they coexist with other values and beliefs. Culture is multifaceted; the effect of one aspect of culture is embedded within the context of other aspects that are also present in the culture. Therefore, depending on the context, the same cultural variable may have differing effects on a given psychological construct. In the United States Rosen and D'Andrede (1959) found that parental emphasis on mastery promotes achievement motivation in children. This parental emphasis on mastery in white middle-class Protestant families—the cultural context in which most contemporary psychological studies have been conducted—often coincides with parental emphasis on individual independence. Recent studies of ethnic minorities in the United States have found that for Afro-Americans, a sense of solidarity with one's ethnic group is positively related to persistence in achievement-related tasks (Oyerman, Ager, & Grant, 1995). In Oyerman, Ager, and Grant's study, it was interdependence rather than independence that was positively correlated with the motivation to achieve. Could it then be that within the collectivist context, the individual's motivation to achieve is fostered and positively supported by a sense of belongingness (see, e.g., Ramirez & Price-Williams, 1976)? These studies point to the possibility that the relationship between achievement and collectivism depends on the context of a network of other variables in which the relationship takes place.

Singapore is a modern Confucian state (Tu, Hejtmanek, & Wachman, 1992) and has maintained some values traditionally considered Chinese. Chang and Wong (1998) found that highest among the values endorsed by Singaporeans is a cluster of intertwined values denoting industry and civic harmony. This value orientation constitutes the cultural context in which the motivation to achieve assumes its unique meaning and psychological significance. In Singapore, achievement is not only an individual endeavor, it is also relevant to the people who form the social network of the individual (Chang & Mohammed, 2000). It is therefore not surprising to find that in Singapore the motivation to achieve is positively correlated with the motivation for affiliation (Ang & Chang, 1999), in contrast to findings on the relationship in the West (Mehrabian, 1970). These findings suggest that individual collectivism in Singapore may not have a negative impact on the motivation to achieve.

COLLECTIVISM AND SITUATIONAL VARIATION

Taking a broader view of culture, Triandis (1995) proposed that researchers might look at collectivism as both an internalized belief toward a group, and a principle with which a society is organized. The second meaning of collectivism refers to it as a way of using the collective as a unit for social transaction and economic analysis. In other words, collectivism may be a way in which work and reward are organized and distributed in society. It is now maintained by most researchers (Triandis, 2000) that a society is not exclusively individualistic or collectivistic. Collectivist societies are those in which there are more situations that call for collectivist actions, while individualist societies are those in which there are more situations that call for individualist actions. A more sophisticated conceptualization of the relationship between collectivism and individualism and the motivation to achieve is therefore possible. Instead of asking whether achievement motivation develops in collectivist cultures, it is possible to ask whether achievement motivation is higher or lower when the group is the unit of analysis or when the individual is the unit of analysis. In other words, instead of analyzing the culture, analysis of the situations in which achievement motivation may be induced or activated is likely to produce more relevant results.

Disposition and Situational Interactions
Related to the Motivation to Achieve

In this study, situations are used to study the variation in the motivation to achieve. Since the first achievement motivation study, achievement motives have been considered a trait of the individual; that is, individuals vary from each other in terms of their dispositional levels of achievement motivation. However, for a given individual, motivation can be activated or deactivated by the situation. In other words, motivation can be raised or lowered by perceived incentives in the situation (McClellend, 1953). To test this proposition, this study addressed the following questions: Can situational variables in work organization and reward distribution bring about changes in the motivation to achieve? Do people of high or low collectivism respond to different situational cues in activating motivation?

Four styles of work–reward structure commonly applied in school-related work in Singapore have been identified: teamwork–team reward, individual work–individual reward, teamwork–individual reward, and individual work–team reward. In other words, though Singapore is considered collectivist in general (Hofstede, 1980), schoolwork in Singapore is not always a team effort. Within each class, grades are distributed according to individual performance. More important, an individual's grade is assessed on the relative standing of the student's performance against members in the cohort. In addition to individual grades, rewards can be in the form of a team or class prize awarded to the entire class. Some times in group projects, one individual may do the work for the entire group, though the prize is given to the whole group. In other occasions, individuals may work together as a group to complete a project, knowing that only one member of the team may be given the reward, such as in class production of drama where the leading man or woman may be identified to receive the praise or blame for the entire cast. Therefore, both work organization and reward distribution can be either group-based or individual-based in Singapore. Scenarios were developed to simulate each of these realistic work and reward practices in the empirical study presented later.

MULTIDIMENSIONS OF
THE MOTIVATION TO ACHIEVE

The motivation to achieve has been found to incorporate both task-related motives (Murray, 1938; White, 1959), as well as the ego–socially-related motives, such as competitiveness (Chang, Wong, & Teo, 2000). In Singapore, the motivation to achieve is also a mixture of task- and ego-related motives. Similarities and differences have been found between Singaporean's and American's conceptualization and manifestation of the motivation to achieve (Chang & Mohammed, 2000). We modified an extensively validated scale, the Work and Family Orientation Scale (Spence, 1983) to reflect the conceptualization and manifestation of the motivation to achieve in Singapore more validly. This new scale was labeled the Attitude Toward Work (ATW) (see Appendix 1) scale; it was used in this study to measure the general need for achievement (nAch).[3] The dimensions of ATW can be further grouped into the task-related dimensions: Work Ethics, Mastery, and Meeting Challenges; and the socially related dimension, Competitiveness.

Contemporary research in the motivation to achieve takes into consideration this multidimensional conceptualization of the concept (Baron & Harachiewicz, 2001). The task versus social dichotomy in the basic motivation to achieve has also been investigated by Harackiewicz, Barron, Lehto, Carter, and Elliot (1997). Their studies indicated that task-related motives to achieve and socially-related motives to achieve produce different consequences. It would be logical to assume that the task-related dimensions and the social-related dimension of achievement motivation might be activated by different antecedents. These antecedents would include both cultural variables and situational variables.

THIS STUDY

With reference to the recent advances in understanding of collectivism and the motivation to achieve, this study asks the following research questions: Focusing on the individual level of analysis, does high or low allocentrism affect an individual's basic motivation to achieve? Do situational variations in task or reward distribution affect an individual's achievement motivation? We postulate the following hypotheses: (1) Within the context of Singapore, contrary to the McClellend–Winterbottom hypothesis regarding individual levels of collectivism allocentrism predict the motivation to achieve. However, the effect of allocentrism differs from one dimension of the ATW to another. Among the different dimensions, people with high collectivism show higher levels of the work ethic and lower levels of competitiveness. (2) The motivation of

Singaporeans to achieve is affected by manipulation of the different ways in which work and reward are organized. Situational variables that involve work organization and reward distribution influence the motivation with respect to the work ethic and competitiveness. We hypothesized that the work ethic would be higher when there is a clear contingency between work and reward. As suggested by the classical Skinnerian paradigm, behavior–reward contingency leads to higher action potential and motivation for the behavior. (3) Individual or group-based work organization and reward distribution influence the competitiveness of the individual. (4) There is an interaction effect between work–reward organization and allocentrism: People with lower allocentrism are more affected by the unit of analysis used in work and reward distribution than people with higher allocentrism.

No specific hypotheses were made concerning the dimension of meeting challenges or the dimension of mastery. The concept of mastery is related to intrinsic interest in the task (Deci, 1975). Since the task itself was not varied, but only the situational context of the task changed, the mastery dimension is not expected to vary with the work–reward structures. Similarly, the amount of uncertainty involved in the task was not varied, so no specific hypotheses about the effect of situations on the dimension of meeting challenges were made.

Method

Study Design

A two (allocentrism) × four (individual work–individual reward, group work–group reward, individual work–group reward, and group work–individual reward) mixed factorial design was used. Allocentrism was the between-subject independent variable. Scenarios depicting different work–reward organizations were the within-subject factor.

Participants

A randomized stratified sampling was conducted in a neighborhood secondary school in Singapore to select a sample that matched the ethnic composition of Singapore according to national statistics. Eighty students were sampled (forty males and forty females, sixty-two Chinese, eleven Malays, and seven Indians). The students ages ranged from 14 to 17 years old, with a mean age of 15.1. Based on their scores on the Singapore Collectivism scale (Singh & Vasoo, 1994) they were grouped, using median split, into high allocentrist and low allocentrist groups.

Instruments

Two scales were used: (1) the Singapore Collectivism scale (Singh & Vasoo, 1994), a measure that specifically addresses the manifestation of collectivism in Singapore, and (2) the Attitude Toward Work scale, a measure of the motivation to achieve. Internal reliability of each measure was assessed prior to the study using a group of university students in Singapore. The internal reliability of the Singapore Collectivism scale was found to be 0.90, and the internal reliability of the Attitude Toward Work scale was found to be 0.81 for the entire scale, and 0.62 for Mastery 1–Quality of Work, 0.71 for Mastery 2–Meeting Challenges, 0.70 for Work Ethics, and 0.77 for Competitiveness. All were within the acceptable range. In addition, scenarios were developed to simulate realistic work and reward practices.

Procedure

The experiment was conducted in a classroom on the participants campus during a recess period. Each participant read a booklet containing all four conditions. After reading each condition, the participants rated themselves on the Attitude Toward Work scale. The order of presentation of the four scenarios was counterbalanced across the participants to control for order effect. The scenarios are presented in Appendix 2.

Results

Descriptive statistics of the study are presented in Table 8.1.

Effects of Allocentrism

We took the average of the Attitude Toward Work measure across the four situations as the trait or individual difference measure of the motivation to achieve, designated as nAch. The means and standard deviations for the high and low collectivists are presented in Table 8.1. High and low allocentrics differed marginally on their overall nAch. The mean of high allocentrics was 3.65; the mean of low allocentrics was 3.51, $F(1,78) = 1.90$, $p = 0.06$. High allocentrics showed a slightly higher motivation to achieve than low allocentrics.

As hypothesized, allocentrism had different effects on different dimensions of the motivation to achieve. The main effect was significant for mastery, $F(1, 78) = 9.95$, $p < 0.005$, and meeting challenges, $F(1, 78) = 4.38$, $p < 0.05$; but not significant on competitiveness, $F(1, 78) = 0.78$, $p > 0.05$, or work ethic, $F(1, 78) = 2.79$, $p > 0.05$. High allocentrics scored higher on task-related dimensions of the ATW, although lower on the competitiveness dimension than the low allocentrics.

Attitude Toward Work—nAch

Different work–reward organizations were found to affect the overall motivation to achieve, $F(3, 76) = 3.67$, $p < 0.05$. In descending order, the mean for individual work–individual reward was 3.63, for group work–group reward was 3.58, for group work–individual reward, 3.57, and for individual work–

Table 8.1
Means and Standard Deviations of Competitiveness, Mastery, Meeting Challenges, Work Ethics, and nAch

	Work-Reward Distribution			
	IW-IR	GW-IR	IW-GR	GW-GR
Low Allocentrics				
Competitiveness	3.17 (.90)	3.09 (.88)	3.00 (.86)	3.05 (.87)
Mastery	4.04 (.45)	4.01 (.44)	4.02 (.40)	4.02 (.44)
Meeting Challenges	3.12 (.57)	3.09 (.65)	3.03 (.67)	3.10 (.56)
Work Ethics	3.92 (.69)	3.90 (.64)	3.72 (.71)	3.89 (.57)
nAch	3.57 (.41)	3.52 (.43)	3.44 (.40)	3.51 (.35)
High Allocentrics				
Competitiveness	2.93 (.82)	2.93 (.78)	2.93 (.84)	2.90 (.77)
Mastery	4.35 (.42)	4.31 (.47)	4.33 (.43)	4.26 (.50)
Meeting Challenges	3.38 (.49)	3.28 (.53)	3.31 (.52)	3.32 (.50)
Work Ethics	4.10 (.52)	3.98 (.56)	4.01 (.49)	4.15 (.51)
nAch	3.69 (.32)	3.62 (.36)	3.64 (.33)	3.66 (.31)

Key: IW = individual work; IR = individual reward; GW = group work; GR = group reward.

group reward, 3.54 (see Figure 8.1). The interaction effect between allocentrism and work–reward organization was small and did not reach statistical significance, $F(3, 76) = 1.20, p > 0.05$.

Since different effects were found on different dimensions of the motivation to achieve, these results are presented separately for each dimension (see Figure 8.2).

Competitiveness

Though there was no overall effect across the four work–reward conditions on competitiveness, $F(3, 76) = 1.31, p > 0.05$, comparisons across individual cells revealed interesting differences. Effect of individual versus group reward distribution was found in competitiveness $F(1, 78) = 6.41, p < 0.05$. When reward was

Figure 8.1
Means of nAch on Work–Reward Distribution

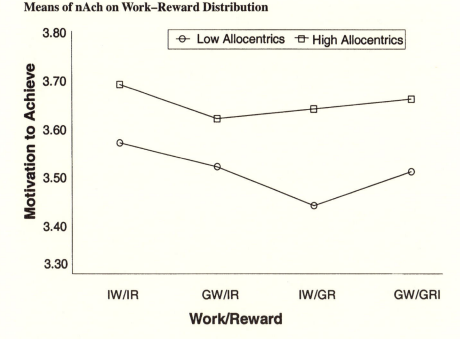

distributed on an individual basis, competitiveness was higher, $M = 3.03$. When reward was distributed on a group basis, competitiveness was lower, $M = 2.97$. No other comparisons were significant. There was no interaction effect between allocentrism and work–reward organizations, $F(3, 76) = 0.94, p > 0.05$.

The Work Ethic

There was an overall effect of work–reward distribution on the work ethic, $F(3, 76) = 4.60, p < 0.01$. Interaction effect between allocentrism and work–reward distribution was not significant, $F(3, 76) = 2.16, p > 0.05$. As with competitiveness, further investigation suggested that when reward and work are consistent, that is, group work–group reward and individual work–individual reward, the work ethic is higher ($M = 4.0$). When there is inconsistency, the work ethic is lower ($M = 3.85$), $F(1, 78) = 11.42, p < 0.001$.

Mastery and Meeting Challenges

As predicted, no significant situational effects were found, $F(3, 76) = 1.39$, $p > 0.05$. Neither were any situation-allocentrism interaction effects found on meeting challenges, $F(3, 76) = 1.40, p > 0.05$.

Figure 8.2
Means of Competitiveness, Mastery, Meeting Challenges, and Work Ethics on Work–Reward Distribution

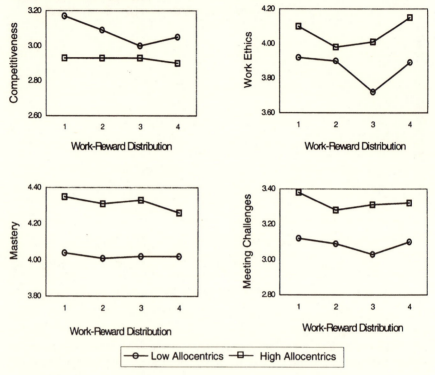

Key: 1 = individual work–individual reward; 2 = group work–individual reward; 3 = individual work–group reward; 4 = group work–group reward.

No significant situation effects were found on mastery, $F(3, 76) = 1.10, p > 0.05$, and no significant allocentrism and situation interaction effect was found either, $F(3, 76) = 0.39, p > 0.05$.

Discussion

This study addresses the question of whether collectivism matters in an individual's motivation to achieve. The answer has long eluded cross-cultural researchers. This study used a cultural psychology approach by treating collectivism as a within-culture variable. Collectivism was operationalized in two ways: (1) as allocentrism, an individual difference variable, and (2) as a situational variable, which varied as the unit of analyses in work–reward organization. Using this approach, the findings should also be interpreted by taking into consideration the general cultural context in which the relationship unfolded.

Within the collectivist culture of Singapore, individuals with high allocentrism showed higher overall motivation to achieve. Differences found in the various dimensions of motive were small. Especially where the work ethic and competitiveness were concerned, the differences did not reach statistical significance. In addition, with the exception of competitiveness on which high allocentrists scored lower than low allocentrists, the high allocentrists scored higher on all dimensions of the motive to achieve. These results cannot be interpreted without taking into consideration the general value orientation of the Confucian cultural context, in which both individual achievement and collectivism are highly valued (Chang & Wong, 1998). The finding that high allocentrists scored higher on achievement motivation can be seen as reflecting the culture's dual emphasis. Within this context, it is also logical to expect that the competitiveness dimension would be lower in those with high allocentrism. In other words, the relationship between collectivism and achievement motivation might be context dependent. In other collectivist cultures in which individual mastery and competence are not emphasized, individual differences in allocentirsm may be unrelated to achievement motivation.

Fiske (1992) suggested that collectivism and individualism are related to how resources are distributed in a society. Applying this theoretical conceptualization of collectivism, we tested the effect of four scenarios of individual versus group emphasis in work and reward distribution. For the overall level of the motivation to achieve, results suggested that individual-based work and rewards seem to be the most effective in activating the motivation to achieve, followed by group-based work and rewards. Inconsistency in work organization and reward distribution seem to be the least motivating. Even within a highly collectivist society such as Singapore, individual-based work and rewards are still the most motivating.

The results revealed that the two task-related dimensions—mastery and meeting challenges—were not affected by the work and reward distribution. This finding may suggest that these two dimensions might be the intrinsic motivation proposed by Deci (1975). They are motives somewhat immune to variation in work and reward structure.

We found that the work ethic, a dimension related to an individual's effort expenditure, is highly susceptible to variations in the incentive structure. Specifically, when there is high contingency between work and reward, the work ethic was high. When the contingency was inconsistent, the work ethic was low. This result can be easily explained in terms of the operant conditioning principle, which suggests high contingencies between behavior and reward lead to an increase in the rewarded behavior. This principle seems to apply to both high and low collectivists somewhat equally.

Competitiveness was found to vary with reward distribution but not work organization. When reward was given on an individual basis, competitiveness was high. When given on the group basis competitiveness was low. This result seems to be self-explanatory. Individuals compete when there is incentive to compete. They compete when only one member of the group could emerge to receive the recognition and reward. Outperforming the others, breaking out from the pack, becomes necessary for the reward in these situations. Based on this finding, the paradoxical phenomenon of the competitive student often observed in East Asian schools can be explained. If students are graded according to their relative standing in the class, and if opportunities for career placement (reward) are based on school grades, even students in the most collectivist societies become highly competitive. Many Confucian societies practice meritocracy in performance evaluation and reward distribution. Meritocracy in many of these Confucian societies is based on individual performance evaluation. No wonder Asian students are highly competitive in their achievement pursuits.

In summary, the question of whether collectivism has an effect on the motivation to achieve can be answered with the current conceptual advances. With a finer differentiation of the motivation to achieve and a broader definition of collectivism, this study has identified how the dimensions of achievement motivation are differentially related to collectivism. In addition, the relationships seem to be context dependent. An individual's motivations to achieve is positively predicted by the individual's allocentrism in Singapore, a collectivist society. Variations in the dimensions of the motive were related to situational variations in the unit of analysis. This last finding reinforces a current trend in seeing culture in situations whereby the traditional cultural differences can sometime be seen in different situations within the same cultural community (Gardner, Gabriel, & Lee, 1999; Hong, Morris, Chiu, & Benet-Martinez, 2001).

APPENDIX 1

Scale Items of the Attitude Toward Work Scale

Competitiveness

10. I will not be satisfied with good performance unless I perform better than others.
14. It is important to me to perform better than others on a task.
16. It annoys me when other people perform better than I do.
17. I feel bad when I do not outperform others even if I did a good job.
19. I feel winning is important in life.
22. I work harder when I am in competition with others.

Mastery

9. I find satisfaction in exceeding my past performance even if I do not outperform others.
13. When I am engaged in a task I like to find the most efficient ways to get the job done.

15. I take pride in a job well done.
21. I feel good when I complete a task that requires a high level of skills.
23. I like to work on problems that will really make me learn.
24. I like to work in situations where there are obstacles to overcome in order to reach a higher goal.

Meeting Challenges

1. It excites me to work on a new and unfamiliar task.
3. I like to try new and innovative projects that will really test my efforts.
5. I would rather do a job with high uncertainty of outcome and high reward than a secure job with low reward.
8. I avoid projects with uncertainty of success.
12. I more often attempt difficult tasks that I am not sure I can do than easier ones I believe I can do.
20. I would rather do something at which I feel confident and relaxed than something which is challenging and difficult.

Work Ethics

1. I like to work.
2. I feel good when I am working.
6. It is bad to be idle.
7. Once I undertake a task I persist.
11. I take pride in working hard.
18. I believe hard work is the key to success.

APPENDIX 2

Group Versus Individual Work and Reward Scenarios

Group Work and Group Reward

Your teacher has just given the class a project to do. The project is to be done in groups. The project topic can be anything of your group's choice. Only one group with the best project performance will be awarded. In addition, each member of the group with the best project will get a Swatch watch.

Individual Work and Individual Reward

Your teacher has just given the class a project to do. The project topic can be anything of your choice. Only one student with the best project will be awarded for good performance. In addition, the student with the best project will get a Swatch watch.

Group Work and Individual Reward

Your teacher has just given the class a project to do. The project is to be done in groups. The project topic can be anything of your group's choice. Though it is a group project, individual performance is assessed. Only one student with the best performance will be awarded with a distinction for good performance. In addition, the student with the best performance will get a Swatch watch.

Individual Work and Group Reward

Your teacher has just given the class a project to do and divided the class into small groups. Each student is to work on one part of a project alone. Members of the group will then put the parts together to complete the project. The entire project will then be assessed. Only the group with the best project will be awarded for good performance. In addition, each member of the group with the best overall performance will get a Swatch watch.

NOTES

1. This chapter was presented at the Third International Conference of the Asian Association for Social Psychology, August 4–6, 1999, Academia Sinica, Nankang, Taiwan.

2. Preparation for this chapter was partially supported by the National University of Singapore, Faculty of Arts and Social Sciences, Faculty Research Grant RP 390006 given to the first author.

3. We use the conventional abbreviated form, nAch (Murray, 1938), for achievement motivation, to indicate the overall or scale score of the entire scale of the Attitude Toward Work.

REFERENCES

Ang, R., & Chang, W. C. (1999) Achievement and affiliative motivation in a collective context. *Journal of Social Psychology, 139* (4), 527–529.

Barron, K. E., & Harachiewicz, J. M. (2001). Achievement goals and optimal motivation: Testing multiple goal models. *Journal of Personality and Social Psychology, 80* (5), 706–721.

Chan, P. U., & Koh, J.B.K. (2000). Individualism and collectivism in Singapore. *Asian Psychologist, 2* (1), 15.

Chang, W. C. (2001, February 22–24). *A cultural model of achievement and achievement motivation.* Paper presented at the Thirtieth Annual Conference of the Cross-Cultural Research Association, San Diego, CA.

Chang, W. C., & Mohammed, B. (2000) What makes Chuming learn: Achievement motivation and goals in a secondary school English class in Singapore. In *Work values and organizational behavior toward the new millennium* (pp. 71–76). Jerusalem: Bar-Ilan University, School of Management.

Chang, W. C., & Wong, W. K. (1998). Rational traditionalism: Chinese values in Singapore. In H. Lim & R. Singh (Eds.), *Values and development: A multidisciplinary approach with some comparative studies* (pp. 295–308). Singapore: Center for Advanced Studies, National University of Singapore.

Chang, W. C., Wong, W. K., & Teo, G. (2000) Individual-oriented and social-social oriented achievement motivation of Singaporean Chinese. Special issue on Chinese achievement motivation. *Journal of Psychology in Chinese Societies, 1* (2), 39–63.

Chang, W. C., Wong, W. K., Teo, G., & Fam, A. (1997). Achievement motivation in Singapore: In search of a transcultural construct. *Personality and Individual Differences, 23* (5), 885–859.

D'Andrade, R. G. (1992). Schemas and motivation. In R. G. D'Andrade & C. Strauss (Eds.), *Human motives and cultural models* (pp. 23–44). Cambridge: Cambridge University Press.

Deci, E. L. (1975). *Intrinsic motivation*. New York: Plenum Press.

Fiske, A. P. (1992). The four elementary forms of sociality: Framework for a unified theory of social relations. *Psychological Review, 99*, 689–723.

Gardner, W. L., Gabriel, S., & Lee, A. Y. (1999). "I" value freedom, but "we" value relationships: Self-construal priming mirrors cultural differences in judgment. *Psychological Science, 10* (4), 321–326.

Harackiewicz, J., Barron, K. E., Carter, S. M., Lehto, A. T., & Elliot, A. J. (1997). Predictors and consequences of achievement goals in the college classroom: Maintaining interest and making the grade. *Journal of Personality and Social Psychology, 73* (6), 1284–1295.

Hofstede, G. (1980). *Culture's consequences*. Thousand Oaks, CA: Sage.

Hong, Y. Y., Morris, M. W., Chiu, C., & Benet-Martinez, V. (2001). Multicultural minds: A dynamic constructivist approach to culture and cognition. *American Psychologist, 55* (7), 709–720.

Maehr, M. L., & Nicholls, J. G. (1980). Culture and achievement motivation: A second look. In N. Warren (Ed.), *Studies in crosscultural psychology* (vol. 2, pp. 221–267). New York: Academic Press.

McClelland, D. C. (1953). *The achievement motive*. New York: Appleton-Century-Crofts.

McClelland, D. C. (1961). *The achieving society*. Princeton, NJ: Van Nostrand.

Mehrabian, A. (1970). Questionnaire measures of affiliative tendency and sentitivity to rejection. *Educational and Psychological Measurement, 30*, 417–428.

Mischel, W., & Shoda, Y. (1995). A cognitive-affective system theory of personality: Reconceptualizing situations, dispositions, dynamics, and invariance in personality structure. *Psychological Review, 102* (2), 246–268.

Murray, H. A. (1938). *Explorations in personality: A clinical and experimental study of fifty men of college age*. New York: Oxford University Press.

Oyerman, D., Ager, J., & Grant, L. (1995). A socially contextualized model of African American identity: Possible selves and school persistence. *Journal of Personality and Social Psychology, 69* (6), 1216–1232.

Ramirez, M., III, & Price-Williams, D. R. (1976). Achievement motivation in children of three ethnic groups in the United States. *Journal of Cross-Cultural Psychology, 7*, 29–69.

Rosen, B. C., & D'Andrede, R. (1959). The psychosocial origins of achievement motivation. *Sociometry, 22*, 185–218.

Sagie, A., Elizur, D., & Yamaguchi, N. (1996). The structure and strength of achievement motivation: A cross-cultural comparison. *Journal of Organizational Behavior, 17,* 431–444.

Singh, R., & Vasoo, S. (1994). *Singapore collectivism scale.* Working paper, Department of Social Work and Psychology, National University of Singapore.

Sinha, D., & Tripathi, R. C. (1994). Individualism in a collectivist culture: A case of coexistence of opposites. In U. Kim, H. C. Triandis, C. Kagitcibasi, S. C. Choi, & G. Yoong (Eds.), *Individualism and collectivism: Theory, method, and applications* (pp. 123–136). Newbury Park, CA: Sage.

Spence, J. T. (1983). *Achievement related motives and behaviors.* San Francisco: W. H. Freeman.

Spence, J. T. (1985). Achievement American style. *American Psychologist, 40* (12), 1285–1295.

Triandis, H. C. (1995). *Individualism and collectivism.* Boulder, CO: Westview Press.

Triandis, H. C. (2000). Recent development in the study of collectivism and individualism. *Asian Psychologist, 2* (1), 10–14.

Tu, W., Hejtmanek, M., & Wachman, A. (Eds.). (1992). *The Confucian world observed: A contemporary discussion of Confucian humanism in East Asia.* Honolulu, HI: Program for Cultural Studies, East–West Center.

White, R. (1959). Motivation reconsidered: The concept of competence. *Psychological Review, 66,* 297–323.

Yu, A. B., & Yang, K. S. (1994). The nature of achievement motivation on collectivistic societies. In U. Kim, H. C. Triandis, C. Kagitcibasi, S. C. Choi, & G. Yoon (Eds.), *Individualism and collectivism: Theory, method, and applications* (pp. 239–251). Newbury Park, CA: Sage.

CHAPTER 9

An Indigenous Analysis of Success Attribution: Comparison of Korean Students and Adults

Uichol Kim and Young-Shin Park

The twentieth century has often been called the *Pacific Era* to characterize the phenomenal achievements in economics, education, and nation building. At the turn of this century, however, Asian societies were far behind in science and technology, lacking in educational, social, economic, and political infrastructure, and experiencing national turmoil. Despite limited natural resources, East Asian governments and businesses were able to design appropriate educational, political, and economic policies to kinetically transform latent human resources into powerful economies. In the Pacific region, South Korea (henceforth abbreviated as Korea) emerged from the devastation of the Japanese colonial rule and Korean War to become one of the fastest growing economies in the world.

At the beginning of the 1960s, Korea had all the problems of a resource-poor, low-income, underdeveloped nation. The vast majority of people were dependent on agricultural products produced on scarce farmland. The literacy rate and educational level was one of the lowest in the world. Korea's per capita gross product in 1961 stood at a meagre $82, and it was considered one of the poorest nations in the world. From 1965, however, Korea experienced a phenomenal transformation in the economic, social, and political sectors. The Korean economy has been dramatically transformed, with the economy growing at an average annual rate of over 8%. The per capita GNP increased to $1,640 by 1981. By 1997, the per capita GNP had increased to $10,000, and

Korea joined the elite circle of the Organization of Economic Cooperation and Development.

The economic miracle in Korea is closely tied to the educational aspiration and investment made by adolescents and parents. Currently, the literacy rate is over 97%, one of the highest in the world. By 1983, Korea had the highest percentage of adolescents wishing to obtain a university degree and in terms of Korean parents' desired educational level for their children, the vast majority wanted their children to at least graduate from university and they were willing to provide the necessary financial and social support for their children (Kim & Park, 2000).

The purpose of this chapter is to investigate the nature and process of achievement as perceived by a cross-section of Korean participants: students, teachers, salaried employees, and housewives. The first part of this chapter briefly reviews the attribution literature and its limitations. The second section outlines the indigenous psychologies approach. The third section provides a conceptual framework for understanding educational and occupational achievement in Korea by focusing on three major influencing factors: (1) socialization and the role of parents, (2) the role of schools and teachers, and (3) organization and corporate culture. The fourth section reviews an empirical study conducted by the authors that explores the nature of achievement in Korea. The final part of this chapter discusses the type of structural reforms and transformations that are necessary for Korean society to become an active contributor and leader in the global community.

ACHIEVEMENT AND ATTRIBUTION

Current research on attribution can be traced to the seminal work by Heider (1958). Heider pointed out that people attempt to make sense of their world by making attributions about the cause of a certain outcome. He made a distinction between personal and situational causes. Heider further divided the personal and situational causal attribution into the following four categories using the two dimensions of internality–externality and stability: ability, effort, task difficulty, and luck. Ability is stated to be an internal stable factor, while effort is believed to be an internal unstable factor. Luck is believed to be an external unstable factor, while task difficulty is believed to be an external stable factor.

Nisbett and Ross (1980) found that subjects in the United States are more likely to attribute success to personal ability and failure to situational factors; this phenomenon has been labeled as "self-serving bias." In an analysis of Chinese culture, however, Wan and Bond (1982) found the opposite pattern: a modesty or self-effacing bias. Muramoto, Yamaguchi, and Kim (in press) replicated the self-serving bias in the United States, but found self-effacing bias in Japan and Korea. They found that in the United States those individuals who are self-serving are viewed as competent, while self-effacing persons are viewed as less competent. In Japan and Korea, the opposite results were obtained. Subjects did not take the self-effacing attribution at face value, but concluded that the self-effacing individuals were actually very competent. These studies point out the limitations of attribution studies conducted in the United States, especially those focused on self-serving bias and fundamental attribution error (Park & Kim, 1997, 1998, 1999).

Bandura (1997) pointed out the limitation of Heider (1958) and Weiner's (1986) conceptualization. He indicated the need to distinguish between innate ability and acquired ability. He found that people believe that ability can be incrementally increased through hard work, perseverance, and efficacy belief. Many athletes, musicians, and scholars have shown that achievements in athletic, artistic, and scholarly arenas are a combination of innate ability and ability acquired through incremental skill development.

Levenson (1974) argued that powerful others could play an important role in determining the success and failure of an outcome. Park and Kim (1997) further pointed out the need to distinguish powerful others into ingroup or outgroup members. This distinction is especially important in collectivistic societies (Hofstede, 1991; Kim, 1994). Moreover, Park and Kim (1997) note that task difficulty cannot be considered to be a stable factor since it is hard to predict the difficulty of the task before it is actually given to the respondents. They note that rather than task difficulty, fate or destiny is a better stable external factor.

Integrating these refinements, the first author developed six types of attributional belief based on the 2 × 3 categorization (i.e., stable versus unstable, and internal, mediated, and external) (see Table 9.1). Innate ability is a stable internal factor, while effort is an unstable external factor. Fate is a stable internal factor, while luck is an unstable external factor. Ingroup support is a relatively stable mediated factor, while outgroup influence is an unstable mediated factor. Based on this conceptualization, the first author developed a seventy-two-item attributional scale and collected data in a series of studies conducted with samples of Korean students and adults. The results indicate that contrary to previous conceptualizations, ability loaded with other external factors such as fate, luck, outgroup influence, and ingroup support. Effort loaded on a separate factor with achievement motivation, academic grade, and life

Table 9.1
Six Attributional Styles

	Internal	Mediated	External
Stable	Innate ability	Ingroup support	Fate
Unstable	Effort	Outgroup influence	Luck

satisfaction (Park & Kim, 1997, 1998, 1999). These results challenge previous conceptualizations, which may not accurately reflect indigenous beliefs and attributional styles. The contradiction highlights the need for an indigenous psychologies approach that can better capture how people think, feel, behave, and make sense of their physical and social world (Kim, 1999, 2000).

Indigenous Psychologies Approach

The indigenous psychologies approach advocates examining the knowledge, skills, and beliefs people have about themselves, and studying these aspects in their natural contexts. It represents a bottom-up approach in which the goal of psychology is to understand how people function in their natural context and to examine how they interact with their natural and human world. It recognizes that human psychology is complex, dynamic, and generative. It advocates a transactional model of human functioning that recognizes the importance of agency, meaning, intention, and goals (Kim, 1999). Epistemology, theories, concepts, and methods must be developed to correspond with psychological phenomena (Kim, 1999; Kim, Park, & Park, 1999). The goal is not to abandon science, objectivity, experimental method, and a search for universals, but to create a science that is firmly grounded in the descriptive understanding of human beings. The goal is to create a more rigorous, systematic, universal science that can be theoretically and empirically verified, rather than naively assumed.

Molding lay knowledge into institutionalized psychological theories is an example of the external imposition that can distort understanding of psychological phenomena. For example, Heider (1958) pointed out, "the ordinary person has a great and profound understanding of himself and of other people which, though unformulated or vaguely conceived, enables him to interact in more or less adaptive ways" (p. 2). Based on Heider's preliminary work, J. Rotter developed his theory of locus of control and B. Weiner developed his attribution theory (Hewstone, 1989). These theories are, however, far removed from ordinary people's conception of attribution and control. More important, they possess low internal and external validity (Bandura, 1997; Park & Kim, 1997, 1998, 1999). The main problem with these approaches is that they have eliminated the influence of context and agency, which are central to understanding people's conceptions of control and belief systems (Bandura, 1997; Park & Kim, 1997, 1998, 1999). Kim, Park, and Park (2000) contend that current psychological theories represent psychologists' conceptions, interpretations, and explanations rather than an accurate representation of human psychology. In other words, current psychological knowledge can be described as the psychology of psychologists, and not the psychology of the lay public (Harré, 1999; Koch & Leary, 1985).

In the indigenous psychologies approach, concepts and methods are developed internally, and indigenous information is considered to be a primary source of knowledge (Kim, 1999). The indigenous psychologies approach recognizes the existence of two types of knowledge: analytical, semantic, and declarative knowledge on the one hand, and phenomenological, episodic, and procedural knowledge on the other. Analytical, semantic, and declarative knowledge represent information based on objective, impartial, third-person analysis. Phenomenological, episodic, and procedural knowledge represent the subjective, first person experience. For example, adult native English speakers can freely express their thoughts in English (i.e., procedural knowledge), but may not know the grammatical syntax or structure of the spoken words (i.e., semantic knowledge). In other words, the person knows how to produce the sentences, but may lack the ability to describe them analytically. This situation occurs because "description of the grammar of a word is of no use in everyday life; only rarely do we pick up the use of a word by having its use described to us; and although we are trained or encouraged to master the use of the word, we are not taught to describe it" (Ludwig Wittgenstein, in Budd, 1989, pp. 4–5). Wittgenstein pointed out that "the meaning of a word is its use in the language" and not in the description of the word (Budd, 1989, p. 21). In everyday life, people may know how to perform certain actions, but may not have the analytical ability to describe how they were done.

Analytical knowledge, like grammar, is taught as a part of formal education in most cultures. For example, a mother can raise a child efficaciously, but she may lack the analytical ability to describe how it was done. In contrast, a developmental psychologist can analyze and document successful mothering skills, but she may lack the procedural skills in implementing that knowledge in raising her own child. The task of indigenous psychologists is to translate the first person phenomenological, episodic, and procedural experience into analytical, semantic, and declarative knowledge.

Another important aspect of the indigenous psychologies approach is the separation of different levels of analysis: physiological, psychological, and cultural. Although all actions must have a physiological or neurological basis, behavioral explanations cannot be reduced to that level. Our physiology and genetics can be reduced to four basic atoms (carbon, nitrogen, hydrogen, and oxygen) that we share with all other organic life forms. This information does not help us to understand, predict, and manage human behavior. Also, the important distinction between life and death cannot be defined through genetics, since the genetic makeup of a person who has just died is the same as when the person was alive. Athletic, artistic, and scientific feats cannot be reduced to physiological, neurological, or genetic levels. Harré and Gillet (1994) pointed out that "the brain, for any individual human being, is the repository of meaning in that it serves as the physical medium in which mental content is realized and plays a part in the discursive activities of individuals" (p. 81).

Finally, characteristics of collective entities, such as groups, societies, and cultures are emergent properties that cannot be reduced to the mere sum of individual characteristics. Culture, language, philosophy, and science are products of collective human effort. The relationship between an individual and a group needs to be viewed as a dynamic, interactive system of mutual influence. Culture is defined as a "rubric of pattern variables" and represents a "collective utilization of natural and human resources to achieve desired outcomes" (Kim, 1999).

To understand the educational and economic achievements of Korean students and adults and their attributional beliefs, it is important to first examine the cultural context of these achievements. Second, it is important to examine important factors that have led to such achievements.

EDUCATIONAL AND ECONOMIC ACHIEVEMENT: THE KOREAN CONTEXT

The key to understanding the educational and economic achievement of modern Korea lies in understanding the influence of Confucianism (Kim, 1998). Although Korea shares the Confucian heritage with other East Asian societies, Confucianism became indigenized, being modified by the ecological, social, and political conditions in Korea.

Confucianism was adopted in Korea about two thousand years ago. At the early stage, the influence of Confucian philosophy was limited to political and academic spheres. In 1392, when the Yi Dynasty was newly established, neo-Confucianism was chosen as the state's guiding philosophy, influencing not only scholarship and politics, but also all aspects of individual and social life, especially the educational system.

With the adoption of the neo-Confucian political system, individuals of merit were selected through regional examinations. Successful applicants were eligible to compete in the civil service examination (*kwago*). Those candidates who successfully passed the national examination were given an official position as a government, military, or local official. In return for their government services, they were given a tract of land from which they could acquire a stable income. The land grant lasted for three generations. Thus, in order for the family members to maintain their gentry status, by the third generation a descendant of the family had to pass another civil service examination.

With the adoption of neo-Confucianism, economic, military, and political power became centralized and success on the civil service examination became the most viable access to power. Success on the civil service examination was an indication of knowledge, wisdom, and moral integrity. Moreover, those who passed were provided with social, economic, and political power. Educational success not only benefited the individuals, but also their family members and succeeding generations and soon it became a vehicle of fulfilling one's filial piety. Since education was the most viable means of social mobility and recognition and an indicator of moral superiority, education became not only a means to an end, but an end in itself.

The neo-Confucian stronghold on the Korean educational, economic, and political system was maintained until the late nineteenth century. With Western encroachment and colonization of East Asia, Korea attempted to maintain its independence by curtailing all Western influences and by reifying its staunch support of neo-Confucian ideals. As a result, Korea became known as the "hermit kingdom" by the end of the nineteenth century (Lee, 1984).

The enlightenment movement (*kyehwa undong*, also known as moderniza-tion movement) was initiated in the late nineteenth century to reform the eco-nomic, political, and educational system (Lee, 1984). Many reformers saw the conservative neo-Confucian ideology as a major obstacle in promoting national progress. They argued for the adoption of Western education, economic, and po-litical systems as a viable solution to its backward status. During this time, a na-tionwide movement to promote enlightenment through education was initiated. With the aid of North American missionaries, many Western-style primary and secondary schools were built. These schools educated both men and women with new Western knowledge and about the world beyond its borders.

The enlightenment movement was curtailed with the Japanese annexation of Korea in 1910. With Japanese colonization, the Japanese style of education system was forcefully implemented. The goal of the educational system was not to enlighten the general public but a vehicle of colonial dominance. Ko-rean history, geography, and culture were systematically distorted to justify Japanese colonization of Korea.

The exploitation suffered during the Japanese colonization and the ravages of the Korean War (1950–1953) left Korea totally devastated in all strata of society. Transition from a war-torn country to a rapidly developing country was interrupted by numerous social and political upheavals. But by 1997 Ko-rea had moved from being a highly illiterate and impoverished nation to join the elite circle of developed nations.

In 1998, Korea experienced a severe economic crisis and the economy shrank more than 30%. From 1999, the Korean economy gradually recovered and in early 2002, the Korean economy recovered its pre-1997 crisis level.

Korea has faced dramatic changes in all aspects of society in the modern era. Koreans had to learn to change from an agrarian to an industrial society, from rural to urban communities, from conservative to progressive ideologies, from being past-oriented to future-orientation, from choosing the middle-path values to achievement values, from sentimentalist and reflective thinking to practical and analytical thinking, from hierarchical to democratic political or-ganization, from acceptance of nature and harmony to controlling nature and its forces and becoming its master. In brief, Koreans had to adapt to the forced colonial rule of Japan, to the dislocations and ravages of the Korean War, to the reality of a divided Korea, and to the harsh realities of bleak economic, political, and social crises all in one lifetime. Although the nature of Korean society has significantly changed, the desire to become educated has remained a top priority. Even in modern Korea, people view education as the most vi-able way to achieve personal, familial, and national prosperity. Moreover, the spirit of Confucianism, viewing education not only as a means to an end, but as an end itself, still persists. It has become a moral imperative that all individuals, regardless of sex or social class, acquire higher education.

Societal influence of attribution is mediated by familial and school influence. The following section examines the role that the parents and teachers play in instilling a strong achievement motivation.

EDUCATIONAL ATTAINMENT: THE ROLE OF FAMILY AND SCHOOL

Korean parents are instrumental in motivating their children to achieve a high level of educational success. Through socialization and enculturation practices values are transmitted to their children. The goal of socialization and enculturation is to create a common viewpoint and lifestyle so that when children become adults these socialized aspects become supremely "natural" (Wirth, 1946). The goal of socialization in Korea is to create a sense of interdependence, relatedness, and common fate.

Traditional Socialization Beliefs and Practices

In traditional Korea, socialization for interdependence starts at the prenatal stage and continues throughout a person's life (see Kim & Choi, 1994, for a review). *T'aekyo* (prenatal care) contains rigorous guidelines for pregnant women outlining desirable and undesirable attitudes, emotions, and behaviors during pregnancy. These prescriptive guidelines are based upon a belief that a mother's experiences during her pregnancy will directly affect the baby inside her womb and leave lasting impressions on the child. The goal of *t'aekyo* is to heighten a sense of awareness of the unique psychological and biological bonds between the mother and the unborn child.

When a child was born, many mothers believed that children needed more than just their milk. They needed symbolic "dew" emanating from the mother, who needed to remain close to the child in order to indulge the child with this essential psychological nutrient. The belief was that the maternal dew propagates the existence of an unseen but powerful bond between a mother and her child. Both *t'aekyo* and maternal dew created a strong and undifferentiated interpersonal bond.

Modern Era

Although the influence of Confucianism has declined with modernization, researchers (Choi, 1990; Kim & Choi, 1994; Kim & Park, 2000) agree that two important features of the interdependence still persist: devotion and indulgence. Mothers in modern Confucian cultures view unselfish devotion to their children as a critical feature of their personhood and motherhood. Choi

(1990) found that Korean mothers' personal identities are often defined by their role as mothers. They become closely tied to their children and see their children as extensions of themselves. Children's accomplishments and failures become their own, and children vicariously fulfil their own dreams and goals. Attaining this vicarious gratification is one of the most important aspects of motherhood, and it is the most valued meaning that Korean mothers have in raising their children.

When a child is born, a Korean mother remains close to the child to make the child feel secure, to make the boundary between herself and the child minimal, and to meet all of the child's needs, even if that means a tremendous sacrifice on her own part. Children's strong dependency needs, both emotional and existential, are satisfied by their mother's indulgent devotion. As children mature, they sense that it is through the mother that they obtain gratification, security, and love. As such, children become motivated to maintain a close relationship and they do so by gradually taking a more active role in pleasing their mothers and behaving according to their mothers' wishes. Thus, the feeling of interdependence helps children to assimilate their mothers' values and beliefs as their own. Similar patterns of socialization have been also found in China and Japan (Ho, 1986; Azuma, 1986).

SCHOOL ENVIRONMENT
AND EDUCATIONAL ATTAINMENT

Phenomenal educational attainment, especially in mathematics, in East Asian societies has been systematically documented (Stevenson & Lee, 1990; Stevenson, Azuma, & Hakuta, 1986). In addition to the supportive environment that parents provide, an important aspect of educational success has been attributed to social-oriented achievement motivation (SOAM) (Yu & Yang, 1994). SOAM emphasizes the following four qualities: (1) interdependence, (2) effort, (3) substantive goals, and (4) compatibility of values between the home environment and the school environment.

Interdependence

As documented in the previous section, mothers in Korea inculcate interdependence. As children grow up they are expected to transfer such identification and loyalty from their mothers to other family members, friends, and teachers. A mother's job is to use her interdependence with her child to prepare her child for adult life. She becomes a mediator between the home environment and the school environment and she gradually implants appropriate social values in her children (Kim & Choi, 1994; Kim & Park, 2000).

In Korea, the relationship between teachers and their students is seen as an extension of the mother–child relationship. The typical climate in Korean schools affirms the strong relational bond between teacher and students, pressures the student to strive for personal excellence, and encourages students to cooperate in a group (Kim & Choi, 1994; Kim & Park, 2000). Children are motivated to please the teacher and their attention is focused on the teacher. Even in a class size that is as large as forty or fifty, Korean students are attentive and devoted to doing their schoolwork and homework (Kim & Choi, 1994; Kim & Park, 1999a).

Effort

The second important value is the emphasis on effort. In East Asian societies, effort (an internal and controllable factor) is believed to lead to success, especially in education (Park & Kim, 1997; Stevenson & Lee, 1990; Yu & Yang, 1994). Lebra (1976) found in a free-association task that over 70% of Japanese respondents (both young and old, men and women) attribute success to diligence, effort, and endurance, and only 1% attributed it to ability. Park and Kim (1997, 1998, 1999) similarly found that Korean adolescents and adults attribute educational success to effort.

Consistent with Confucian philosophy, individual striving is viewed as a necessary component of the self-cultivation process. Excellence in performance provides evidence that a child has developed a moral character through perseverance and persistence. It is a visible demonstration that a child has deeper abilities to be a virtuous person. Furthermore, Holloway, Kashiwagi, and Azuma (1986) pointed out that "the emphasis on individual effort includes a sense of responsibility to the group to which one belongs" (p. 272). In virtue-based societies, individuals are pressured to contribute to the group and success is collectively defined and shared.

Compatibility

Finally, in Korea, there is a greater congruence between the values emphasized in the home environment and those learned in the school environment than there is in the United States. In the United States, individualistic values are often in conflict with a relatively rigid classroom structure, curriculum, and the teacher–student relationship. In addition, students, parents, teachers, and administrators often hold different views about the meaning of success and factors that lead to success. This diversity of viewpoints is considered to be the strength of individualistic societies. In Korea, there is greater congruence among all parties about the goals of education and the method of achieving this goal. As noted in the results section below, most Korean adults and adolescents view educational success as one of the most important facets of their life. This collective agreement is a fundamental requirement of virtue-based societies.

ORGANIZATION BEHAVIOR

According to U. M. Kim (1994), organizations in Japan and Korea are perceived as extensions of a family. In these societies, companies and the government encourage paternalism and communalism. To examine the nature of paternalism and communalism in Korea, surveys were obtained from personnel managers from mining and manufacturing firms with more than one hundred employees at a 90% response rate (i.e., 985 out of 1,097 company personnel managers completed the questionnaire). U. M. Kim (1994) found that the vast majority (over 80%) of the managers strongly endorsed the ideas of paternalism and communalism. He found that many companies provide services to foster paternalism and communalism, which are believed in turn to enhance production, efficiency, solidarity, loyalty, job satisfaction, and social control. Additional studies also confirm the belief that companies are an extension of a family and affirm the values of paternalism and human relatedness (Kim, 1998).

EMPIRICAL STUDY

An empirical study was conducted during the summer of 1997 to explore Korean students' and adults' perception of success and the personal, relational, social factors that contributed to their success. Using the indigenous psychologies approach (Kim, 2000; Kim, Park, & Park, 1999), an open-ended questionnaire was developed and administered to a sample of Korean students and adults. The indigenous psychologies method differs from existing qualitative methodology by providing a context and by forcing participants to articulate and analyze the factors that contribute to success. The goal of this study is to capture the pattern of analysis that the participants have provided and to capture the implicit values and attributional style outlined by the participants.

Method

Questionnaire

Participants were asked, in an open-ended format, to list three accomplishments, achievements, or successes in their life. From the three, they were then asked to select the achievement that they are most proud of and that is very important for them. The purpose of these two steps was to provide a context for answering the subsequent questions. Respondents were then asked the following series of questions: (1) Why are you proud of the above accomplishment, achievement, or success? (2) Were there people around who supported and helped you? If so, please list the person and specify your relationship to the person. (3) Specifically, what type of support did you receive from the person? (4) Overall, what do you consider to be the most important factor contributing to your success?

Sample

The student sample consisted of 486 high school students (from vocational and preparatory high school) and 244 university students. For the adult sample, a total of 167 housewives, 126 salaried employees, and 134 teachers completed the survey (see Table 9.2).

Coding

For each question, all responses from the participants were typed into a master list. From the master list similar responses were grouped together and categorized. The coding scheme was finalized when all three coders agreed that a particular response belonged to a particular category. A response that could not be slotted into an existing category was pooled into the "Other" category, as were categories with a frequency less than 3% of the total response. Based on the categories, a quantitative coding scheme was then cre-

Table 9.2
Sample

Group		Men	Women	Total
Student	High school	273	209	486 (no response-4)
	University	113	127	244 (no response-4)
	Subtotal	386	336	730 (no response-8)
Adult	Employee	100	12	126 (no response-14)
	Housewife	-	167	167
	Teacher	47	86	134 (no response-1)
	Subtotal	147	265	427 (no response-15)
	Total	533	601	1,157 (no response-23)

ated with specific categories numbered in ascending order. The original survey responses were each coded with a number from the coding scheme. Table 9.3 lists the specific categories.

Results

Background Information

The average age of salaried employees was thirty-six years (ranging from eighteen to sixty-eight), housewives averaged forty years (ranging from twenty to sixty-seven), and teachers were thirty-five years old (ranging from twenty-three to fifty-eight) (see Table 9.2).

Table 9.3 lists the most proud achievement as articulated by the respondents. The results are given in frequencies and in percentages (in brackets). The total frequency is further subdivided into student and adult samples and into men and women.

For the student sample, the category that was mentioned most frequently was educational attainment, followed by self-development, friendship, social relationship, occupation, and hobbies. Within educational attainment, entry into a particular high school or university was mentioned most frequently. In the self-development category, activities that promote independence, positive outlook, goal-fulfillment, and trying one's best were mentioned. Maintaining a good relationship with friends and meeting new friends were the next most frequent responses. It appears that for students, getting into a university and doing well in school is their most important task at hand. Personal interests and preferences such as hobbies were mentioned by onlt 7% of the students.

For the adult sample, occupational success was mentioned most frequently, followed by family life, self-development, and education. Compared to the student sample, occupational achievement replaced educational success as their most important achievement. In contrast to the student sample, which listed self-development and social relationships as being very important, the adult sample listed family life and child rearing as more important.

In terms of sex differences, both men and women agreed that educational and occupational achievement, self-development, family, and social relationships were very important. However, more women reported occupational success and family life as important achievements as compared to men. In contrast, more men reported self-development as being important as compared to women. Since the majority of women in the sample were not employed, having an occupation could be seen as more significant for employed women than for employed men.

Table 9.4 lists the reasons the respondents are proud of their achievements. Students mentioned that they were proud of their achievements because it was the result of their persistent effort and because they overcame difficulties. They also mentioned satisfaction and gratification derived from achieving their de-

Table 9.3
The Most Proud Achievement: Frequency and Percentages

Category	Total (%)	Student (%)	Adult (%)	Men (%)	Women (%)
Educational attainment	286 (26.2)	140 (28.0)	19 (5.0)	140 (28.1)	145 (25.3)
Entry: high school	90 (8.2)	90 (12.7)	00 (0.0)	37 (7.4)	52 (9.1)
Entry: university	83 (7.6)	68 (9.6)	15 (3.9)	31 (6.2)	52 (9.1)
Rise in grade	83 (7.6)	82 (11.5)	1 (0.3)	57 (11.4)	26 (4.5)
Better grade than others	30 (2.7)	27 (3.8)	3 (0.8)	15 (3.0)	15 (2.6)
Occupation	195 (17.9)	52 (7.3)	143 (37.6)	82 (16.4)	108 (18.8)
Finding a job	73 (6.7)	7 (0.0)	66 (17.4)	21 (4.2)	51 (8.9)
Receiving a certificate	52 (4.8)	40 (5.6)	12 (3.2)	17 (3.4)	34 (5.9)
Job satisfaction	32 (2.9)	0 (0.0)	32 (8.4)	24 (4.8)	6 (1.0)
Economic security	28 (2.6)	5 (0.7)	23 (6.1)	11 (2.2)	16 (2.8)
Promotion	10 (0.9)	0 (0.0)	10 (2.6)	9 (1.8)	1 (0.2)
Self-development	145 (13.3)	108 (15.2)	37 (9.7)	78 (15.6)	63 (11.0)
Independent activity	37 (3.4)	33 (4.6)	4 (1.1)	23 (4.6)	13 (2.3)
Positive thinking	29 (2.7)	23 (3.2)	6 (1.6)	16 (3.2)	13 (2.3)
Self-development	27 (2.5)	12 (1.7)	15 (3.9)	13 (2.6)	14 (2.4)
Goal- fulfillment	26 (2.4)	20 (2.8)	6 (1.6)	16 (3.2)	10 (1.7)
Tried my best	26 (2.4)	20 (2.8)	6 (1.6)	10 (2.0)	13 (2.3)
Friendship	100 (9.2)	88 (12.4)	12 (3.2)	43 (8.6)	54 (9.4)
Good relationship	53 (4.9)	46 (6.5)	7 (1.8)	19 (3.8)	33 (5.8)
Met good friends	47 (4.3)	42 (5.9)	5 (1.3)	24 (4.8)	21 (3.7)

sired goal. Beyond attaining their desired goal, it also led to harmonious social and family relationships and provided them with social recognition. There were no discernable sex or group differences.

For the adult sample, the satisfaction derived from their achievement was mentioned most frequently, followed by the response that it was the result of effort, goal attainment, or harmonious family life. Housewives stressed harmonious family life more, and the teachers and employees emphasized the result of effort more than housewives did. As for sex differences, men mentioned the result of effort more often than women, who mentioned satisfaction more often.

Table 9.3 (*continued*)

Category	Total (%)	Student (%)	Adult (%)	Men (%)	Women (%)
Family life	97 (8.9)	2 (0.3)	95 (25.0)	26 (5.2)	69 (12.0)
Harmonious family	36 (3.3)	2 (0.3)	34 (8.9)	9 (1.8)	26 (4.5)
Marriage	31 (2.8)	0 (0.0)	31 (8.2)	13 (2.6)	17 (3.0)
Birth of children	18 (1.6)	0 (0.0)	18 (4.7)	2 (0.4)	16 (2.8)
Education of children	12 (1.1)	0 (0.0)	12 (3.2)	2 (0.4)	10 (1.7)
Human relations	76 (7.0)	64 (9.0)	12 (3.2)	41 (8.2)	34 (5.9)
Good relations	54 (4.9)	44 (6.2)	10 (2.6)	30 (6.0)	23 (4.0)
Social recognition	22 (2.0)	20 (2.8)	2 (0.5)	11 (2.2)	11 (1.9)
Hobbies	57 (5.2)	49 (6.9)	8 (2.1)	29 (5.8)	27 (4.7)
Hobbies	37 (3.4)	29 (4.1)	8 (2.1)	20 (4.0)	16 (2.8)
Interest groups	20 (1.8)	20 (2.8)	0 (0.0)	9 (1.8)	11 (1.9)
Other	135 (12.4)	81 (11.4)	54 (14.2)	60 (12.0)	73 (12.7)
Religious experience	46 (4.2)	13 (1.8)	33 (8.7)	10 (2.0)	35 (6.1)
Other	45 (4.1)	27 (3.8)	18 (4.7)	26 (5.2)	18 (3.1)
Received award	32 (2.9)	30 (4.2)	2 (0.5)	12 (2.4)	20 (3.5)
Army life	12 (1.1)	11 (1.5)	1 (0.3)	12 (2.4)	0 (0.0)

Adults were proud of their educational success and hobbies because they were the results of their effort. For occupational success, satisfaction was most frequently mentioned. For friendship and social relations, good relations and satisfaction were most frequently reported. For family life, harmonious family was most frequently listed.

Table 9.5 lists the person who provided the necessary support for success. Both students and adults mentioned parents as being the most supportive person. For the student sample, friends, teachers, and other family members followed. For the adult sample, other family members, colleagues, friends, and teachers followed. Women mentioned other family members more frequently than men. Men mentioned colleagues more frequently than women did.

Table 9.6 lists the frequency of the type of social support received. For both groups emotional support was most frequently mentioned, followed by advice. For the student sample good surroundings was mentioned next, followed by cooperation and financial support. For the adult sample, financial support

Table 9.4
Reasons for Being Proud: Frequency and Percentages

Category	Total (%)	Student (%)	Adult (%)	Men (%)	Women (%)
Result of effort	323 (30.1)	235 (33.6)	88 (23.5)	158 (32.0)	159 (28.3)
Result of effort	133 (12.4)	113 (16.2)	20 (5.3)	65 (13.2)	67 (11.9)
Overcame difficulties	116 (10.8)	69 (9.9)	47 (12.5)	54 (10.9)	58 (10.3)
Overcame it by myself	49 (4.6)	36 (5.2)	13 (3.5)	30 (6.1)	19 (3.4)
Did not give up	25 (2.3)	17 (2.4)	8 (2.1)	9 (1.8)	15 (2.7)
Satisfaction	266 (24.8)	162 (23.2)	104 (27.7)	118 (23.9)	144 (25.7)
Pride	68 (6.3)	60 (8.6)	8 (2.1)	39 (7.9)	28 (5.0)
Important life goal	57 (5.3)	31 (4.4)	26 (6.9)	22 (4.5)	34 (6.1)
Satisfaction	39 (3.6)	9 (1.3)	30 (8.0)	20 (4.0)	18 (3.2)
Gratification	37 (3.4)	18 (2.6)	19 (5.1)	12 (2.4)	25 (4.5)
Hope	33 (3.1)	22 (3.1)	11 (2.9)	10 (2.0)	22 (3.9)
Happiness	32 (3.0)	22 (3.1)	10 (2.7)	15 (3.0)	17 (3.0)
Goal attainment	173 (16.1)	116 (16.6)	57 (15.2)	82 (16.6)	89 (15.9)
Achieved desired goal	121 (11.3)	74 (10.6)	47 (12.5)	48 (9.7)	73 (13.0)
Accomplished objective	20 (1.9)	10 (1.4)	10 (2.7)	9 (1.8)	9 (1.6)
Rise in grade	17 (1.6)	17 (2.4)	0 (0.0)	14 (2.8)	3 (0.5)
Entry: desired university	15 (1.4)	15 (2.1)	0 (0.0)	11 (2.2)	4 (0.7)
Human relationship	79 (7.4)	62 (8.9)	17 (4.5)	31 (6.3)	46 (8.2)
Good relationship	60 (5.6)	49 (7.0)	11 (2.9)	25 (5.1)	33 (5.9)
Emotional security	19 (1.8)	13 (1.9)	6 (1.6)	6 (1.2)	13 (2.3)
Family life	64 (6.0)	20 (2.9)	44 (11.7)	21 (4.3)	40 (7.1)
Harmonious family	28 (2.6)	2 (0.3)	26 (6.9)	10 (2.0)	16 (2.9)
Parents are happy	23 (2.1)	18 (2.6)	5 (1.3)	9 (1.8)	14 (2.5)
Children's progress	13 (1.2)	0 (0.0)	13 (3.5)	2 (0.4)	10 (1.8)
Social recognition	56 (5.2)	39 (5.6)	17 (4.5)	30 (6.1)	26 (4.6)
Others	113 (10.5)	65 (9.3)	48 (12.8)	54 (10.9)	57 (10.2)
Others	86 (8.0)	58 (8.3)	28 (7.5)	49 (9.9)	35 (6.2)
Religious strength	27 (2.5)	7 (1.0)	20 (5.3)	5 (1.0)	22 (3.9)

Table 9.5
Most Supportive Person: Frequency and Percentages

Category	Total (%)	Student (%)	Adult (%)	Men (%)	Women (%)
Parents	340 (32.2)	242 (34.9)	98 (27.1)	155 (31.6)	182 (33.1)
Parents	210 (19.9)	156 (22.5)	54 (14.9)	96 (19.6)	113 (20.5)
Mother	95 (9.0)	69 (9.9)	26 (7.2)	39 (8.0)	55 (10.0)
Father	35 (3.3)	17 (2.4)	18 (5.0)	20 (4.1)	14 (2.5)
Friend	206 (19.5)	177 (25.5)	29 (8.0)	107 (21.8)	95 (17.3)
Teacher	125 (11.8)	104 (15.0)	21 (5.8)	59 (12.0)	63 (11.5)
Teacher/school	104 (9.8)	85 (12.2)	19 (5.2)	50 (10.2)	51 (9.3)
Teacher/institute	21 (2.0)	19 (2.7)	2 (0.6)	9 (1.8)	12 (2.2)
Family member	123 (11.6)	41 (5.9)	82 (22.7)	37 (7.6)	84 (15.3)
Spouse	62 (5.9)	0 (0.0)	62 (17.1)	12 (2.4)	48 (8.7)
Family member	61 (5.8)	41 (5.9)	20 (5.5)	25 (5.1)	36 (6.5)
None	52 (4.9)	39 (5.6)	13 (3.6)	30 (6.1)	22 (4.0)
Colleagues	39 (3.7)	9 (1.3)	30 (8.3)	28 (5.7)	9 (1.6)
Others	171 (16.2)	82 (11.8)	89 (24.6)	74 (15.1)	95 (17.3)
Senior	35 (3.3)	24 (3.5)	11 (3.0)	20 (4.1)	14 (2.5)
People around me	32 (3.0)	19 (2.7)	13 (3.6)	16 (3.3)	15 (2.7)
Relative	26 (2.5)	7 (1.0)	19 (5.2)	12 (2.4)	14 (2.5)
God	26 (2.5)	11 (1.6)	15 (4.1)	5 (1.0)	21 (3.8)
Myself	23 (2.2)	16 (2.3)	7 (1.9)	14 (2.9)	9 (1.6)
Minister	22 (2.1)	4 (0.6)	18 (5.0)	4 (0.8)	18 (3.3)
Others	7 (0.7)	1 (0.1)	6 (1.7)	3 (0.6)	4 (0.7)

was the third most frequent response, followed by good surroundings and cooperation. For both samples, women mentioned emotional support more frequently than men.

Table 9.7 lists what the respondents consider to be the most important factor contributing to their success. The most important factor for everyone was self-regulation. For the student sample, it was followed by family environment, social support, positive thinking, personality, and friends. For the adult

Table 9.6
Type of Support Received: Frequency and Percentages

Category	Total (%)	Student (%)	Adult (%)	Men (%)	Women (%)
Emotional support	341 (34.7)	227 (34.9)	114 (34.3)	135 (29.5)	201 (39.6)
Praise	109 (11.1)	79 (12.2)	30 (9.0)	40 (8.7)	68 (13.4)
Emotional support	91 (9.3)	61 (9.4)	30 (9.0)	37 (8.1)	52 (10.2)
Provide confidence	41 (4.2)	29 (4.5)	12 (3.6)	12 (2.6)	29 (5.7)
Love	37 (3.8)	21 (3.2)	16 (4.8)	18 (3.9)	18 (3.5)
Comfort	32 (3.3)	18 (2.8)	14 (4.2)	12 (2.6)	19 (3.7)
Security	31 (3.2)	19 (2.9)	12 (3.6)	16 (3.5)	15 (3.0)
Advice	290 (29.5)	208 (32.0)	82 (24.7)	148 (32.3)	138 (27.2)
Advice	124 (12.6)	84 (12.9)	40 (12.0)	61 (13.3)	61 (12.0)
Teach	111 (11.3)	98 (15.1)	13 (3.9)	65 (14.2)	46 (9.1)
Information	29 (3.0)	21 (3.2)	8 (2.4)	17 (3.7)	11 (2.2)
Good messages in Bible	26 (2.6)	5 (0.8)	21 (6.3)	5 (1.1)	20 (3.9)
Good surroundings	108 (11.0)	72 (11.1)	36 (10.8)	48 (10.5)	58 (11.4)
Served as a model	44 (4.5)	23 (3.5)	21 (6.3)	16 (3.5)	27 (5.3)
Control the environment	29 (3.0)	23 (3.5)	6 (1.8)	18 (3.9)	11 (2.2)
Family environment	20 (2.0)	13 (2.0)	7 (2.1)	8 (1.7)	12 (2.4)
Competition	15 (1.5)	13 (2.0)	2 (0.6)	6 (1.3)	8 (1.6)
Financial support	97 (9.9)	49 (7.5)	48 (14.5)	41 (9.0)	56 (11.0)
Financial and spiritual	50 (5.1)	25 (3.8)	25 (7.5)	17 (3.7)	33 (6.5)
Financial	47 (4.8)	24 (3.7)	23 (6.9)	24 (5.2)	23 (4.5)
Cooperation	81 (8.2)	55 (8.5)	26 (7.8)	45 (9.8)	32 (6.3)
Cooperation	50 (5.1)	31 (4.8)	19 (5.7)	31 (6.8)	18 (3.5)
Work together	31 (3.2)	24 (3.7)	7 (2.1)	14 (3.1)	14 (2.8)
Other	65 (6.6)	39 (6.0)	26 (7.8)	41 (9.0)	23 (4.5)
Other	48 (4.9)	28 (4.3)	20 (6.0)	31 (6.8)	16 (3.1)
None	17 (1.7)	11 (1.7)	6 (1.8)	10 (2.2)	7 (1.4)

sample, personality was the next most frequent response, followed by faith, family environment, social support, and positive thinking.

Discussion

Overall, Korean students place prime importance on educational attainment. They view education as the most important life goal to achieve. Once an individual has achieved a high level of educational success, he or she has access to social and economic rewards. In order to succeed in Korea, whether it is academic or occupational, people believe that self-regulation is the most effective strategy. In other words, if they work hard and try their best, they believe they can accomplish their desired objectives. This belief in effort has contributed to phenomenal educational and economic achievements in Korea.

As found in other studies, Korean respondents agree that the most important factor in success is self-regulation, especially the belief that effort will contribute to success. The second most frequent response was social support received from significant others, especially parents. Even adults considered social support received from their parents as being very important. The type of support they received was affective in nature.

In contrast to the importance in self-regulation and social support, ability and environment factors were mentioned infrequently. Personality was mentioned frequently, but it was mainly for maintaining good social relationships in the work setting. Overall, it appears that Korean respondents believe that success is contingent on self-regulation and support received from significant others, and they play down the role of innate ability and environmental factors.

CONCLUSION AND IMPLICATIONS

The current results point to the limitation in the current theories and concepts developed in the West. First, contrary to the emphasis on ability and personality in the West, very few Korean participants emphasized ability or personality, instead they believed self-regulation to be the most important factor that led to their success. Second, contrary to developmental theories that focus on parental influence only in the early years, in Korea parental influence is very strong during adolescence and remains strong even in adulthood. Third, in Korea close ingroup members are highly influential, especially family members, while professional relationships (such as the teacher–student relationship, superior–subordinate relationship, or relationship among colleagues at the workplace) did not emerge as important contributing factors to participants' success attribution. Fourth, Western theories have focused on informational support and a problem-focused coping style and have not fully examined the positive aspects of emotional support. In Korea, emotional support emerged as the most influential factor in participants' attribution of their success.

Table 9.7
The Most Important Reason for Success: Frequency and Percentages

Category	Total (%)	Student (%)	Adult (%)	Men (%)	Women (%)
Self-regulation	416 (41.4)	300 (44.6)	116 (35.0)	201 (42.8)	208 (40.2)
Effort	188 (18.7)	139 (20.7)	49 (14.8)	84 (17.9)	100 (19.3)
Will	71 (7.1)	52 (7.7)	19 (5.7)	37 (7.9)	34 (6.6)
Desire	43 (4.3)	32 (4.8)	11 (3.3)	21 (4.5)	22 (4.2)
Patience	34 (3.4)	20 (3.0)	14 (4.2)	16 (3.4)	17 (3.3)
Positive attitude	33 (3.3)	24 (3.6)	9 (2.7)	17 (3.6)	14 (2.7)
Belief	27 (2.7)	14 (2.1)	13 (3.9)	12 (2.6)	15 (2.9)
Persistence	20 (2.0)	19 (2.8)	1 (0.3)	14 (3.0)	6 (1.2)
Personality	112 (11.2)	50 (7.4)	62 (18.7)	58 (12.3)	52 (10.0)
Sincerity	48 (4.8)	14 (2.1)	34 (10.3)	27 (5.7)	21 (4.1)
Unique attribute	43 (4.3)	24 (3.6)	19 (5.7)	21 (4.5)	21 (4.1)
Overall personality	21 (2.1)	12 (1.8)	9 (2.7)	10 (2.1)	10 (1.9)
Family environment	107 (10.7)	76 (11.3)	31 (9.4)	44 (9.4)	62 (12.0)
Parent	71 (7.1)	63 (9.4)	8 (2.4)	32 (6.8)	38 (7.3)
Family environment	26 (2.6)	13 (1.9)	13 (3.9)	11 (2.3)	15 (2.9)
Spouse	10 (1.0)	0 (0.0)	10 (3.0)	1 (0.2)	9 (1.7)

The results of this study can be linked to the current educational and economic crisis that Korea is currently experiencing. At the end of 1997, Korea experienced a dramatic economic crisis in which the national economy shrank more than 30% (the per capita GNP shrank from $10,000 to $6,800) and more than one million people became unemployed. Although Korea was able to achieve phenomenal educational and economic achievement during the past thirty years, the financial crisis reflected fundamental structural problems inherent in Korean society and mentality. About one-hundred years ago, many Koreans believed that the external challenges they faced could be resolved internally through regulating themselves and supporting ingroup members; such a pattern of belief still persists in Korea.

The economic crisis arose due to a fundamental bias in Korean mentality: the overemphasis on self-regulation and trusting only ingroup members, focusing mostly on family members. Furthermore, Koreans focus on affective domains and not on cognitive or problem-solving approaches. Similar responses

Table 9.7 (*continued*)

Category	Total (%)	Student (%)	Adult (%)	Men (%)	Women (%)
Help from others	89 (8.9)	59 (8.8)	30 (9.1)	39 (8.3)	49 (9.5)
People around me	60 (6.0)	47 (7.0)	13 (3.9)	30 (6.4)	30 (5.8)
Trust in people	29 (2.9)	12 (1.8)	17 (5.1)	9 (1.9)	19 (3.7)
Positive thinking	77 (7.7)	52 (7.7)	25 (7.6)	39 (8.3)	37 (7.1)
Confidence	38 (3.8)	28 (4.2)	10 (3.0)	18 (3.8)	19 (3.7)
Positive attitude	27 (2.7)	15 (2.2)	12 (3.6)	13 (2.8)	14 (2.7)
Self-understanding	12 (1.2)	9 (1.3)	3 (0.9)	8 (1.7)	4 (0.8)
Faith	59 (5.9)	23 (3.4)	36 (10.9)	16 (3.4)	42 (8.1)
Friends	49 (4.9)	46 (6.8)	3 (0.9)	22 (4.7)	26 (5.0)
Ability	23 (2.3)	20 (3.0)	3 (0.9)	18 (3.8)	5 (1.0)
Others	72 (7.2)	47 (7.0)	25 (7.6)	33 (7.0)	37 (7.1)
Others	32 (3.2)	18 (2.7)	14 (4.2)	18 (3.8)	12 (2.3)
Environment	15 (1.5)	10 (1.5)	5 (1.5)	6 (1.3)	9 (1.7)
None	14 (1.4)	12 (1.8)	2 (0.6)	5 (1.1)	9 (1.7)
Luck	11 (1.1)	7 (1.0)	4 (1.2)	4 (0.9)	7 (1.4)

have also been found for stressful events. In others words, Koreans utilize more emotion-focused coping styles than problem-focused coping styles, even though problem-focused coping styles are much more effective than emotion-focused coping styles (Kim & Park, 1997; Kim & Park, 1999a). Moreover, for most respondents the coping style tends to be passive (such as self-regulating negative emotions) and relationship focused (e.g., seeking social support, avoiding the situation) (Kim & Park, 1997; Kim & Park, 1999b).

The major weakness that Korean society faces is its inability to control the external environment and working with strangers. The existing coping strategy focuses on emotions, self-regulation, and social support among ingroup members, not in understanding and controlling the larger social context (i.e., the societal and global market).

A collective in Korea and East Asia is an exclusive ingroup and not an inclusive entity (Kim, 1995). In Korea, people maintain harmony within the ingroup and a separate orientation, one of apathy, exploitation, and neglect, exists for outgroup members. Such discrimination has historically become the basis of factionalism, regionalism, and nepotism, and blocked the creation of a well-functioning civil and democratic society.

Korean people have invested their energy and hopes in people that they know well (i.e., family members and ingroup members) and have excluded outgroup members. For example, although women are included as ingroup members as sisters, wives, and mothers, they are not given equal opportunity to participate and contribute to the larger society. The challenge that Korean society faces is to create a system in which everyone can participate on an equal footing and have equal access to various opportunities. In Korea, interpersonal connections through regional networks, familial ties, and school ties, and even gender, have excluded competent individuals from full participation. This exclusive membership and emphasis on harmony creates homogeneity of thought and action that has limited the diversity of ideas that could be utilized in creatively transforming Korean society.

It is tempting to blame Confucianism for the ingroup favoritism and nepotism, but many people have misunderstood and misused Confucianism. First, Confucius was a forceful advocate of selecting government officials based on merit and in no way advocated, supported, or justified nepotism or ingroup favoritism. Second, Confucius emphasized the importance of family, but at the same time he believed that a person of merit should also serve the nation. Confucius felt that a person who has cultivated virtue (*te*) should become a government official and should serve the public and serve the country upholding integrity, morality, and principles. In Confucianism learning and holding a government position are considered a twin activity (Lau, 1979). In other words, "When a man in office finds that he can more than cope with his duties, then he studies; when a student finds that he can more than cope with his studies, then he takes office" (Confucius, 1979, XIX.13). As Confucius (1979, XV.32) pointed out: "To give these qualities their fullest realization the gentleman must take part in government."

Although the success of Korean education is based on a system where individuals are objectively evaluated and are given opportunities based on individual merit (consistent with Confucian philosophy), this is not the case in the economic and financial sector. In the economic arena, outcomes are often based on personal, social, and political favoritism and are not contingent upon performance or merit. For this reason, many employees distrust the system and do not invest their effort in developing the necessary skills for improving performance, but rather they develop political skills to maintain and enhance their social network (Kim, 1998). In order to compete in the international arena, Korean society must create a system that people can trust and that ensures equal access to everyone, including women, people without a college degree, and non-Koreans. Korean society must respect differential outcomes that are based on merit and performance rather than simply dividing the outcome equally to maintain superficial harmony.

Although role-based paternalism has merit for families and tight ingroups, it can be dysfunctional in public settings (e.g., large groups such as companies, nation, and in the international context). Thus, Korea needs to adopt a dual-based system to deal with the complexity of modern life: a role-based system for families and tight ingroups and a principle-based merit system for public settings. This is not a novel idea or a Western one, but an idea inherent in East Asian philosophy of separating the private from the public and having two contrasting rules for inside and outside (Kim, 1998, 2001). In other words, in families and tight ingroups, individuals utilize role-based and virtue-based morality. In larger settings, people utilize principle-based ethics in which individuals have equal access to opportunities and in which they are evaluated and rewarded based on merit and performance. This dual system may be problematic for Westerners, but East Asians have traditionally incorporated dual systems, such as the opposing forces of *yin* and *yang*.

In order to participate fully in the international arena, a balance between self-regulation and controlling the environment must be created. Furthermore, Korean society must move away from a nepotistic, closed, and discriminatory system to a system that is fair, just, open, accountable, and harmonious. It must be a system that people can trust, that everyone has equal access to, and that can incorporate diversity of ideas and lifestyles.

REFERENCES

Azuma, H. (1986). Why study child development in Japan? In H. Stevenson, H. Azuma, & K. Hakuta K (Eds.), *Child development and education in Japan* (pp. 3–12). New York: W. H. Freeman.

Bandura, A. (1997). *Self-efficacy: The exercise of control*. New York: W. H. Freeman.

Budd, M. (1989). *Wittgenstein's philosophy of psychology*. London: Routledge.

Choi, S. H. (1990). Communicative socialization process: Korea and Canada. Unpublished Ph.D. diss., University of Alberta, Edmonton, Canada.

Confucius (1979). *The analects*. (D. C. Lau, Trans.). New York: Penguin Books.

Harre, R. (1999). The rediscovery of the human mind: The discursive approach. *Asian Journal of Social Psychology, 2*, 43–63.

Harré, R., & Gillet, G. (1994). *The discursive mind*. Thousand Oaks, CA: Sage.

Heider, F. (1958). *The psychology of interpersonal relations*. New York: John Wiley and Sons.

Hewstone, M. (1989). *Causal attribution: From cognitive processes to collective beliefs*. Oxford: Blackwell.

Ho, D.Y.F. (1986). Chinese patterns of socialization: A critical review. In M. H. Bond (Ed.), *The psychology of the Chinese people*. Oxford: Oxford University Press.

Hofstede, G. (1991). *Cultures and organizations: Software of the mind*. New York: McGraw-Hill.

Holloway, S., Kashiwagi, K., & Azuma, H. (1986). Causal attribution by Japanese and American mothers and children about performance in mathematics. *International Journal of Psychology, 21*, 269–286.

Kim, U. (1994). Individualism and collectivism: Conceptual clarification and elaboration. In U. Kim, H. C. Triandis, C. Kagitcibasi, S. C. Choi, & G. Yoon, G. (Eds.), *Individualism and collectivism: Theory, method, and applications* (pp. 19–40). Thousand Oaks, CA: Sage.

Kim, U. (1995). Psychology, science, and culture: Cross-cultural analysis of national psychologies in developing countries. *International Journal of Psychology, 30*, 663–679.

Kim, U. (1998). Understanding Korean corporate culture: Analysis of transformative human resource management. *Strategic Human Resource Development Review, 2*, 68–101.

Kim, U. (1999). After the crisis in social psychology: Development of the transactional model of science. *Asian Journal of Social Psychology, 1*, 1–19.

Kim, U. (2000). Indigenous, cultural, and cross-cultural psychology: A theoretical, conceptual, and epistemological analysis. *Asian Journal of Social Psychology, 3* (3), 265–287.

Kim, U. (2001). Analysis of democracy and human rights in cultural context: Psychological and comparative perspectives. In H. S. Aasen, U. Kim, & G. Helgesen (Eds.), *Democracy, human rights, and peace in Korea: Psychological, political, and cultural perspectives* (pp. 53–94). Seoul: Kyoyook Kwahasa.

Kim, U., & Choi, S. C. (1994). Individualism, collectivism, and child development: A Korean perspective. In P. M. Greenfield & R. Cocking (Eds.), *Cognitive socialization of minority children: Continuities and discontinuities*. Hillsdale, NJ: Lawrence Erlbaum.

Kim, U., & Park, Y. S. (1997). Stress, appraisal and coping: An indigenous analysis. *Korean Journal of Health Psychology, 2*, 96–126.

Kim, U., & Park, Y. S. (1999a). Psychological and behavioral pattern of Korean adolescents: With specific focus on the influence of friends, family, and school. *Korean Journal of Educational Psychology, 13*, 99–142.

Kim, U., & Park, Y. S. (1999b). The experience of stress during the economic crisis in Korea: An indigenous analysis. *Korean Journal of Health Psychology, 4* (1), 57–79.

Kim, U., & Park, Y. S. (2000). Confucian and family values: Their impact of educational achievement in Korea. *Zeitshrift fur Erziehungswissenschaft (Journal of Educational Science), 3*, 1–21.

Kim, U., Park, Y. S., & Park, D. H. (1999). The Korean indigenous psychology approach: Theoretical considerations and empirical applications. *Applied Psychology: An International Review, 45*, 55–73.

Kim, U. M. (1994). Significance of paternalism and communalism in the occupational welfare system of Korean firms: A national survey. In U. Kim, H. C. Triandis, C. Kagitcibasi, S. C. Choi, & G. Yoon (Eds.), *Individualism and collectivism: Theory, method, and application*. Thousand Oaks, CA: Sage.

Koch, S., & Leary, D. E. (Eds.). (1985). *A century of psychology as science*. New York: McGraw-Hill.

Lau, D. C. (1979). Introduction to Confucius. In *The analects*. New York: Penguin Books.

Lebra, T. S. (1976). *Japanese patterns of behavior*. Honolulu: University of Hawaii Press.

Lee, K. B. (1984). *A new history of Korea* (E. W. Wagner & E. J. Shultz, Trans.). Seoul: Ilchokak.

Levenson, H. (1974) Activism and powerful others: Distinction within the concept of internal–external control. *Journal of Personality Assessment, 38*, 377–383.

Muramoto, Y., Yamaguchi, S., Kim, U., & Kosaka, A. (in press). Perception of self-effacing and group-serving attributes: A cross-cultural study. In U. Kim, S.

Choi, & G. Cho (Eds.), *Post-modern psychologies: Cognitive, social and cultural perspectives*. Seoul: Hana Medical.

Nisbett, R. E., & Ross, L. (1980). *Human inference: Strategies and shortcomings of social judgements*. Englewood Cliffs, NJ: Prentice Hall.

Park, Y. S., & Kim, U. (1997). Attributional style of Korean students: Comparative analysis of primary, secondary and university students. *Korean Journal of Educational Psychology, 11*, 71–97.

Park, Y. S., & Kim, U. (1998). The relationship among attributional style, home environment, and behavioral outcome: Comparative analysis of delinquent adolescents and high school students. *Korean Journal of Psychological and Social Issues, 4* (1), 29–54.

Park, Y. S., & Kim, U. (1999). Conceptual and empirical analysis of attributional style: The relationship among six attributional styles in Korea. *Korean Journal of Educational Psychology, 137* (3), 119–165.

Stevenson, H., Azuma, H., & Hakuta, K. (Eds.). (1986). *Child development and education in Japan*. New York: W. H. Freeman.

Stevenson, H., & Lee, S. Y. (1990). Context of achievement: A study of American, Chinese, and Japanese children. *Monographs of the Society for Research in Child Development, 55*.

Wan, K. C., & Bond, M. H. (1982). Chinese attributions for success and failure under public and anonymous conditions of rating. *Journal of Consumer Research, 24*, 23–31.

Weiner, B. (1986). *An attribution theory of motivation and emotion*. New York: Springer-Verlag.

Wirth, L. (1946). Preface to K. Manheim, *Ideology and utopia: An introduction to sociology of knowledge*. New York: Harcourt, Brace.

Yu, A. B., & Yang, K. S. (1994). The nature of achievement motivation in collectivistic societies. In U. Kim, H. C. Triandis, C. Kagitcibasi, S. C. Choi, & G. Yoon (Eds.), *Individualism and collectivism: Theory, method, and applications* (pp. 239–250). Thousand Oaks, CA: Sage.

Part IV

GROUP
AND INTERGROUP
DYNAMICS

CHAPTER 10

Effects of Communication Medium and Goal Setting on Group Brainstorming

Asako Miura

New technology has created new forms of communication. Computer-assisted environments represent a fundamental shift in technology available for group interaction, and their use may substantially alter group processes and performance. Researchers have paid much attention to the effect of new types of communication media in group process and performance. In this study focus is on the effects of two different communication styles in brainstorming tasks in terms of group performance and member perceptions of process. The first style is the conventional form, namely face-to-face communication (FTF), and the second is a new form, computer-mediated communication (CMC). The effect of group goal setting as a contextual determinant of group performance is of particular interest.

PREVIOUS THEORY AND RESEARCH

Computer-Mediated Communication

Research on computer-mediated communication systems has been going on for nearly twenty years. Different theoretical frameworks have been developed in order to explain patterns of communication and social relations between the interlocutors in computer-mediated communication.

As seen in past research, one of the most striking features of CMC is the combination of rapidity and restriction. There is a relatively fast exchange of messages, while at the same time written language is the primary medium of communication. The most obvious feature of FTF communication that is lacking in CMC is physical presence. The fact that the interlocutors cannot see or hear each other means that they cannot exchange many of the tacit signs that play an important role in resolving ambiguities and establishing social control (Feenberg, 1987). This observation is relevant also for multimedia applications (Hapeshi & Jones, 1992), although they present other forms of information beside text, such as pictures, sound, diagrams, and so on. In a review of computer-mediated communication research, Hiltz and Turoff (1993) noted that computer-based media produce a sense of impersonality and that this effect is further increased by user anonymity. Rice (1993) also suggested that CMC has been seen as extremely limited in terms of "social presence" because text-based communication lacks many nonverbal cues. These nonverbal and interpersonal cues are more likely to be transmitted via nonverbal and paraverbal cues that are extremely constrained in a text-based CMC medium.

In this context, one of the most intriguing questions studied has been the effect of the loss of "richness" of nonverbal cues in this medium of communication (Daft & Lengel, 1984) and how such constrained interpersonal communication cues might affect group development.

Group Task and Communication Media

The "task" has been an important factor in group-work research. There is the question of which type of task the CMC medium is best suited for. Most small group researchers would agree that one cannot fully understand group processes or performance without taking into account the nature of the task being performed (see, e.g., Hackman & Morris, 1975). Numerous scholars have proposed theoretical frameworks that classify tasks on the basis of critical features. For example, a classification scheme for task variables comes from McGrath (1984) who proposed a circumplex model that discriminates tasks according to two dimensions: (1) demands for cooperation versus competition, and (2) cognitive versus behavioral activities. McGrath and his associates (McGrath, 1984; McGrath, Arrow, Gruenfeld, Hollingshead, & O'Connor, 1993; Straus & McGrath, 1994) predicted a relationship among task type, the medium used to perform the task, and indicators of group performance and satisfaction. McGrath and Hollingshead (1993) suggested that computer systems would be suitable for creativity tasks such as idea generation. When groups communicate via a computer network, group members are only able to compose, transmit, and receive text messages. Many channels through which face-to-face groups communicate—auditory, visual, nonverbal, and paraverbal—are greatly reduced or eliminated. As tasks requiring groups to generate ideas, such as brainstorming, require only the transmission of specific ideas, the paraverbal and nonverbal cues that provide emotional, attitudinal, normative, and other meanings beyond the literal denotations of the text are not necessarily needed or may inhibit group performance. In generating ideas, the distraction of other channels of communication are nonessential for effective task performance. To summarize, information richness is not required and may be considered a hindrance to brainstorming tasks.

Group Creativity

There are perhaps as many definitions and perspectives on creativity as there are people who choose to comment on the subject (which is perhaps as it should be, given the nature of the subject). In almost all definitions, however, there is an implication that creativity includes or involves a combination of originality and feasibility. The choices made during a creative process or the resultant products are not necessarily the most logically obvious, at least to most observers. Most research and theory on creativity processes focuses on individual creativity. However, the development of original ideas requires some basic level of knowledge in a variety of areas and such knowledge is often attained in a group context. Group interaction provides a basis for the exchange of information among group members. This information can be in the form of knowledge, skills, or new perspectives. Effective groups should have individuals with a diversity of knowledge and skills and be motivated for a full exchange of ideas. Although there might be a number of factors inhibiting groups from attaining this ideal, groups have much potential to facilitate creativity. From this point of view, creativity can be regarded as a social phenomenon and almost all creativity involves group processes.

Since so much creative activity relies on having a pool of ideas, coming up with those ideas is an important part of the creative process. Ideation, defined as "idea generation without evaluation," strategies are not only being used by practitioners in applied settings but also are being refined, tested, and evaluated in laboratory and field research (Jarboe, 1999). Brainstorming developed by Osborn (1957) is the classic and still influential divergent ideation strategy.

Brainstorming is a widely studied creativity task that is often an early phase of many group activities. Generating divergent ideas, not just routine notions is an important part of the problem-solving process, perhaps the most important since it is so difficult and unpredictable. Seeking better ways to facilitate the idea generation process, researchers have compared the performance of interactive groups with individuals or nominal groups. During the past forty decades, more than fifty studies have made this comparison, and most of these studies have shown that interactive groups are less effective than individuals (McGrath, 1984, p. 131), disproving the popular saying "two heads are better than one." In an attempt to identify which process losses are most consequential for group idea generation, Diehl and Stroebe (1987) examined this problem using a series of laboratory experiments. They found that production blocking (the fact that only one person can effectively talk at a time in verbal communication) inhibits performance most seriously for verbal group idea generation. They also identified other inhibitors (i.e., evaluation apprehension and free riding), the effects of which are often a function of the task being performed and the group composition.

Effects of Information Technology

While past research has shown interacting groups to be less effective than individuals or nominal groups, an experiment by Dennis and Valacich (1993) showed that electronically interacting groups can produce better results. The study demonstrated that not only could process losses be overcome but that process gains do exist. One of the most popular computer-based technologies designed to improve group performance is a group support system (GSS; Bostrom, Watson, & Kinney, 1992; Jessup & Valacich, 1993), which is of immense use in systems development, and also in support groups engaged in a variety of tasks requiring collaboration and coordination. A GSS is typically set up on personal computers and local area networks or computers linked over a network (e.g., LAN, Internet). Group members may interact either in real time (i.e., synchronously) or asynchronously; and may be either colocated or geographically dispersed. GSSs typically incorporate tools for capturing ideas generated by members of groups, and for organizing and evaluating them. GSSs are particularly well suited for group creativity tasks (Fellers & Bostrom, 1993).

GSS researchers have paid attention to the phenomenon of idea generation and there is considerable evidence of the support provided by GSSs for creativity tasks. Several studies have confirmed that groups using a GSS generate significantly more ideas than either nominal groups (individuals silently generating ideas) or verbally interacting groups (Dennis & Valacich, 1993; Gallupe, Bastianutti, & Cooper, 1991; Valacich, Dennis, & Connolly, 1994). The performance difference has been linked to GSS structural features (Gallupe, Bastianutti, & Cooper, 1991): (1) simultaneous generation of inputs which allows participants to express themselves without having to wait their turn; (2) anonymity (in some systems) which promotes candor in the comments made and thereby encourages "out-of-the-box" thinking; and (3) a common repository, or group memory, that continuously records all inputs directly on the system which permits the rapid and direct capture of input in the original form without interpretation by a facilitator. Consequently, participants in group sessions involving the use of a GSS, more often than not, speak their minds, and consistently generate more input in a given period of time than groups not using a GSS. There is likely to be more balanced participation with even the more taciturn members contributing to a discussion.

Of course there has been much research about GSSs, but the vast majority has focused on GSS usage in American and European cultures. Briggs, Nunamaker, and Sprague (1998) raised the question as to how many of past findings about GSS could be generalized to Asian or other non-European cultures. This study answers this question, examining whether it is possible for

CMC to be more suitable for group brainstorming than FTF in Japan as in Western countries.

Goal Setting

Very little is known about the contextual determinants of creative behavior in groups. The majority of work to date on creativity has been in two main areas: research that has focused on individual characteristics in an attempt to identify the "creative personality" (Cattell & Butcher, 1968; MacKinnon, 1975) and work focused on ways to increase or nurture creativity (Barron, 1965; Osborn, 1957). Less attention has been focused on ways in which the environment may affect creativity (Amabile, 1983; Simonton, 1975), and most of these studies focused on not group but individual creativity. The purpose of this study is to examine the creativity issue by looking at the effects of one of the important contextual factors, goal setting, on group performance. As creativity is one of the most critical phases in the group innovation process, there may be the need to examine environmental factors that might enhance or stifle group creativity. If the environment can be structured to encourage creativity, this creative innovativeness may contribute to higher group performance and even the long-term productivity and innovativeness of the organization (Galbraith, 1982).

Numerous past studies have found that goals that are both specific and difficult lead to a higher level of task performance than vague (do-your-best) goals, low goals, or no goals (Locke, Shaw, Saari, & Latham, 1981; Mento, Steel, & Karren, 1987). Also, a meta-analysis on group goals by O'Leary-Kelly, Martocchio, and Frink (1994) revealed that specific, difficult group goals lead to better performance than other types of goals, just as in the case of individual goals. Although many investigations have been done on goal-setting theory, there seems to have been no study that focused on the effects of goal setting in a computer-mediated context.

On the other hand, in recent years, interest in stimulating group creativity has grown as innovation, creativity, learning, and team development have become important ingredients for competition (Woodman, Sawyer, & Griffin, 1993). Many organizations have deployed advanced information technology such as a GSS to address the need to enhance group creativity. Most prior research done on GSS has focused on examining how technical aspects, such as anonymity and parallel communication, influence group creativity (Jessup, Connolly, & Galegher, 1990; Valacich, Dennis, & Nunamaker, 1992; Cooper, Gallupe, Sandra, & Cadsby, 1998). Recently, a growing number of researchers have become interested in examining the soft processes that can also affect a group's performance under computer-mediated conditions. For example, Sosik, Avolio, and Kahai (1998) examined the effect of the leadership process on creativity in GSS groups. Sosik, Avolio, and Kahai regarded goal setting as a main factor of transactional leadership and suggested that it was positively related to group creativity. But the goal expressed by transactional leaders in their study was only a do-your-best one and they did not focus on the difference of assigned goal style. As mentioned, the impact of specific and difficult goals on group creativity would be more positive than a do-your-best goal. This study examines how different goal styles may affect group creativity in a computer-mediated context. Given that CMC groups are more task-focused than FTF groups (Schmitz & Fulk, 1991), the impact of goal setting on group creativity is expected to be more positive under CMC than FTF conditions. A 2 × 2 factorial design was used to compare the number of nonredundant ideas and their creativity generated by CMC versus FTF groups. The two factors were communication medium (computer mediation versus face-to-face) and goal setting (assigned goal and do one's best).

METHOD

Participants

Ninety-six undergraduate and graduate students (fifty-six males and forty females) volunteered to participate in the experiment. The mean age of the participants was 21.8 years with a range of 19 to 24. All the participants had some familiarity with the computer network and all had already acquired touch-typing skills before this experiment. Participants were not acquainted with one another prior to the experiment. The participants were randomly assigned to one of 32 three-person ad hoc groups. Each group was randomly assigned to one of four experimental conditions (eight for each condition). Twenty-four of the groups were two-male and one-female groups and eight were one-male and two-female groups. There was no gender difference in dependent variables.

Task

The brainstorming task was the Unusual Uses Task (UUT), which has been used extensively as a creativity task. Participants are asked to generate ideas about unusual uses for a wire hanger, which is usually used for hanging clothes.

Experimental Manipulation

Goal Setting

Participants were assigned a difficult assigned productivity goal (twenty ideas) or a do-your-best productivity goal (generate as many ideas as possible) to work toward during the fifteen-minute experimental session. Each group received the goal orally from an experimenter. The difficult goal level was set on the basis of results of the pilot study in which 15% of groups in FTF condition generated twenty or more ideas. Prior research has defined a difficult goal as one for which the objective probability of attainment is relatively low (e.g.,

$p = 0.14$, Frost & Mahoney, 1976; $p = 0.20$, Motowidlo, Dunnette, & Loehr, 1978; $p = 0.12$, Shalley, 1991). Thus, this goal was within the appropriate difficulty range.

Communication Medium

Participants in the CMC condition communicated over a computer network. The four computers were connected using a Windows 95 operating system. The network software included a communication tool that allowed users to type and send messages to other group members. All messages remained on the screen throughout the task, thereby allowing participants to review previous messages. Each window for the task scrolled down automatically as the number of messages increased. Thus, the most recent messages were always in view. They were instructed to use the computer for all interaction; no verbal communication among members occurred. The ideas were entered by participants and stored by group. Participants in the FTF condition communicated verbally in the same room and wrote their ideas on paper while communicating those ideas to the other members.

Experimental Procedures

All experimental sessions took place in the laboratory of the Department of Social Psychology, Osaka University. In the FTF condition, upon arrival in the lab, participants were seated around a table with the two other participants. They were given place cards with their first names printed on them. In the CMC condition, members of each group were introduced to one another at the start of experiment, and after that they were escorted out of sight of each other and seated at computer terminals connected to a local area network as shown Figure 10.1. Each participant had access to a small, laptop computer during the experimental session. Each comment they typed during the experiment was automatically identified by the author's name, so that each participant could see who had made each previous comment. It was clear to the members that their group was made up of the participants to whom they had been introduced, but no group members communicated verbally to any other members during the session.

Participants of all the conditions first completed a presession questionnaire that asked their age, gender, prior experience with computers and computer-mediated group work. Typing ability was asked about only in the CMC condition. Participants were then given task instructions as follows:

1. In this study you will work on a creativity task.
2. You should work as a group. Express all your ideas to the group.
3. You will have fifteen minutes for the creativity task. I will keep track of the time for you. I will give you the name of a common object and you are to list as many unusual uses for that item as you can. For example, if I said "hairpin," you might

conceive an idea such as "to pick a lock," since that would be an unusual use for a hairpin. You would not write down "to hold hair in place" since that is the intended use of a hairpin. Before we begin I'd like to make some suggestions for improving your performance. First, try to avoid criticizing ideas or uses, no matter how wild they may seem. Second, remember that wild ideas are welcome, because they can be toned down much more easily than new ideas can be generated. Third, try to produce as many ideas as possible. Fourth, try to combine and improve your ideas by using one idea as a steppingstone to another. In other words, you should make an effort to make ideas presented by other members a clue to generating a new idea.

4. 1. (FTF condition) In order to prevent duplicate listing of ideas, each of you should write down only those ideas you came up with yourself. However, all ideas should be expressed aloud, for you are to work as a group.

4. 2. (CMC condition) Each of you should type all ideas you come up with. You have to use the computer for all interactions within the group and not express any ideas or related comments aloud.

Groups were given a five-minute practice session and after that they were given fifteen minutes in which to generate ideas. The common object in the task was a coat hanger made of wire. After finishing the fifteen-minute task, participants completed the postsession questionnaire and were debriefed.

Figure 10.1
Experimental Room of the CMC Condition (overhead view)

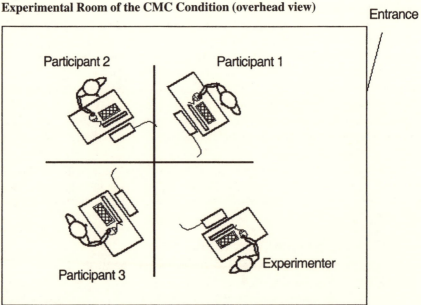

DEPENDENT VARIABLES

Productivity

The main dependent variable was the number of nonredundant ideas produced per group. The data were coded and two experienced coders who were unaware of the hypotheses and treatment assessed the number of nonredundant ideas. The interater correlation of the coders was 0.94.

Creativity

The second dependent variable was the creativity of the generated idea, which was operationalized into novelty, originality, and feasibility. Novelty was defined as the degree of uncommonness compared with an original use. Originality was defined as the degree of uniqueness in its usage and object. Feasibility was defined as the degree of actual applicability. Two experienced coders assessed each of the previously coded nonredundant ideas. They were both hypotheses- and treatment-blind. The degree of agreement between the two coders was acceptable ($r = 0.84$, $p < 0.01$), so the average score of the two coders was calculated for each idea. Then the average score of each group was used as the measure of the second dependent variable.

Postsession Questionnaire

Responses to the items on the postsession questionnaire were also used to assess additional differences among the conditions. Two variables, perceived motivation and contribution to the task, were assessed on five-point scales that had verbal anchors at each response option. Each variable was assessed with a four-item scale. Motivation was assessed with items such as "How motivated were you to generate ideas?" (1 = definitely motivated, 5 = very motivated; *alpha* = 0.85). Contribution was assessed with items such as "Did you feel you had sufficient opportunity to express your ideas during the idea generation session?" (1 = little opportunity, 5 = ample opportunity; *alpha* = 0.82). With reference to the high Cronbach's alphas, scores for these items were summed at the individual level to form a scale for perceived motivation and contribution.

RESULTS

Manipulation Checks

Checks on the goal-setting manipulation were included in a postsession questionnaire. The manipulation was checked by one item: "Our group was provided one clear goal for the task." Items were anchored by 1 (No, not at all) and 5 (Yes, very much). Individual-level responses to this item were analyzed with a two-factor (communication medium × goal setting) ANOVA. The assigned goal groups (*Average* = 4.48) more often responded that they made an effort toward one clear goal than the do-your-best groups (*Average* = 1.33). The communication medium manipulation had no effect on this measure. Thus the goal-setting manipulation appears to have been successful.

Substantive Findings

Table 10.1 presents the scale means, standard deviations of all the group–individual dependent variables for each of the four experimental conditions.

Table 10.2 summarizes results of a series of two-way ANOVAs using communication medium and the goal-setting condition as independent variables and idea productivity and creativity as dependent variables. This analysis was conducted at the group level ($n = 32$). An ANOVA of the number of nonredundant ideas revealed a significant main effect for communication medium. The CMC groups produced more nonredundant ideas than FTF groups (CMC = 18.69, FTF = 15.38). In contrast, there were no main effects for communication medium on idea creativity. The other manipulation, assigned goal or do your best, did not affect idea productivity and creativity. In addition, marginally significant communication medium × goal setting interactions were found for the number of nonredundant ideas and idea originality. In the FTF condition, assigned goal groups (*Average* = 16.88) generated more ideas than do-your-best groups (*Average* = 13.88), while there was no difference in the CMC condition (assigned goal = 18.63, do your best = 18.75). In the case of idea originality, there was not the same interaction pattern as with idea productivity. In the FTF condition, do-your-best groups (*Average* = 3.25) generated more original ideas than assigned goal groups (*Average* = 2.78), while there was no difference in the CMC condition (assigned goal = 3.05, do your best = 2.90).

The results of two-way ANOVAs, using communication medium and goal-setting condition as independent variables and the two scales of the postsession questionnaire as dependent variables, are also shown in Table 10.2. This analysis was conducted at the individual level ($n = 96$). An ANOVA of perceived motivation revealed a marginally significant communication medium effect, no effect for goal setting, and no interaction effect. CMC groups were marginally more motivated (*Average* = 16.33) to the task than the FTF groups (*Average* = 15.44). An ANOVA of perceived contribution revealed a significant communication medium effect, a significant interaction effect, and no effect for goal setting. The members of the CMC groups felt that they could contribute to their task more actively (*Average* = 15.56) than the members of the FTF groups (*Average* = 14.75). The interaction effect showed that the CMC × do-your-best groups (*Average* = 16.08) felt they had contributed the most in the idea-generation process of all the conditions.

Table 10.1
Means and Standard Deviations for Dependent Variables

Dependent variable	n	FTF		CMC	
		Assigned goal	Do your best	Assigned goal	Do your best
No. of nonredundant ideas	32 groups				
M		16.88	13.88	18.63	18.75
SD		2.70	2.42	2.39	2.71
Novelty	32 groups				
M		3.10	3.21	2.90	3.17
SD		0.66	0.47	0.72	0.71
Originality	32 groups				
M		2.78	3.25	3.05	2.90
SD		0.60	0.36	0.54	0.37
Feasibility	32 groups				
M		3.02	3.57	3.19	3.19
SD		0.58	0.72	0.66	0.86
Motivation	96 participants				
M		15.08	15.79	16.42	16.25
SD		2.59	2.15	2.06	2.51
Contribution	96 participants				
M		14.96	14.54	15.04	16.08
SD		1.46	1.61	1.57	1.82

DISCUSSION

Results from this study add evidence to previous research demonstrating that CMC groups are more productive than FTF groups in an idea-generation task (Dennis & Valacich, 1993; Valacich, Dennis, & Connolly, 1994). Group brainstorming on CMC achieved more productivity than FTF in Japan as in North America and European countries. Study findings also provide support for the notion that creative behavior is influenced not only by dispositional

Table 10.2
F Values for Dependent Variables for 2 × 2 ANOVA

Dependent Variables	n	Communication Medium (CM)	Goal setting (GS)	CM x GS
No. of nonredundant ideas	32	13.42[**]	2.53	2.99[†]
Novelty	32	0.26	0.70	0.13
Originality	32	0.06	0.85	3.16[†]
Feasibility	32	0.19	1.30	1.09
Motivation	96	3.53[†]	0.32	0.84
Contribution	96	6.03[*]	0.89	4.86[*]

$†p < 0.10$; $*p < 0.05$; $**p < 0.01$.

attributes, but also by contextual or situational influences (Kasof, 1995). Electronic interaction produced numbers of ideas equivalent to those produced in the FTF condition and participants in the CMC condition were more motivated and actively participated in the discussion. Thus, it was found that the use of computers could free people's ability to produce ideas, replicating earlier research (Gallupe, Bastianutti, & Cooper, 1991; Dennis & Valacich, 1993; Gallupe, Cooper, Grise, & Bastianutti, 1994).

Electronic technology yielded greater productivity in terms of the quantity of generated ideas but had no significant effect on the quality. Despite representative benefits of computer-mediated communication such as the elimination of production blocking, no gains in group creativity were shown in the CMC condition. There has been a long unsolved debate in the context of creativity research as to whether productivity can be resolved into creativity (Homma, 1996). If evaluation apprehension (one of the major inhibitors of group creativity) is mitigated and more creative ideas are generated in the CMC condition, the difference between the medium conditions would also be seen in group creativity. However, it has been suggested that these results did not support our prediction but the significant improvement of performance occurred only in terms of group productivity. At least in this study, it must be concluded that a larger number of responses does not result in more creative responses.

In an individual-level analysis of postsession questionnaires, results were in general as expected. In the CMC condition, members tended to be highly motivated and more eagerly confront the brainstorming task. This result replicates the finding of Zigurs, Poole, and DeSanctis (1988) that task motivation of members is higher in the CMC setting than the FTF setting. It implies that members tend to increase task-oriented behavior in a computer-mediated context (Schmitz & Fulk, 1991). We found a significant interaction effect on perceived contribution. Especially the do-your-best groups in the CMC condition perceived that they had more sufficient opportunity to participate in the task than any other groups. This is clear evidence that some process gains (Dennis & Valacich, 1993) on group productivity exist in the CMC condition, which does not have as much pressure to achieve the goal. In the case of computer brainstorming, all participants have their own computer, which enables them to contribute simultaneously. That is, members need not wait for others to finish before contributing ideas. Members can read all generated ideas on their own screen and respond by building them into new ideas, by ignoring them and generating unrelated ideas, or, of course, by doing nothing. These characteristics of computer brainstorming may lighten the cognitive load of members and lead to some process gains on group performance. For further investigation of process gain on CMC, the characteristics of this communication style must be explored through content analysis.

These results indicate that setting a productivity goal did not enhance both productivity and creativity in the CMC condition. Although it has been shown that a difficult specific goal had a positive effect on group performance in many previous studies, the manipulation of goal setting in this study might have established a favorable context only in the FTF condition. These unexpected results might have been caused by a ceiling effect of CMC on group productivity. As shown in Table 10.1, groups in the CMC condition produced more than eighteen ideas on average. The range of generated ideas was sixteen to twenty-five in the CMC condition and six of sixteen groups (three groups in each goal condition) generated over twenty ideas, whereas only two of sixteen groups in the FTF condition did so. This result suggests that the assigned goal was not necessarily a difficult one in the CMC × assigned-goal condition. I predicted that the assigned-goal condition would perform better than the do-your-best condition. However, the predicted effect was not obtained. On the one hand, groups in the do-your-best condition might have had some process gain in their performance, but on the other, groups in the goal-setting condition did not remarkably exceed their performance goal. Consequently, no significant difference between goal-setting conditions was found. In future research, through more elaboration of proper level of the assigned goal, the effect of goal setting on CMC group brainstorming should be reconsidered.

Future research can address certain limitations of this study. First the number of groups studied was relatively small ($n = 32$). Although it was adequate for statistical analysis, this sample size may have led to a restriction in the range of responses, reduced variance in the study variables, and a masking of relations among communication medium, goal setting, and group process (productivity, creativity, and response to the postsession questionnaire). Future studies should examine these relations with a larger number of groups.

Second, participants in this experiment worked in temporary ad hoc groups, which were not well established, to perform a short-term laboratory task. Although prior familiarity was intentionally controlled because of the limited number of participants, at the same time, this short-term nature of their relationship may serve as a potential limitation to the generalizability of our findings. For example, adult work groups that have a history of interaction with each other may import norms or styles of interaction into brainstorming sessions. Also prior research indicates that group history and the expectation of future interaction may be important factors in moderating the effects of communication medium on group process and performance (Weisband, Schneider, & Connolly, 1995). Thus, the findings of this study should be interpreted as being most applicable to temporary ad hoc groups. In future research the history and experience that groups have with each other, and how it is imported into group brainstorming sessions should be examined. It would also be important to compare these results in ad hoc groups with findings of intact groups attempting to accomplish complex, long-term tasks in future research.

Third, the effect of group size and member characteristics may also be considered in future research. For example, Valacich, Dennis, and Nunamaker (1992) reported a laboratory experiment that examined the effect of group size (three and nine members) on the performance of groups using a computer-mediated idea generation system. They found that larger groups generated significantly more and higher-quality ideas than did smaller groups. Although it is possible to examine the positive effect of CMC on group performance even in relatively small-size groups, the optimal group size that can be adequately supported in computer brainstorming is worthy of further investigation.

Clearly, much more research is needed to provide a more complete understanding of the effects of computer mediation on group interaction and task performance, and the effects of these advanced technologies on group process, structure, and outcomes. In this study, the effect of communication medium on group performance was examined, especially paying attention to the difference of style. Of course, in the next study, close investigation of the characteristics of each media (especially CMC) with qualitative analysis (e.g., protocol analysis, conversational analysis) is necessary. Communication technology might be the key to making a breakthrough in group creativity research. Advances in communication technology have provided the tools and capabilities needed to expand the group creativity process beyond the horizon of a face-to-face environment and verbal brainstorming. It is time to seize this opportunity and push group creativity to the next stage of development.

NOTE

This study was funded, in part, from the Kayamori Foundation of Informational Science Advancement.

REFERENCES

Amabile, T. M. (1983). *The social psychology of creativity*. New York: Springer-Verlag.

Barron, F. (1965). The psychology of creativity. In T. Newcomb (Ed.), *New direction in psychology* (vol. 2, pp. 1–34). New York: Holt, Rinehart & Winston.

Bostrom, R. P., Watson, R. T., & Kinney, S. T. (1992). *Computer augmented teamwork: A guided tour*. New York: Van Nostrand Reinhold.

Briggs, R. O., Nunamaker, J. F. Jr., & Sprague, R. H. Jr. (1998). 1001 unanswered research questions in GSS. *Journal of Management Information Systems, 14*, 3–21.

Cattell. R. B., & Butcher, H. J. (1968). *The prediction of achievement and creativity*. New York: Bobbs-Merrill.

Cooper, W. H., Gallupe, R. B., Sandra, P., & Cadsby, J. (1998). Some liberating effects of anonymous electronic brainstorming. *Small Group Research, 29*, 147–178.

Daft, R. L., & Lengel, R. H. (1984). Information richness: A new approach to managerial behavior and organizational design. *Research in Organizational Behavior, 6*, 191–233.

Dennis, A. R., & Valacich, J. S. (1993). Computer brainstorms: More heads are better than one. *Journal of Applied Psychology, 78*, 531–537.

Diehl, M., & Stroebe, W. (1987). Productivity loss in brainstorming groups: Toward the solution of a riddle. *Journal of Personality and Social Psychology, 53*, 497–509.

Feenberg, A. (1987). The planetary classroom. In E. Strefferud, O. J. Jacobsen, & P. Schicker (Eds.), *Proceedings of IFIP symposium on message handling systems and distributed publications*. North-Holland: Elsevier Science.

Fellers, J. W., & Bostrom, R. P. (1993). Application of group support systems to promote creativity in information systems organizations. In T. Mudge, V. Milutinovic, & L. Hunter (Eds.), *Proceedings of the 26th Annual Hawaiian International Conference on System Sciences* (pp. 332–341). Los Alamitos, CA: IEEE Computer Society Press.

Frost, P. J., & Mahoney, T. A. (1976). Goal setting and the task process: I. An interactive influence on individual performance. *Organizational Behavior and Human Decision Processes, 17*, 328–350.

Galbraith, J. R. (1982). Designing the innovating organization. *Organizational Dynamics, 10*, 5–25.

Gallupe, R. B., Bastianutti, L. M., & Cooper, W. H. (1991). Unblocking brainstorms. *Journal of Applied Psychology, 76*, 137–142.

Gallupe, R. B., Cooper, W. H., Grise, M. L., & Bastianutti, L. M. (1994). Blocking electronic brainstorms. *Journal of Applied Psychology, 79*, 77–86.

Hackman, J. R., & Morris, C. G. (1975). Group tasks, group interaction process, and group performance effectiveness: A review and proposed integration. In L. Berkowitz (Ed.), *Advances in experimental social psychology* (vol. 8, pp. 47–100). San Diego, CA: Academic Press.

Hapeshi, K., & Jones, D. M. (1992). Interactive multimedia for instruction: A cognitive analysis of the role of audition and vision. *International Journal of Human Computer Interaction, 4*, 79–99.

Hiltz, S. R., & Turoff, M. (1993). *The network nation: Human communication via computer*. Cambridge, MA: MIT Press.

Homma, M. (1996). Reconsidering group productivity in brainstorming. *Japanese Psychological Review, 39*, 252–272.

Jarboe, S. (1999). Group communication and creativity process. In R. F. Lawrence (Ed.), *The handbook of group communication theory and research* (pp. 335–368). Thousand Oaks, CA: Sage.

Jessup, L., & Valacich, J. S. (1993). *Group support systems: New perspectives.* New York: Macmillan.

Jessup, L., Connolly, T., & Galegher, J. (1990). The effects of anonymity on group process in an idea generating task. *MIS Quarterly, 14*, 313–321.

Kasof, J. (1995). Social determinants of creativity: Status expectations and the evaluation of original products. In M. Barry, K. Heimer, & J. O'Brien (Eds.), *Advances in group processes* (vol. 12, pp. 167–220). Greenwich, CT: JAI Press.

Locke, E. A., Shaw, K. N., Saari, L. M., & Latham, G. P. (1981). Goal setting and task performance: 1969–1980. *Psychological Bulletin, 90*, 125–152.

MacKinnon, D. W. (1975). IPAR's contribution to the conceptualization and study of creativity. In I. Taylor & J. Getzels (Eds.), *Perspectives in creativity* (pp. 60–89). Chicago: Aldine.

McGrath, J. E. (1984). *Groups: Interaction and performance.* Englewood Cliffs, NJ: Prentice Hall.

McGrath, J. E., & Hollingshead, A. B. (1993). Putting the "group" back in group support systems: Some theoretical issues about dynamic processes in groups with technological enhancements. In L. M. Jussup & J. S. Valacich (Eds.), *Group support systems: New perspectives.* New York: Macmillan.

McGrath, J. E., Arrow, H., Gruenfeld, D. H., Hollingshead, A. B., & O'Connor, K. M. (1993). Groups, tasks, and technology: The effects of experience and change. *Small Group Research, 24*, 406–420.

Mento, A. J., Steel, R. P., & Karren, R. J. (1987). A meta-analytic study of the effects of goal setting on task performance: 1966–1984. *Organizational Behavior and Human Decision Processes, 39*, 52–83.

Motowidlo, S. J., Dunnette, M. D., & Loehr, V. (1978). A laboratory study of the effects of goal specificity on the relationship between probability of success and performance. *Journal of Applied Psychology, 63*, 172–179.

O'Leary-Kelly, A. M., Martocchio, J. J., & Frink, D. D. (1994). A review of the influence of group goals on group performance. *Academy of Management Journal, 37*, 1285–1301.

Osborn, A. F. (1957). *Applied imagination* (2d ed.). New York: Scribner.

Rice, R. E. (1993). Media appropriateness: Using social presence theory to compare traditional and new organizational media. *Human Communication Research, 19*, 451–484.

Schmitz, J., & Fulk, J. (1991). Organizational colleagues, media richness, and electronic mail. *Communication Research, 18*, 487–523.

Shalley, C. E. (1991). Effects of productivity goals, creativity goals, and personal discretion on individual creativity. *Journal of Applied Psychology, 76*, 179–185.

Simonton, D. K. (1975). Sociocultural context of individual creativity: A transhistorical time-series analysis. *Journal of Personality and Social Psychology, 32*, 1119–1133.

Sosik, J. J., Avolio, B. J., & Kahai, S. S. (1998). Inspiring group creativity: Comparing anonymous and identified electronic brainstorming. *Small Group Research, 29*, 3–31.

Straus, S. G., & McGrath, J. E. (1994). Does the medium matter: The interaction of task and technology on group performance and member reactions. *Journal of Applied Psychology, 79*, 87–97.

Valacich, J. S., Dennis, A. R., & Connolly, T. (1994). Idea generation in computer-based groups: A new ending to an old story. *Organizational Behavior and Human Decision Processes, 57*, 448–467.

Valacich, J. S., Dennis, A. R., & Nunamaker, J. F. (1992). Group size and anonymity effects on computer-mediated idea generation. *Small Group Research, 23*, 49–73.

Weisband, S., Schneider, S. K., & Connolly, T. (1995). Computer mediated communication and social information: Status salience and status differences. *Academy of Management Journal, 38*, 1124–1151.

Woodman, R. W., Sawyer, J. E., & Griffin, R. W. (1993). Toward a theory of organizational creativity. *Academy of Management Review, 18*, 293–321.

Zigurs, I., Poole, M. S., & DeSanctis, G. L. (1988). A study of influence in computer-mediated group decision making. *MIS Quarterly, 12*, 625–644.

CHAPTER 11

Coexistence of Equity and Interpersonal Harmony among Recipients: Reward Allocation as an Instrument for Group Management

Fumio Murakami

Since Adams's (1965) pioneering work, research on reward allocation has been conducted from various theoretical perspectives (for reviews, see Deutsch, 1983; Cook & Hegtvedt, 1983). In the equity theory tradition, which was dominant at an earlier stage, reward allocation is conceptualized within exchange theory (e.g., Walster, Berscheid, & Walster, 1976). Equity in this tradition means that each recipient receives resources (outcome) in proportion to contribution (input). Equity theory focuses on fair compensation for contribution.

It has also been claimed that the goal of reward allocation affects the preference for a particular allocation rule (Deutsch, 1975). Deutsch hypothesized that equitable allocation is dominant when economic productivity is the primary goal, whereas equal allocation is dominant when interpersonal harmony is the primary goal. Based on Deutsch's hypotheses, equitable allocation can be considered an inappropriate means of maintaining interpersonal harmony. The main purpose of this study is to investigate whether equitable allocation, reflecting productivity goals, can coexist with maintenance of interpersonal harmony among recipients.

MOTIVATIONS IN REWARD ALLOCATION: HARMONY MAINTENANCE AND PRODUCTIVITY PROMOTION

A considerable amount of empirical evidence supports Deutsch's (1975) hypotheses that preferred choice of allocation principle depends on the goal of allocation. Leventhal, Michaels, and Sanford (1972) showed that when participants were told to avoid conflict, they reduced the difference in reward between high and low performers. Allocators preferred the equality rule when they made the allocation decision publicly, but they did not prefer the equity rule when they made the decision secretly (e.g., Lane & Messe, 1971; Reis & Gruzen, 1976). It has been suggested that allocators believe that the equity rule might damage harmonious relationships in the group. Cross-cultural studies have also supported Deutsch's hypotheses. Leung and Bond (1984) showed that the Chinese, who are assumed to be collectivistic, prefer the equal distribution of rewards among ingroup members to a greater extent than among strangers. They explained that for collectivists harmonious relationships among ingroup members are more important than among strangers. Mahler, Greenberg, and Hayashi (1981) showed that the Japanese prefer the equality principle in reward allocation, whereas Americans prefer the equity principle.

In an attempt to test Deutsch's (1975) hypotheses directly, Leung and Park (1986) examined whether reward allocation is affected by perception of the interaction goals. If the participants perceived that promotion of productivity was the primary goal, they allocated a larger share of the rewards to a high performer and judged equitable allocation as fairer. On the other hand, if maintenance of harmonious relationships was perceived as the primary goal, they allocated a smaller share to the high performer and judged equal allocation as fairer. This empirical evidence suggests that primacy of goals affects choice of allocation rule. In other words, environmental factors affect the allocator's orientation.

According to Deutsch's (1975) hypotheses, the equity principle and interpersonal harmony can be considered mutually exclusive, at least concerning the preference for reward allocation rule. If an allocator intends to maintain harmonious relationships among recipients, equal allocation must be chosen. However, equitable allocation and equal allocation are incompatible when there is a difference of recipients' contribution. So, based on Deutsch's (1975) argument, when an allocator adopts an equitable allocation, it means that the allocator disregards harmony maintenance.

Conceptually, harmony orientation and productivity orientation are mutually independent and can coexist. Yamaguchi, Inoue, Muramoto, and Ozawa (1997) investigated the importance of interpersonal harmony and productivity by asking participants to indicate how much they cared about these two goals in an allocation situation described in a vignette. The results indicated that harmony maintenance and productivity enhancement motives are independently related to reward allocation; people can have harmony and productivity goals at the same time.

As Leventhal (1980) argued, reward allocation is based on conditional decision standards such as the allocator's role, the importance of an allocator's other goals, and so on. Especially in East Asia, the social role is one of the powerful motives determining reward allocation (Chiu & Hong, 1997; Zhang & Yang,

1998). Thus, the two goals, maintenance of harmony and promotion of productivity, are related to the expected social role of the allocator. The allocator's choice of reward allocation rule is affected more by the required social role than consistent justice concerns. In this study, both promotion of productivity and maintenance of harmony are treated as the required roles of the allocator.

MAINTENANCE OF INTERPERSONAL HARMONY WITH EQUITABLE ALLOCATION

Harmony orientation can coexist with productivity orientation. In this study, investigation focuses on whether equitable allocation, which is assumed to promote productivity, is preferred when interpersonal harmony must also be maintained. When an allocator must maintain interpersonal harmony and promote productivity at the same time, both goals cannot be fulfilled through reward allocation because each goal leads to a different allocation rule. A harmony goal leads to equal allocation, whereas productivity goals lead to equitable allocation. However, if harmonious relationships can be maintained without equal allocation, productivity goals can be obtained through equitable allocation and both goals achieved. In order to investigate how interpersonal harmony can be maintained without equal allocation, it is necessary to know how equal allocation works to enhance harmonious relationships.

Theorists have argued that equal allocation works to maintain interpersonal harmony by decreasing the sense of relative deprivation (Deutsch, 1975), and emphasizing common fate and group solidarity (Leventhal, 1976; Mikula, 1980). The common factors among these functions are disregarding individual differences and perceiving the group as a unit. People prefer equal allocation when they perceive the group as a unit (Markham, 1988), suggesting that group solidarity is closely related to the choice of equal allocation. Equal allocation makes individual differences in contribution less important (Mikula, 1980). In contrast, equitable allocation works to promote productivity because it enhances recipients' motivation to work hard as individual differences in contribution are reflected in allocated rewards. Thus, harmony goals lead to focus on the group as a unit, whereas the productivity goals lead to focus on individual recipients.

This study is focused on whether equitable allocation is more acceptable to recipients if the allocator also uses an additional strategy to promote harmony than if an allocator does not use such a strategy. I hypothesize that if the allocator can maintain harmonious relationships using alternative strategies recipients will feel less need to maintain harmonious relationships through equal allocation.

In order to investigate how the strategy to maintain harmonious relationships affect individuals' evaluation of allocation rules, the effect of the reward allocation on recipients' feelings was examined. Satisfaction with the allocated rewards reflects a decreased sense of relative deprivation. The allocator should feel less need to keep harmonious relationships through equal distribution when recipients are perceived as being satisfied with the equitable allocation because emphasis on group solidarity will enhance the recipients' sense of membership and ease emotional hardships that could be generated by individual differences in allocated rewards. In sum, I hypothesize that people consider an equitable distribution of rewards more acceptable when group solidarity is enhanced than when it is not. Before testing this prediction, a preliminary study was conducted to investigate the characteristics of productivity and harmony orientation.

PRELIMINARY STUDY

A preliminary correlational study using a scenario was conducted for two purposes. First, it attempted to replicate the two-factor structure of allocation orientation reported in Yamaguchi and colleagues (1997). If productivity orientation and harmony orientation are mutually independent, different strategies can fulfill each orientation at the same time. Second, the relationship between causal attribution of differences in performance and the two allocation orientations was examined. Previous research has shown that people prefer equity when performance is determined by effort, which is controllable, whereas they prefer equality when performance is uncontrollable or to luck (Utne & Kidd, 1980; Farwell & Weiner, 1996). Productivity orientation would motivate an allocator to distribute rewards in proportion to workers' performance, unless their performance is attributed to luck. Harmony orientation would motivate the allocator to distribute rewards equally regardless of differences in performance or how the allocator attributes the differences.

Method

Participants

Participants were recruited from an introductory psychology class at a university in Tokyo. There were 162 undergraduate students (92 males) voluntarily participating in the study.

Procedure

The participants were presented with a scenario along with a questionnaire at a regular class meeting. They were asked to assume the role of the person in charge of allocating rewards at a workplace.

Scenario

The job was to get interviews with passersby on the street. The number of the interviews was counted as the performance of the interviewer. The manager allocated the rewards for one month, 180,000 yen (US$1,600) to three part-time interviewers. The three interviewers contributed 50%, 33%, and 17% of the total interviews, respectively. Four allocation alternatives were available to the manager.

Dependent Variables

The questionnaire contained items concerning the participants' choice of allocation, orientation in allocation, and the attribution of difference in performance.

1. *Allocation of rewards.* The participants were asked to choose an allocation method from the four choices given in the questionnaire. The four options included the equitable allocation, the equal allocation, and two intermediate allocations.

2. *Allocation orientation.* Participants were asked to indicate how much consideration they gave to each of nine issues. Of the nine issues, five were relevant to harmony orientation: (1) maintaining good relationships among people; (2) not dissatisfying the low performance member; (3) not dissatisfying anyone; (4) satisfying everyone; and (5) not making people dislike the allocator. The other four issues were relevant to productivity orientation: (6) satisfying members who worked hard; (7) not rewarding members who did not work hard; (8) letting people fully use their abilities; and (9) not deteriorating recipients' motivation.

3. *Attribution of performance.* The participants were asked to indicate how they would attribute the recipients' performance in terms of ability, effort, and luck on a seven-point scale. Then they were asked to indicate the relative proportion in percentage that ability, effort, and luck played in the worker's results. Percentages had to equal 100.

Results and Discussion

Allocation Orientation

The participants were asked nine questions regarding what they had considered in their reward allocation. A principal component factor analysis was conducted on their responses. Because the scree plot of the resulting eigenvalues indicated a two-factor structure, the two factors were extracted and rotated by means of the varimax procedure. As can be seen in Table 11.1, the first factor represents Harmony Orientation, and the second represents Productivity Orientation. This result is consistent with the findings in Yamaguchi and colleagues (1997). Harmony and productivity orientation items were each summed to yield two composite scores representing the participant's harmony orientation and productivity orientation. The correlation coefficient between the two composite scores was very small and not significant, $r = 0.03$. The coefficient *alphas* for the harmony orientation and the productivity orientation scores were 0.78 and 0.81, respectively.

Table 11.1
Factor Loadings of Nine Consideration Items on Allocation Orientations (Varimax Rotated)

Item	Harmony Orientation	Productivity Orientation
Not dissatisfy anyone	*0.75*	0.04
Maintain good relationship among people	*0.72*	-0.25
Not dissatisfy low performance member	*0.70*	-0.29
Satisfy everyone	*0.69*	-0.03
Not make people have a grudge against the allocator	*0.62*	-0.16
Satisfy members who make efforts	0.18	*0.78*
Not reward the members who do not work hard	-0.03	*0.77*
Let people give full play to their abilities	0.11	*0.74*
Not decrease recipients' motivation	0.50	*0.53*
Eigenvalue	2.72	2.20
Proportion (%)	30.3	24.5

Note: Factor loadings greater than 0.5 are italicized.

Correlational Analyses

The relationship among the participant's reward allocation, allocation orientation, and performance attribution was examined. Harmony orientation was positively correlated with the choice of equal distribution of reward, $r = 0.47$, $p < 0.001$, whereas the correlation of productivity orientation with the choice of equal distribution was negative, $r = -0.41$, $p < 0.01$. As expected, people with a higher harmony orientation tended to allocate equally. People with a higher productivity orientation tended to allocate equitably. Also as expected, the more participants attributed the recipients' performance to effort, the more they tended to prefer the equity rule, $r = 0.21$, $p < 0.01$, whereas, the more they attributed the recipients' performance to luck, the more they tended to prefer the equality rule, $r = 0.24$, $p < 0.01$.

The correlations between the harmony and productivity orientations and attributions are presented in Table 11.2. Attribution to effort was positively correlated

Table 11.2
Correlations between the Orientations and the Attributions

Attribution of Performance	Harmony Orientation		Productivity Orientation	
Effort	-0.07	n.s.	0.23	$p < .01$
Ability	0.11	n.s.	-0.05	n.s.
Luck	-0.04	n.s.	-0.24	$p < .01$

with the productivity orientation, whereas attribution to luck was negatively correlated with the productivity orientation. As predicted, consideration of the individual differences was related only to productivity orientation.

In the preliminary scenario, there was no cue as to the reason for differences in the workers performance, thus participants' attributions likely reflect their implicit theories. Causal relations between reward allocation and attribution of performance could not be examined in this study. However, none of the performance attributions had any relation to harmony orientation, suggesting that harmony orientation is not related to assessment of individual differences in performance.

In the main study, whether the allocator intended to promote harmonious relationship was manipulated in the scenario, while ignoring individual differences in performance. The effect of an additional specific strategy for harmony maintenance (dinner for the workers) on the evaluation of allocation rules was examined.

MAIN STUDY

Method

Participants

There were 109 participants (twenty-two males and eighty-seven females) recruited from an open university in Tokyo. The mean age of the participants was 39.4.

Procedure

The participants were presented with a scenario along with a questionnaire during regular class hours. There were four types of scenarios corresponding to four conditions. Participants were randomly assigned to each condition.

Participants read a scenario describing a workplace situation: Two workers were paid by an employer to work on a task, and one of the workers completed three times as much work as the other. The manager allocated ¥20,000 (US$180) between these two workers using either the equity rule or the equality rule. In the harmony maintenance condition, the manager offered the two workers a dinner intended to maintain harmony among the workers. They enjoyed the dinner and the conversation, becoming friends.

Measure

Participants rated the importance of the goal of promoting productivity and the goal of maintaining harmonious relationships. They also evaluated the allocation described in their scenario on dimensions of fairness, prevalence, appropriateness, satisfaction of the high performer, and satisfaction of the low performer. The participants were then asked to play the manager's role and allocate the rewards for the two workers, and whether they would also engage in the harmony maintenance behavior as a manager did. Finally, participants rated the employer on nine bipolar adjective scales, which included friendly–unfriendly, not competitive–competitive, biased–unbiased, likable–unlikable, efficient–inefficient, unfair–fair, warm–cold, clever–foolish, and objective–subjective. The participants answered all the questions on a seven-point scale.

Results

Importance of the Goals

A two-factor factorial design was employed with two allocation rules (equality and equity), and two situations (whether the employer offered the dinner for harmony maintenance or not). An analysis of variance (ANOVA) was performed on the two items that measured participants' perception of the importance of the two goals in the two conditions. The goal of maintaining harmonious relationships was rated more important in the dinner condition than in the no-dinner condition, $F(1, 107) = 4.62, p < 0.05$, whereas the goal of promoting productivity was rated similarly in both conditions, $F(1, 107) = 0.34$, *n.s.* That is, the invitation to dinner for harmony affected participants' perception of the importance of the goal of maintaining harmonious relationships. The degree of importance of the two goals was not correlated ($r = 0.01$, *n.s.*), thus these two goals can be interpreted as independent of each other.

Assumed Satisfaction of the Recipients

Two ANOVAs were performed on the items that measured participants' estimates of the recipients' satisfaction with the allocation. The high performer's satisfaction was estimated to be higher in the equity condition than in the equality condition, as shown in Figure 11.1. That is, the equity rule was estimated to satisfy the high performer to a greater extent than the equality rule, $F(1, 107) = 151.46$, $p < 0.001$. The effect of the allocation rule was qualified by the significant interaction effect between the allocation rule and the manipulation of the dinner, $F(1, 107) = 5.36$, $p < 0.05$. The interaction effect indicates that the equity rule was estimated to satisfy the high performer more in the dinner condition than in the no-dinner condition (M's = 6.34 versus 5.71), whereas the equality rule was estimated to satisfy the high performer more in the no-dinner condition than in the dinner condition (M's = 3.56 versus 3.19). Participants judged that the difference between the high performer's satisfaction with equity and equality would be smaller in the dinner condition than in the no-dinner condition.

As expected, the low performer's satisfaction was estimated to be higher in the equality condition than in the equity condition, as shown in Figure 11.1, $F(1, 107) = 105.88$, $p < 0.001$. There was also a significant interaction effect between the allocation rule and the strategy for harmony, $F(1, 107) = 4.39$, $p < 0.05$. The interaction effect indicates that the equity rule was estimated to satisfy the low performer more in the dinner condition than in the no-dinner condition (M's = 3.34 versus 2.85), whereas the equality rule was estimated to satisfy the low performer more in the no-dinner condition than in the dinner

Figure 11.1
Estimate of Recipients' Satisfaction

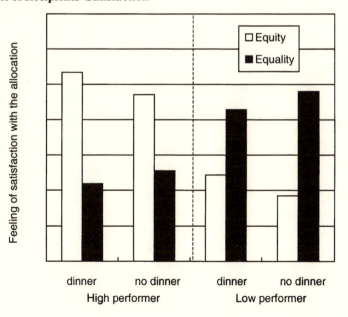

condition (*M*'s = 5.80 versus 5.29). Participants judged that the low performer's relative satisfaction with equity compared to equality would be higher in the dinner condition than in the no-dinner condition.

Evaluations of the Allocation

Participants were asked to evaluate the fairness, prevalence, and appropriateness of the allocation described in the scenario. An ANOVA did not yield any significant effect of the manipulations on the evaluation of the fairness, $F(3, 104) = 0.76$, *n.s.*, or appropriateness, $F(3, 104) = 0.31$, *n.s.* A significant main effect was found for prevalence. The participants in the equality condition rated the allocation in the scenario more prevalent than those in the equity condition, $F(1, 106) = 56.75$, $p < 0.001$. No other effects were significant.

Hypothetical Allocation of the Rewards

Participants were asked to assume the role of the manager and to allocate the rewards for the two workers, and to decide whether they would offer the dinner for harmony maintenance or not. More than half of the participants answered that they would offer the dinner for harmony maintenance. Based upon the answer to this question, the participants were divided into two groups: harmony maintenance group (N = 65) and nonharmony maintenance group (N = 44). An ANOVA on the allocated share in percentage given to the high performer, using these groups as an independent variable, revealed that the participants allocated a larger share to the high performer in the harmony maintenance group than in the nonharmony maintenance group, $F(1, 107) = 2.92$, $p < 0.10$ (*M*'s = 58.52% versus 55.79%). Note that if the equity rule is strictly followed, the share given to the high performer should be 75%, and the share for both workers should be 50% under the equality rule. This result suggests that most participants had the tendency to use the equity rule whether they offered dinner for harmony maintenance. Again, no other effects were significant.

Person Perception Items

A principal component factor analysis was run on the nine person-perception items. Only factors with eigenvalues greater than one were rotated to orthogonal structure by means of the varimax procedure.

As shown in Table 11.3, two factors emerged from the overall factor analysis. The first factor was named Productive Ability. Items with a loading greater than 0.50 included "fair," "efficient," "clever," "likable," and "objective." The second factor was labeled Affective Evaluation. Items that loaded greater than 0.50 on the second factor included "friendly," "warm," and "not competitive." The two factors accounted for 40.0% and 24.4% of the total variance, respectively. A

Table 11.3
Factor Loadings of Person Perception Items (Varimax Rotated)

Item	Productive Ability	Affective Evaluation
Efficient-inefficient	0.77	-0.36
Clever-foolish	0.75	0.34
Likable-unlikable	0.71	0.49
Objective-subjective	0.68	-0.03
Unfair-fair	-0.82	-0.20
Warm-cold	0.16	0.84
Friendly-unfriendly	0.10	0.85
Not competitive-competitive	-0.16	0.81
Biased-unbiased	-0.31	-0.46
Eigenvalue	3.60	2.20
Proportion (%)	40.00	24.40

composite score for each factor was obtained by summing up the appropriate items that loaded on each factor. Coefficient *alphas* for the resulting two composite scores for the productive ability and the affective evaluation were 0.82 and 0.81, respectively. How these two personality factors were affected by the reward allocation and the strategy for harmony was then investigated.

Productive Ability

As to the productive ability score, there were no significant effects of experimental conditions, F's$(1, 107) < 1$. That is, judgment of the allocator's productive ability was neither affected by the reward allocation nor use of dinner as a strategy for harmony.

Affective Evaluation

Two significant main effects were found. First, allocators using the equality rule were judged higher on the affective evaluation dimension than those using the equity rule, $F(1, 107) = 86.6$, $p < 0.001$ (M's = 16.12 versus 11.16). Second, allocators offering the dinner for harmony maintenance were rated higher on the affective evaluation dimension than those who did not offer the dinner, $F(1, 107) = 13.64$, $p < 0.001$ (M's = 14.50 versus 12.49). The range of affective evaluation score was from three to twenty-one.

A marginally significant interaction effect was found between the allocation rule used and the dinner, $F(1, 107) = 3.52$, $p < 0.07$. The allocator who adopted the equity rule was rated as higher on the affective evaluation dimension in the dinner condition than the one in the no-dinner condition, whereas the allocator who adopted the equality rule was rated as almost same on the affective evaluation dimension in both the dinner condition and the no-dinner condition.

DISCUSSION

As predicted, participants judged that recipients would be satisfied with the reward allocation to a greater extent in the dinner condition than in the no-dinner condition. Participants' evaluations of fairness, prevalence, and appropriateness of the allocation showed no significant differences between the dinner conditions, although evaluation of the prevalence of the allocation rule adopted was higher for the equal allocation than for the equitable allocation in both dinner conditions. As previously argued, the results indicated that the equity rule was more acceptable for recipients when interpersonal harmony was maintained by other means than when it was not. Also, the participants' hypothetical reward allocation was in line with this argument. That is, participants who said they would offer dinner also allocated rewards more equitably.

These findings are consistent with the findings from the research of organizational justice by Greenberg (1988) that suggest that productivity orientation can be fulfilled without equitable reward allocation. In contrast to the present study, Greenberg (1988) showed that the strategy for promoting productivity, specifically giving high job status without any other incentive, could improve both productivity and worker's satisfaction without increasing monetary reward. It indicated that a strategy for promoting productivity would work well to enhance recipients' satisfaction, even if there is not any change in reward allocation. That is, both harmony and productivity goals can be fulfilled through strategies other than reward allocation. When reward allocation is considered as an instrument for group management, the specific goals of the allocation and the allocator's orientation must be considered separately.

Although use of a harmony maintenance strategy had a relatively smaller effect on participants' estimation of recipients' satisfaction than on the choice of allocation rule, it improved the estimation of both high and low performers' satisfaction. Participants' judgments of recipients' satisfaction was strongly affected by the amount of reward that each recipient received. The effect of the allocation rules applied on the perceived satisfaction of recipients were greater than the effect of the use of a strategy for maintenance of harmony. Even in the dinner condition, participants considered that the low performer would be more satisfied with the equal allocation than the equitable allocation. However, the allocation rule applied had an opposite effect on recipients depending on their performance. Equity will satisfy high performers and dissatisfy low performers. Satisfaction under equitable allocation can be improved by use of a strategy for maintaining harmony. On the other hand, harmony maintenance strategy has an effect that cannot be accomplished by use of a particular allocation rule. Harmony maintenance strategy increased estimated satisfaction with equitable allocation for both high and low performers. By using an additional strategy to maintain harmony, estimated satisfaction with equitable allocation is enhanced.

Findings on the perception of the allocator indicated that allocators who adopted the equity rule were rated higher on affective evaluation in the dinner condition than in the no-dinner condition. This result indicates that use of a strategy for harmony maintenance can affect perceptions regarding the affective evaluation of the allocator to a greater extent under the equity rule than under the equality rule. Thus, it provides indirect support for the argument that the strategy for harmony makes the equity rule more acceptable.

In this study, use of the additional strategy for harmony was assumed to be independent of the amount of the allocated reward. However, an alternative interpretation is that the participants perceived the dinner for harmony as a part of the reward. If this was the case, the dinner for harmony should have been perceived as a part of the equal allocation. However, if the strategy for harmony had been considered a part of the reward, it would not have affected the estimation of the recipients' satisfaction when the reward was allocated equally—the amount of the reward in the dinner condition would have been perceived as more than that in the no-dinner condition. In fact, the results showed that the dinner for harmony made the equal allocation less satisfying for both the recipients. Thus, the results can be interpreted as indicating that the dinner for harmony was not considered part of the allocated reward.

There are some issues that are left for future research. First, hypotheses were tested only in the hypothetical situation described in a scenario. It was assumed that participants' estimate of recipients' satisfaction with the reward allocation corresponds to the degree that allocation goals are fulfilled. But, how those goals were fulfilled by the allocation was not directly examined. Future research should test the findings observed in the present study in a lab setting. Second, the instrumental value of the allocation rules was only indirectly examined in the present study. The observers estimated recipients' satisfaction with the allocation. Also, there is a limitation on the effect of the manipulation on the strategy for harmony. Because the participants were not asked if they believed the dinner improved the relationship among recipients, the possibility of alternative interpretations on the meaning of the dinner cannot be ruled out. Future research needs to examine the responses of the recipients directly. Third, this study was conducted only in Japan. Preferences for particular reward allocation rules are influenced by cultural values or norms. The two-dimensionality of harmony and productivity orientations in reward allocation was shown only in Japan. In other cultures, the two-dimensionality may not be replicated because the importance of interpersonal harmony within a group may vary across cultures. Based on the individualism–collectivism framework, it is proposed that the relationship among recipients will affect the choice of interaction goal (Leung, 1997). In individualistic cultures, members tend to treat groups as transient, so contractual engagement may be important (Leung & Bond, 1984). Thus, it can be assumed that people in individualistic cultures always regard recipients as individuals even when the goal of maintaining harmonious relationships is emphasized. That is, it is quite likely that the meaning of harmony in individualistic cultures refers to harmonious relationships among individuals, not within a whole group. In future research, therefore, cross-cultural comparison of the structure of the two orientations in reward allocation should be conducted.

REFERENCES

Adams, J. S. (1965). Inequity in social exchange. In L. Berkowits (Ed.), *Advances in experimental social psychology* (vol. 2). New York: Academic Press.

Chiu, C., & Hong, Y. (1997). Justice from a Chinese perspective. In H.S.R. Kao & D. Sinha (Eds.), *Asian perspectives on psychology*. New Delhi, India: Sage.

Cook, K. S., & Hegtvedt, K. A. (1983). Distributive justice, equity, and equality. *Annual Review of Sociology, 9*, 217–241.

Deutsch, M. (1975). Equity, equality, and need: What determines which value will be used as the basis of distributive justice? *Journal of Social Issues, 31*, 137–149.

Deutsch, M. (1983). Current social psychological perspectives on justice. *European Journal of Social Psychology, 13*, 305–319.

Farwell, L., & Weiner, B. (1996). Self-perception of fairness in individual and group contexts. *Personality and Social Psychology Bulletin, 22*, 867–881.

Greenberg, J. (1988). Equity and workplace status: A field experiment. *Journal of Applied Psychology, 73*, 606–613.

Lane, I. M., & Messe, L. A. (1971). Equity and the distribution of the rewards. *Journal of Personality and Social Psychology, 21*, 228–233.

Leung, K. (1997) Negotiation and reward allocations across cultures. In P. C. Earley & M. Erez (Eds.), *New perspective on international industrial/organizational psychology* (pp. 641–675). San Francisco: New Lexington Press.

Leung, K., & Bond, M. H. (1984). The impact of cultural collectivism on reward allocation. *Journal of Personality and Social Psychology, 47*, 793–804.

Leung, K., & Park, H. J. (1986). Effects of interactional goal on choice of allocation rule: A cross-national study. *Organizational Behavior and Human Decision Processes, 37*, 111–120.

Leventhal, G. S. (1976). The distribution of rewards and resources in groups and organizations. In L. Berkowits & E. Walster (Eds.), *Advances in experimental social psychology*, vol. 9: *Equity theory: Toward a general theory of social interaction* (pp. 91–131). New York: Academic Press.

Leventhal, G. S. (1980). What should be done with equity theory? New approaches to the study of fairness in social relationship. In K. J. Gergen, M. S. Greenberg, & R. H. Willis (Eds.), *Social exchange: Advances in theory and research* (pp. 27–53). New York: Plenum.

Leventhal, G. S., Michaels, J. W., & Sanford, C. (1972). Inequity and interpersonal conflict: Reward allocation and secrecy about reward as methods of preventing conflict. *Journal of Personality and Social Psychology, 23*, 88–102.

Mahler, I., Greenberg, L., & Hayashi, H. (1981). A comparative study of rules of justice: Japanese versus American. *Psychologia, 24*, 1–8.

Markham, S. E. (1988). Pay-for-performance dilemma revisited: Empirical example of the importance of group effects. *Journal of Applied Psychology, 73*, 172–180.

Mikula, G. (1980). On the role of justice in allocation decisions. In G. Mikula (Ed.), *Justice and Social Interaction* (pp. 127–166). Wien: Huber.

Reis, H. T., & Gruzen, J. (1976) On mediating equity, equality, and self-interest: The role of self-presentation in social exchange. *Journal of Experimental Social Psychology, 12*, 487–503.

Utne, M. K., & Kidd, R. (1980). Equity and attribution. In G. Mikula (Ed.), *Justice and social interaction* (pp. 63–93). Wien: Huber.

Walster, E., Berscheid, E., & Walster, G. W. (1976). New direction in equity research. In L. Berkowitz & E. Walster (Eds.), *Advances in experimental social psychology* (vol. 9). New York: Academic Press.

Yamaguchi, S., Inoue, H., Muramoto, Y., & Ozawa, S. (1997). Reward allocation among groups and individuals: A vignette study. In K. Leung, U. Kim, S. Kashima, & S. Yamaguchi (Eds.), *Progress in Asian social psychology* (vol. 1). Singapore: John Wiley and Sons.

Zhang, Z., & Yang, C. (1998). Beyond distributive justice: The reasonableness norm in Chinese reward allocation. *Asian Journal of Social Psychology, 1*, 253–269.

CHAPTER 12

Overcoming the Ironic Rebound: Effective and Ineffective Strategies for Stereotype Suppression

Tomoko Oe and Takashi Oka

People make intentional efforts to avoid applying stereotypes because stereotypes sometimes color social perceptions against their will (Devine, 1989; Gilbert & Hixon, 1991; Monteith, 1993). In doing so, people sometimes attempt to control their biased or prejudiced responses by suppressing their stereotypic thoughts. Contrary to their intentions, however, such attempts can lead them to fail in suppressing the prejudiced response due to heightened accessibility of the stereotypes (e.g., Macrae, Bodenhausen, Milne, & Jetten, 1994; Macrae, Bodenhausen, & Milne, 1998; for a review, see Monteith, Sherman, & Devine, 1998). This detrimental outcome of suppression is termed the *ironic rebound effect* (Wegner, Schneider, Carter, & White, 1987).

To explain this rebound effect, Wegner (1994; Wegner & Erber, 1992) proposed the model that two cognitive processes in thought suppression increase the accessibility of unwanted thoughts: the controlled distractor search process and the automatic target search process. The model posits that the two processes in combination lead suppressors (those who attempt to suppress their unwanted thoughts) to the ironic rebound effect. The controlled distractor search is an intentional process in which suppressors search for something unrelated to their unwanted thought (thinking about beautiful roses to suppress a dreadful crime). The automatic target search process is assumed to operate without conscious attention, simply monitoring the unwanted thought to be suppressed and activating it throughout suppression allowing it to continue functioning even after suppression. For this reason, a suppressor is likely to have higher accessibility to the unwanted thought than a person who consciously uses the thought, and thus may use the thought without intention. Consistent with this model, the rebound effect in suppression has been found to occur when suppressors have few cognitive resources (Wegner & Erber, 1992) or when their attention to suppress is distracted (Macrae, Bodenhausen, Milne, & Jetten, 1994). In those situations, suppressors cannot afford to keep the controlled distractor search process operating, and the ironic rebound effect occurs because the automatic target search repeatedly primes the unwanted thought (Macrae, Bodenhausen, Milne, & Jetten, 1994).

Although previous studies have demonstrated the existence of the ironic rebound effect, not all attempts to suppress unwanted thoughts lead to the rebound effect (Kelly & Kahn, 1994; Monteith, Spicer, & Tooman, 1998). Monteith, Spicer, and Tooman (1998) showed that low-prejudice students in the United States could succeed in inhibiting the accessibility of their unwanted prejudiced thoughts. Thus, there must be an effective way to suppress stereotypes without suffering from the rebound effect. It is important to know in what circumstances individuals can effectively suppress prejudiced thoughts. The main purpose of this study is to identify conditions in which individuals can effectively suppress their unwanted stereotypic thoughts.

Blair and Banaji (1996) attempted to specify conditions under which the automatic priming effect of a stereotype may be moderated. Participants in their experiments responded to a male or female name (e.g., Jane or James) immediately preceded by a stereotypic or counterstereotypic prime (e.g., pretty or ambitious). When a presented prime-target pair was stereotypic (i.e., pretty Jane), participants responded faster to the target name than when the pair was a counterstereotypic (e.g., ambitious Jane). In their experiments (Experiments 3 and 4), this priming effect of stereotypes was not found when participants were instructed to have a counterstereotypic expectancy. Their findings suggest that participants with counterstereotypic expectancies can inhibit the priming effect of stereotypes. Monteith, Sherman, and Devine (1998) interpreted this expectancy manipulation as a thought replacement in which participants replaced gender stereotypic thoughts (pretty Jane) with counterstereotypic ones (ambitious Jane). This kind of thought replacement may also be effective in extinguishing the heightened accessibility of stereotypes.

Researchers have postulated that a stereotype is represented in an abstract network of semantic relations between a group label and a stereotypic trait (Banaji & Greenwald, 1995; Blair & Banaji, 1996; Dovidio, Evans, & Tyler, 1986; Hamilton & Sherman, 1994). This distinction between a group label and a stereotypic trait enables focus on two thought-replacement strategies for stereotype suppression: trait-replacement and group-replacement strategies. In the trait-replacement strategy, suppressors attempt to replace the stereotypic trait, whereas suppressors in the group-replacement strategy would think about a replacement group. The trait-replacement strategy is effective in stereotype suppression because nonstereotypic traits are activated during suppression and thus the accessibility of the stereotypes is not heightened. This suppression strategy may be adopted by low-prejudice people who can avoid the rebound effect in stereotype suppression (Monteith, Spicer, & Tooman, 1998) because they judge a person in a stereotyped group by replacing their stereotypic thoughts with nonstereotypic ones. In the group-replacement strategy the story is different because the stereotypic traits are not assumed to be replaced with nonstereotypic traits. In this strategy, the automatic target search process heightens the accessibility of the stereotypic traits as Wegner explained (Wegner, 1994; Wegner & Erber, 1992). We hypothesize that the trait-replacement strategy successfully suppresses stereotypic thoughts, whereas the group-replacement strategy suffers from the rebound effect.

In Experiment 1, the effect of the two strategies for suppression (i.e., the trait-replacement and the group-replacement strategies) is examined in contrast to two control conditions. In one of the control conditions, gender stereotypes are activated (the stereotype activation condition), and in the other, the gender stereotypes are activated and also thoughts about gender are replaced with thoughts about a dog (the thought replacement without suppression condition). These two control strategies are expected to heighten the accessibility of stereotypes more than the trait-replacement strategy, but less than the group-replacement strategy.

EXPERIMENT 1

Method

Overview

Participants performed a sentence-stem completion task that simulated one of four cognitive processes (group replacement with suppression, trait replacement with suppression, stereotype activation, and thought replacement without suppression). Then they performed a lexical decision task in which they judged whether a letter string presented on a computer screen was a word or a nonword. The decision latencies (ms) were taken as a measure of the accessibility to stereotypic and nonstereotypic concepts about females. It was assumed, as in previous studies (e.g., Devine, 1989; Higgins, Bargh, & Lombardi, 1985; Macrae, Bodenhausen, Milne, & Jetten, 1994) that response latency would be shorter when the accessibility to a concept is higher.

Participants and Design

Forty-seven volunteer students (twenty-four females, twenty-three males) at the University of Tokyo served as participants in a 4 (questionnaire: group replacement with suppression, trait replacement with suppression, stereotype activation, thought replacement without suppression) × 3 (word type: group label, stereotypic adjective, nonstereotypic adjective) mixed design with re-peated measures on the second factor.

Procedure and Materials

Participants were seated individually in a soundproof experimental booth. At the beginning of each session, an experimenter informed participants that the purpose of this study was to investigate mental processes by focusing on stereotypes, and that they would be asked to perform several tasks. Then they received a questionnaire containing a sentence-stem completion task. Partici-pants were randomly assigned to one of the four questionnaire conditions.[1] The experimenter informed them of the task and asked them to answer two practice questions in front of the experimenter. Participants were encouraged to ask questions of the experimenter, and the experimenter confirmed that par-ticipants had understood how to answer the questionnaire. After the experimenter left the booth, the participant answered the subsequent questions. In the ques-tionnaire, each of four conditions were manipulated as follows:

Group replacement with suppression condition. This questionnaire simulated the mental process of stereotype suppressors who think of stereotypes of women and then think of another group unrelated to women to suppress the stereotypes of women. On each page of the questionnaire participants answered two questions. The first question required them to complete the sentence beginning with the words "Women are . . ." by providing a stereotypic adjective describing women. In the second question, they were asked to complete a sentence beginning with "Dogs are . . ." without using stereotypes of women. Participants repeated the same six pairs of questions. We expected that the first question would activate stereotypic thoughts, as when one meets a woman or when one is asked to judge a woman, and the second question would suppress the activated stereotypic thoughts about women as when one inten-tionally avoids using stereotypes of women.

Trait replacement with suppression condition. This questionnaire was expected to simu-late the trait-replacement strategy. Participants answered two questions, the first of which was identical to that used in the group-replacement condition. The second question required them to complete a sentence beginning with the words "Women are . . ." without using stereotypes of women. It was expected that participants in this condition would generate nonstereotypic traits as instructed. As in the group-replacement condition, they answered six pairs of questions.

Stereotype activation condition. In this condition, the questionnaire simulated a situa-tion in which people think of stereotypes of women without suppressing them. On each page of the questionnaire, only one sentence-stem completion trial (identical to the first question in the previous two conditions) was included.

Thought replacement without suppression condition. The thought-replacement ques-tionnaire simulated another strategy as when a person thinks of a stereotype of women and then happens to think of a group unrelated to women without suppression. Par-ticipants in this condition answered two questions identical to those used in the group-replacement condition, except that no mention was made to the use of stereo-types of women in the second question.

After completing the questionnaire, each participant was instructed to face the screen of a tachistscope and perform a lexical decision task. Participants were told that they would see an orienting stimulus (+) followed by a letter string in Japanese hiragana characters. They were instructed to indicate whether the letter string was a word or nonword by pressing a key as quickly and accurately as possible. The orienting stimulus (+) and the letter string were presented in the center of the screen as white letters on a black background and were easily visible to each participant. Lexical decision latencies (ms) were recorded as well as the accuracy of each judgment. Participants were instructed that if they made a mistake, they should continue to perform the next trial without minding the mistake. For all trials, an orienting stimulus (+) was presented for 1,000 ms, followed by a letter string, which remained on the screen until the participant made a response. Trials were separated by a blank screen of 1,000 ms, resulting in a 2,000 ms interval between the offset of a letter string and the onset of the next one.

The list of letter strings comprised ten nonwords and fifteen words. The words included three stereotypic adjectives and a group label of women and three nonstereotypic adjectives. Of the fifteen words, men's and dog's stereotypic adjectives were used as fillers. All the stereotypic adjectives were selected on the basis of a preliminary test and earlier pilot experiments. Participants performed three blocks of judgment trials, each consisting of forty trials (fifteen words and ten nonwords were presented twice and once, respectively). Presentation of the letter strings was randomized in each block, for each participant by a computer. A thirty-second break and brief instructions that reminded participants of how they should perform the lexical decision task were given between the blocks.

Finally, participants rated the stereotypicality of twelve adjectives in the lexical decision task. They were asked to what extent they thought the adjectives were stereotypic for women on a seven-point scale. Following these questions, they were asked to answer additional questions, including the manipulation checks, and then they were fully debriefed.

Results and Discussion

The dependent measures were mean response latencies (ms) of judgment on the lexical decision task. Each participant made six judgments on each of the five words (i.e., one group label, two stereotypic adjectives, and two nonstereotypic adjectives), yielding a final data set containing thirty judgments.[2] Because the error rate was low (0.91% across all judgments for stereotypic and nonstereotypic words), incorrect classifications of the letter strings were included in the following analyses. When a participant's response latency was longer than the mean response latency of the participant by four standard deviations, it was replaced by that participant's average response latency (0.76% of all judgments). Finally, natural logarithm transformation was used to normalize the distribution of latencies. Hereafter, *response latency* indicates the log-transformed response latency.

To determine whether the predicted effects of suppression strategies on the accessibility to stereotype concepts were obtained, we submitted the participants' response latencies to a Questionnaire × Word Type mixed-model ANCOVA with repeated measures on the second factor, treating the mean response latency on practice trials and the stereotypicality of each adjective as covariates. As predicted, this analysis revealed a significant Questionnaire × Word Type interaction effect, $F(6, 76) = 2.41, p < 0.05$. As shown in Figure 12.1, planned t-tests revealed that participants in the group-replacement strategy condition responded faster to stereotypic adjectives ($p < 0.05$) and a group label ($p < 0.10$) than those in the stereotype activation condition. These results support the prediction that the group-replacement strategy results in the rebound effect. Moreover, participants in the group-replacement strategy condition responded faster to stereotypic adjectives than those in the thought-replacement strategy condition ($p < 0.05$), and participants in the thought-replacement strategy condition responded faster to stereotypic adjectives ($p < 0.10$) and a group label ($p < 0.05$) than those in the trait-replacement strategy condition. These results support the prediction that the trait-replacement strategy does not heighten the accessibility of stereotypes of women whereas the group-replacement strategy results in the rebound effect.

Follow-Up Data Collection

These findings raise the question as to why the trait-replacement strategy did not result in the rebound effect. Although this question is beyond the scope of the model proposed by Wegner (Wegner, 1994; Wegner & Erber, 1992), one possible explanation would be that newly generated nonstereotypic thoughts in the trait-replacement strategy condition inhibited the rebound effect. The sentence-stem completion task used in Experiment 1 required participants in the trait-replacement condition to generate nonstereotypic adjectives. In this process, the newly generated nonstereotypic concepts (i.e., replacement concepts) may have had some influence on the accessibility of the stereotypic concepts.

To examine the validity of this explanation, we asked another fifteen participants to rate the counterstereotypicality of the seventy-two replacement concepts generated by the suppressors in Experiment 1. The mean rating of the counterstereotypicality of each adjective was used to calculate the counterstereotypicality of adjectives generated by each participant in the two suppression conditions (trait-replacement strategy and group-replacement strategy). Then we examined the correlation coefficients between the counterstereo-

Figure 12.1
Log Response Latencies by Questionnaire and Word Type in Experiment 1

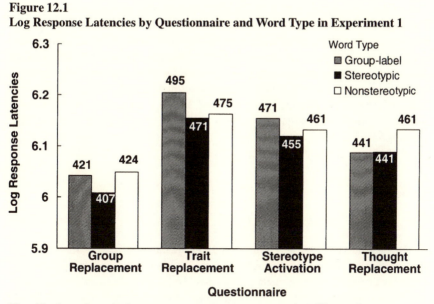

Note: Numbers above the bars represent mean response scores in milliseconds.

typicality of the replacement adjective and the response latency of the participant in the two suppression conditions. In the group-replacement strategy condition, the counterstereotypicality was not correlated with the response latency or nonstereotypic concepts. However, in the trait-replacement condition, the counterstereotypicality was positively correlated with both the response latency for stereotypic concepts [r (12) = 0.58, p < 0.05] and nonstereotypic concepts [r (12) = 0.58, p < 0.05].[3] The fewer counterstereotypic adjectives the participant in the trait-replacement condition generated, the slower they responded to stereotypic and nonstereotypic concepts. This result suggests that the more neutral adjectives were used in the trait-replacement condition, the less accessible the stereotypic concepts may have become. This possibility was examined in the next experiment.

EXPERIMENT 2

The follow-up correlational analyses in Experiment 1 brought out the question of whether the accessibility of stereotypes after suppression depends on the type of adjectives that people used in stereotype suppression. The main purpose of Experiment 2 was to test the suppressing effect of adjectives by directly manipulating the type of adjectives. Specifically, we divided the trait-replacement with suppression strategy into two possible substrategies: counterstereotypic-trait and neutral-trait replacement strategies. The former replacement represents a strategy in which suppressors generate counterstereo-typic traits of a target group, whereas in the latter strategy suppressors gener-ate neutral traits (i.e., neither stereotypic nor counterstereotypic traits) when they attempt to suppress their stereotypes. We hypothesize that adoption of the counterstereotypic-trait replacement strategy will heighten the accessibil-ity of stereotypes as compared to the group-replacement strategy, which trig-gers the rebound effect. On the other hand, we expect suppressors who adopt the neutral-trait replacement strategy to respond more slowly to the stereo-types than those who adopt the group-replacement strategy because neutral concepts would inhibit the rebound effect as suggested by Experiment 1.

Method

Participants and Design

Thirty-nine volunteer students (twenty-four males, fifteen females) at the University of Tokyo served as participants in a 3 (strategy: group replacement, counterstereotypic-trait replacement, neutral-trait replacement) × 2 (word type: stereotypic, nonstereotypic) mixed design with repeated measures on the sec-ond factor.

Procedure and Materials

As in Experiment 1, participants performed practice trials of a lexical deci-sion task and a sentence-stem completion task, and then main trials of a lexi-cal decision task. Procedures and materials in this experiment were different from those in Experiment 1 in three ways. First, participants were not pro-vided with the first question of the pair used in Experiment 1. Second, in the sentence-stem completion task, the strategy for suppression was manipulated as follows:

Group-replacement condition. In this condition, participants were asked to complete a sentence beginning with the words "Dogs are . . ." without using stereotypes of women.

Counterstereotypic-trait replacement condition. Participants were asked to complete a sentence beginning with the words "Women are . . ." without using stereotypes of women but with traits counter to such stereotypes.

Neutral-trait replacement condition. Participants were asked to complete a sentence be-ginning with the words "Women are . . ." using neither stereotypes of women nor traits counter to such stereotypes. All participants answered the same question six times.

Finally, in a lexical decision task, letter strings were selected from a differ-ent preliminary test from Experiment 1 and comprised ten nonwords and fif-teen words. The words included two stereotypic and two nonstereotypic adjectives for women and some fillers. Participants performed four blocks of judgment trials, each consisting of twenty-five randomized trials. On completion of all the tasks, participants rated on a seven-point scale the stereotypicality of the stereotypes of women on the fifteen adjectives that had been presented in the lexical decision task.

Results and Discussion

As in Experiment 1, mean response latency in the lexical decision task was the main dependent variable in Experiment 2. Because the error rate was low (i.e., 1.28% across all judgments for the two stereotypic and two nonstereotypic adjectives), incorrect classifications of the letter strings were included in the analyses. When a participant's response latency was longer than the mean response latency of the participant by four standard deviations, it was replaced by that participant's average response latency (0.96% across of all judgments). The response latencies were log transformed as in Experiment 1. Then, we submitted participants' response latencies to a Strategy × Word Type mixed-model ANCOVA with repeated measures on the second factor, treating the mean response latency of practice trials as a covariate. The analysis revealed a significant Strategy × Word Type interaction effect on participants' response latencies, $F(2, 35) = 7.05$, $p < 0.005$. As shown in Figure 12.2, planned t-tests revealed that participants with the counterstereotypic-trait replacement strategy

Figure 12.2
Log Response Latencies by Strategy and Word Type in Experiment 2

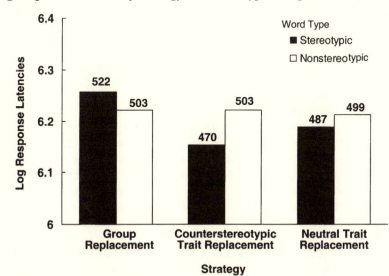

Note: Numbers above the bars represent mean response scores in milliseconds.

responded faster to the stereotypic adjectives than those with group-replacement strategy ($p < 0.05$). On the other hand, contrary to our prediction, participants with the neutral-trait replacement strategy had a tendency to respond faster to the stereotypic adjectives than those with the group-replacement strategy ($p = 0.10$).

Both the counterstereotypic-trait and the neutral-trait replacement strategies caused a stronger rebound effect than the group-replacement strategy. In these conditions, the participant's response latency was shorter than in the group-replacement strategy condition. This result suggests that the same cognitive processes may have operated in both the counterstereotypic-trait replacement and the neutral-trait replacement strategies. Not just participants in the counterstereotypic-trait replacement condition but also those in the neutral-trait replacement condition may have intentionally searched for counterstereotypic traits in order not to use stereotypic or counterstereotypic traits. On the other hand, the trait-replacement strategy in Experiment 1, which did not produce the rebound effect, may not have directed the participants to intentionally search for counterstereotypic traits. Searching for counterstereotypic traits may heighten the accessibility of stereotypes because these traits have close semantic relation to stereotypes. In addition to this cognitive process, the process that automatically monitors stereotypes is also ironically contributing to the heightened accessibility of stereotypes (Wegner, 1994; Wegner & Erber, 1992). Searching for counterstereotypic traits may trigger dual cognitive processes, both of which increase the accessibility of stereotypes. Therefore, these two strategies result in the stronger rebound effect than the other strategies.

GENERAL DISCUSSION

In Experiment 1, we found an effective way to suppress stereotypes when participants in the trait-replacement strategy condition replaced stereotypic traits with nonstereotypic traits. This kind of cognitive process may work to inhibit the accessibility of suppressed stereotypic thoughts. Similar cognitive processes may be at work in people who can suppress their stereotypic thoughts successfully, such as low-prejudice people who participated in Monteith, Spicer, and Tooman's (1998) study.

We found in Experiment 2 that a strong rebound effect was triggered by means of both the counterstereotypic-trait and the neutral-trait replacement strategies in which participants replaced stereotypic traits with counterstereotypic and neutral traits, respectively. Participants with these strategies may have intentionally searched for both stereotypic and counterstereotypic traits during suppression, and this cognitive process may have easily heightened the accessibility of stereotypic thoughts. This finding is inconsistent with the results of Experiment 1 and several previous studies that demonstrated the effectiveness of counterstereotype strategies (Blair & Banaji, 1996; Thompson, Roman, Moskovitz, Chaiken, & Bargh, 1994). However, this apparent contradiction can be resolved in terms of the difference in cognitive processing of counterstereotypes between these strategies. Counterstereotypes may have been automatically searched in the successful strategies such as the trait-replacement strategy in Experiment 1 and those in the other studies, whereas counterstereotypes may have been intentionally searched in the strategies in Experiment 2.

For example, in Blair and Banaji's (1996) experiments, participants with the counterstereotype strategy performed a judgment task following an instruction to motivate them to expect counterstereotypes. This strategy moderated the automatic priming effect of stereotypes. Blair and Banaji (1996) explained that the counterstereotype strategy may have changed the cognitive representation of the target group by automatically heightening the accessibility of counterstereotypic concepts. This automatic activation of counterstereotypes may have counteracted the automatic activation of stereotypes. If so, participants using the counterstereotype strategy may not have paid much attention to counterstereotypes and may not have intentionally searched for counterstereotypic traits. This interpretation of automatically activated counterstereotypic and stereotypic concepts can be applied to the results shown for participants in the trait-replacement condition in Experiment 1, most of whom paid little attention to counterstereotypic traits in the sentence-stem completion task. On the other hand, counterstereotypic traits may have been intentionally searched for in the counterstereotypic-trait and the neutral-trait replacement strategies in Experiment 2. Participants with these strategies could not lose their attention to counterstereotypic traits throughout the sentence-stem completion task, which may have heightened the accessibility to stereotypes because counterstereotypic concepts have close semantic relation to stereotypic ones.

The idea of consciously and nonconsciously acquired associations supports this interpretation. As Hill and his colleagues demonstrated, people are sensitive to detecting a covariation of stimuli and events nonconsciously, and a nonconsciously aquired association has a strong effect on subsequent judgment (Hill, Lewicki, Czyzewska, & Boss, 1989; Hill, Lewicki, Czyzewska, & Schuller, 1990). Effective counterstereotype strategies, such as the trait-replacement strategy in Experiment 1, may have contributed to establishing a nonconsciously acquired association between the group label and counterstereotypic traits because participants with these strategies paid little attention to the traits. This association may have inhibited the rebound effect. On the other hand, participants using the counterstereotypic-trait and the neutral-trait replacement strategies in Experiment 2 paid much attention to counterstereotypes, and this consciously acquired association may not have been enough to inhibit the rebound effect.

In sum, we offer two explanations for the effective and ineffective strategies. One is from a cognitive search process and the other is from association. Whichever explanation applies, automatic counterstereotype activation may be effective, whereas intentional counterstereotype activation may be ineffective.

CONCLUSIONS

We simulated four strategies for stereotype suppression in a laboratory setting. The findings indicate that the trait-replacement strategy is the most effective in suppressing stereotypic thoughts without causing the rebound effect. Trait-replacement strategies with an intentional search for counterstereotypes, on the other hand, trigger off a strong rebound effect. These findings afford a glimpse of effective and ineffective cognitive processes in stereotype suppression, suggesting the importance of automatic counterstereotype activation in successful suppression. Future research should systematically examine the various automatic and intentional cognitive processes involved in stereotype suppression. Moreover, the explanation of automatic counterstereotype activation invites further speculation on the successful cognitive process of low-prejudice people. They may automatically adopt the counterstereotype strategy by thinking of an existing counterstereotypic member of a group or by having an expectancy that a member of a group is a counterstereotypic person. These cognitive processes may be automatized through frequent repetition (Bargh, 1996, 1997). Still, considerable obscurities are attached to these speculations. Future research is needed to step into the obscurities to clarify the full configuration of stereotype suppression.

NOTES

We are thankful to Susumu Yamaguchi, Takashi Yokoi, Chikako K. Ueki, Hiroko Akiyama, Yoshiko Onuma, Isao Sakuma, Megumi Ohashi, Yuriko Zemba, and anonymous reviewers for their helpful comments on an earlier draft of this manuscript. We also thank the more than three hundred participants in our two experiments and additional studies.

1. Before performing the sentence-stem completion task, participants performed practice trials of a lexical decision task. The covered purposes of this task were to give some practice judgment trials to participants and to measure the mean decision latency of each participant before the strategy manipulation. This mean decision latency was used in later analysis to control individual differences in response latency.

2. We calculated the intercorrelation between the ratings for adjectives to confirm whether each adjective was equally recognized as stereotypic or nonstereotypic for women. As a result, of the three adjectives presented as stereotypic words, the two most highly correlated adjectives were used in the following analyses, and of the three adjectives presented as nonstereotypic words, the one that was highly correlated with one of the stereotypic adjectives was excluded from the analyses.

3. In addition to counterstereotypicality, stereotypicality for men was also assessed for each concept because participants in the trait-replacement condition may have used male stereotypes as one of the replacement strategies. Another fifteen students who had not given ratings of the counterstereotypicality for women were asked to judge the extent to which the list of words were stereotypic for men. There was no significant correlation between the stereotypicality for men and the response latency for either stereotypic or nonstereotypic concepts for women, although suppressors showed a

high correlation between counterstereotypicality for women and stereotypicality for men [$r\,(24) = 0.74, p < 0.01$]. This result suggests that stereotypes for men are similar to counterstereotypes for women, but the stereotypes for men did not affect the accessibility of stereotypes of women in this case.

REFERENCES

Banaji, M. R., & Greenwald, A. (1995). Implicit gender stereotyping in judgment of fame. *Journal of Personality and Social Psychology, 68,* 181–198.

Bargh, J. A. (1996). Automaticity in social psychology. In E. T. Higgins & A. W. Kruglanski (Eds.), *Social psychology: Handbook of basic principles* (pp. 169–183). New York: Guilford Press.

Bargh, J. A. (1997). The automaticity of everyday life. In R. S. Wyer (Ed.), *Advances in social cognition* (vol. 10, pp. 1–61). Hillsdale, NJ: Erlbaum.

Blair, I. V., & Banaji, M. R. (1996). Automatic and controlled processes in stereotype priming. *Journal of Personality and Social Psychology, 70,* 1142–1163.

Devine, P. G. (1989). Stereotypes and prejudice: Their automatic and controlled components. *Journal of Personality and Social Psychology, 56,* 5–18.

Dovidio, J., Evans, N., & Tyler, R. (1986). Racial stereotypes: The contents of their cognitive representation. *Journal of Experimental Social Psychology, 22,* 22–37.

Gilbert, D. T., & Hixon, J. G. (1991). The trouble of thinking: Activation and application of stereotypic beliefs. *Journal of Personality and Social Psychology, 60,* 509–517.

Hamilton, D. L., & Sherman, J. W. (1994). Stereotypes. In R. S. Wyer, Jr. & T. K. Srull (Eds.), *Handbook of social cognition* (2d ed., vol. 2, pp. 1–68). Hillsdale, NJ: Erlbaum.

Higgins, E. T., Bargh, J. A., & Lombardi, W. (1985). The nature of priming effects on categorization. *Journal of Experimental Psychology: Learning, Memory, and Cognition, 38,* 369–425.

Hill, T., Lewicki, P., Czyzewska, M., & Boss, A. (1989). Self-perpetuating development of encoding biases in person perception. *Journal of Personality and Social Psychology, 57,* 373–387.

Hill, T., Lewicki, P., Czyzewska, M., & Schuller, G. (1990). The role of learned inferential encoding rules in the perception of faces: Effects of nonconscious self-perpetuation of a bias. *Journal of Experimental Social Psychology, 26,* 350–371.

Kelly, A. E., & Kahn, J. H. (1994). Effects of suppression of personal intrusive thoughts. *Journal of Personality and Social Psychology, 66,* 998–1006.

Macrae, C. N., Bodenhausen, G. V., & Milne, A. B. (1998). Saying no to unwanted thoughts: Self-focus and the regulation of mental life. *Journal of Personality and Social Psychology, 74,* 578–589.

Macrae, C. N., Bodenhausen, G. V., Milne, A. B., & Jetten, J. (1994). Out of mind but back in sight: Stereotypes on the rebound. *Journal of Personality and Social Psychology, 67,* 808–817.

Monteith, M. J. (1993). Self-regulation of prejudiced responses: Implications for progress in prejudice-reduction efforts. *Journal of Personality and Social Psychology, 65,* 469–485.

Monteith, M. J., Sherman, J. W., & Devine, P. G. (1998). Suppression as a stereotype control strategy. *Personality and Social Psychology Review, 2,* 63–82.

Monteith, M. J., Spicer, C. V., & Tooman, G. D. (1998). Consequences of stereotype suppression: Stereotypes on and not on the rebound. *Journal of Experimental Social Psychology, 34*, 355–377.

Thompson, E. P., Roman, R. J., Moskovitz, G. B., Chaiken, S., & Bargh, J. A. (1994). Accuracy motivation attenuates covert priming effects: The systematic reprocessing of social information. *Journal of Personality and Social Psychology, 66*, 474–489.

Wegner, D. M. (1994). Ironic processes of mental control. *Psychological Review, 101*, 34–52.

Wegner, D. M., & Erber, R. (1992). The hyperaccessibility of suppressed thoughts. *Journal of Personality and Social Psychology, 63*, 903–912.

Wegner, D. M., Schneider, D. J., Carter, S. III, & White, L. (1987). Paradoxical effects of thought suppression. *Journal of Personality and Social Psychology, 58*, 409–418.

CHAPTER 13

The Effects of Nationality, Length of Residence, and Occupational Demand on the Perceptions of "Foreign Talent" in Singapore

Anna Lim and Colleen Ward

With the Singapore economy expected to face a rising mismatch between the job market and the local labor market ("Low Skilled Jobs," 1999), there is currently a need for Singapore to recruit people who possess the occupational skills that the country lacks. As part of the government's aim to develop a world-class workforce that will propel Singapore into the top league of developed nations in the twenty-first century, concerted efforts have been made to attract high quality workers from international sources. Concrete plans were formulated, and the government's "welcome foreign talent" policy was unveiled by the country's prime minister in August 1997.

The active recruitment of foreign labor came at a difficult time given the economic slowdown in Singapore and the regional financial crisis in Asia. In the late 1990s the Singapore economy shed more jobs than it created, and unemployment rose markedly for the first time since 1986. By the end of 1998 a record 28,300 people were retrenched, bringing the unemployment rate to 4.3%, considerably more than during the 1985 recession ("Lay-Offs Soar," 1999). This retrenchment is striking in that prior to the introduction of the 1997 "foreign talent" policy, there were already half a million foreigners working in Singapore, making up one-quarter of the country's total labor force ("Are Foreign Workers," 1998).

Social psychological theory suggests that in-group favoritism and out-group prejudice increase in relation to scarcity of resources, and surveys conducted by Forbes Research indicate that about one-third of Singaporeans polled agree that there are too many foreign workers in the country. In addition, one in four believe that foreign workers take away jobs from locals ("Most Neutral," 1998). Despite the controversial nature of the government recruitment policy and the poll, relatively little is known about Singaporeans' perceptions of expatriate workers. How do Singaporeans view foreign talent, and what influences these perceptions? These applied questions are the focus of this research.

FOREIGN TALENT IN SINGAPORE: OCCUPATIONAL DEMAND, RESIDENCE, AND NATIONALITY

A number of questions may be raised about the presence of foreign talent in Singapore. First and most fundamentally, "Why is foreign talent needed in Singapore?" The government has largely justified its intention to attract an international labor force on economic grounds. For example, it has argued that millions of dollars of business opportunities, the creation of hundreds of jobs, and increased spending power are consequences of the employment of an international labor force. The openness to employ foreign talent is seen as an incentive for multinational investment, and the willingness to hire the best workers is believed to make Singapore more competitive in the international arena. A more fundamental argument, however, is that the jobs that are lost and the ones that are created are not in the same areas. In reality, expatriate labor is used to fill immediate needs in growth areas when there is a mismatch between the posts that are available and what Singaporeans are willing or able to do. Consequently, whether an occupational skill is in adequate supply or in high demand should affect the perception of expatriate workers.

Realistic conflict theory offers an economic interpretation of this situation based on the assumption that conflicts arise because of competition for scarce resources (Campbell, 1965). There is an abundance of social psychological research that demonstrates that positive attitudes toward out-group members relate to feelings of economic and political security (e.g., Berry, Kalin, & Taylor, 1977; Stephan & Stephan, 1996). In contrast, threat of job loss is a strong predictor of negative attitudes toward migrants and migration (Esses, Jackson, & Armstrong, 1998; Stephan, Ybarra, & Bachman, 1999). If it is the case that foreign professionals are occupying jobs that cannot be filled by locals, there would be little reason for Singaporeans to feel threatened or to reject the foreigners. Consequently, international workers who possess skills that are in high demand, and therefore pose little threat to Singaporeans, are likely to be perceived more favorably than those who have skills that are in adequate supply.

A second question concerns benefits: "What does foreign talent offer?" The government has highlighted the significance of the contributions that foreign laborers make to the country as well as the commitment demonstrated by the foreign nationals. For example, a person's type of skills and duration of stay in Singapore are considered in determining eligibility for permanent residence status ("A Points System," 1998). Generally speaking, longer-term residents would be seen as having demonstrated more service and commitment to the country. In addition, as they would have remained productive throughout the recent economic crisis, they may be seen to share a common fate with Singaporeans. This common fate is likely to result in more positive evaluation of long-term residents as awareness of interdependent contact is known to enhance out-group perceptions and reduce intergroup conflict (Amir & Ben-Ari, 1988; Grzelak, 1988).

Equity theory offers additional clues to the probable effects of length of residence and occupational demand on the evaluation of foreign talent in Singapore. This theory concerns perceptions of fairness that are based on notions of economic exchange. At the most elementary level interactions are seen to be equitable when the ratio between inputs and outputs is balanced. In other words, people are rewarded in proportion to their contribution (Adams, 1965). However, the notion of economic exchange permeates human interactions to such an extent that equity theory has also been used to explain interpersonal and intergroup relations (Messick & Cook, 1983; Walster, Walster, & Berscheid, 1978). Equity theory would suggest that foreign talent in Singapore could maximize their input in at least two ways: by providing highly demanded skills and by rendering a longer period of service. These inputs should result in enhanced output; that is, more favorable evaluations of foreign talent by Singaporeans.

A final issue relates to appropriate sources of foreign talent for employment in Singapore. Official statistics are difficult to obtain, but the popular media suggest that citizens of the United States represent one of the largest groups of employment pass holders in Singapore. It is also widely known that there is a large influx of Chinese nationals, encouraged by government initiatives, who have relocated to Singapore with the intention of obtaining permanent residence. Given the salience of Americans and P.R.C. Chinese in the country, these groups obviously merit inclusion in a contemporary investigation of perceptions of foreign talent in Singapore.

Consequently, the third question considered here is "Which ethnic or cultural group is preferred?" The acculturation literature discusses the notion of *cultural distance* noting that native-borns prefer migrants who are culturally and ethnically similar to themselves (Ho, Niles, Penney, & Thomas, 1994; Ward, Bochner, & Furnham, 2001). This finding may be broadly interpreted in terms of the similarity-attraction hypothesis discussed in the mainstream social psychological literature and applied widely to explain the evaluative differences found across ethnocultural groups. For example, King, King, Zhermer, Posokhova, and Chiker (1997) reported that Ukrainians, who share common Slavic ancestry, religion, and culture with Russians, are thought to be more similar and are perceived more positively by Russians than are residents of other ex-Soviet states such as Moldavia or Georgia. In the Singaporean context, both the shared ethnocultural heritage and government's current emphasis on the maintenance of Asian values suggest that there is greater similarity between Chinese Singaporeans and P.R.C. nationals than between Chinese Singaporeans and Americans and that a preference for the Chinese would result.

In some instances the preference for members of ethnically and culturally similar groups may also be related to social categorization and the distinction of in-groups and out-groups as elaborated by Social Identity Theory (SIT). Chiu and Hong (1999), for example, suggested that for most ethnic Chinese in Hong Kong, "Chinese" is a superordinate identity which encompasses regional subtypes. If the same is true in Singapore, both local and P.R.C. Chinese may be seen to share an inclusive in-group identity that could contribute to intergroup bias and Chinese favoritism.

Although the similarity-attraction hypothesis and aspects of social identity theory suggest a preference for Chinese, rather than American, foreign talent in Singapore, there is an alternative possibility to consider. A number of scholars have remarked upon an old colonial syndrome whereby citizens of formerly colonized and developing nations hold unduly positive perceptions of Western expatriates. This syndrome has been broadly discussed as inverse resonance by Carr, Ehiobuche, Rugimbana, and Munro (1996) in relation to the evaluation of expatriate effectiveness in Africa. Empirical support for this syndrome has also been offered by Eze (1985) who found a consistent preference for European versus local doctors, managers, and engineers in Nigeria. Further evidence has been provided by Marin and Salazar (1985) who reported that students from Brazil, Columbia, Dominican Republic, Mexico, and Peru had more positive stereotypes of the nationals from more developed countries, whether culturally similar or dissimilar to their own. In addition, socioeconomic development was found to be a significant predictor of positive national stereotyping.

These themes reflect elements of Social Dominance Theory (SDT) by Sidanius (1993). SDT arises from the premise that all societies are organized by hierarchies, that stratification is often based on groups defined by nations, races, and classes, that individuals make consistent and highly consensual judgments about social status, that discrimination and reward allocation are influenced by these hierarchies within and across social groups, and that most prejudice is directed toward subordinate groups (Sidanius, 1993; Sidanius & Pratto, 1993; Sidanius, Pratto, & Mitchell, 1994). If it is perceived that the United States is a leading world power, as evidenced by its socioeconomic development and political influence, SDT, like inverse resonance theory, would suggest that Singaporeans should express a preference for American expatriates.

The research reported here has been clearly prompted by the pressing need to address a contemporary social issue. How do Singaporeans perceive foreign talent, and which factors (nationality, occupational demand, and length of stay) affect the evaluations of international professionals? Social psychological theories offer some predictions of anticipated results, and although the research is considered exploratory, the hypotheses are as follows:

1. Workers with skills that are in high demand will be perceived more favorably than those with low-demand skills.

2. Workers who have resided in Singapore for a long period will be perceived more favorably than those who have stayed for a shorter duration.

It is also expected that there will be significant differences in the evaluations of American and Chinese workers, although the direction of these differences is not specified due to competing theoretical predictions.

METHOD

Participants and Procedures

Singaporean Chinese working in the private sector were invited to take part in research concerning perceptions of foreign talent. Of the 158 questionnaires that were distributed, 140 were returned, with 134 valid cases. Six of the questionnaires were rejected as the respondents were non-Chinese. The gender composition was 41.4% male and 58.6% female with ages ranging from twenty-one to sixty-five years ($M = 32.90$, $SD = 9.26$). The educational qualifications of the respondents were as follows: 36.8% were college graduates; 29.3% were high school diploma holders; and 4.5%, 28.6%, and 0.8% had preuniversity, secondary, and primary education, respectively.

Survey forms were initially distributed through personal contacts with Singaporean adults working in the private sector, and a snow-balling technique was used to expand the recruitment base. Respondents were drawn from a range of employment sectors and included both professional and skilled workers. Participation in the research was voluntary and anonymous.

Materials

Participants were first presented with the excerpt of a resume that described an employee working as a project coordinator in the information technology industry in Singapore. The employee was described either as Mr. Smith from the United States or as Mr. Tan from the People's Republic of China. Length of employment (three months versus three years) and occupational demand (in adequate supply or in demand) were also varied. Educational background and work experience were held constant (e.g., degree and occupation) but were set in the country of origin. Other details that were presented in the resume but held constant included hobbies and personal particulars, such as marital status.

After reading the resume, participants were asked to rate the employee on six dimensions. As in most studies of interpersonal attraction, these included likability and competence evaluations, specifically social domains (social skills and likability) and occupational competence (job competence and ability to work with Singaporeans). Furthermore, as government initiatives have emphasized the benefits of foreign talent for economic, technological, and national development, contributions to the company and to Singapore were also evaluated. In addition to these six dimensions, participants were asked to consider their behavioral intentions with respect to the likelihood that they would employ and retrench the worker. All ratings were made on seven-point scales (endpoints: very low/very high) with higher scores indicating more favorable evaluations except in the case of the retrenchment (i.e., redundancy) appraisal.

RESULTS

Analyses of variance with a 2 (nationality: People's Republic of China, United States) × 2 (length of stay: three months, three years) × 2 (occupational skills: adequate supply, demand) design were conducted for the eight dependent measures. The results demonstrated clear main effects ($p < 0.05$) for nationality on the evaluations of social skills [$F (1, 126) = 5.34$]; job competence [$F (1, 126) = 4.55$]; ability to work with Singaporeans [$F (1, 126) = 7.90$]; contribution to the company [$F (1, 126) = 4.02$]; contribution to the country [$F (1, 126) = 5.80$]; likelihood of employment [$F (1, 126) = 4.72$]; and likelihood of retrenchment [$F (1, 126) = 4.49$]. In all cases Singaporeans rated the American employee more favorably than the Chinese. The ratings for likability, though not statistically significant, were also in the direction of favoritism toward the American [$F (1, 126) = 3.16, p < 0.10$]. The mean scores are presented in Table 13.1.

These main effects were qualified by interactions with type of skills for the employment [$F (1, 126) = 5.45, p < 0.02$] and retrenchment [$F (1, 126) = 6.03, p < 0.02$] intentions. The greater likelihood of employing Americans [$F (1, 130) = 4.35, p < 0.04$] and retrenching Chinese [$F (1, 130) = 10.50, p < 0.002$] held only when their occupational skills were in demand (see Table 13.2). Note that, on the whole, the evaluations of foreign workers were fairly neutral with a grand mean of 4.24 on a seven-point scale.

Contrary to hypotheses 1 and 2, there were no significant main effects for either length of stay or type of occupational skills; however, interaction effects between these two variables were found for contributions to the company [$F (1, 126) = 8.04, p < 0.05, MSE = 10.38$, effect size = 0.80] and to Singapore [$F (1, 126) = 4.07, p < 0.05, MSE = 5.51$, effect size = 0.52]. Simple effects showed that when skills were in adequate supply, those who had stayed in Singapore for a longer period of time were perceived to have contributed more to the company and to Singapore [$F (1, 130) = 5.47$ and 7.90, respectively, $p < 0.05$] than those who had stayed in Singapore for a shorter period of

Table 13.1
Mean Evaluations of American and Chinese Employees

	American		Chinese	
Social skills	4.44	(1.20)	3.95	(1.27)
Likability	4.32	(1.04)	3.95	(1.18)
Job competence	4.51	(1.08)	4.05	(1.28)
Ability to work with locals	4.44	(0.94)	3.85	(1.31)
Contributions to company	4.59	(1.22)	4.18	(1.07)
Contributions to country	4.48	(1.26)	3.93	(1.12)
Likelihood of employing	3.99	(1.46)	3.44	(1.41)
Likelihood of retrenching	3.88	(1.48)	4.34	(1.32)

Note: Figures in parentheses are standard deviations.

time. Simple effects also showed that when foreign employees had resided in Singapore for a shorter period of time, those who possessed skills in demand were perceived to have contributed more to the company and to Singapore [F (1, 130) = 9.38 and 8.67, respectively, $p < 0.01$] than those whose skills were in adequate supply (see Table 13.3). There were no other significant second-order interaction effects.

DISCUSSION

The study revealed main effects of nationality and interaction effects of length of residence and occupational demand on the perceptions of foreign talent in Singapore. Specifically, Americans were perceived more favorably than P.R.C. Chinese in terms of job competence, social skills, ability to work with Singaporeans, contribution to the company, and contribution to the country. They were also more likely to be employed and less likely to be retrenched (made redundant) than the Chinese, although this was confined to the high-demand condition. Professionals who had resided longer in Singapore were

Table 13.2
Mean Ratings of Behavioral Intentions to Employ and Retrench Foreign Talent as a Function of Nationality and Occupational Demand

	Occupational Skills			
	Adequate Supply		In Demand	
Nationality	Chinese	American	Chinese	American
Employment	3.65 (1.39)	3.61 (1.37)	3.19 (1.42)	4.30 (1.47)
Retrenchment	4.03 (1.43)	4.18 (1.38)	4.74 (1.06)	3.63 (1.53)

Note: Figures in parentheses are standard deviations.

seen to have made a greater contribution to their company and the country than those who had remained for a shorter period, but only if the skills were in adequate supply. In addition, those with skills in demand were seen has having made a greater contribution than those with skills in adequate supply, but only when the period of residence was short.

Why did Singaporean Chinese express an overwhelming preference for American employees? These data reflect the inverse resonance effect and the previously reported finding that positive evaluations of out-group nationals are predicted by level of socioeconomic development (Carr et al., 1996; Marin & Salazar, 1985; Kashima, 1999). The results also converge with predictions made by social dominance theory; that is, societies are stratified into hierarchical groups; the order of stratification is widely recognized and consensually validated; and individuals make choices that reflect and reinforce established hierarchical patterns. These processes have been specifically discussed in the context of occupational role attainment by Pratto, Stallworth, Sidanius, and Siers (1997). Their research showed that the recommendations of employers for the placement of candidates in status-enhancing and status-attenuating occupations were consistent with the position of the candidate's group in the social dominance hierarchy. Although the research of Pratto and colleagues was focused on gender imbalances and the preference for men in high status occupations, its underlying rationale and guiding principles may also be applied to national groups. If it is widely perceived that the United States holds a disproportionate balance of power in the international arena, it would similarly be expected that its nationals would be favored over those from the People's Republic of China in prestigious or lucrative occupational domains.

Table 13.3
Mean Evaluations of Employee Contributions as a Function of Occupational Demand and Length of Residence

	Occupational Skills			
	Adequate Supply		In Demand	
Residence	Three Months	Three Years	Three Months	Three Years
Contributions to Company	3.95 (1.27)	4.60 (1.07)	4.76 (1.21)	4.33 (0.92)
Contributions to Country	3.65 (1.34)	4.47 (1.11)	4.46 (1.26)	4.43 (0.94)

Note: Figures in parentheses are standard deviations.

The ethnic-preference findings reported here appear at odds with predictions made by the similarity-attraction hypothesis; however, these results warrant further consideration in light of more recent research. Although Singaporean and P.R.C. Chinese share common ethnic roots, there are other dimensions of similarity that may be evaluated. In subsequent research we relied upon multidimensional scaling to investigate both perceived value similarity and preference for various groups of foreign residents in Singapore (Leong & Ward, 2000). Our data indicated that Singaporean Chinese saw themselves as no less similar to Americans than to P.R.C. Chinese, and they expressed a strong preference for immigrants from the United States. Clearly, the undifferentiated similarity ratings suggest that comparative evaluations of American and Chinese employees may not be an adequate test of the similarity-attraction hypothesis.

Questions can also be raised with reference to the utility of social identity theory and the validity of its underlying assumptions about an inclusive Chinese in-group. If Singaporean Chinese do not see themselves as sharing similar values with P.R.C. Chinese, there is little basis for the formation of an overarching ethnocultural in-group identity. Consequently, there would be minimal reason to expect favoritism toward the P.R.C. Chinese.

Of the three competing theories, similarity-attraction, social identity, and social dominance, SDT best explains Singaporeans' preference for American employees. It assumes that societies are organized into hierarchies, that socially, politically, and economically advantaged groups are positioned at the top of the dominance chain, and that prejudice is commonly directed toward subordinate social groups. To date, SDT research has been confined to the study of within-country groups. Our work expands investigation to the international setting, and our findings suggest that there is a world order that influences intergroup perceptions. With increasing internationalization of the world-wide labor force, this suggestion deserves further attention in future research.

Contrary to predictions based on realistic conflict theory, occupational demand did not exert a main effect on the evaluations of expatriate workers in Singapore. It may be the case that Singaporeans have yet to perceive the influx of foreign workers to be a significant threat to their rice bowls. Although unemployment has increased somewhat in recent years, it is still low compared to rates in many Western developed countries where the bulk of the immigration research has been undertaken. In these settings opposition to immigrant labor is more widespread. In Canada, for example, almost half (49%) of those responding to an opinion poll believed that immigration increases unemployment (Angus Reid poll, cited in Esses, Jackson, & Armstrong, 1998) and in Australia 44% believe that immigration deprives Australians of jobs (Goot, 1993). In contrast, this belief is true for only about one in four Singaporean workers ("Most Neutral to Foreign Talent," 1998).

Length of residence did affect perception of international employees, but only in combination with occupational demand. Residing in Singapore more long term can enhance the perception of those who possess skills that are in adequate supply, while having skills that are highly demanded can boost the evaluation of those who have been in Singapore for a short period of time. These findings are roughly in accordance with equity theory (Adams, 1965) and are consistent with cross-cultural findings that suggest the equity rule, rather than the equality rule, is more frequently adopted by Chinese when resources are limited (Hui, Triandis, & Yee, 1991), and when dealing with outgroup members (Leung & Bond, 1984). It is worth noting, however, that the effects of skills and length of stay were confined to evaluations of contribution rather than to more personal qualities such as likability and competence.

Given this pattern of results, it is recognized that overall support for equity theory is not strong. Statistically significant outcomes were limited to interaction effects and to only two of the eight dependent variables. This outcome is not completely surprising in that the equity principle is known to operate specifically in conjunction with reward allocation, and rewards are most frequently operationalized in terms of monetary benefits in cross-cultural research (Leung, 1988). Perceptions of fairness or deservingness may be less relevant to the appraisal of personal characteristics such as likability or competence. Nevertheless, it remains puzzling as to why equity effects were limited to the perception of workers' contributions to the company and the country and were not observed in connection with behavioral intention to hire and retrench workers, particularly when employment in a tight labor market could be seen as reward allocation.

Although the research reported here is one of the few studies on perceptions of foreign talent in Singapore, and it has provided some interesting results, the investigation is subject to two major limitations. First, the study concerned the appraisal of foreign talent in a single occupational setting. The extent to which the favoritism displayed for American employees in information technology would generalize to other employment domains remains unknown. Furthermore, the study tells us nothing about the perception of Chinese and Americans outside of work settings. This is an obvious topic for further research.

A second limitation concerns the choice of language. Our survey was conducted in English, which, although generally more appropriate for communication and research in the private sector, may highlight issues of language fluency and disadvantage nonnative speakers in evaluative studies. In addition, choice of language can prompt both ethnic accommodation and affirmation in survey research with bilinguals (Bond & Yang, 1982), and this may limit the external validity of our findings. It would be particularly useful to know if these results would generalize to Mandarin-speaking respondents. This question should be explored in future research.

In conclusion, this study has investigated Singaporeans' perceptions of foreign workers. The results suggest that perceptions are largely neutral and that evaluations of expatriate professionals are affected by nationality, occupational demand, and length of residence. The findings are relevant to government policymakers, local and multinational companies, and foreign workers themselves. However, the research is limited in that it has been confined to a single occupational domain, to work as opposed to social contexts, and to English rather than bilingual survey materials. As the country continues to increase its international labor force, it is recommended that future research be systematically expanded to include a wider variety of stimulus persons, occupations, contexts, and respondents in order to gain greater insight into Singaporeans' perceptions of foreign talent.

REFERENCES

Adams, J. S. (1965). Inequity in social exchange. In L. Berkowitz (Ed.), *Advances in experimental social psychology* (vol. 2, pp. 267–300). New York: Academic Press.

Amir, Y., & Ben-Ari, R. (1988). A contingency approach for promoting intergroup relations. In J. W. Berry & R. C. Annis (Eds.), *Ethnic psychology: Research and practice with immigrants, refugees, native peoples, ethnic groups and sojourners* (pp. 287–296). Lisse, The Netherlands: Swets & Zeitlinger.

Are foreign workers taking away local jobs? (1998, September 6). *The Sunday Times*, p. 33.

Berry, J. W., Kalin, R., & Taylor, D. (1977). *Multiculturalism and ethnic attitudes in Canada*. Ottawa: Ministry of Supply and Services.

Bond, M. H., & Yang, K.-S. (1982). Ethnic affirmation versus cross-cultural accommodation: The variable impact of questionnaire language on Chinese bilinguals. *Journal of Cross-Cultural Psychology, 13*, 169–185.

Campbell, D. T. (1965). Ethnocentric and other altruistic motives. In D. Levine (Ed.), *Nebraska symposium on motivation* (pp. 283–311). Lincoln: University of Nebraska Press.

Carr, S. C., Ehiobuche, I., Rugimbana, R., & Munro, D. (1996). Expatriates' ethnicity and their effectiveness: "Similarity-attraction" or "inverse resonance?" *Psychology and Developing Societies, 8*, 177–197.

Chiu, C.-Y., & Hong, Y.-Y. (1999). Social identification in a political transition: The role of implicit beliefs. *International Journal of Intercultural Relations, 23*, 297–318.

Esses, V. M., Jackson, L. M., & Armstrong, T. L. (1998). Intergroup competition and attitudes toward immigrants and immigration. *Journal of Social Issues, 54*, 699–724.

Eze, N. (1985). Sources of motivation among Nigerian managers. *Journal of Social Psychology, 125*, 341–345.

Goot, M. (1993). Multiculturalists, monoculturalists and the many in between: Attitudes to cultural diversity and their correlates. *Australian and New Zealand Journal of Sociology, 99*, 226–253.

Grzelak, J. (1988). Conflict and cooperation. In M. Hewstone, W. Stroebe, J.-P. Codol, & G. M. Stephenson (Eds.), *Introduction to social psychology* (pp. 288–312). Oxford: Basil Blackwell.

Ho, R., Niles, S., Penney, R., & Thomas, A. (1994). Migrants and multiculturalism: A survey of attitudes in Darwin. *Australian Psychologist, 29*, 62–70.

Hui, C. H., Triandis, H. C., & Yee, C. (1991). Cultural differences in reward allocation: Is collectivism the explanation? *British Journal of Social Psychology, 30*, 310–323.

Kashima, E. (1999, August). *"Asian" and "Pacific Rim" identities among Australians, Chinese, Japanese and North Americans.* Poster presented at the Third Conference of the Asian Association of Social Psychology, Taipei, Taiwan.

King, E. H., King, D. H., Zhermer, N., Posokhova, S., & Chiker, V. (1997). In-group favoritism and perceived similarity: A look at Russians' perceptions in the post–Soviet era. *Personality and Social Psychology Bulletin, 23*, 1013–1021.

Lay-offs soar to record high. (1999, February 26). *The Straits Times*, p. 2.

Leong, C.-H., & Ward, C. (2000, September). *Chinese Singaporeans' perceptions of "Chineseness," immigration and identity.* Paper presented at the International Conference on Immigrant Societies and Modern Education, Singapore.

Leung, K. (1988). Theoretical advances in justice behavior: Some cross-cultural implications. In M. H. Bond (Ed.), *The cross-cultural challenge to social psychology* (pp. 218–229). Newbury Park, CA: Sage.

Leung, K., & Bond, M. H. (1984). The impact of cultural collectivism on reward allocation. *Journal of Personality and Social Psychology, 47*, 793–804.

Low skilled jobs in Singapore going. (1999, February 7). *The Sunday Times*, p. 2.

Marin, G., & Salazar, J. (1985). Determinants of hetero- and auto-stereotypes. *Journal of Cross-Cultural Psychology, 16*, 403–422.

Messick, D. M., & Cook, D. S. (Eds.). (1983). *Equity theory: Psychological and sociological perspectives.* New York: Praeger.

Most neutral to foreign talent. (1998, August 19). *The Straits Times*, p. 33.

A points system to decide PR status. (1998, December 31). *The Straits Times*, p. 1.

Pratto, F., Stallworth, L. M., Sidanius, J., & Siers, B. (1997). The gender gap in occupational role attainment: A social dominance approach. *Journal of Personality and Social Psychology, 72*, 37–53.

Sidanius, J. (1993). The psychology of group conflict and the dynamics of oppression: A social dominance perspective. In S. Iyengar & W. J. McGuire (Eds.), *Explorations in political psychology* (pp. 183–219). Durham, NC: Duke University Press.

Sidanius, J., & Pratto, F. (1993). The dynamics of social dominance and the inevitability of oppression. In P. Sniderman & P. E. Tetlock (Eds.), *Prejudice, politics and race in America today* (pp. 173–211). Stanford, CA: Stanford University Press.

Sidanius, J., Pratto, F., & Mitchell, M. (1994). Group identity, social dominance orientation, and intergroup discrimination: Some implications of social dominance theory. *Journal of Social Psychology, 134*, 151–167.

Stephan, W. G., & Stephan, C. W. (1996). Predicting prejudice. *International Journal of Intercultural Relations, 20*, 409–426.

Stephan, W. G., Ybarra, O., & Bachman, G. (1999). Prejudice towards immigrants: An integrated threat theory. *Journal of Applied Social Psychology, 29*, 2221–2237.

Walster, E., Walster, G. W., & Berscheid, E. (1978). *Equity: Theory and research.* Boston: Allyn & Bacon.

Ward, C., Bochner, S., & Furnham, A. (2001). *The psychology of culture shock.* London: Routledge.

PART V

DEVIANT BEHAVIOR
AND REHABILITATION

CHAPTER 14

The Effects of School Violence on the Psychological Adjustment of Korean Adolescents: A Comparative Analysis of Bullies, Victims, and Bystanders

Kye-Min Yang, Hyun-hee Chung, and Uichol Kim

Over the last several years, school violence has increased at an alarming rate in Korea. National statistics indicate that a substantial number of adolescents have reported being victims of school violence. For example, 41.3% of students in Korea experienced school violence in 1998 (Korean Foundation for Prevention Youth Violence, 1998). The Korean Institute of Criminology (1996) also found that 56.8% of students reported being bullied by their peers. About one-third (33%) of students were abused physically at least once, 18.1% of students experienced serious physical attack, and 6.5% of students were hospitalized, and 1.0% died as the result of physical assault (Korean Foundation for Prevention Youth Violence, 1996). In terms of psychological outcome, 56% of students experienced anxiety, 11% refused to attend school, 3.2% received psychological treatment, 0.5% attempted suicide, and 0.6% actually succeeded in committing suicide. These statistics show that school violence has become a serious problem in terms of both the physical and psychological well-being of adolescents.

According to a study conducted by the Korean Youth Center, social exclusion has become a more serious problem in Korea than physical or verbal violence (Korean Youth Center, 1998). The study surveyed 1,088 high school students in Korea. Results indicated that 19.8% of the students experienced social exclusion during the past year, and 51.2% worried about being excluded by their peers. For girls, 59.2% feared social exclusion, which was higher than for boys (43%). Students experiencing social exclusion experienced the following reaction: desire to take revenge (46.7%), not wanting to go to school (39.5%), increased fear of friends (36.5%), and increased social phobia (7.5%) (Korean Youth Center, 1998).

Although victims of school violence and social exclusion suffer from physical and psychological problems, bullies also experience social and psychological problems. Bullies are more likely to drop out of school, and they are also more likely to participate in delinquent behavior, even as adults. In Korea, empirical studies focusing on school violence are very limited, and relatively few have assessed the psychological and behavioral characteristics of bullies and victims. The aim of this study is to examine the problem of bullies and victims and the negative impact school violence has on their school and personal adjustment.

DEFINITION OF BULLYING

Traditionally, school violence has been defined as an act of assault, theft, or vandalism. However, school violence has been redefined more broadly to include any condition or act that creates a hostile environment for students (Batsche & Knoff, 1994). According to Hazler, Hoover, and Oliver (1992), bullying is defined as a form of aggression in which one or more students physically and/or psychologically (and more recently, sexually) harasses another student repeatedly over time. Typically, the action is unprovoked and the bully is perceived as stronger than the victim (Hazler, Hoover, & Oliver, 1992; Olweus, 1991b). Tattum and Herbert (1990) defined bullying as a conscious desire to hurt others physically and psychologically and to put them under stress. Moreover, Olweus (1993) stated that a student is bullied or victimized when he or she is exposed repeatedly to negative actions on the part of one or more other students. It must be stressed that the term bullying is not used when two students are of approximately the same strength and are quarreling with one another. Use of the term bullying indicates an imbalance in terms of strength and power. In this definition, school violence includes both physical violence (such as beating or kicking) and psychological bullying in the form of social exclusion and abuse. For this study, the definition of bullying as physical aggression, social exclusion, and stealing other students' money or possessions is adopted.

CHARACTERISTICS OF BULLIES AND VICTIMS

Bullies

A distinctive characteristic of the typical bully is aggressive behavior toward peers (Olweus, 1978). Generally, bullies have a more positive attitude toward violence and use of violent means than other students. They are often characterized by being impulsive and have a strong need to dominate others. They have little empathy toward victims. Male bullies are likely to be physically stronger than other boys of the same age, especially as compared to victims (Olweus, 1978).

Olweus (1993) distinguished three patterns that are related to bullies. First, bullies have a strong need for power and dominance; they seem to enjoy being in control and need to subdue others. Second, they grew up in an unhealthy family environment in which they experienced a high degree of hostility and as such they derive satisfaction from inflicting injury and suffering upon others. Finally, there is a benefit component to their behavior. Bullies often coerce their victims into giving them money, cigarettes, beer, and other valuables (Patterson, Littman, & Bricker, 1967). Aggressive behaviors in many situations are rewarded in the form of social prestige (Bandura, 1973).

There is a lack of evidence indicating that bullies are anxious, insecure, or have low self-esteem. Instead, bullies are reported as being liked by other students and perceive their actions as justified (Greenbaum, 1988). Bullies believe that they pick on their victim because they are provoked or because they do not like the victim. A study in Korea also showed that bullies tend to regard themselves as a judge, hence, they engage in the role of punishing bad boys and girls and unusual students (I. K. Kim, 1996). In addition, they assume that they are superior to their victims.

Victims

Victimized adolescents have low self-esteem. Moreover, they are more likely to experience depression, loneliness, and anxiety (Olweus, 1993; Boulton & Smith, 1994; Craig, 1998; Hawker & Boulton, 1998). O'Moore and Hillery (1991) also found that victims have low self-esteem, high-anxiety, low happiness and satisfaction, and lower popularity than peers.

Olweus (1978) identified two types of victims: the passive victim and the provocative victim. Passive victims are described as being anxious and insecure. They do nothing to provoke attacks and they do not defend themselves. They are lonely and feel abandoned at school. They are also recognized as being without friends. They are described as being nonaggressive and are likely to be physically weaker than same-age peers (in the case of boys). Therefore, these children often have a negative attitude toward violence as well as the usage of violent means in any situation. In contrast, provocative victims are described as being hot-tempered, restless, anxious, and will attempt to retaliate when attacked. These students often have problems concentrating. They behave in ways that may cause irritation and tension around them. Perry, Kusel, and Perry (1988) identified victims in a similar manner, using the terms *high-aggressive* and *low-aggressive* victims. However, they found that the number of provocative and passive victims was approximately equal, whereas Olweus (1984) found fewer than one in five victims were provocative.

The purpose of this study is to examine the experiences of school violence among Korean adolescents to determine the negative impact on school adjustment for three groups: bullies, victims, and bystanders. The second purpose is to examine whether psychological and behavioral patterns found in other countries are also found in Korea.

METHOD

Subjects

A total of 2,565 Korean adolescents from ten junior and senior high schools participated in this study: 1,226 were junior high school students (514 male and 712 female) and 1,339 were senior high school students (698 male and 641 female). The participants were enrolled in grades seven through eleven, and their ages ranged from twelve to eighteen years old (see Table 14.1).

Procedure

Participants completed the survey in their classrooms. The survey was comprised of the following measures: Stress, Social Anxiety, Self-Esteem, Depression, Suicide Idealization, Loneliness, Life Satisfaction, Delinquent Behavior, and Grade Point Average (Grade). Participants were assured that the information would be kept confidential.

Measures

School Violence

Six items assessed the extent to which adolescents experience peer aggression as a bully or victim. They responded to questions such as how often they hit or hurt other students, socially excluded other students, or stole possessions from other students. They were also asked how often they were hit or

Table 14.1
The Demographic Characteristics

School	Female	Male	Total
Junior High School	514	712	1226
Preparatory School	438	508	946
Vocational School	203	190	393
Total	1155	1410	2565

hurt by other students, were socially excluded by other students, or had their possessions stolen by other students. They responded to these questions on a four-point scale defined by *never, sometimes, often*, and *very often*.

Stress

Two subscales developed by Byun (1995) were used to measure adolescents' stress (e.g., stress toward school or teacher and stress toward friends). The Cronbach *alpha* was 0.83 for stress toward school or teacher and 0.84 for stress toward friends.

Social Anxiety

Participants responded to six items from the social anxiety subscale on a Self-Consciousness Scale (Scheier & Carver, 1985). This scale assesses subjective anxiety, reticence in social context, and performance difficulty. Participants responded on a four-point scale, ranging from *never* to *very much*. The Cronbach *alpha* for the scale was 0.77.

Self-Esteem

The participants completed the Rosenberg Self-Esteem Scale (1965). They responded using a four-point scale, ranging from *never* to *very much*. The Cronbach *alpha* for the scale was 0.86.

Depression

This scale was derived from the Center for Epidemiological Studies in Depression Scale (Randloff, 1977) to measure the participants' depression. This scale assesses the depression symptoms experienced during the past week on a four-point scale ranging from *always* to *never*. The Cronbach *alpha* for the scale was 0.91.

Suicide Idealization

Harlow, Newcomb, and Bentler's (1986) scale was used for suicide idealization. This scale uses five points ranging from *never* to *always*. The Cronbach *alpha* for this scale was 0.85.

Loneliness

Twenty-four items were used to measure adolescents' loneliness (Asher, Hymel, & Renshaw, 1984) with a scale that assessed loneliness experiences among peers and dissatisfaction in social contexts. Participants responded to each item on a five-point scale ranging from *always* to *never*. The Cronbach *alpha* for the scale was 0.78.

Life Satisfaction

The participants responded to a ten-item scale developed by Taft (1986) and adapted by Kim and Park (1999). The scale assesses adolescents' satisfaction with school life, academic achievement, relationship with teacher, economic status, relationship with friends, leisure time, and general satisfaction. The Cronbach *alpha* was 0.85.

Delinquent Behavior

The scale consisted of eight items including violation of school rules, stealing, skipping class, running away, and watching pornography. The scale was developed by the present authors to assess the behavioral problems that may appear in a school setting. Participants indicated how many times they experienced behavioral problems during the past year.

Academic Achievement

Academic achievement consisted of rank order in the class and grade point average (GPA).

RESULT

Group Classification Procedure

Cluster analysis identified four groups: victims, bullies, bystanders, and mixed. This categorization was based on the students' scores on the following six behavior measures: (1) students beat me, (2) students excluded me, (3) students stole my possessions from me, (4) I beat other students, (5) I excluded other students, and (6) I stole other students' possessions. The K-Means method (Dilon & Goldstein, 1984) was employed as the algorithm since the sample size of this study was over 2,000, and the produced clusters were set in advance into four. School violence was categorized into four groups: (1) victim, (2) bully, (3) mixed group (both victim and bully), and (4) bystanders. The number of final clusters was set in advance according to our theoretical assumptions.

The means and standard deviations of the four clusters for the school violence–related behavior measures are presented in Table 14.2. Cluster 1 includes 5% of the sample (N = 128). Cluster 1 shows high scores on the three items related to the victim, and low scores on the items related to bullies. Thus, this group is classified as the victim group. Cluster 2 consists of 6.8% of the students (N = 175) and is characterized by relatively high scores on the three

Table 14.2
The Mean and Standard Deviation of the Items in Each Cluster

Item	Cluster 1	Cluster 2	Cluster 3	Cluster 4	Total mean	F
	Victim	Bully	Bystander	Mixed		
	(n = 128)	(n = 175)	(n = 2245)	(n = 7)		
1. Students beat me.	2.62 (0.92)	1.18 (0.40)	1.03 (0.17)	3.86 (0.38)	1.13 (0.47)	1482.72**
2. Students exclude me.	2.16 (0.94)	1.18 (0.41)	1.07 (0.25)	3.57 (1.13)	1.14 (0.43)	545.62**
3. Students steal my possessions from me.	1.54 (0.94)	1.10 (0.41)	1.03 (0.17)	3.86 (0.38)	1.06 (0.33)	389.96**
4. I beat other students.	1.38 (0.60)	2.25 (0.67)	1.07 (0.26)	3.43 (1.13)	1.18 (0.33)	788.86**
5. I exclude other students.	1.29 (0.53)	2.12 (0.66)	1.10 (0.29)	3.57 (1.13)	1.18 (0.45)	574.66**
6. I steal other students' possessions.	1.03 (0.22)	1.19 (0.56)	1.01 (0.00)	3.14 (1.46)	1.03 (0.22)	347.17**

Note: **$p < 0.01$.

items relating to bullies, but low scores on the items related to victims. Thus this group is classified as bullies. Cluster 3 consists of 87.8% of the sample (N = 2,245), and showed uniformly low scores across all the items. This group is thus classified as bystanders. Cluster 4 includes 0.3% of the sample (N = 7), and scores are uniformly high across all items, which suggests that they are both victims and bullies. An analysis of variance indicated that the four clusters differed significantly on each of the six items. Since only a small number of adolescents belonged to the mixed group, they were excluded from additional analyses.

The Demographic Characteristics of Victims and Bullies

For the victim group (N = 128), 83.6% of students (N = 107) were male, and 16.4% of the students were female (N = 21). Junior high school students made up 71.9% (N = 92) of the group, and the remaining 28.1% of the students were in senior high school (N = 36).

For the bully group (N = 175), 80.6% of the students were male (N = 141), and 19.4% were female (N = 34), 61.1% of the students were in junior high school (N = 107), and 38.9% were in senior high school (N = 68). These results show that the victim–bully problem is most serious for boys attending junior high school (see Table 14.3).

Table 14.3
The Frequency and Percentage of the Victim Group and Bully Group by Sex and School

	Group	Victim	Bully
Gender	Male	107 (83.6)	141 (80.6)
	Female	21 (16.4)	34 (19.4)
School	Junior High School	92 (71.9)	107 (61.1)
	Senior High School	36 (28.1)	68 (38.9)
	Total	128 (100.0)	175 (100.0)

Psychological Adjustment of the Victim and the Bully

For the three groups (victim, bully, bystander), analysis revealed significant differences in terms of stress (school and teacher), stress toward friends, self-esteem, depression, loneliness, life satisfaction, delinquent behavior, and grade. There were no significant differences across groups in terms of social anxiety and suicide idealization. More specifically, victims showed the highest scores of the three groups in stress for school and teacher, stress for friends, depression, and loneliness. They had the lowest scores on self-esteem, life satisfaction, and grade. In contrast, bullies showed no significant differences with the bystander groups on any of the scales, except that they scored the highest in delinquent behavior and lower in academic achievement. This result indicates that the psychological adjustment of bullies is relatively better than that of victims.

CONCLUSION

The goal of this study is to examine psychological adjustment among victims, bullies, and bystanders (who are neither victims nor bullies). Four conclusions can be drawn from this study.

First, school violence is most prevalent in junior high school. This result is consistent with the other studies in Korea (K. A. Kim, 1996; Korean Youth Center, 1998; Ahn, 1998). More important, this result highlights that school violence prevention programs are critical during the early stage of schooling.

Second, victims experience a high degree of stress in school, and from teachers and friends (see Table 14.4). This result is consistent with prior research

Table 14.4
The Mean and Standard Deviation of the Psychological Variables among the Three Groups

Variable	Victim (1) (N=128)	Bully (2) (N=175)	Bystanders (3) (N=2245)	F	Post Hoc
Stress: School and teacher	3.31 (0.76)	3.12 (0.73)	3.06 (0.72)	6.52**	1 > 2,3
Stress: friend	3.27 (0.79)	2.86 (0.83)	2.89 (0.80)	14.23**	1 > 2,3
Social Anxiety	2.06 (0.47)	1.98 (0.46)	1.97 (0.45)	n.s.	n.s.
Self-Esteem	2.69 (0.61)	2.77 (0.60)	2.86 (0.57)	7.28**	1 < 3
Depression	2.27 (0.68)	1.84 (0.57)	1.81 (0.54)	40.52**	1 > 2,3
Suicide Idealization	1.97 (0.91)	1.91 (0.79)	1.84 (0.75)	n.s.	n.s.
Loneliness	2.89 (0.86)	2.24 (0.70)	2.23 (0.65)	59.28**	1 > 2,3
Life Satisfaction	56.12 (17.76)	61.34 (15.98)	62.24 (15.44)	8.96**	1 < 2,3
Delinquent Behavior	1.36 (0.36)	1.56 (0.53)	1.30 (0.39)	46.31**	2 > 1,3
Grade	8.76 (1.37)	9.06 (1.40)	9.39 (1.39)	16.60**	3 > 1,2

Note: **$p < 0.01$.

suggesting that victims tend to avoid school, and have unstable and maladjusted relationships with their peers (Olweus, 1994; Sharp & Smith, 1994). Victims perceive their teachers as sources of stress and not as being supportive. Victims, therefore, perceive their school climate as being hostile and unsafe. In addition, victims show higher depression and loneliness, and lower self-esteem and life satisfaction than the other two groups. These findings suggest that victims are experiencing psychological problems. Moreover, the level of academic achievement of victims is the lowest among the three groups. These results support previous findings that victims may suffer from a lack of concentration and benefit little from learning (Sharp & Smith, 1994). These results also show that victims are maladjusted psychologically and socially, and they may need professional help.

Third, students in the bully group were not significantly different from the bystander group, except for their higher scores in delinquency and lower scores in academic achievement. This result is interesting in that it is inconsistent with previous studies that show juvenile delinquency and violence are related to low self-esteem (Kwok & Moon, 1993, 1995), and that violence is the sign that these bullies are in psychological pain and appealing to the people around them for help (Coser, 1967). However, our findings are consistent with other studies that found no indication that bullies are anxious, insecure, or lack self-esteem (Greenbaum, 1988; Olweus, 1991a).

This result does not mean that the bullies are psychologically well adjusted or healthy; it may indicate that their psychological state is problematic. For instance, even if they attack their peers physically or exclude them socially, they do not feel stress or anxiety, but are actually satisfied with themselves and with their lives. They do not feel guilt since they feel that their behavior is justified. This result is consistent with other studies in which students who engage in school violence morally disengage from their actions, and as a result, do not take responsibility for them (Bandura, 1973; Park & Kim, 2001a, 2001b). This result was also found in a Korean study in which bullies regarded themselves as "a kind of judge," and were entitled to control "the bad students," and thus felt superior and viewed violence positively (I. K. Kim, 1996). As Greenbaum (1988) indicated, bullies enjoy acts of violence as well as the byproducts of their actions (e.g., elevating their status in the group), and they are able to justify their behavior. As a result, their violent behavior is reinforced. Therefore, bullies may also need professional help, but would likely refuse such intervention.

Fourth, the results of this study indicate that prevention is urgently needed to treat the problem of school violence for Korean adolescents. As pointed out in this study, school violence is multifaceted, and requires a multipronged approach to address it. Therefore, intervention for adolescents who are involved in school violence should be developed and administered in diverse aspects according to the level of the problem, the student's age, and the environment. This type of multipronged approach needs to be administered not independently, but interdependently to maximize the effect of prevention (Coie et al., 1993). More specifically, in order to prevent school violence, proactively applying prevention programs for adolescents that involve parents, teachers, and peers is more effective than implementing secondary or tertiary prevention programs.

Finally, there are several limitations to this study. First, we did not test the causal relationship among the variables included in this study. That is, we did not determine whether the psychological maladjustment of the victims is the result of the school violence or vice versa. The causal relation of victimization and psychological maladjustment needs to be investigated in future longitudinal studies, as it is very important to understanding victims and bullies and to developing prevention and intervention programs. The second limitation of this study is related to methodology. This study is based on self-report. Since school violence is a subtle and sensitive issue, it is possible that the students did not answer violence-related items honestly or seriously. Therefore, in the future studies, ratings from parents, peers, and teachers should be included. Third, the variables included in this study are limited in explaining the diverse aspects of school violence and adolescent functioning.

Even with these limitations, the findings show that victimized students as well as bullies are clearly at risk for a variety of adjustment problems. They are in need of proactive intervention programs that address and resolve these problems. The public needs to recognize that school violence is a serious problem and that psychological intervention is crucial for the well-being and success of adolescents.

REFERENCES

Ahn, S. O. (1998). The alternatives and synthetic analysis of school violence. *Present states and alternatives of school violence.* Seoul: Association of Korean Adolescents Mental Health.

Asher, S. R., Hymel, S., & Renshaw, P. D. (1984). Loneliness in children. *Child Development, 55,* 1456–1464.

Bandura, A. (1973). *Aggression: A social learning analysis.* Englewood Cliffs, NJ: Prentice Hall.

Batsche, G. M., & Knoff, H. M. (1994). Bullies and their victims: Understanding a pervasive problem in the school. *School Psychology Review, 23* (2), 165–174.

Boulton, M. J., & Smith, P. K. (1994). Bully/victim problem in middle-school children: Stability, self-perceived competence, peer perceptions and peer acceptance. *British Journal of Developmental Psychology, 12,* 315–329.

Byun, Y. J. (1995). *Parents' child rearing attitude, and irrational belief and stress of adolescents.* Unpublished master's thesis. Yonsei University, Seoul, South Korea.

Coie, J. D., Watt, N. F., West, S. G., Hawkins, J. D., Asarnow, J. R., & Markman, H. J. (1993). The science of prevention: A conceptual framework and some directions for a national research program. *American Psychologist, 48,* 1013–1022.

Coser, L. (1967). Some social functions of violence. In *Continuities in the study of social conflict.* New York: Free Press.

Craig, W. M. (1998). The relationship among bullying, victimization, depression, anxiety, and aggression in elementary school children. *Personality and Individual Difference, 24,* 123–130.

Dilon, W. R., & Goldstein, M. (1984). *Multivariate analysis-methods and application.* New York: John Wiley and Sons.

Greenbaum, S. (1988). *School bully and victimization* (Resource Paper). Malibu, CA: National School Safety Center.

Harlow, L. L., Newcomb, M. D., & Bentler, P. M. (1986). Depression, self-derogation, substance use, and suicide ideation: Lack of purpose in life as a mediational factor. *Journal of Clinical Psychology, 42,* 5–21. Reprinted at Center on Evaluation, Development, and Research: Hot Topics Series (1988). *Adolescent suicide* (pp. 97–113). Bloomington, IN: Phi Delta Kappa.

Hawker, D. S., & Boulton, M. J. (1998). Peer victimization: Cause and consequence of psychological adjustment. *Child Development, 66,* 710–722.

Hazler, R. J., Hoover, J. H., & Oliver, R. (1992, November). What kids say about bullying. *The Executive Educator*, pp. 20–22.

Kim, I. K. (1996). The bullies. In Korean Youth Center (Ed.), *The victim and bully* (pp. 97–105). Seoul: Korean Youth Center.

Kim, K. A. (1996). *Study for describing the state of school violence and searching alternatives in Korea*. Unpublished master's thesis. Dong-Kuk University, Seoul, South Korea.

Kim, U., & Park, Y. S. (1999). Psychological and behavioral pattern of Korean adolescents: With specific focus on the influence of friends, family, and school. *Korean Journal of Educational Psychology, 13*, 99–142.

Korean Foundation for Prevention Youth Violence. (1996). *I hate violence: The prevention and instruction of school violence*. Seoul: Korean Foundation for Prevention Youth Violence Press.

Korean Foundation for Prevention Youth Violence. (1998). *The field research report for prevention of school violence*. Research report no. 4. Seoul: Korean Foundation for Prevention Youth Violence Press.

Korean Institute of Criminology. (1996). *Statistics of school violence and solution*. Research report no. 96-12. Seoul: Korean Institute of Criminology Press.

Korean Youth Center. (1998). *The alternative model of adolescents' violence—Prevention program for violence focusing on community network development*. Seoul: Korean Youth Center Press.

Kwok, K. J., & Moon, U. Y. (1993). Psychological characteristics and the relationship between depression and delinquency. *Korean Journal of Psychology: Development, 6* (2), 29–43.

Kwok, K. J., & Moon, U. Y. (1995). Psychological characteristics, depression and delinquency (2). *Korean Journal of Psychology: Development, 8* (1), 1–11.

Olweus, D. (1978). *Aggression in the schools: Bullies and whipping-boys*. London: Willy Hasted.

Olweus, D. (1984). Aggressors and their victims: Bullying at school. In N. Frude & H. Gault (Eds.), *Disruptive behavior disorders in schools* (pp. 57–76). New York: John Wiley and Sons.

Olweus, D. (1991a). Bullying at school: Basic facts and effect of a school-based intervention program. In D. Pepler & K. Rubin (Eds.), *The development and treatment of childhood aggression*. Hillsdale, NJ: Erlbaum.

Olweus, D. (1991b). Bully/victim problems among school children: Basic facts and effects of a school based intervention program. In I. Rubin & D. Pepler (Eds.), *The development and treatment of childhood aggression* (pp. 411–447). Hillsdale, NJ: Erlbaum.

Olweus, D. (1993). *Bullying at school: What we know and what we can do*. Oxford: Blackwell.

Olweus, D. (1994). Annotation: Bullying at school: Basic facts and effect of a school-based intervention program. *Journal of Child Psychology, 5* (7), 1171–1190.

O'Moore, A. M., & Hillery, B. (1991). What do teachers need to know? In M. Elliott (Ed.), *Bullying: A practical guide to coping for schools* (pp. 56–69). Harlow: Longman.

Park, Y. S., & Kim, U. (2001a). Influence of environmental and psychological factors on school violence: Comparative analysis of high school students and adolescents under institutional supervision. *Korean Journal of Educational Psychology, 15* (2), 25–52.

Park, Y. S., & Kim, U. (2001b). Psychological, behavioral, and relational characteristics of school violence: Comparative analysis of victims, bullies, nonparticipants of aggression. *Korean Journal of Psychological and Social Issues, 7* (1), 63–89.

Patterson, G. R., Littman, R. A., & Bricker, W. (1967). Assertive behavior in children: A step toward a theory of aggression. *Monographs of the Society for Research in Child Development, 32* (5), 1–43.

Perry, D.G.M., Kusel, S. J., & Perry L. C. (1988). Victims of peer aggression. *Developmental Psychology, 24*, 807–814.

Randloff, L. S. (1977). The CES-D scale: A self-report depression scale for research in the general population. *Applied Psychological Measurement 1*, 385–401.

Rosenberg, M. (1965). *Society and the adolescent self-image: Self-esteem scale.* Princeton, NJ: Princeton University Press.

Scheier, M. F., & Carver, C. S. (1985). Revised scale for noncollege populations. The self-consciousness scale: A revision for use general populations. *Journal of Applied Social Psychology, 15*, 687–699.

Sharp, S., & Smith, P. K. (1994). *Tackling bullying in your school.* New York: Routledge.

Taft, R. (1986). The psychological study of the adjustment and adaptation of immigrants to Australia. In N. T. Feather (Ed.), *Survey of Australian psychology: Trend for research.* Sydney: George Allen and Unwin.

Tattum, D., & Herbert, G. (1990). *Bullying: A positive response.* Cardiff: South Glamorgan Institute of Higher Education.

CHAPTER 15

Does Media Coverage of Capital Punishment Have a Deterrent Effect on the Occurrence of Brutal Crimes? An Analysis of Japanese Time-Series Data from 1959 to 1990

Akira Sakamoto, Kiyoko Sekiguchi,
Aya Shinkyu, and Yuko Okada

Although many countries have abolished capital punishment, some countries still practice it, including Japan, China, and the United States. This situation is probably due in part to support from public opinion in those countries, which the governments are unable to ignore (Amnesty International, 1989). For example, a survey conducted by the Prime Minister's Office of Japan (1999) revealed that 79.3% of Japanese think that capital punishment should be retained, whereas 8.8% of Japanese think that it should be abolished. Those who are in favor of capital punishment seem to believe that capital punishment has a deterrent effect on brutal crimes such as homicide, robbery, arson, and rape. In fact, the same survey showed that 54.4% of Japanese think that abolishment of capital punishment would lead to an increase in brutal crime, whereas only 8.4% of Japanese think it would not increase it. While public belief in a deterrent effect is clear, controversy is evident in the academic world.

Most studies on this issue have been conducted in the United States. These studies may be classified into three groups. The first group consists of studies that examined whether the murder rate changed when executions were carried out. These studies use time-series analysis methods (Bailey, 1998; Bower & Pierce, 1975; Cochran, Chamlin, & Seth, 1994; Ehrlich, 1975; Layson, 1985; Sorensen, Wrinkle, Brewer, & Marguart, 1999). The second group of studies examine the difference in murder rate between states in which executions are carried out and ones in which executions are not carried out (Bailey, 1980, 1984; Black & Orsagh, 1978; Ehrlich, 1977; Peterson & Bailey, 1988). The third group consists of studies investigating how media coverage of executions and capital punishment sentences influenced the homicide rate (Bailey, 1990, 1998; Bailey & Peterson, 1989, 1994; Dann, 1935; King, 1978; Phillips, 1980; Phillips & Hensley, 1984; Peterson & Bailey, 1991; Savitz, 1958; Stack, 1987, 1990). This third group of studies has presented mixed results without any clear conclusion with regard to the deterrent effect of capital punishment.

As Stack (1990) wrote, the third group of studies is important when examining the impact of capital punishment. The public usually only finds out if someone was executed or sentenced to death through media coverage, meaning that the impact of the execution or sentence is mediated by the media coverage, if there is any effect. To evaluate possible effects of capital punishment on the homicide rate, researchers need to examine the change in the murder rate when executions and death sentences are publicized in the media. Studies showing no effect of capital punishment may not have looked at the media coverage, and instead simply focused on the executions themselves.

In this study, we examined whether and how media coverage of capital punishment has affected the occurrence of brutal crimes through an analysis of Japanese data. The Japanese data are particularly useful for the following reasons. First, capital punishment is still practiced in Japan (Figure 15.1), whereas most highly industrialized countries have abolished it. Japanese data therefore may be helpful to understand the effect executions might have in similarly industrialized countries. Second, three major newspapers (*Asahi,*

Figure 15.1
A Change in the Number of Executions in Japan

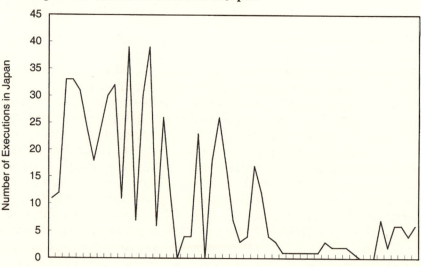

Year

Mainich, and *Yomiuri*) are available in Japan, and a large number of Japanese people read them. Sales for each paper run up to several million copies per day. Almost all households in Japan subscribe to at least one of these newspapers. If publicity of capital punishment influences the occurrence of brutal crimes, the publicity provided by these newspapers should have a significant effect on the crime rate.

Third, results of this study will add a cross-cultural perspective to the impact of capital punishment since most research on the topic is American (see Layson, 1983; Wolpin, 1978, for exceptions). Cross-cultural confirmation of results would increase the robustness of the findings. In addition, if cross-cultural results differ, they may still promote understanding of contributing factors. A Japanese time-series study should be helpful in examining the generality of the effect of capital punishment from a cross-cultural perspective.

This study also has three novel aspects. First, not only the impact of publicity of executions and capital sentences were examined, but also the impact of other publicity surrounding judicial affairs such as life sentences and judgments of innocence. It is important to compare the impact of capital punishment with the impact of imprisonment for life to discern whether capital punishment should be abolished or not. An argument for abolishing capital punishment can only be made when the impact of capital punishment is larger than the impact of imprisonment for life. Only a small number of studies have examined the impact of imprisonment for life (Bailey, 1977; Phillips & Hensley, 1984).

Second, we examined not only the impact on the homicide rate, but also on the rate of other crimes, including robbery, arson, and rape. Most previous studies examined only the impact on the homicide rate.

Third, as measures of the publicity of the affairs, not only the number of judicial affairs (execution, death sentence, imprisonment for life, and innocence judgments) publicized in newspapers, but also the number of characters and the number of photographs printed in the articles were examined as a measure of media attention. As Bailey and Peterson (1994) indicated, few previous studies measured the amount of media attention devoted to executions. Media attention reflects the degree of importance attached to the event by the media. When newspapers consider an event important, they usually publish a large article containing many characters and photographs.

Specifically, we examined how the amount of judicial affairs publicity (execution, death sentences, imprisonment for life, and innocence judgments) in the three major newspapers (*Asahi, Mainichi,* and *Yomiuri*) influenced the occurrence of brutal crimes (homicide, robbery, arson, and rape) in Japan from 1959 through 1990. Data from over 360 time periods (months) were analyzed.

Many factors affect the occurrence of brutal crimes in a complicated manner. In this study, the effects of the publicity itself were assessed as accurately as possible using time-series analysis to remove other explanatory factors. Strictly speaking, an experiment with a randomized group design is the ideal for testing causality, but time-series analysis of data from many periods is also regarded as an excellent method for revealing causality (Cook & Campbell, 1979).

METHOD

Publicity

We collected all articles published on the four types of judicial affairs from the three major newspapers between 1959 and 1990. We also collected articles appearing between October and December 1958 to examine a possible lag effect of capital punishment.

We used three measures for the publicity of each type of judicial affair from the 387 months of articles. The first measure was the monthly number of publicized judicial affairs. If one affair was repeatedly publicized in a newspaper on a particular day, we counted only the first appearance. The second and third measures were the number of characters and photographs per month devoted to articles on judicial affairs.

We first obtained the scores of these measures for each of the three newspapers, and then added the scores across newspapers. We analyzed only this total score. As shown in Table 15.1, correlation coefficients between the newspapers for each measure were mostly high, and therefore, it is unlikely that important information was lost by using the total score.

Brutal Crimes

Hanzaitoukeisho (criminal statistics) was consulted for the number of brutal crimes: that occurred each year. *Hanzaitoukeisho* is the periodical the Japanese National Police Agency publishes once a year to report criminal statistics. In volumes published after 1978, the agency reports the frequency of crimes that occurred during previous years but that were not reported in previous volumes because they were not discovered when the volume was published. To obtain the most accurate number of crimes for any particular year, three volumes must be consulted—those published one, two, and three years after the target year. We added the data in three volumes to determine the frequency of occurrence of a given crime in a given month. In the volumes from 1964–1966 only the annual data are described, so we could not analyze the complete data for these three years. Thus, we eventually decided to analyze the data for only twenty-nine years.

Analysis

The impact of capital punishment on the occurrence of brutal crimes was examined, using autoregression analysis (cf. Box & Jenkins, 1976; Ostrom, 1978; Johnston, 1984; Vandaele, 1983)—the AUTOREG procedure of the Statistical Analysis System (SAS). Three stages were used to perform the AUTOREG.

Table 15.1
Correlation Coefficients for the Publicity Items between Major Japanese Newspapers

	Affairs	Characters	Photographs
Execution			
Asahi-Mainichi	0.62	0.22	0.20
Asahi-Yomiuri	0.54	0.18	0.06
Mainichi-Yomiuri	0.78	0.30	0.40
Death sentence			
Asahi-Mainichi	0.75	0.69	0.57
Asahi-Yomiuri	0.80	0.90	0.80
Mainichi--Yomiuri	0.74	0.69	0.61
Imprisonment for life			
Asahi-Mainichi	0.59	0.86	0.54
Asahi-Yomiuri	0.67	0.84	0.87
Mainichi-Yomiuri	0.54	0.87	0.65
Innocence judgment			
Asahi-Mainichi	0.73	0.93	0.88
Asahi-Yomiuri	0.70	0.93	0.89
Mainichi-Yomiuri	0.76	0.91	0.86

Note: $n = 384$.

First, we determined the stationarity of the mean, variance, and autocorrelation of the data for a dependent time-series variable. *Stationarity* means that the mean, variance, and autocorrelation are constant across periods, each of which contains one datum. This is a requisite precondition for autoregression analysis as it is not possible to estimate a real mean, variance, and autocorrelation for each period and examine the autoregressive process for time-series data if the data do not have stationarity.

The stationarity of the dependent variable can be estimated by observing a trend or a drift in a plot of the data. The data of the variable do not have stationarity if there are trends and drifts in the data. Stationarity can also be assessed by measuring autocorrelations for the variable. The data of the variable have stationarity if a higher-order autocorrelation is weaker than another lower-order autocorrelation. The data must be transformed if they do not have stationarity.

Second, we investigated whether some autocorrelations of the dependent variable were significant and evaluated the autoregressive process of the variable. Significant autocorrelations can bias the estimated values of parameters obtained through a regression analysis; we needed to find significant autocorrelations before we could conduct the regression analysis.

Finally, we conducted a regression analysis to examine the effect of the independent variables on the dependent variable. If significant autocorrelations were found at the second stage, the effect of the autocorrelations should be controlled. This control is actualized by adding the lag of the dependent variable to a set of independent variables.

RESULTS

Publicity

The publicity data for the four judicial affairs were first summarized. Figures 15.2, 15.3, and 15.4 show annual changes in the number of affairs, characters, and photographs, respectively.

Brutal Crimes

Next the crime rates were summarized. Figure 15.5 shows annual changes in the rate. There are trends and drifts in these plots, and it is obvious that these data do not have stationarity. The data therefore required transformation. Seasonal differencing was chosen as the technique for transformation. This technique is used to transform time-series data by subtracting the value of the datum from one year previous (month t-12) from the datum for each month (month t). This technique is recommended when a seasonal cycle exists among the data (Vandaele, 1983). Our data, especially the arson and rape data, suggested the presence of seasonal cycles (Figure 15.6). In addition, the results of an analysis of variance showed that the effect of the month on the occurrence of homicides, arsons, and rapes was significant (F (11, 480) = 3.79, 19.96, and 9.87, $p < 0.01$, respectively). With regard to robbery, the results of the analysis of variance did not show a significant effect (F (11, 480) = 0.28, ns), but we used the technique for this crime, too, to permit comparisons across types of crimes.

Autocorrelations for lag periods ranging from t-1 through t-12 from the difference data transformed with this technique were examined. We found that the higher-order autocorrelation was weaker than other autocorrelations. This shows that we were successful in obtaining stationarity in the data.

Figure 15.2
A Change in the Number of Publicized Judicial Affairs

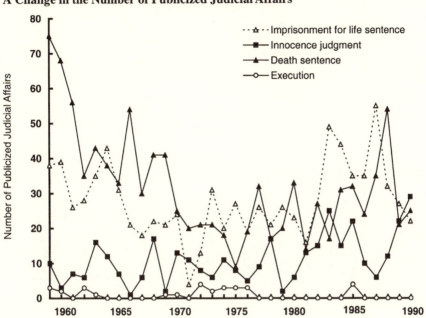

Autoregression Analysis

We conducted an autoregression analysis to examine the impact of the publicity of judicial affairs on the occurrence of brutal crimes. We first computed partial autocorrelations for lag periods ranging from t-1 to t-12 from the difference data. Partial autocorrelations are considered more important than simple correlations to detecting autoregressive effects that should be controlled (Vandaele, 1983).

We found some significant partial autocorrelations; that is, the 4th- and the 12th-order autocorrelations for homicide, the 1st-, 2nd-, 4th-, and 12th-order ones for robbery, the 1st-, 5th-, 8th-, 10th-, and 12th-order ones for arson, and the 1st-, 2nd-, 6th-, 11th-, and 12th-order ones for rape. We conducted the autoregression analysis with these autocorrelative effects removed by adding the lag in the occurrence of brutal crimes into the set of the independent variables.

As for independent variables, we used not only (1) the data of judicial affairs publicized in the month of the occurrence of the brutal crimes, but also (2) the data from affairs publicized a month before the month of the occurrence, (3) the data of the affairs publicized two months before, and (4) the data of the affairs publicized three months before. If the number of judicial affairs publicized the previous month has a significant effect on the crime rate, it suggests that publicity influences the occurrence of brutal crimes the month

Figure 15.3
A Change in the Number of Characters in Newspaper Articles on Judicial Affairs

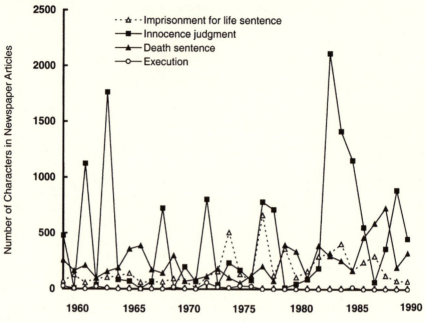

Figure 15.4
A Change in the Number of Photographs in Newspaper Articles on Judicial Affairs

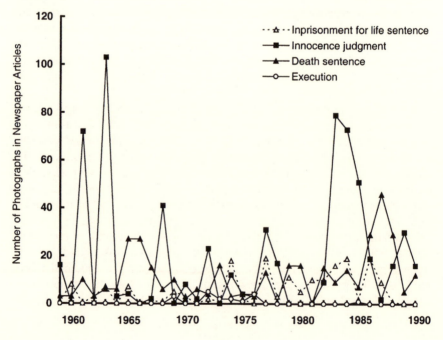

Figure 15.5
The Number of Occurrences of Brutal Crimes in Each Year

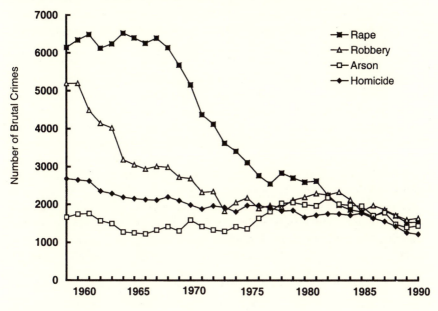

Figure 15.6
The Number of Occurrences of Brutal Crimes in Each Month

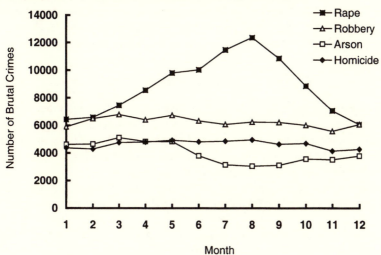

following the publicity. In this way, the lag effects of media publicity can be examined.

This analysis was conducted for each of the forty-eight combinations in a matrix of four (judicial affairs: execution, death sentence, life sentence, and innocence judgment) by four (brutal crimes: homicide, robbery, arson, and rape) by three (measures of publicity: number of publicized judicial affairs, number of characters, and number of photographs).

Table 15.2 shows the results for homicides. We describe only significant and marginally significant effects. The values in Table 15.2 are unstandardized regression coefficients indicating the amount of change in the crime rate caused by one judicial affair, one thousand characters, or one photograph appearing in a newspaper. For example, the value (4.59) found in the homicide cell and the number of publicized judicial affairs in Table 15.2 shows that one affair publicized in a newspaper is related to an increase of 4.59 homicides. The lag results are omitted from the table for brevity. All the effects of the lags were highly significant.

As shown in Table 15.2, for executions, the number of publicized affairs and photographs had significantly positive effects on the number of homicides that occurred one and two months after publicity, respectively. This result suggests that the publicity of executions does not reduce the occurrence of homicide, but augments it.

Similar results were found for death sentences. The number of characters and photographs had significantly positive effects on the number of homicides that occurred one month after the publicity. The number of publicized affairs had marginally significant effects. Thus, the publicity of a death sentence also seems to augment the occurrence of homicide. On the other hand, the publicity of life sentences and innocence judgments rarely showed significant effects. As for the other brutal crimes of robbery, arson, and rape, we detected no significant effects of media coverage on their occurrence.

DISCUSSION

The results suggest that media coverage of capital punishment does not decrease the homicide rate, but rather augments it. In addition, media coverage of life sentences does not have this augmentative effect. Therefore, it seems unlikely that the homicide rate would increase in Japan if capital punishment were abolished and imprisonment for life used instead.

No significant effect was found for the number of characters in the articles concerning executions on the homicide rate. It is doubtful that the media coverage itself in the three newspapers influenced the homicide rate. Coverage from other media, for example, television, radio, magazines, other newspapers, computer networks, and personal communications, would contribute to the influence of these three newspapers. However, although the number of publicized judicial affairs is likely to correspond with the number presented in other media, the number of characters would not likely be highly correlated

Table 15.2
The Results of Autoregression Analysis for Homicides

	Affair		Characters		Photographs	
	b	t	b	t	b	t
Execution						
The same month	0.24	0.11	- 0.10	- 0.43	- 0.63	- 0.28
One month after	2.97	1.37	0.28	1.25	4.82	2.12*
Two months after	4.59	2.10*	0.35	1.53	3.53	1.56
Three months after	-1.16	- 0.54	- 0.12	- 0.52	- 0.18	- 0.08
Death sentence						
The same month	- 0.10	- 0.28	0.00	0.09	0.21	0.54
One month after	0.65	1.86+	0.05	2.33*	0.89	2.35*
Two months after	- 0.52	-1.46	- 0.00	- 0.11	0.12	0.31
Three months after	- 0.12	- 0.34	- 0.00	- 0.18	- 0.18	- 0.48
Imprisonment for life						
The same month	0.26	0.70	0.04	1.74+	0.66	1.21
One month after	- 0.10	- 0.26	0.03	1.28	0.70	1.28
Two months after	- 0.09	- 0.23	- 0.03	1.15	0.47	0.86
Three months after	- 0.19	- 0.50	0.03	- 0.19	0.06	0.11
Innocence						
The same month	- 0.50	- 0.90	0.00	0.12	0.09	0.69
One month after	- 0.54	- 0.99	0.00	0.21	- 0.06	- 0.44
Two months after	- 0.70	-1.28	- 0.01	- 0.78	- 0.14	-1.12
Three months after	- 0.54	-1.00	0.00	0.08	0.03	0.21

Notes: $*p < 0.05$; $+p < 0.1$.

with the amount of coverage in other media. In fact, as Table 15.1 shows, the number of characters in a particular newspaper is not highly correlated even with other newspapers. If the number of characters is not highly correlated with the amount of coverage in other media, it cannot be regarded as representing the amount of coverage of all media. We found no significant effect of the number of characters in the articles on execution partly because it was not possible to detect the influence of coverage of all media due to the lack of representativeness.

The results of this study are different from those of some previous American studies. Several American studies supported the deterrent effect of capital punishment (Ehrlich, 1975, 1977; Layson, 1985; Stack, 1987, 1990). Some of them (Ehrlich, 1975; Stack, 1987) have been criticized (Bowers & Pierce, 1975; Yunker, 1976; Bailey & Peterson, 1989), while others (Ehrlich, 1977; Layson, 1985; Stack, 1990) have not yet been criticized. If the deterrent effect is valid in the United States, why the American effect is different from the Japanese one found in this study must be explained.

We offer a possible explanation. King (1978) speculated about a mechanism underlying the augmentative effect and proposed a hypothesis, writing that "The use of the death penalty as a punishment deadens people's respect for life by the state and thus increases the incidence of homicide." However, if people's respect for life has already been deadened by daily murders, their respect will not be deadened any more when they encounter publicity of capital punishment. Murders are committed much more frequently in the United States than in Japan. Therefore, the respect for life by people living there has possibly been deadened already, and previous American studies have therefore not shown the augmentative effect. On the other hand, it seems unlikely that Japanese people's respect for life is deadened by murders, because murder incidents are much more unusual in Japan. This lower incidence might be one of the reasons why the augmentative effect was obtained in this study. A similar explanation is also possible. Capital punishment itself may be regarded as a violent behavior performed by a country to solve problems. The modeling of this behavior might more easily occur for Japanese people, because the impression made by that violent behavior is made stronger by the infrequency of murder in Japan. Further research on these hypotheses is warranted.

Finally, the data of this study have some limitations. We analyzed the data from 1959–1990. We cannot be certain whether our findings can be generalized to the current situation. We also admit the limitation of the present methodology to detect causality, although time-series data analysis is regarded as an excellent method for revealing causality (Cook & Campbell, 1979).

Future studies should address these problems. In addition, some other questions should be investigated. For example, how can the effects of media coverage found in the present study be generalized to other countries? If some differences between countries are found, how can they be explained? How do mediating factors such as the criminal's gender and age influence the effect of media coverage? Although a quantitative research method was used in this study, qualitative research methods would also be useful.

In summary, our results indicate that the publicity of capital punishment does not decrease the homicide rate but increases it in Japan. If the problems concerning generalization of periods and causality detection can be minimized, these results imply that abolishment of capital punishment will not increase the homicide rate but decrease it. Therefore, retention of capital punishment is not meaningful in Japan if its deterrent effect is the major reason for its retention. In Japan, no studies have been conducted to examine the effect of capital punishment, but public opinion has supported the deterrent effect and thus its retention. Although the data of this study have limitations, we argue that they are meaningful enough to make Japanese people consider the lack of evidence for public opinion. At present, Japanese people do not seem to have strong reasons for believing in the deterrent effect of capital punishment.

NOTE

We want to express our thanks for Professor Masayuki Tamura (Institute of Scientific Research for the Police) and Professor Fumio Mugishima (Teikyo University) for their assistance in this study. We also greatly appreciate Professor Junko Tanaka-Matsumi (Kwansei Gakuin University) for her very helpful comments on an earlier version of this chapter.

REFERENCES

Amnesty International. (1989). *When the state kills: The death penalty v. human rights.* London: Amnesty International Publications.

Bailey, W. C. (1977). Imprisonment vs. the death penalty as a deterrent to murder. *Law and Human Behavior, 1*, 239–260.

Bailey, W. C. (1980). Deterrence and the celerity of the death penalty: A neglected question in deterrence research. *Social Forces, 58*, 1308–1333.

Bailey, W. C. (1984). Murder and capital punishment in the nation's capitol. *Justice Quarterly, 1*, 211–233.

Bailey, W. C. (1990). Murder and capital punishment: An analysis of television execution publicity. *American Sociological Review, 55*, 628–633.

Bailey, W. C. (1998). Deterrence, brutalization, and the death penalty: Another examination of Oklahoma's return to capital punishment. *Criminology, 36*, 711–733.

Bailey, W. C., & Peterson, R. D. (1989). Murder and capital punishment: A monthly time series analysis of execution publicity. *American Sociological Review, 54*, 722–743.

Bailey, W. C., & Peterson, R. D. (1994). Murder, capital punishment, and deterrence: A review of the evidence and an examination of police killings. *Journal of Social Issues, 50*, 53–74.

Black, T., & Orsagh, T. (1978). New evidence on the efficacy of sanctions as a deterrent to homicide. *Social Science Quarterly, 58*, 616–631.

Bower, W. J., & Pierce, G. (1975). The illusion of deterrence in Isaac Ehrlich's research on capital punishment. *Yale Law Journal, 85*, 187–208.

Box, G.E.P., & Jenkins, G. M. (1976). *Time series analysis: Forecasting and control.* (Rev. ed.). San Francisco: Holden-Day.

Cochran, J. K., Chamlin, M. B., & Seth, M. (1994). Deterrence or brutalization? An impact assessment of Oklahoma's return to capital punishment. *Criminology,*

32, 107–134.

Cook, T. D., & Campbell, D. T. (1979). *Quasi-experimentation: Design and analysis issues for field settings*. Boston: Houghton Mifflin.

Dann, R. H. (1935). The deterrent effect of capital punishment. *Friends' Social Service Series Bulletin, 29*, 1–20.

Ehrlich, I. (1975). The deterrent effect of capital punishment: A question of life or death. *American Economic Review, 65*, 397–417.

Ehrlich, I. (1977). Capital punishment and deterrence: Some further thoughts and additional evidence. *Journal of Political Economy, 85*, 741–788.

Johnston, J. (1984). *Econometric methods* (3d ed.). New York: McGraw-Hill.

King, D. R. (1978). The brutalization effect: Execution publicity and the incidence of homicide in South Carolina. *Social Forces, 57*, 683–687.

Layson, S. K. (1983). Another view of the Canadian time-series evidence. *Canadian Journal of Economics, 16*, 52–73.

Layson, S. K. (1985). Homicide and deterrence: An examination of the United States time-series evidence. *Southern Economic Journal, 52*, 68–89.

Ostrom, C. (1978). *Time series analysis*. Beverly Hills, CA: Sage.

Peterson, R. D., & Bailey, W. C. (1988). Murder and capital punishment in the evolving context of the post–Furman era. *Social Forces, 66*, 774–807.

Peterson, R. D., & Bailey, W. C. (1991). Felony murder and capital punishment: An examination of the deterrence question. *Criminology, 29*, 367–395.

Phillips, D. (1980). The deterrent effect of capital punishment: Evidence on an old controversy. *American Journal of Sociology, 86*, 139–148.

Phillips, D., & Hensley, J. (1984). When violence is rewarded or punished: The impact of mass media stories on homicide. *Journal of Communication, 34*, 101–116.

Prime Minister's Office of Japan. (1999). *Kihon teki hou seido nikansuru seron chousa [A public opinion survey on fundamental law systems]*. Tokyo: Author.

Savitz, L. D. (1958). A study in capital punishment. *Journal of Criminal Law, Criminology, and Police Science, 49*, 338–341.

Sorensen, J., Wrinkle, R., Brewer, V., & Marguart, J. (1999). Capital punishment and deterrence: Examining the effect of executions on murder in Texas. *Crime and Delinquency, 45*, 481–493.

Stack, S. (1987). Publicized executions and homicide, 1950–1980. *American Sociological Review, 52*, 532–540.

Stack, S. (1990). Execution publicity and homicide in South Carolina: A research note. *Sociological Quarterly, 31*, 599–611.

Vandaele, W. (1983). *Applied time series and Box–Jenkins Models*. New York: Academic Press.

Wolpin, K. (1978). Capital punishment and homicide in England: A summary of results. *American Economic Review: Papers and Proceedings*, 422–427.

Yunker, J. (1976). Is the death penalty a deterrent to homicide? Some time series evidence. *Journal of Behavioral Economics, 5*, 1–32.

CHAPTER 16

Eastern and Western Perspectives in Social Psychological Research on Rehabilitation

Sing-fai Tam, Wai-kwong Man, and Jenny Yuen-yee Ng

Social psychology is the art and science of people's belief and behavior in relation to their existence, interpersonal interaction, and social groups. Rehabilitation, in a broad sense, is the restoration of the fullest physical, mental, social, vocational, and economic usefulness of which the individual is capable. The ultimate objective is to integrate people with disabilities in sensory, physical, mental, psychosocial, or other functional aspects into the community with optimal independence and productivity. Medical, educational, vocational, and social rehabilitation services help persons with disabilities to achieve their rehabilitation objectives maximally. The rehabilitation outcome is indicated by the degree of the individual's ultimate functional independence. However, since the rehabilitation process happens at the individual, interpersonal, and social organizational levels, understanding how to enhance oneself on all these levels is essential for a quality rehabilitation process.

For example, a person's level of independence may not directly relate to the degree of disability. Similarly, the relationship between disability and personality is varied, because what a disability means to a person depends on how the person interprets that disability, not just how severe the disability is. Wright (1983) explained that persons with a mild disability might, because they are almost normal, have a greater need to hide and deny the disability, thereby frustrating adjustment, whereas persons for whom disability is so severe that it cannot be denied may have little recourse. They need to face the problem of accepting themselves as a person with a disability. Consequently, through better acceptance of disability and more active striving toward further independence, the adjustment outcome of a person with more severe disabilities may be better than that of those with a milder disability.

To achieve independence in daily living tasks, a person with a disability must overcome environmental and social challenges. To achieve the goal of participating in society or being accepted by others requires a positive body image and psychological well-being. Also, the more competence a person has in carrying out daily living activities the better that person demonstrates to himself or herself and others that success in improving the situation in spite of the disability is possible. Success brings a feeling of being more self-actualized and allows a more positive self-assessment. An enhanced self-assessment allows more self-confidence in other areas of life, such as with the family or on the job.

DISABILITY AND REHABILITATION

In common usage, terms such as *impairment, disability*, and *handicap* are often confounded. In this research, the definitions of the World Health Organization are adopted. These terms differentiate between functional levels as follows:

Impairment refers to any loss or abnormality of psychological, physiological, or anatomical structure or function. *Disability* refers to any restriction or lack (resulting from impairment) of ability to perform an activity in the manner or within the range considered normal for a human being. Whilst, *handicap* refers to a disadvantage for a given individual, resulting from an impairment or disability, that limits or prevents the fulfillment of a role that is normal, depending on age, sex, social and cultural factors, for that individual.

Handicap is therefore a function of the relationship between disabled persons and their environment. It occurs when they encounter cultural, physical or social barriers that prevent their access to the various systems of society that are available to other citizens. Thus handicap is the loss or limitation of opportunities to take part in the life of the community on an equal level with others. With these definitions in mind, the principle of rehabilitation is to maximize the degree of ability in the presence of disability. (Working Party on Rehabilitation Policies and Services, 1992, p. 8)

From these definitions of impairment, disability, and handicap, it is clear that a person's impairment is more related to functioning in various life aspects and levels of social behavior. Impairment can be a transient or a permanent phenomenon and depends on the disease or injury recovery outcome, which relates to the quality of healthcare service available. Disability of a person largely depends on the occupational role and task performance that the person needs to undertake. Role performance has close relationships both with individual behavior and interpersonal interaction. For example, a wheelchair user can manage a job as a computer operator independently. However, architectural barriers in the office such as stairs or narrow throughways may disable mobility. A person with permanent impairment or functional disability may not necessarily be handicapped at the end. The living environment, including cultural practices and social organizational issues, is a significant determinant in this aspect. For example, wheelchair users can have fully independent living in a community without architectural and attitudinal barriers.

Functional independence of persons with disabilities has always been the most important aim of the rehabilitation process. For people with disabilities functional independence allows more productive living, greater acceptance from others and of themselves, and the opportunity to demonstrate competence in daily living tasks, thus receive positive appraisal from peers. More positive performance feedback also leads to higher self-efficacy and thus better behavioral intention to overcome the various limitations encountered. This process is called *normalization*. It is similar to the *acculturation process* as mentioned in cross-cultural psychology (Berry, 1998). The rehabilitation process, like acculturative stresses, drive persons with disabilities to develop more adaptive physical and psychological characteristics and come into contact with real-life encounters, including new people, tasks, objects, and culture.

In addition to the normalization process, successful adjustment to disability also requires another major process called *integration*. In this process, persons with disabilities are helped to integrate and resettle within their living environment. They can have a normal working life in remunerative work suited to their capacity and make the best use of their available skills. Although residual disability remains, they can accept their own limitations and feel consistently positive about their personal worth and experience dignity as a human being.

Rehabilitation professionals help persons with disability to exert a maximum of control over their daily lives, thereby increasing their freedom and dignity. In the rehabilitation process, people explore their own potential and build up performance competence through intervention in role and habit reformation. A person's functional independence is thus rebuilt with optimal self-concept and volition to pursue further life-role demands. Though a person may have quite a severe disability, the rehabilitation effort aims to actualize potential to achieve maximal independence, self-acceptance, and social acceptance. The person can integrate in the community and have the right to access facilities and the freedom to develop.

There are no fixed norms or standards in achieving the rehabilitation objectives of individuals. Adjustment to disability is an important concept and the goal of rehabilitation. According to Adler (1917), the presence of disability will lead to striving for superiority feelings, compensation, and achieving an optimal lifestyle. An individual's personality develops in the direction of self-realization or self-actualization. Adler called this development "the individual's style of life," which follows concrete modes to achieve perfection to some degree. Individuals may attempt to achieve the original goal of superiority through the manipulation and domination of others. On the other hand, they may attempt to strengthen other organs in order to compensate for the weakened ones (cf. McDaniel, 1976).

CULTURAL IMPACTS ON
ADJUSTMENT TO DISABILITY

In many cultures, it is traditionally believed that the disability is the principal cause of the unique lifestyle of the individual with the disability. In order to maintain an adjusted self, individuals attain new ways of expression and discard old ones, but their lifestyles may remain the same. Several laws of disability have been identified as common in the adjustment of persons with disabilities. *Compensation* is one of the most common concepts adopted. For example, a person may attempt to strengthen a defective limb to compensate for its weakness. Or a person may attempt to strive for superiority in other aspects to lessen feelings of inferiority regarding a particular body part (McDaniel, 1976).

Illness or disability produces incapacity and therefore limits or inhibits the performance of accustomed tasks. According to Social Role Theory (Parsons, 1958), disability disrupts the role patterns of the family, and the need for someone else to perform such tasks can lead to a reorganization of the fundamental social system of the family. This reorganization has special implications for Chinese people who have a disability, as the family is the most fundamental and important social system to which an individual may belong. According to this theory, rehabilitation refers to any treatment or service that is designed to restore or at least optimize the person's capacity for appropriate role performance. Successful rehabilitation leads to both physical and psychological health that represents a state of optimum capacity for the performance of valued tasks. However, rehabilitation or skills training can only take place when the individual is ready for it (Dodds, 1989). A thorough understanding of the person's life values and needs within his or her own social system is essential for rehabilitation planning.

Unique cultural characteristics significantly impact the development of disability adjustment patterns as well as public attitudes toward disability. Scheer and Groce (1988) mentioned that the presence of persons with disability is a constant; the social context across time influences the culturally shared response in different ways. Therefore an understanding of cultural beliefs that shape attitudes toward disability is essential for the success of any rehabilitation efforts that aim at the person's normalization and integration. The following are some examples of the impact of traditional Chinese culture on the disability adjustment process that may also be common in other Asian cultures that have a strong heritage of Confucianism. From the perspective of the Chinese concept of "nourishment of life" (*yang-shen*), what one should really pursue in life is good health (Lao, 1981). This concept emphasizes health promotion and disease prevention. Disability reflects violation of the proper way of living. A model human being knows how to avoid and prevent injury, failure to do so means the person has failed to be a model to others. In comparison with other cultures, the Chinese placed a strong emphasis on health promotion. Disease prevention is emphasized over curative techniques. A person with physical disabilities is considered careless, lacking knowledge and a proper way of living (Koo, 1989).

From the perspective of filial piety, disability means failure to value and keep the life that was given by one's parents. From early childhood, children are taught that they have an obligation to be healthy and to keep the body undamaged; that is, "You should not do any harm to the body and not even your hair or skin because you get them from your father and mother." Doing harm to the body, either deliberately or through carelessness is considered to be inexcusable because it could bring bad luck to the family from the ancestors (Koo, 1989, p. 51). Misattribution of the causes and effects of disability leads to social prejudice in Chinese society. For example, a person who has impaired body parts or has disfigurements will be regarded as being punished by society or heaven due to having committed crimes. Strong social prejudice causes socially isolated behavior of the persons with disabilities in Chinese society. Disability also means failure to resume daily productivity and pursue wealth. It is an obvious disadvantage in Hong Kong Chinese society in which the major normative orientation emphasizes material values (Redding & Wong, 1985). Disability contrasts with productivity and leads to being deprived of materials. Persons with disabilities are expected to be lacking in wealth, which acts as a resource for security. They have less ability to fulfill obligations to the family, are unable to gain a reputation attributable to success at work, and thus lose the sense of belonging due to being barred from work and related social activities.

Persons with physical disability in Chinese society are likely to have a lower self-concept, as they will probably be the only individual with a disability in their family. They lack opportunities to gain mutual support from peers with disabilities through interaction. They can rarely gain successes or positive experiences for self-concept enhancement as they can only compare themselves with their counterparts without visible disabilities. Persons with disabilities experience constant disability-related environmental and social stresses, for example, architectural and attitudinal barriers which bar them from integrating into family activities satisfactorily. The constant lack of positive experiences and of respect from people, including significant others, will probably cause low self-concept.

The traditional social circle of the Chinese was so family-centered that few secondary groups outside of the kinship boundary developed. Persons with disabilities lacked interaction with peers with disabilities. Due to the absence of these experiences, they could not explore ways of better acceptance of their own disability, for example, through the experience of being accepted and of demonstrating competence among other people with disabilities through mutual support and shared feelings. Social interaction and self-esteem are significantly related; the greater the opportunities for interaction, the higher the esteem (Anderson, 1967). Through interaction with peers more social acceptance and higher self-concept can be achieved (Hardman, Drew, & Egan, 1987; Kirk & Gallagher, 1983; Starr & Heiserman, 1977).

Many Chinese values and beliefs were developed from an agriculturally oriented perspective. Emphasis was on physical rather than intellectual competence. Persons with physical disabilities often had greater disadvantages than those with a mental handicap as they were generally barred from major productive roles in an agricultural society. From the viewpoint of social psychology, unemployment causes lower financial status, deteriorating physical well-being, unsatisfactory interpersonal relationships, and decreased social interests and activities (Fraser, 1980). This situation can effect the overall psychological feelings of adequacy of an individual.

The humanistic rehabilitation concept is not well developed in Chinese society, which has the concept of offering welfare and care to dependent groups, for example, the young, aged, and disabled, but does not consider needs for rehabilitation and self-actualization. Unlike Western society, Chinese society generally lacks concern for unfortunate minority groups. It tends to classify persons with disabilities with other unfortunate minority groups such as criminals, prostitutes, and drug addicts. As with these other groups, the general public tends to attribute problems of people with disabilities as being due to moral–ethical offenses and regards the disability as a kind of punishment from heaven for immorality.

To sum up, persons with physical disabilities in a Chinese society generally lack positive experiences as the disability acts as a stigma for an underprivileged social position. Through a successful rehabilitation and adjustment process, persons with disabilities can gain better competence and higher self-actualization that can compensate for the disability-related negative experiences. Consequently, they can come to have a more positive self-concept. A successful rehabilitation and disability adjustment process that brings about a higher self-concept can help them to function more adaptively, to have greater opportunities, and guide them toward need satisfaction and higher self-actualization.

Through rapid cultural exchange, the Chinese and other Asian societies are receiving strong influence from Western cultures and values. The socialization and expectation of the Asian people have moved from the highly collectivistic to the more individualistic in nature (Ho, 1986). It is expected that the group pressures experienced by persons with disabilities in a traditional collectivistic society are lessened. The social participation of persons with disabilities should increase with societal changes, as Hanks and Hanks (1948) suggested. They suggested that "the social participation of persons with disabilities would increase in societies where the standard of living is high, or in societies where the economic hierarchy is less competitive, where criteria for achievement acknowledge individual capacity, and where standards are relative rather than absolute."

Also, through the all too gradual development of social rehabilitation services, persons with disabilities gain many more opportunities to interact with peers. They have many more opportunities to experience the self-serving downward social comparison through social interactions with peers and offering help to others. Also, as the public becomes more educated, they have more accurate knowledge of the cause and effect of disability. Through more contact with persons with disabilities, the misattributions of disability have become clarified and so there is less social pressure and stigmatism toward them. The society generally gives more allowance to persons with disabilities in fulfilling their life goals. As the public generally has lower expectations of persons with disabilities, once they achieve more than is expected, they are praised and rewarded more explicitly. The positive feedback contributes significantly to enhance their self-concept.

As society becomes more and more affluent, competition for resources is not so critical, so more resources are distributed to develop and improve healthcare and social welfare services. The public has a better concept of humanity and recognizes these services as essential and justified in a modern society. The responsibility to take care of persons with sickness or disabilities has shifted somewhat from the family to the government. Disability-related stresses of the individual and their family have been relieved gradually. Together with better education opportunities, the major job types in many Asian countries have changed in the last two decades from agriculturally oriented to production oriented and then to service oriented jobs. Now there are more new jobs that stress intellectual functions rather than physical capabilities. This new situation brings more favorable employment opportunities to persons with physical disabilities. As they become better educated and more productive, they are enabled to secure an independent living which forms an important basis for privileged social interaction and upward social mobility. However, in contrast, persons with mental retardation will face increasing barriers in a society with a knowledge-based economy and expanding information usages.

SOCIAL PSYCHOLOGY FOR REHABILITATION

Based on this understanding of disability adjustment according to well-defined social psychology theories like individual psychology, self-concept, social role, and social comparison, it is understandable that the application of social psychology in rehabilitation has become increasingly common and recognized. Rehabilitation professionals like occupational therapists and physiotherapists apply theories and intervention strategies that originated from social psychology to help the persons to remobilize their personal and social resources to promote maximal functioning and thus life quality.

Traditionally, there has been a lack of research and appropriate instruments to investigate the social psychology of persons with disability. This lack persists despite the importance of social psychology in the understanding and rehabilitation in terms of self-concept and self-efficacy enhancement, empowerment, social comparison, and coping skills. Recently, more researchers have conducted studies to explore understanding of disability attitudes, beliefs, and behavior. We conducted several studies to explore and compare the self-concept of persons with different disabilities. Unique self-concept dimensions were identified for specific disability groups. Due to the prominent and unique impact of disability type, persons with similar disabilities would develop a self-concept with particular structure and content reflecting the influence of the disability and their adjustment outcome.

For example, in a study of Tam and Watkins (1995), persons with physical disabilities showed a prominent functional independence self-concept dimension as compared to subjects without a disability. This difference reflects that being functionally independent can become the core of a person with disability self-concepts and that this dimension significantly influences life satisfaction. For those without a disability, being independent in daily living activities is natural and does not impact self-concept formation. In another study, persons with cardiac diseases perceived their physical abilities as an important self-concept dimension, as they impacted life quality in many ways, including socialization (Tam & Ng, 2000). For persons with mental illness, social integrity, including being honest, helpful, and law abiding are important to their self-concept (Tam, Tsang, Ip, & Chan, 2000). The positive valuation of social self-concept helps them to enhance or at least to preserve their self-concept, which may be hampered by relatively less advantageous self-appraisals in areas such as personal achievement, work, family responsibilities, and materials.

SELF-PSYCHOLOGY: CULTURAL AND CROSS-CULTURAL PERSPECTIVES

Some social scientists believe that there ought to be great homogeneity in the sense of self among individuals from widely different societies as a consequence of maturational and cognitive universals (Kennedy, Scheier, & Rogers, 1984; Sampson, 1989; Shweder & Bourne, 1984). They argue that cultural influence is not essential in explaining development of self-understanding. However, there is a growing belief that cultural assumptions in self-concept development can profoundly shape one's experience of self. Cultural assumptions provide useful and important information in studying and understanding self-concept. Culture is also important in understanding the concept of personal agency, which emphasizes individual self-development and achievement (Andersen, 1987; Hart & Edelstein, 1991). It is commonly believed that people in different cultures have different bases of self-perception. This basis consists of various individual life experiences including cognition, emotion, motivation, and socialization (Markus & Kitayama, 1991). The dimension that seems to differentiate most clearly between cultures in terms of self-concept formation is individualism and collectivism. The former usually characterizes Western cultures and the later characterizes many Eastern and other non-Western cultures. Individualism focuses attention on attainment of personal goals (Georgas, 1989; Triandis, 1987). The importance of striving for self-enhancement and self-actualization is highlighted, and the self is viewed as the basic unit of survival (Hui & Villareal, 1989; Markus & Kitayama, 1991). Collectivism focuses on maintenance of social norms and performance of social duties as defined by one's in-group. The group is viewed as the basic unit of survival and the importance of cooperation with in-group members is highlighted (Georgas, 1989; Hui & Triandis, 1985; Markus & Kitayama, 1991).

In order to understand the development of self-concept, an understanding of the person's cultural background is essential. Markus and Kitayama (1991) summarized the key differences between an independent (individualistic) and interdependent (collectivistic) construal of self by defining the independent self as separate from its social context and its structure as bounded, unitary, and stable. The independent self is unique and expressive. It is internal and private, with an emphasis on abilities, thoughts, and feelings. A person with an individualistic self performs tasks according to personal goals. Goal setting is direct and self-evaluation is made through social comparison and reflected appraisal from others. The basis and level of self-esteem is determined by the ability to actualize the self and validate internal attributes. For example, American teenagers tend to hold the common attitude that they have the right to do whatever they want with their life, since they own their life. The structure of the interdependent self is comparatively flexible and variable. Its definition is concerned with social context, and the important features of self are external and public. The self emphasizes status, roles, relationships, and belonging. People with an interdependent self will try to promote others goals by performing tasks that fit into the related social context. The person will read other people's minds before setting a goal. The self is defined by the person's relationships with others in specific contexts. The basis and level of self-esteem are determined by whether the person can show self-restraint to maintain harmony within the social context. For example, the Chinese define self as a configuration of roles expressed in self–other expectations and observable in self–other interactions, especially with significant others (Chu, 1985). The Chinese believe that as one's parents gave one a body, hair, and skin, one is not at liberty to do harm to them.

SELF-CONCEPT AND ADJUSTMENT TO DISABILITY

A person's assigned meaning of a particular disability determines what and how the disability affects that person's self-concept. For example, one will accept disability more easily if that particular disability does not trespass the core of one's self-concept. Therefore, the degree of impact of a physical disability is related to the weight a person puts on the physical component of self-concept. Wright (1983) mentioned that the self-concept of persons with a physical disability would be affected by interpersonal relationships and the attitudes of others. When one accepts one's own disabilities, others are likely to view one as self-respecting and worthwhile. Cordaro and Shontz (1969) found that, like other people, a person with a disability searches for identity not only from within but also from others. Relationships and attitudes of persons closest to the person with a disability have particular significance. In the same vein, Pringle (1964) found that parental attitudes toward disability are a particularly important determinant of a child's adjustment to disability. Further, the attitudes of rehabilitation healthcare professionals are thought to have a significant impact on the self-evaluation by their patients. The influence of social comparisons on adjustment to disability is also prominent (Molleman, Pruyn, & van Knippenberg, 1986; Schulz & Decker, 1985; Wood, Taylor, & Lichtman, 1985). The effect is especially explicit with in-group comparisons, for example, relatives of those who also have a disability (Major, Sciacchitano, & Crocker, 1993). A person's lifestyle and self-concept can be affected by disability, but the extent and the way in which the effects are manifested are also determined by several factors, such as predisability self-concept characteristics, the person's perception of the disability, interpersonal relationships, and life experiences. Socioeconomic factors and differences in disability conditions should also be taken into consideration.

Disability impacts the formation of a unique self-concept structure and self-concept levels. In a study by Tam and Watkins (1995), it was found that an additional facet of functional independence is needed to convey adequately the self-conceptions of people with physical disabilities. Also, independence as an internal aspect of achievement is important in the self-concept of persons with physical disabilities. This achievement is self-oriented, which means the persons with disabilities themselves determine the standard of achievement. The independence self-concept of persons with physical disabilities is determined by their rehabilitation outcome, which also reflects their ability to compare and interact with others equally. Also, disability is definitely a salient factor that influences the formation of self-concept. The presence of physical disability would cause a person to have specific feelings about life dimensions. According to self-enhancement theory, people are motivated to maintain and enhance their self-esteem (Allport, 1937; Greenwald, 1980; James, 1890; Rogers, 1959; Taylor & Brown, 1988; Tesser, 1988). When given sufficient leeway, people define positive traits, abilities, and outcomes in a way that makes them self-descriptive (Banaji & Prentice, 1994). Similarly, people with disabilities also weigh and interpret their life perspectives in ways that may be different from those without visible disabilities, but these specific life perceptions would probably make them happier. For example, they may discount the importance of certain life areas in which they are less likely to achieve high satisfactions, for instance, grooming or good looks.

The results of a study conducted by Tam and Watkins (1995) showing that the Chinese population with physical disabilities in Hong Kong tends to have a relatively low self-concept can be explained in several ways. Those with disabilities generally rated physical abilities as more salient than did people without disabilities. Those with physical disabilities in Chinese society generally lack positive experiences as the disability places them in a stigmatized and underprivileged social position. In general, physical disability acts as a negative stimulus and leads to social discrimination. These types of experiences would predispose individuals toward feeling inferior to the able bodied.

From analysis of the open-ended question, "What makes you feel bad?" it was found that those with disabilities believe that the life events that made them feel bad were mainly due to unfavorable feelings caused by an unsatisfactory rehabilitation process and outcome, being discriminated against, and being dependent in daily living activities. These responses constitute nearly 50% of the total responses to the question. This result reflects the inadequacy of rehabilitation services in Hong Kong. The other responses included (in rank order): health and disability, work, social relationships, study, family relationships, money and material wealth, personal aspirations, and social events. Also, from content analysis of the life-satisfaction items, the participants with disabilities ranked satisfaction with their physical condition and earnings lower than participants without disabilities did. Those without disabilities rated themselves more satisfied with their physical abilities, grooming, ability to meet family responsibilities and personal goals, money-earning ability, and ability to exert personal influence. Failure to meet family responsibilities is likely to be a serious blow to the pride of those with physical disabilities because, compared to participants without disabilities, this was one of the most salient areas of their life. They also rated physical abilities as more salient than did those without disabilities, so again this all too unavoidable deficiency would probably strongly influence overall self-concept.

Future research might identify the relationship between the self-concept of persons with disabilities, social beliefs, and attitudes toward disability in contemporary Eastern and Western societies. Study results would have significant implications for the social and healthcare service delivered to those with a disability or perhaps even chronic illness. Also, cross-cultural comparisons of these disability-related psychological processes can be performed to investigate the existence of possible underlying universal processes or concepts in understanding disability and rehabilitation that may contribute significantly to improving the quality of life of this minority group.

SELF-EFFICACY AND REHABILITATION OF PERSONS WITH DISABILITY

Self-efficacy refers to one's confidence in one's ability to behave in such a way as to produce a desirable outcome in a particular situation (Bandura, 1977). Self-efficacy theory stresses the influence of personal expectations on subsequent performance and maintains that the expectation of personal competence greatly affects one's behavior. Self-beliefs of efficacy have been shown to be important proximal determinants of human motivation, affect, thought, and action. They exert their effects on functioning through intervening motivational, cognitive, and affective processes. Self-efficacy beliefs also serve as intervening influencers of action and shape performance outcomes by influencing choice of pursuits and selection of environments.

The implication of applying self-efficacy theories in rehabilitation planning for persons with disabilities is that the planning will be more effective and efficient if the need for self-efficacy enhancement is considered carefully. Also, if persons with disabilities have better self-efficacy regarding their own functional independence and adjustment, this accomplishment will facilitate the generalization of functional skills and then ultimate independence. On the whole, the study of self-efficacy in a person's rehabilitation aims at mobilizing resources intrinsically and extrinsically to achieve maximal outcome. As Thompson (1981) mentioned, *perceived control* refers to the belief that one can influence the aversiveness of an event.

Self-efficacy enhancement can enable a person, even those with disabilities, to achieve higher functional independence, and is likely to generalize to having a higher self-concept. Bandura (1977) claimed that greater persistence and success could result through raising a person's self-efficacy. Associated with increases in self-efficacy may be gains in other coping mechanisms necessary for successful training performance and rehabilitation outcome. For example, several researchers have suggested that trainees with high self-efficacy exhibit low anxiety, more positive affect (e.g., less anger or fatigue), and better working styles (higher retention and better task focus; Bandura, 1982; Brockner, 1979). Recently, field experimenters have begun targeting self-efficacy as an effective way to increase motivated performance of work behaviors. In a self-management-training program conducted by Frayne and Latham (1987), the workers' absenteeism was reduced through raising their work self-efficacy. Gist, Schwoerer, and Rosen (1989) demonstrated the performance advantage of a computer software-training program designed to increase university administrators' computer self-efficacy. Caplan, Vinokur, Price, and van Ryn (1989) and Eden and Aviram (1990) have shown that training unemployed workers in a manner designed to boost their self-efficacy increased their likelihood of finding subsequent reemployment.

There are several effective methods to mobilize resources of persons with disabilities both intrinsically and extrinsically to achieve maximum rehabilitation outcomes. These methods include persuasion, performance feedback, live modeling, and downward social comparison. Identifying the ability level of the individual and then explaining the rehabilitation objective in terms of those abilities assures the individual that the rehabilitation task is not complex and that systematic feedback will be given. This process would facilitate appropriate outcome expectancy and goal setting. Also, persuasion could effect changes in the individual's internal self-attribution to the achievement of rehabilitation objectives. Positive performance feedback should be given explicitly and frequently for attainment beyond baseline performance to ensure the person knows whether the expected level of mastery of a particular learning task has been achieved. This method has the strongest influence on self-efficacy because seeing oneself attain success at a job is incontrovertible evidence of one's ability to do the job. Vicarious experience can be obtained through live modeling to demonstrate successful performance to others. This method demonstrates to the person that peers have also achieved the rehabilitation goal successfully. Moreover, self-efficacy can be enhanced by social comparisons. One may select a reference group in which one can see oneself in a more favorable light, even if one has experienced a loss of self-esteem.

We conducted a study to illustrate the application and implication of social psychology constructs in the rehabilitation process and outcome for people with brain damage. Evidence from this scientific study is intended to support the integration of social psychology theories in this area to enable a more effective and humanistic approach to help populations with rehabilitation needs to achieve a better quality of life.

EMPOWERMENT PROGRAM: A REHABILITATION STRATEGY FOR CHINESE CARING FOR A FAMILY MEMBER WHO HAS EXPERIENCED BRAIN DAMAGE

Chinese Families Coping with a Disability

Discussion on how Chinese families cope with family members with disabilities has centered on existing Western literature and findings. However, it is important to examine the relevance of Western thinking to the experience of Chinese families, especially in light of the characteristic features of Chinese beliefs about disabilities and rehabilitation. Chinese persons with disabilities and their families may face extra difficulties as compared to those from other cultures in understanding the meaning of disability and their coping efforts in the complex problem-solving process. For example, in comparison with other Asian families (Indian and Malay) in caring for relatives who are mentally ill, it has been found that Chinese use much less helpful coping strategies, and do not use either formal or informal support networks (Bentelspacher, Chitran, & Marziyanna, 1994). These findings may explain partly why Chinese families in Hong Kong do not advocate their needs or ask for services from the community, which may further compound the problem.

Application of disability and stress-coping studies from the Western literature could pose difficulty from both conceptual and implementation perspectives. This study explores empowerment of Chinese families who are caring for their brain-damaged members to understand better how Chinese react to caring for a member with a disability and to develop intervention strategies suitable for Chinese.

Empowerment and Rehabilitation of Persons with Disabilities

There are some undeniably negative characteristics associated with severe disability such as brain damage. For instance, uncertainty, a declining physical trajectory, dependence, role transition, and feelings of powerlessness may coexist in the person with the disability and their family system. Empowerment philosophy, suggesting an expanded perception of rehabilitation, takes into account the rich attributes of human life, such as the ability to think, create, rationalize, experience joy, and learn, as motivators for coping. All persons are assumed to have a capacity for coping. Zimmerman and Rappaport (1988) broadly summed up the many definitions of empowerment as the process through which individuals gain mastery and control over their own lives. Family resources such as social support, psychological stability, knowledge, self-esteem, energy, and hope can be considered, developed, and maintained to empower the coping process for families in trouble. Thus both the persons who have a disability and their caregivers are viewed as having multiple resources enabling them to control their lives. (Schaefer, Coyne, & Lazarus, 1981; Mischel & Braden, 1988; Miller, 1992).

Coping with perceived powerlessness might be considered a major demand of individuals who have suffered from brain damage as well as their families. The purpose of rehabilitation may imply striking a balance between dependence and independence, being satisfied with self, being at peace, having a feeling of self-worth, having energy to enjoy life's special pleasures, coping effectively, and having hope. By translating these ideas into working principles, it is possible to conceptualize persons with brain damage and their families as having deficits in several power resources, such as physical strength and energy. Intervention should be designed around developing the remaining power components within the family, so as to prevent or overcome powerlessness.

Empowerment as an Alternate Rehabilitation Strategy

When families are in trouble, their coping strategies compensate for deficient resources or enable them to become empowered so as to cope. There is an increasing recognition of the influential role played by the family in rehabilitation. Although families are expected to take up the burden of care, they are usually ill-prepared to face this long-term process, especially in Chinese culture (Pearson & Chan, 1993; Philips, 1993). The concept of empowerment, a coping strategy commonly used in Western societies, has been explored with respect to Asian cultures for possible development of a conceptual framework, and thus application (Hwang, 1977; Shek & Mak, 1987).

Empowerment is thus hypothesized as a working model through which Chinese families may also develop strengths and strategies to face problems associated with having brain damage or in caring for a brain-damaged family member (Dunst & Trivette, 1987). A recent local study of an empowerment framework applicable to Hong Kong Chinese families was conducted with

211 families. Through explorative factor analysis, the construct validity of family empowerment was studied and a fifty-two-item empowerment questionnaire developed. It yielded four interpretable factors (efficacy, knowledge, support, and aspiration), which accounted for 48.8% of the variance (Man, 1998). The internal consistency of the questionnaire, in terms of *alpha* coefficients and the four dimensions of the conceptual framework ranged from 0.76–0.96, indicating the questionnaire measured the construct in a reliable manner.

However, there is a paucity of studies on the effectiveness of the empowerment approach (concept and actual implementation) on disability groups and in a Chinese family context. This study is designed to contribute to this important objective.

Family Empowerment: An Illustrated Example

We designed a community-based empowerment program for people with brain damage and their families. The long-term effects of the program were also evaluated in a three-month postprogram follow-up study.

Methodology

Sampling

All the families had members who had experienced brain damage resulting from traumatic brain injury, cerebral vascular accidents, arteriovenous malformation (AVM), or a brain tumor. They were recruited through information pamphlets in hospitals, rehabilitation centers, self-help groups, the local Community Rehabilitation Network, and newspaper advertisements. A total of seventy-two families applied and out of them sixty were selected to join the program. Fifty of the applicants successfully accomplished the program. The drop-out rate was mainly due to personal-arrangement problems. Of the sample, 82% were females who played an important role as wife (48%) and key caregiver. The resources these families possessed in empowering themselves were not abundant. Diagnoses of the people with brain damage were balanced across major diagnostic groups: stroke (30%), brain tumor (28%), AVM (20%), and traumatic brain injury (22%). Characteristics of the families are presented in Table 16.1. The fifty family members were divided into six groups with eight or nine people per group.

Implementation

The Empowerment Program Description

The problems of the families were first summarized from the literature, and then confirmed through interviews with members of self-help groups. For consistency in categorization, information collected was grouped under the four

Table 16.1
Empowerment Program Outline

Program session (session theme)	Empowerment factor			
	Knowledge	Efficacy	Support	Aspiration
Session 1 (briefing, icebreaking)	knowing the group, knowing each other			
Session 2 (understand empowerment)	what is empowerment and how to empower?	analyzing own stress and coping mechanism, family strength as empowerment	learn to mutually support in common issues of impact of brain damage on family	introduce positive thinking
Session 3 (implication of brain injury)	types and level of problems associated with brain damage	learn to relax from and cope with stress induced by caring for the brain damaged member	manage own emotion, experience self-help and help others in a group	realize possible ways to estimate situations and gain control
Session 4 (physical deficit)	questions and answers related to medical issues and physical deficits associated with brain damage	management of physical deficits such as self care	learn to listen to others, impact of physical deficits on family, education, work, and leisure	use successful experiences of member(s) directly or indirectly to instill hope in others
Session 5 (cognitive deficits)	questions and answers related to cognitive issues	management of cognitive deficits such as memory	experience the importance of support from others in dealing with cognitive problems in family, education, work, and leisure	encourage the estimation of difficulties in a solid way rather than use guesswork
Session 6 (behavioral problems)	questions and answers related to emotional and behavioural deficits associated with brain damage	management of emotional and behavioural deficits associated with brain damage	further interaction in issues of behavioural problems in family, education, work, and leisure	develop a personal plan to solve problems
Session 7 (social resources and problemsolving)	understand need and importance of future planning	utilization of social resources in long-term caring, personal planning	acknowledge existing resources and aware of the group as another important resource	extend the idea of empowerment into future life
Session 8 (roundup)	Summarizing, planning of follow-up and reunion activities			

postulated empowerment components for Chinese families (efficacy, knowledge, support, and aspiration). Eight sessions of two hours each were constructed to form a program that would cover the major concerns of most families with brain-damaged members. Selected characteristics of the program content are listed in Table 16.1. Typical methods used included games, role play, discussion, audio–visual materials, demonstration and skill practice, review of written articles and books on families coping with brain injury, sharing of logbook information over the previous weeks, and home assignments.

Instrumentation

The major outcome indicator was the theory-driven empowerment questionnaire (Man, 1998). Other empowerment-related indicators adopted in this study include the following: the Chinese version of the General Health Questionnaire (GHQ; Shek, 1989), a tailor-made self-efficacy rating scale to monitor families' abilities in tackling physical self-care activities (such as dressing, feeding), behavioral and emotional problems (such as impulsive behavior), cognitive deficits (memory, attention) and social problems (social groups and interaction) of their brain damaged members. Individual questions on families' subjective feelings of the burden and the amount of support they had obtained were also asked. These tools were used to monitor changes in empowerment status before, immediately after, and three months after the program.

Results

The relationship between the demographic variables of the families and indicators of their successful coping during different stages of the intervention were first studied. No significant relationships were found for any of the intervention stages. Using one-way ANOVA to test the relationship between the education level of the family and their empowerment level as represented by GHQ scores during the preprogram, postprogram, and three-month follow-up again showed no significant difference. These results seem to suggest that the groups of Chinese caring for a brain-damaged family member changed their psychological well-being and empowerment levels irrespective of their age, sex, and background.

Chinese family members' empowerment changes were investigated by analyzing individual and total scores on the four empowerment components as reflected in the empowerment questionnaire. The pair *t*-test statistics of empowerment differences between different periods of intervention are presented in Table 16.2. The intervention was effective in significantly improving all empowerment components ($p < 0.01$).

After joining the empowerment program, families showed an increase in total empowerment to levels higher than previous stages. Similar patterns were

Table 16.2
Paired t-Test Results of Changes in Empowerment during Different Stages of Intervention

Intervention stage	Empowerment change				
	Efficacy	Knowledge	Support	Aspiration	Total
Pre-program and Post-program	6.01 *	6.4 *	5.47 *	6.16 *	6.13 *
Post-program and 3 month follow-up	1.10 (0.29)	0.60 (0.55)	0.80 (0.43)	0.82 (0.42)	0.91 (0.38)

Note: $p < 0.01$.

again observed in the four individual empowerment components. After three months, families' empowerment dropped a little, but maintained a higher level than in the preprogram stage. Long-term effects of empowerment in these families seem to be supported.

In using paired *t*-tests to compare the improvement in psychological well-being (reflected in a drop of GHQ scores) during the preprogram and postprogram period, the *t*-value was 2.4 ($p < 0.01$), meaning the GHQ score was significantly lower than before. But the *t*-value for the postprogram and the three months after program was not significantly different ($t = 0.86$, $p < 0.409$). Though GHQ scores increased after three months (psychological well-being deteriorated slightly), during the program Chinese families were considerably relieved and did not present so much discomfort as before. It is not so clear why these families' GHQ scores did not decrease further after three months, but it might be related to increasing life challenges after a longer period of caring, and in tackling more difficult problems and beginning to confront the reality of the permanent disability of brain damage.

The families were also asked to indicate the level of support they received during different stages. The changes in support, in the form of substantial assistance and emotional support are presented as a summary in Table 16.3.

From Table 16.4, it is concluded that the families subjectively experienced less stress associated with physical caring, cognitive dysfunction, and behavioral disturbances after joining the empowerment program. There was, however, no significant difference in the three-month follow-up.

Similar to the subjective experience of burden, families' self-efficacy improved very significantly after joining the empowerment program ($p < 0.01$), such as in handling problems in physical caring and cognitive deficits. However, families did not show significant improvement in behavioral and social problem areas. Thus Chinese families caring for their relatives seemed to have

Table 16.3
Percentage of Families Showing Changes in the Amount of Support System Changes during Preprogram, Postprogram, and Three-Month Follow-Up

Support system	Intervention stage					
	Pre-program		Post-program		3-month follow-up	
	Percentage of Families Perceiving Changes					
	yes	no	yes	no	yes	no
Substantial assistance	68%	32%	72.3%	27.7%	58.3%	41.7%
Emotional support	66%	34%	83.3%	16.7%	86.2%	13.8%

derived selective benefits from the eight-week empowerment program. They tended to improve faster and more in training skills and arousing family members' mental abilities within the short period of the program (see Table 16.5). Further improvement after three months in self-efficacy in tackling any or all of the four problem areas was, however, not proven.

Though the overall results showed the program to be effective in empowering Chinese families, it is unclear why some individual family participants were not empowered through the program. As it would be useful to develop principles for successful empowerment of all family participants, postgroup and three-month follow-up empowerment scores were used as dependent variables, and possible demographic characteristics were identified as a list of independent variables for multiple regression analysis. The beta coefficients suggested that the order of predictors of empowerment were GHQ, sex, age, financial situation, preprogram empowerment, and education level. The findings seemed to suggest that order of predictive power would be as follows: lower preprogram GHQ scores, female and older family members, free from financial difficulties, and higher education level. This implied that initial screening of participants using these predictors might guarantee a better success rate of empowerment within a short period of time. Similar to previous analyses of postprogram empowerment, the empowerment scores after three months could be predicted by the six variables.

In short, the programs were initially found to be effective in empowering Chinese family members in the four postulated empowering dimensions, and improving all other outcome measures. The follow-up studies also reflect stability in empowerment, though there was no further improvement. From re-

Table 16.4
Changes in Families' Subjective Feelings of Burden Related to Brain Injury and Intervention Stages

		Wilcoxon Matched-Pairs Signed-Rank Test†	
Subjective Burden Associated with Brain Damage Problems	Stages	z-score†	2-tail probability‡
Physical Problems	preprogram and postprogram	3.00	0.0027**
	postprogram and 3-month follow-up	0.40	0.69
Cognitive Problems	preprogram and postprogram	2.56	0.011*
	postprogram and 3-month follow-up	12.00	0.22
Emotional and behavioral problems	preprogram and postprogram	3.63	0.0005**
	postprogram and 3-month follow-up	0.00	1.00

Notes: Wilcoxon Matched Pairs Signed Rank Test (as n > 25 z-score used rather than *t* values); ‡*p* value; **p* < 0.05; ***p* < 0.01.

gression analysis, it was suggested that, for optimum empowerment to take place, important predictors included the education levels of carers, age ranges, and work status.

Discussion

The results of this study suggest that Hong Kong Chinese families benefited from the empowerment program even though Chinese people have been conceptualized as less able to communicate their needs, recruit social resources, and as lacking the concept of rehabilitation. Moreover, the program families showed more positive outcomes in their physical caring and handling of cognitive problems associated with brain damage. This result may reflect the deep-rooted Chinese ways of showing concern to others through physical means, instead of overt expression of emotion. This result seems to be further supported by the less favorable progress in families' handling of the behavioral and social problems of their brain-damaged members. They viewed the empowerment program as a possible way of recruiting resources and an efficient way of getting information to care for members with a disability. The Chinese families demonstrated flexibility to shift their focus from a personal- or family-centered situation to a more social-oriented situation (similar to people from

Table 16.5
Self-Efficacy in Handling Problems Associated with a Brain-Injured Family Member in Different Intervention Stages

Self efficacy in management	Stages	Paired Difference / SD	t-value	2-tail probability
Physical self-caring	preprogram and postprogram	-2.77 / 3.73	-3.49	0.002**
	postprogram and 3 month follow-up	1.33 / 327	1.00	0.363
Cognitive deficits	preprogram and postprogram	-11.29 / 26.61	-1.99	0.06*
	postprogram and 3 month follow-up	-10.57 / 11.04	-2.34	0.07*
Behavioral problems	preprogram and postprogram	-6.46 / 22.19	-0.71	0.51
	postprogram and 3 month follow-up	-1.42 / 34.11	-0.19	0.85
Social difficulties	preprogram and postprogram	11.13 / 47.72	1.09	0.286

Note: $*p < 0.05$; $**p < 0.01$.

Western cultures). Thus they can improve by establishing support systems and relieving their subjective feelings of burden. Reducing negative psychological characteristics (GHQ scores), Chinese families were able to deviate from the unhealthy family stereotype of lack of communication and few sharing channels. The improvement of empowerment indicators did not continue in the postprogram period, and deteriorated slightly over a period of three months. Lack of further empowerment actions within a powerful group dynamic might have contributed to this outcome. However, empowerment status was maintained at a higher level than before joining the empowerment program. This stability implies the likelihood of achieving empowerment over time. It would be considered feasible for Chinese families facing problems associated with brain damage to achieve an optimum level of empowerment.

The experience of running the empowerment program leads to the suggestion of empowering Chinese family participants in several ways:

1. *Knowledge empowerment.* Recovery from brain damage is an uncertain and sometimes very long process. Chinese families, who are unfamiliar with the concept of disability and rehabilitation, need to be informed so they are realistically prepared to deal with changes in the future. Similar to Western families, Chinese family members can be empowered through increased knowledge of the situation. They can be relieved from uncertainty and be active in making decisions so

that they can take appropriate action for emerging and anticipated problems. Knowledge was not purely transmitted to Chinese family members in a didactic manner. But rather, they were expected to be reflective in exploring meaningful answers by themselves. Peer group discussion, sharing of experiences, and self-study of reading materials all contributed to a better grasp of the idea of brain damage and its implication for family life.

2. *Efficacy empowerment.* Typical methods of demonstration, role-play, and practice have been found to be useful in Chinese families. However, the emphasis should first center on specific problems and their solution. Instead of sharing information on self-care skills, for example, reference to a particular behavioral problem in bathing could be discussed, group suggestions given, and real practice at home could then be achieved. Constant feedback about the performance should be encouraged and cultivated.

3. *Support empowerment.* Within the group situation, Chinese families seem to demonstrate better awareness and realization of hope as empowerment, though it takes a longer time to develop. They find the new experience of meeting with other people who not only know what life with persons with brain damage is like but also experience much the same themselves empowering. They are able to share a common experience and bring with that a unique companionship. For example, a family member may be empowered through the positive experience of being really listened to, being allowed to express feelings, sensing these feelings being truly understood, being valued by others in the group, and then given time to talk around the issue, challenge the despair, and displace it.

4. *Aspiration empowerment.* For positive changes and empowerment to occur, members have to recognize what they have become and discover that they themselves are responsible for a needless retreat. Life can be lived in a determined, outgoing way with positive experiences in a forward direction. It is a matter of changing perceptions and developing understanding within the group that facilitates changes. This brings motivation to change, a challenge to reinforce thought and perceptions, and eventually mutual encouragement as other family members struggle to develop similar new coping behaviors.

Development of the empowerment questionnaire and program through further study of Chinese families is needed. The empowerment concept seems to be a useful model for understanding Chinese families in trouble and guiding the development of coping strategies with brain damage. It is of equal importance to suggest the agenda on how healthcare professionals can contribute to the empowerment process of Chinese families caring for their members with brain damage.

CONCLUSION

Disability is a salient factor that influences the formation of a person's life perception. The presence of physical disability causes a person to have specific feelings about life dimensions. Independence is an internal achievement that is self-oriented, which means that a person determines the standard of achievement for himself or herself. However, in a collectivistic culture, the standard may be strongly influenced by significant others and socialization.

This chapter has illustrated social psychology perspectives that influence the rehabilitation process and outcome of persons with disability. Certainly, this is an area worthy of more investigation and development. It is always controversial to define normal in a society. For example, wearing glasses seems to be a norm of university students. Disability itself can be a cultural category and its meaning is determined by the existing norms. Moreover, disability is regarded as a special feature and also bears different meanings in different cultures; for example, in some African tribes, like the Bushman, the child with disability is relatively well-treated (Marshall, 1976; Scheer & Groce, 1988).

Since the individual must live according to the social context, rehabilitation efforts should therefore not only enhance the lives of persons with disabilities, but also aim at changing the way that context is perceived and understood by the individual. Studies of self-efficacy enhancement and empowerment strategies in rehabilitation are good illustrations of this consideration. Furthermore, rehabilitation should also aim at changing the social context to facilitate more promising rehabilitation outcomes. Legitimate mobilization of community resources and changing of societal attitudes would help persons with disabilities to integrate into their communities. They will feel consistently positive about their personal worth and experience dignity as a human being. We believe that social psychology theories and strategies, of both cultural and transcultural perspectives, can be integrated with rehabilitation practices to enhance the quality of life for persons with disabilities.

REFERENCES

Adler, A. (1917). *Study of organ inferiority and its compensations*. New York: Nervous and Mental Diseases Publishing.

Allport, G. W. (1937). *Personality: A psychological interpretation*. New York: Harcourt.

Anderson, N. N. (1967). Effects of institutionalization on self-esteem. *Journal of Gerontology, 22*, 313–317.

Andersen, S. M. (1987). The role of cultural assumptions in self-concept development, In K. Yardley & T. Honess (Eds.), *Self and identity: Psychosocial perspectives* (pp. 231–246). John Wiley and Sons.

Banaji, M. R., & Prentice, D. A. (1994). The self in social contexts. *Annual Review of Psychology, 45*, 297–332.

Bandura, A. (1977). Self-efficacy: Toward a unifying theory of behavioural change. *Psychological Review, 84*, 191–215.

Bandura, A. (1982). The self and mechanisms of agency. In J. Suls (Ed.), *Psychological perspectives on the self* (vol. 1, pp. 3–39). Hillsdale, NJ: Erlbaum.

Bandura, A. (1986). *Social foundations of thought and action: A social cognitive theory*. Englewood Cliffs, NJ: Prentice Hall.

Bandura, A. (1992). Exercise of personal agency through the self-efficacy mechanism. In R. Schwarzer (Ed.), *Self-efficacy: Thought control of action* (pp. 3–38). Washington: Hemisphere.

Bandura, A., & Schunk, D. H., (1981). Cultivating competence, self-efficacy, and intrinsic interest through proximal self-motivation. *Journal of Personality and Social Psychology, 41*, 586–598.

Bentelspacher, C. E., Chitran, S., & Marziyanna, B.A.R. (1994). Coping and adaptation patterns among Chinese, Indian, and Malay families caring for a mentally ill relative. *Families in Society, 75* (5), 287–294.

Berry, J. W. (1998). Acculturative stress. In P. B. Organista, K. M. Chun, & G. Marin (Eds.), *Readings in ethnic psychology* (pp. 117–122). New York: Routledge.

Brockner, J. (1979). Self-esteem, self-consciousness, and task performance. *Journal of Personality and Social Psychology, 37*, 447–461.

Caplan, R. D., Vinokur, A. D., Price, R. H., & van Ryn, M. (1989). Job seeking, reemployment and mental health: A randomized field experiment in coping with job loss. *Journal of Applied Psychology, 74*, 759–769.

Chu, G. C. (1985). The changing concept of self in contemporary China. In A. J. Marsella, G. Devos, & L. K. Hsu (Eds.), *Culture and self: Asian and Western perspectives* (pp. 252–277). New York: Tavistock.

Cordaro, L. L., & Shontz, F. C. (1969). Psychological situations as determinants of self-evaluations. *Journal of Counselling Psychology, 16*, 575–578.

Dodds, A. G. (1989). Motivation reconsidered: The importance of self-efficacy in rehabilitation. *British Journal of Visual Impairment, 7* (1), 11–15.

Dunst, C. J., & Trivette, C. M. (1987). Enabling and empowering families: Conceptual and intervention issues. *Social Psychological Review, 16*, 443–456.

Eden, D., & Aviram, A. (1990). *Self-efficacy training to speed reemployment* (Working Paper no. 72/90). Tel Aviv, Israel: Tel Aviv University, Faculty of Management.

Fraser, C. (1980). The social psychology of unemployment. *Psychology Survey No. 3.* London: George Allen and Unwin.

Frayne, C. A., & Latham, G. P. (1987). Application of social learning theory to self-management of attendance. *Journal of Applied Psychology, 72*, 387–392.

Georgas, J. (1989). Changing family values in Greece: From collectivist to individualist. *Journal of Cross-Cultural Psychology, 20*, 80–91.

Gist, M. E., Schwoerer, C., & Rosen, B. (1989). Effects of alternative training methods on self-efficacy and performance in computer software training. *Journal of Applied Psychology, 74*, 884–891.

Greenwald, A. G. (1980). The totalitarian ego: Fabrication and revision of personal history. *American Psychologist, 35*, 603–618.

Hanks, J., & Hanks, L. M. (1948). The physically handicapped in certain non-Western societies. *Journal of Social Issues, 4* (4), 11–19.

Hardman, M. L., Drew, C. J., & Egan, M. W. (1987). *Human exceptionality: Society, school and family.* Boston: Allyn and Bacon.

Hart, D., & Edelstein, W. (1991). Self-understanding in cross-cultural perspective. In T. M. Brinthaupt & R. P. Lipka (Eds.), *The self definitional and methodological issues* (pp. 291–322). New York: State University of New York Press.

Ho, D.Y.F. (1986). Chinese pattern of socialization: A critical review. In M. H. Bond (Ed.), *The psychology of the Chinese people* (pp. 1–37). Hong Kong: Oxford University Press.

Hui, C. H., & Triandis, H. C. (1985). Measurement in cross-cultural psychology: A review and comparison of strategies. *Journal of Cross-Cultural Psychology, 16* (2), 131–152.

Hui, C. H., & Villareal, M. (1989). Individualism–collectivism and psychological needs. *Journal of Cross-Cultural Psychology, 20*, 296–309.

Hwang, C. H. (1977). Discussing filial piety from a psychological point of view and analyzing the views of youth toward filial behavior. *Bulletin of Educational Psychology, 10*, 11–20.

James, W. (1890). *Principles of psychology* (2 vols.). Chicago: Encyclopedia Britannica.

Kennedy, S., Scheier, J., & Rogers, A. (1984). The price of success: Our monocultural science. *American Psychologist, 39*, 996–997.

Kirk, S. A., & Gallagher, J. J. (1983). *Educating exceptional children*. Boston: Houghton Mifflin.

Koo, L. C. (1989). A journey into the cultural aspects of health and ill-health in Chinese society in Hong Kong—The importance of health and preventive medicine in Chinese society. *Hong Kong Practitioners, 11*, 51–58.

Lao, S. K. (1981). *The history of Chinese philosophy* (vol. 1) [in Chinese]. Taipei: San-Min.

Major, B., Sciacchitano, A. M., & Crocker, J. (1993). In-group versus out-group comparisons and self-esteem. *Journal of Personality and Social Psychology, 19*, 711–721.

Man, D.W.K. (1998). The empowering of Hong Kong Chinese families with a brain damaged member: Its investigation and measurement. *Brain injury, 12*, 245–254.

Markus, H. R., & Kitayama, S. (1991). Culture and the self: Implications for cognition, emotion, and motivation. *Psychological Review, 2*, 224–253.

Marshall, L. (1976). *The Kung of nyae nyae*. Cambridge, MA: Harvard University Press.

McDaniel, J. W. (1976). *Physical disability and human behavior*. New York: Pergamon Press.

Miller, J. F. (1992). Patient power resources. In J. F. Miller (Ed.), *Coping with chronic illness: Overcoming powerlessness*. Philadelphia, PA: F.A. Davis.

Mischel, M. H., & Braden, C. J. (1988). Finding meaning: Antecedents of uncertainty. *Nursing Research, 37*, 98–103.

Molleman, E., Pruyn, J., & van Knippenberg, A. (1986). Social comparison processes among cancer patients. *British Journal of Social Psychology, 25*, 1–13.

Parsons, T. (1958). Definitions of health and illness in light of American values and social structure. In E. Jaco (Ed.), *Patients, physicians, and illness* (pp. 165–187). New York: Random House.

Pearson, V. J., & Chan, T.W.L. (1993). Relationship between parenting stress and social support in mothers of children with learning disabilities: A Chinese experience. *Social Science and Medicine, 37* (2), 267–274.

Philips, M. R. (1993). Strategies used by Chinese families coping with schizophrenia. In D. Davis & S. Harrell (Eds.), *Chinese families in the post-Mao era*. Berkeley and Los Angeles: University of California Press.

Pringle, M. K. (1964). The emotional and social readjustment of physically handicapped children: A review of the literature between 1928 and 1962. *Education Research, 6*, 207–215.

Rogers, C. R. (1959). A theory of therapy, personality and interpersonal relationships as developed in the client-centered framework. In S. Koch (Ed.), *Psychology: A study of science* (vol. 3, pp. 184–256). New York: McGraw-Hill.

Rothman, J., & Thomas, E. L. (1994). *Intervention research: Design and development for the human services*. New York: Haworth Press.

Safilios-Rothschild, C. (1970). *The sociology and social psychology of disability and rehabilitation.* New York: Random House.

Sampson, E. E. (1989). The decentralization of identity: Toward a revised concept of personal and social order. *American Psychologist, 40,* 1203–1211.

Schaefer, C., Coyne, J., & Lazarus, R. (1981). The health-related function of social support. *Journal of Behavioral Medicine, 4,* 381–406.

Scheer, J., & Groce, N. (1988). Impairment as a human constant: Cross-cultural and historical perspectives on variation. *Journal of Social Issues, 44,* 23–37.

Schulz, R., & Decker, S. (1985). Long-term adjustment to physical disability: The role of social support, perceived control, and self-blame. *Journal of Personality and Social Psychology, 48,* 1162–1172.

Shek, D.T.L., & Mak, J.W.K. (1987). *Psychological well-being of working parents in Hong Kong: Mental health, stress and coping responses.* Hong Kong: Hong Kong Christian Service.

Shweder, R. A., & Bourne, E. J. (1984). Does the concept of the person vary cross-culturally? In R. A. Shweder & R. A. LeVine (Eds.), *Cultural theory: Essays on mind, self and emotion* (pp. 158–199). New York: Cambridge University Press.

Starr, P., & Heiserman, K. (1977). Acceptance of disability by teenagers with oral–facial clefts. *Rehabilitation Counseling Bulletin, 20,* 198–201.

Tam, S. F., & Watkins, D. (1995). Towards a hierarchical model of self-concept for Hong Kong Chinese adults with physical disabilities. *International Journal of Psychology, 30,* 1–17.

Tam, S. F., Tsang, W. H., Ip, Y. C., & Chan, C. S. (2000). *Exploring self-concepts of persons with mental illness.* Unpublished Manuscript. Hong Kong: Hong Kong Polytechnic University.

Tam, S. F., & Ng, Y. Y. (2000). *Exploring self-concepts as subjective quality of life of persons with cardiac diseases.* Unpublished Manuscript. Hong Kong: Hong Kong Polytechnic University.

Taylor, S. E., & Brown, J. D. (1988). Illusion and well-being: A social psychological perspective on mental health. *Psychological Bulletin, 103,* 193–210.

Tesser, A. (1988). Toward a self-evaluation maintenance model of social behavior. In L. Berkowitz (Ed.), *Advances in experimental social psychology* (vol. 21, pp. 181–227). San Diego, CA: Academic Press.

Thompson, S. C. (1981). Will it hurt if I can control it? A complex answer to a single question. *Psychological Bulletin, 90,* 89–101.

Triandis, H. (1987). Individualism and social psychological theory. In C. Kagitcibasi (Ed.), *Growth and progress in cross-cultural psychology* (pp. 78–83). The Netherlands: Sweets & Zeitlingler.

Tseng, W. S., & Hsu, J. (1970). Chinese culture, personality information and mental illness. *International Journal of Social Psychiatry, 16,* 237–245.

Wood, J. V., Taylor, S. E., & Lichtman, R. R. (1985). Social comparison in adjustment to breast cancer. *Journal of Personality and Social Psychology, 49,* 1169–1183.

Wright, B. A. (1983). *Physical disability: A psychological approach.* New York: Harper and Row.

Zimmerman, M. A., & Rappaport, J. (1988). Citizen participation, perceived control, and psychological empowerment. *American Journal of Community Psychology, 16,* 725–750.

Name Index

Subject Index

About the Editors and Contributors

Weining C. Chang was born in Nanjing China. She obtained a B.A. in law from National Taiwan University and a Ph.D. in psychology from the University of Houston. Her interest in culture and psychology led her to a postdoctoral research position with the Graduate School of Education, the Institute for International Development at Harvard University. She is currently an associate professor at the National University of Singapore, where she conducts research in the motivation to achieve, and stress-and-coping with reference to the self and self-construction.

Sang-Chin Choi is a professor of psychology at Chung-Ang University, Seoul, Korea. He received his Ph.D. from the University of Hawaii. He is currently the president of the Korean Cultural Psychological Association. He has also served as president of the Asian Association of Social Psychology and the Korean Psychological Association. He published *Korean Psychology* in 2000 and coedited *Psychology of the Korean People* and *Individualism and Collectivism* in 1994. He has devoted himself to developing Korean indigenous psychology for the past twenty years.

Hyun-hee Chung is currently a full-time instructor at Keimyung University in Daegu, Korea. She obtained her doctoral degree from Rutgers University in New Jersey, focusing on school psychology. Her research interests include school adjustment problems, mental health problems of children and adolescents, and intervention and prevention of adolescent problem behaviors.

Ikuo Daibo is a professor of social psychology at Osaka University, Japan. He taught at Sapporo Medical College, Yamagata University, and Hokusei Gakuen University, before going to Osaka in 2000. His research has long focused on interpersonal communication processes and interpersonal closeness. He has also conducted cross-cultural research on facial attractiveness, with an emphasis on cultural background and personal attributes. He is the editor of the *Japanese Journal of Social Psychology*.

Heidi Fung is an associate research fellow of the Institute of Ethnology at Academia Sinica, Taipei, Taiwan. She received her doctoral training in the Committee on Human Development at the University of Chicago. After teaching in the department of psychology at the Chinese University of Hong Kong for four years, she returned to her native Taiwan in 1996 to assume a research position. Dr. Fung has long been interested in understanding how culture and self constitute each other and her research involves the socialization of emotion, disciplinary practices, and moral training at home with young Taiwanese children, parental child-rearing beliefs across cultures, and the methodological issues of situating development in cultural context.

Kwang-Kuo Hwang obtained his Ph.D. in social psychology at the University of Hawaii. He is currently a National Chair professor, awarded by Taiwan's Ministry of Education at National Taiwan University. He has endeavored to promote the indigenization movement of psychology and social science in Chinese society since the early 1980s, and has published eight books and more than one hundred articles on related issues in both Chinese and English. He is president-elect of the Asian Association of Social Psychology.

Kibum Kim obtained his Ph.D. degree from the Chung-Ang University in Korea in 2002. His research interests include the relation between culture and *maum* (mind), interpersonal relationships, and cultural emotion. He has over ten publications in journals and book chapters published in Korea and abroad.

Uichol Kim is a professor of psychology at Chung-Ang University, Seoul, Korea. He taught at the University of Hawaii at Manoa and the University of Tokyo before returning to Korea in 1995. His publications include *Indigenous Psychologies: Experience and Research in Cultural Context* (Sage, 1993); *Individualism and Collectivism: Theory, Method, and Applications* (Sage, 1994); *Progress in Asian Social Psychologies*, vol. 1 (John Wiley and Sons, 1997); and *Democracy, Human Rights, and Peace in Korea: Psychological, Political and Cultural Perspectives* (Kyoyook Kwahaksa, 2001). He has served as an editor of the *Asian Journal of Social Psychology*. He is currently the president of the Division of Psychology and National Development of the International Association of Applied Psychology.

Patrick W. L. Leung is currently a professor in the department of psychology at the Chinese University of Hong Kong. He also serves as the director of Graduate Studies in Clinical Psychology. He was born and raised in Hong Kong. He obtained his Ph.D. from the University of Sheffield, United Kingdom. He was a practicing clinical psychologist for ten years at a children's hospital before assuming his current position in 1992. His main research interests are in child and adolescent psychology and psychiatry.

Eli Lieber currently works as codirector of the Fieldwork and Qualitative Research Laboratory at the Center for Culture and Health at UCLA, developing and supporting integrated methods for social–ecological research. While completing his Ph.D. in psychology at the University of Illinois, Urbana–Champaign, he worked under Dr. Yang Kuo Shu's mentorship as a visiting scholar to National Taiwan University and postdoctoral researcher at Academia Sinica. Collaborations with Taiwanese psychologists and sociologists focused on attributional style, achievement motivation, and child-rearing. Active projects include HIV/STD prevention in China, Asian-American adolescent perception of parental control, and U.S.–Chinese immigrant adjustment and adaptation in child-rearing.

Anna Lim was born and raised in Singapore. She graduated from the National University of Singapore with a major in psychology. She currently provides insights to corporate clients on consumer psychology as an appointed researcher with a multinational market research agency headquartered in London.

Wen-ying Lin received her Ph.D. in educational psychology from Keio University in Tokyo, Japan. She moved to Taiwan where she taught at Catholic Fu Jen University before joining the psychology department of Fo Guang University in 2001. Her research has focused on the social context of parenting behavior with an emphasis on culture and cognition.

James H. Liu was born in Taiwan and immigrated to the United States when he was four. Traveling extensively through the Pacific Rim, he has never lived in one place for longer than eight consecutive years. He received his Ph.D. from UCLA in 1992, and worked as a postdoctoral fellow at Florida Atlantic University before taking a position at Victoria University of Wellington in New Zealand in 1994. He is on the executive committee of the Asian Association of Social Psychology, and is a fellow of SPSSI. He is author of more than thirty-five papers and coeditor of three books. His interests are in developing a culturally and historically grounded approach to the study of social identity and intergroup relations. He currently identifies himself as a Chinese-American New Zealander, and lives in Titahi Bay.

Shu-hsien Liu was born in Shanghai in 1934. He went to Taiwan alone at the age of fifteen in 1949, and earned an M.A. (1958) in philosophy at Natonal Taiwan University. He received his Ph.D. from Southern Illinois University in 1966, and taught there until 1981. He has been Chair Professor in Chinese Philosophy at the Chinese University of Hong Kong since 1981, and is author of many publications in both Chinese and English, including *Understanding Confucian Philosophy: Classical and Sung-Ming* (1998). He is widely recognized as a representative of contemporary neo-Confucianism.

Wai-kwong Man is an assistant professor in the department of rehabilitation sciences at Hong Kong Polytechnic University. He obtained his Ph.D. degree from the University of Hong Kong in 1996. His research interests are brain injury rehabilitation encompassing family intervention strategies, community reintegration programming, vocational rehabilitation, and innovative cognitive rehabilitation. He also developed the Empowerment Questionnaire that is now documented in the Health and Psychosocial Instrument (HaPI) Database. He is an active professional advisor of the Hong Kong Community Rehabilitation Network and a self-help group for Persons with Brain Injury. He has over thirty publications in different journals, book chapters, and conferences.

Asako Miura received a Ph.D. from Osaka University, Japan. Her main research interests are interpersonal and social psychology. She is now concerned with computer mediated communication and group process of creativity.

Fumio Murakami is currently a doctoral student in social psychology at the University of Tokyo. His research interests lie in the area of distributive justice and implicit self-evaluation across cultures.

Jenny Yuen-yee Ng is a registered physiotherapist in Hong Kong. She received her professional diploma in physiotherapy from the Hong Kong Polytechnic University in 1981 and her M.S. in training from the University of Leicester, United Kingdom, in 1995. She has worked for more than twenty years at Grantham Hospital, Hong Kong, which specializes in heart and lung diseases. She is now an honorary lecturer of the department of rehabilitation sciences, Hong Kong Polytechnic University. She has several international publications in psychological and professional journals. Her research interests include the application of social psychology in health services, cardiac and pulmonary rehabilitation, and patient education.

Tomoko Oe is a doctoral student at the University of Tokyo. Her research interests are prejudice, stereotyping, and intergroup perception and behavior. She focuses on the role of the automatic and controlled processes associated with stereotype suppression.

Takashi Oka is an associate professor at the University of Tokyo, where he obtained his Ph.D. in 1992. He teaches and studies various topics related to social cognition. His recent studies concern false consensus effects, cross-categorization effects, linguistic intergroup bias, and stereotype transmission.

Yuko Okada obtained a B.A. from the department of psychology, Ochanomizu University in 1998. She is now working as a systems engineer.

Young-Shin Park is a professor in the department of education at Inha University in Inchon, South Korea. Her research interests include parent–child relationships, adolescent achievement and life satisfaction, self-efficacy, and youth culture. She has served as vice-dean of College of Education, Inha University. She is currently the editor in chief of the *Korean Journal of Psychological and Social Issues*, a consulting editor of the *Asian Journal of Social Psychology*, the editor of the *Korean Journal of Psychology*, and an editor of the *Korean Journal of Educational Psychology*.

Paul B. Pedersen is Professor Emeritus from Syracuse University and a visiting professor at the University of Hawaii, Department of Psychology. He has been on the faculty of the University of Minnesota, University of Hawaii, Syracuse University, and the University of Alabama at Birmingham. He also taught at universities in Indonesia for three years, Malaysia for two years and Taiwan for one year while he was a Senior Fulbright Fellow teaching at National Taiwan University. He is a Fellow in Divisions 9, 17, 45, and 52 of The American Psychological Association. He has published more than 200 books, articles and chapters, mostly in the areas of multicultural counseling and counselor education.

Lilian Quan was born in Singapore. An ethnic Chinese, Lilian grew up speaking both Chinese and English. She is interested in the work-related motivations of Chinese people. She attended the National University of Singapore. After graduation she accepted a position with a social service agency in Singapore as a program officer.

Akira Sakamoto obtained a Ph.D. in sociology from the University of Tokyo and works as an associate professor in the department of psychology at Ochanomizu University, a national women's university in Tokyo. His research areas are social cognition and the impact of media. He is now a consulting editor of the *Asian Journal of Social Psychology*.

Kiyoko Sekiguchi obtained a B.A. from the department of psychology at Ochanomizu University in 1995. She is now working as a systems engineer at TG Information Network Company, Ltd.

Aya Shinkyu obtained a B.A. from the department of psychology at Ochanomizu University in 1996. She is now working as an assistant examiner at the Sagamihara Branch Office of Yokohama Family Court.

Jai B. P. Sinha is a professor of psychology and management at the ASSERT Institute of Management. He received his Ph.D. from Ohio State University, Columbus, Ohio. He has been a visiting professor at Hunter College of the City University of New York, Wake Forest University of Winston-Salem, North Carolina (United States), McGill University of Montreal (Canada), and a UGC national lecturer, a national fellow of the ICSSR, a senior Fulbright fellow, and a member of the executives of the International Association of Applied Psychology and International Association for Cross-Cultural Psychology. Dr. Sinha is a vice president of the World Association for Dynamic Psychiatry. He has published more than 150 research articles in national and international journals, and has written or coauthored a number of books including *Patterns of Work Culture: Cases and Strategies for Culture Building*; *Managing Cultural Diversity for Productivity: The Asian Way* (Ed.); and *The Cultural Context of Leadership and Power*.

Sing-fai Tam is associate professor of rehabilitation sciences at the Hong Kong Polytechnic University. He received his Ph.D. from the University of Hong Kong. He has worked for many years as a front-line occupational therapist in rehabilitation services for clients with mental and physical disabilities. His research interests are in self-concept and the social psychology of persons with disabilities, computer-assisted rehabilitation, cognitive rehabilitation, and outcome measure development and validation. He also investigates the application and implications of self-efficacy and self-concept theories in rehabilitation of persons with disabilities. He is the coordinator of the Centre for East-Meets-West in Rehabilitation Sciences at Hong Kong Polytechnic University. He is the author of more than sixty publications in journals and books.

Colleen Ward was born in New Orleans and started her cross-cultural sojourns as a Ph.D. student at the University of Durham, England. She has since held teaching and research positions at the University of the West Indies (Trinidad), the Science University of Malaysia, Canterbury University (New Zealand), and the National University of Singapore. She is past Secretary-General of the International Association for Cross-Cultural Psychology and serves on the editorial board of the *Journal of Cross-Cultural Psychology* and the *International Journal of Intercultural Relations*. She is also coauthor of *The Psychology of Culture Shock* (forthcoming).

Kuo-Shu Yang is research fellow at the Institute of Ethnology, Academia Sinica, Taipei, Taiwan. He received his doctoral degree from the University of Illinois, Urbana–Champaign. His research interests include the systematic study of Chinese personality and social behavior and changes therein, especially Chinese character, individual modernity, individual traditionality, familism, filial piety, social-oriented achievement motivation, social-oriented self, collectivistic-oriented basic needs, and family socialization from an indigenous perspective. He has orchestrated a group of Chinese psychologists in Taiwan, Hong Kong, and China to promote an academic movement for the indigenization of psychological research in Chinese societies. He has written or edited more than 20 books and published more than 150 academic papers in Chinese and English.

Kye-Min Yang is a Ph.D. candidate at Chung-Ang University in Seoul, Korea. Her interests are culture and acculturation programs, adolescent problem behaviors, and forensic psychology.

Kuang-Hui Yeh is an associate research fellow at the Institute of Ethnology, Academia Sinica, Taipei, Taiwan (Republic of China). He currently also teaches personality and family psychology courses at National Taiwan University. He specializes in social and personality psychology. He is expanding his research areas to family psychology with a systemic perspective and to indigenous psychology with a contextual perspective.

An-Bang Yu is an associate research fellow at the Institute of Ethnology, Academia Sinica, Taipei, Taiwan. He received his Ph.D. from National Taiwan University, where he majored in social and personality psychology. His areas of research interest include emotion, self, and achievement motivation. His indigenous psychological research has focused on Chinese culture and emotion, the Chinese concept of the person, and the Chinese concept of achievement.